CONTENTS

ANSWER KEY

CHAPTER 1 - ALGEBRA

1.1. – ORDER OF OPERATIONS

Math - Pre Algebra Grade 9 Zahra Amir
Nov 4th 2021

1. $5+3\cdot 2 = 11$

2. $2\cdot 3-(-3) = 9$

3. $-5\cdot 5-(-8)\cdot 2 = -9$

4. $-2-5-(-2)+2 = -3$

5. $(-2)(-5)-(-2)\cdot 2 = 14$

6. $25\cdot 2-7 = 43$

7. $15+4/2 = 17$

8. $14/7+3\cdot 6 = 20$

9. $5/5-30/2\cdot 5 = -74$

10. $1+4/2-8/4\cdot 5 = -7$

11. $20/4/2+4 = 13/2$

12. $12\cdot (2+3) = 60$

13. $5(3\cdot 2/3\cdot 2)+2 = 22$

14. $1/2+3/2 = 2$

15. $6/3-20/10 = 0$

16. $5(1+3\cdot 2)+2/2-8/4 = 34$

17. $(15+3)\cdot 2-2 = 34$

18. $0/5+3\cdot 2 = 6$

19. $5/0+3\cdot 2 = 0$

20. $(1+1)\cdot (2-2)\cdot (4\cdot 5\cdot 5) = 0$

21. $(5+3)\cdot 2 = 16$

22. $(5\cdot 3)\cdot 2 = 30$

A+

23. $5\cdot (3\cdot 2) = 30$

24. $5\cdot 3\cdot 2 = 30$

25. $100/2^2+21/3 = 32$

26. $(2+1)^2/3+13 = 16$

27. $2(3^2-4/2)^2-1\cdot 3 = 95$

28. $3(1-4/2^2)^2-4^2/3 = 16/3$

29. $10(2^4/2-1^2+1)/2 = 40$

30. $2+3(2-20/2^2)^2-(5^2+3)/2 =$

31. $5/0 = 0$

32. $0/4 = 0$

33. $0/0 = 0$

34. $(2+4)\cdot 5^2-2/2 = 149$

35. $-1\cdot 5^2-2^2+(-2)^{3-1\cdot 2} = -31$

36. $\left(-2^2-2\right)^2\cdot (-2)^{1-1} = 36$

37. $(4-5\cdot 2)/2-1 = -4$

1.2. – INTRODUCTION TO FRACTIONS

1. Given the following circle, divide it to 2 equal pieces and shade $\frac{1}{2}$

2. Given the following circle divide it to 3 equal pieces and shade $\frac{1}{3}$

3. Given the following circle, divide it to 4 equal pieces and shade $\frac{1}{4}$

4. Given the following circle, divide it to 5 equal pieces and shade $\frac{1}{5}$

5. Given the following circle, divide it to 6 equal pieces and shade $\frac{1}{6}$

6. Given the following circle, divide it to 7 equal pieces and shade $\frac{1}{7}$

7. Given the following circle, divide it to 8 equal pieces and shade $\frac{1}{8}$

8. Given the following circle, divide it to 9 equal pieces and shade $\frac{1}{9}$

9. Given the following circle, divide it to 10 equal pieces and shade $\frac{1}{10}$

10. Given the following circle, divide it to 3 equal pieces and shade $\frac{2}{3}$

11. Given the following circle, divide it to 4 equal pieces and shade $\frac{2}{4}$

12. Given the following circle, divide it to 4 equal pieces and shade $\frac{3}{4}$

13. Given the following circle, divide it to 5 equal pieces and shade $\frac{2}{5}$

14. Given the following circle, divide it to 6 equal pieces and shade $\frac{5}{6}$

15. Given the following circle, divide it to 8 equal pieces and shade $\frac{5}{8}$

16. Given the following circle, divide it to 5 equal pieces and shade $\frac{4}{5}$

17. Given the following circle, divide it to 9 equal pieces and shade $\frac{4}{9}$

18. What fraction of the following circle is shaded:

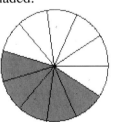

$\frac{5}{11}$

19. What fraction of the following circle is shaded:

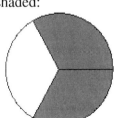

$\frac{2}{3}$

20. What fraction of the following circle is shaded:

$\frac{5}{11}$

21. What fraction of the following circle is shaded:

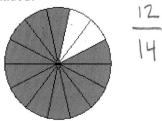

$\frac{12}{14}$

22. What fraction of the following circle is shaded:

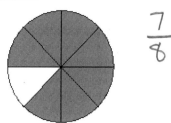

$\frac{7}{8}$

23. What fraction of the following circle is shaded:

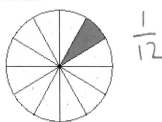

$\frac{1}{12}$

24. What fraction of the following table is shaded:

$\frac{14}{64}$

25. What fraction of the following table is shaded:

$\frac{6}{35}$

26. What fraction of the following table is shaded?

$\frac{9}{24}$

27. What fraction is shaded?

$\frac{5}{16}$

28. What fraction is shaded?

$\frac{1}{3}$ $\frac{1}{3}$ $\frac{1}{3}$ $\frac{2}{3}$

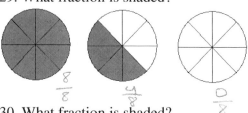

29. What fraction is shaded?

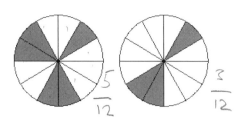

$\frac{8}{8}$ $\frac{4}{8}$ $\frac{0}{8}$

30. What fraction is shaded?

$\frac{5}{12}$ $\frac{3}{12}$

31. There were 12 cookies in the jar. John ate 5, write down the fraction of cookies john ate and the fraction that is left in the jar.

$\frac{5}{12}$ $\frac{7}{12}$

8

32. Lia ate 3 cookies that represented $\frac{3}{4}$ of the cookies in the jar. Write down the number of cookies in the jar before she ate. Make a sketch to show answer.

4 cookies

33. Rami ate $\frac{2}{5}$ of the cookies in the jar, Melissa ate $\frac{1}{4}$ of the cookies. Who ate more? Invent an imaginary jar with a number of cookies that will make the problem easy to solve.

They ate the same amount

34. How much is $\frac{1}{2}$ of 2? Shade to show your answer:

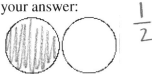

$\frac{1}{2}$

35. How much is $\frac{1}{3}$ of 2? Shade to show your answer:

$\frac{2}{3}$

36. How much is $\frac{1}{4}$ of 2? Shade to show your answer:

$\frac{2}{4}$

37. How much is $\frac{1}{5}$ of 2? Shade to show your answer:

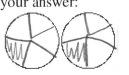

$\frac{2}{5}$

38. How much is $\frac{1}{3}$ of 5? Shade in 2 different ways to show your answer:

$\frac{3}{5}$

39. How much is $\frac{2}{5}$ of 4? Shade in 2 different ways to show your answer:

$\frac{8}{5}$

40. Sketch $\frac{3}{2}$ circles:

41. Sketch $\frac{5}{3}$ circles:

42. Sketch $\frac{7}{4}$ circles:

43. Sketch $\frac{8}{4}$ circles:

44. Sketch $\frac{7}{5}$ circles:

45. Sketch $\frac{8}{3}$ circles:

46. Nathan ate $\frac{2}{7}$ of the cookies in the jar, Melissa ate $\frac{1}{3}$ of the cookies.

    Who ate more? Invent an imaginary jar with a number of cookies that will make the problem easy to solve.

    Mallissa

47. Write down the missing number(s) between 0 and 1:

48. Write down the missing number(s) between 0 and 1:

49. Write down the missing number(s) between 0 and 1:

50. Write down the missing number(s) between 0 and 1:

51. Write down the missing number(s) between 0 and 1:

52. Write down the missing number(s) between 0 and 2:

53. Write down the missing number(s) between 0 and 2:

54. Write down the missing number(s) between 0 and 2:

55. Write down the missing number(s) between 2 and 3:

56. Write down the missing number(s) between 2 and 4:

10

57. Write down the missing fractions(s) and decimal:

58. Write down the missing fractions(s) and decimal: $-\dfrac{6}{5}$ 1.2 $\dfrac{14}{5}$ 2.8

59. Write down the missing fractions(s) and decimal: $-\dfrac{22}{5}$ 4.4 $\dfrac{17}{5}$ 3.4

60. Write down the missing fractions(s) and decimal:

0   **[1/5]**

61. Write down the missing fractions(s) and decimal:

[1/8] $\dfrac{2}{8}$ $\dfrac{3}{8}$ **[1/2]**

62. Write down the missing fractions(s) and decimal: $\dfrac{4}{8}$

[1] $\dfrac{1}{2}$ 1   **[3/2]**   **[5/3]**

63. Write down the missing fractions(s) and decimal:

[13/7]   **[2]** $\dfrac{15}{7}$ $\dfrac{16}{7}$ $\dfrac{17}{7}$ $\dfrac{18}{7}$ $\dfrac{19}{7}$ **[20/7]** $\dfrac{14}{7}$

64. Write down the missing fractions(s) and decimal:

[26/9]   **[3]** $\dfrac{28}{9}$ $\dfrac{29}{9}$ **[10/3]** $\dfrac{27}{9}$

65. Write down the missing fractions(s) and decimal:

[-10/9]   **[-1]** $-\dfrac{8}{9}$ $-\dfrac{7}{9}$ $-\dfrac{6}{9}$ $-\dfrac{5}{9}$ **[-4/9]**   **[-1/3]**

66. Write down the missing fractions(s) and decimal:

[-4] $\dfrac{20}{5}$ $-\dfrac{18}{5}$ $-\dfrac{16}{5}$ $-\dfrac{14}{5}$ $-\dfrac{12}{5}$ $-\dfrac{10}{5}$ **[-2]**   **[-8/5]** $\dfrac{7}{5}$ **[-6/5]**

67. Write down the missing fractions(s) and decimal:

[3/4]   **[3/2]**   **[9/4]**   **[3]** $\dfrac{15}{4}$ $\dfrac{18}{4}$ $\dfrac{21}{4}$ **[6]**   **[27/4]**   **[15/2]** $\dfrac{6}{4}$ $\dfrac{12}{4}$ $\dfrac{24}{4}$ $\dfrac{20}{4}$

Nov 10 2021

Write the fractions as decimals: Math-Pre Algebra, Grade 9 Zahra Ami

1. $\dfrac{1}{10} = 0.1$

2. $\dfrac{1}{100} = 0.01$

3. $\dfrac{1}{1000} = 0.001$

4. $\dfrac{1}{10000} = 0.0001$

5. $\dfrac{2}{10} = 0.2$

6. $\dfrac{5}{100} = 0.05$

7. $\dfrac{-31}{1000} = -0.031$

8. $\dfrac{766}{10000} = 0.0766$

9. $\dfrac{55}{10} = 5.5$

10. $\dfrac{101}{100} = 1.01$

11. $\dfrac{-335}{1000} = -0.335$

12. $\dfrac{20000}{10000} = 2$

13. $\dfrac{1}{2} = 0.5$

14. $\dfrac{1}{5} = 0.2$

15. $\dfrac{1}{4} = 0.25$

16. $\dfrac{1}{3} = 0.333...$

17. $\dfrac{1}{8} = 0.125$

18. $\dfrac{1}{9} = 0.1111...$

19. $\dfrac{2}{5} = 0.4$

20. $\dfrac{2}{4} = 0.5$

21. $\dfrac{3}{5} = 0.6$

22. $\dfrac{4}{5} = 0.8$

23. $\dfrac{3}{4} = 0.75$

24. $\dfrac{7}{5} = 1.4$

25. $\dfrac{5}{4} = 1.25$

26. $\dfrac{9}{5} = 1.8$

27. $\dfrac{2}{9} = 0.2222...$

28. $\dfrac{1}{20} = 00.5$

29. $\dfrac{3}{20} = 0.15$

30. $\dfrac{8}{5} = 1.6$

31. $\dfrac{18}{10} = 1.8$

Write the decimals as fractions:

32. $0.3 = \dfrac{3}{10}$

33. $0.2 = \dfrac{2}{10}$

34. $0.1 = \dfrac{1}{10}$

35. $0.01 = \dfrac{1}{100}$

36. $0.02 = \dfrac{2}{100}$

37. $0.11 = \dfrac{11}{100}$

38. $0.26 = \dfrac{26}{100}$

39. $1.3 = \dfrac{13}{10}$

40. $1.42 = \dfrac{142}{100}$

41. $0.011 = \dfrac{11}{1000}$

42. $0.312 = \dfrac{312}{1000}$

43. $0.16 = \dfrac{16}{100}$

44. $1.4 = \dfrac{14}{10}$

45. $2.043 = \dfrac{2043}{1000}$

46. $43.3 = \dfrac{433}{10}$

47. $4.12 = \dfrac{412}{100}$

48. $1.302 = \dfrac{1302}{1000}$

49. $1.111 = \dfrac{1111}{1000}$

50. $102.32 = \dfrac{10232}{100}$

51. $2.346 = \dfrac{2346}{1000}$

52. Write down the fractions in different ways:

$\dfrac{1}{2} = \dfrac{2}{4}$ 　 $\dfrac{1}{3} = \dfrac{2}{6}$ 　 $\dfrac{1}{4} = \dfrac{2}{8}$ 　 $\dfrac{7}{4} = \dfrac{14}{8}$ 　 $\dfrac{2}{3} = \dfrac{4}{6}$ 　 $\dfrac{11}{8} = \dfrac{22}{16}$

$\dfrac{a}{b} = \dfrac{2a}{2b}$ 　 $\dfrac{3a}{a} = \dfrac{3}{1} = 3$ 　 $\dfrac{a+2}{2+a} = \dfrac{1}{1} = 1$ 　 $\dfrac{x}{7x} = \dfrac{1}{7}$ 　 $\dfrac{1+a}{a-1} = \dfrac{2(1+a)}{2(a-1)} = \dfrac{1+a}{-1+a}$

Fill the blank to make the fractions equal:

53. $\frac{a}{3} = \frac{2a}{6}$ [handwritten: $\frac{2a}{6}_3$]

58. $\frac{a-b}{a-b} = 1$

54. $\frac{a-b}{4} = \frac{3a-3b}{12}$ [handwritten: $\frac{3a-3b}{12_4} \frac{3a-3b}{12} = \frac{3a-3b}{12}$]

59. $\frac{2-a}{-2} = \frac{a-2}{2}$ [handwritten: $\left(\frac{2}{-2}\right) - \left(\frac{-a}{-2}\right)$]

55. $\frac{a}{b} = \frac{2a}{2b}$ [handwritten: $\frac{a}{b}$]

60. $\frac{2a}{b} = \frac{8a}{4b}$

56. $\frac{1}{a} = \frac{3}{3a}$ [handwritten: $= \frac{1}{a}$]

61. $\frac{x^2}{2xy} = \frac{2x^3y}{4y^2}$ [handwritten: $= \frac{2xy}{4y^2}$]

57. $\frac{1}{3} = \frac{a}{3a}$

62. $\frac{2a}{7x} = \frac{4ax}{14x^2}$

[right margin handwritten:]
$\frac{\frac{3a}{12}}{\frac{4}{4}} - \frac{\frac{3b}{12}}{\frac{4}{4}}$
$\frac{a-b}{4}$

Perform the operations using fractions only; give the answer as a decimal and fraction:

63. $50 \cdot 0.1 =$ [handwritten: 5]

77. $2.5 \cdot 1.8 = \frac{25}{10} \cdot \frac{18}{10} = \frac{450}{100} = 4.5$

64. $85 \cdot 0.01 =$ [handwritten: 0.85]

78. $7.2 \cdot 8.8 = \frac{72}{10} \cdot \frac{88}{10} = \frac{6336}{100} = 63.36$

65. $45 \cdot 0.001 =$ [handwritten: 0.045]

79. $0.15 \cdot 2.01 = \frac{15}{100} \cdot \frac{201}{100} = \frac{3015}{10000} = 0.3015$

66. $6 \cdot 0.0001 =$ [handwritten: 0.0006]

80. $87.5 \cdot 0.2 = \frac{875}{100} \cdot \frac{2}{10} = \frac{1750}{1000} = 17.50$

67. $5123 \cdot 0.001 =$ [handwritten: 5123]

81. $31.5 \cdot 0.3 = \frac{315}{100} \cdot \frac{3}{10} = \frac{945}{1000} = 9.45$

68. $435 \cdot 0.01 =$ [handwritten: 4.35]

82. $0.215 \cdot 1.38 = \frac{215}{1000} \cdot \frac{138}{100} = \frac{29670}{100000} = .29670$

69. $15 \cdot 0.001 =$ [handwritten: 0.015]

83. $0.5 \cdot 1.23 = \frac{5}{10} \times \frac{123}{100} = \frac{615}{1000} = .615$

70. $-236 \cdot 0.0001 =$ [handwritten: -0.0236]

84. $1.02 \cdot 2.5 = \frac{102}{100} \cdot \frac{25}{10} = \frac{2550}{1000} = 2.55$

71. $1228 \cdot 0.1 =$ [handwritten: 122.8]

85. $31.7 \cdot 0.18 = \frac{317}{10} \cdot \frac{18}{100} = \frac{5706}{1000} = 5.706$

72. $1085 \cdot 0.01 =$ [handwritten: 10.85]

86. $21.2 \cdot 1.13 = \frac{212}{10} \cdot \frac{113}{100} = \frac{23956}{1000} = 23.956$

73. $4500 \cdot 0.001 =$ [handwritten: 4.5]

87. $0.42 \cdot 5.56 = \frac{42}{100} \times \frac{556}{100} = \frac{23352}{100000} = 23352$

74. $0.16 \cdot 0.0001 =$ [handwritten: 0.000016]

88. $3.1 \cdot 0.642 = \frac{31}{10} \times \frac{642}{1000} = \frac{19902}{10000} = 1.9902$

75. $12 \cdot 1.2 = \frac{12}{1} \cdot \frac{12}{10} = \frac{144}{10} = 1.44$

89. $13.7 \cdot 8.9 = \frac{137}{100} \cdot \frac{89}{10} = \frac{12192}{1000} = 12.192$

76. $25 \cdot 0.22 = \frac{25}{1} \cdot \frac{22}{100} = \frac{550}{100} = 5.5$

90. $1.07 \cdot 0.03 = \frac{107}{100} \cdot \frac{3}{100} = \frac{321}{10000} = 0.0321$

[left margin handwritten:]
$\frac{315}{3 \overline{\smash{)}945}}$

13

Perform the operations <u>using fractions only</u>; give the answer as a decimal and fraction:

91. $\dfrac{1}{0.1} =$ /0

92. $\dfrac{5}{0.01} = 500$

93. $\dfrac{-56}{0.001} = -5600$

94. $\dfrac{-2.3}{0.01} = -230$

95. $\dfrac{3}{0.1} = 30$

96. $\dfrac{0.55}{0.01} = 55$

97. $\dfrac{-31.6}{0.001} = -3160$

98. $\dfrac{0.023}{0.01} =$

99. $\dfrac{15}{0.01} = 150$

100. $\dfrac{-215}{0.01} = -21500$

101. $\dfrac{-45.6}{0.001} = .45600$

102. $\dfrac{-12.3}{0.01} = -1230$

103. $\dfrac{1}{0.02} =$

104. $\dfrac{-2}{0.03} =$

105. $\dfrac{-4.6}{0.05} =$

106. $\dfrac{-1.3}{0.06} =$

107. $\dfrac{1}{0.25} =$

108. $\dfrac{-2}{0.9} =$

109. $\dfrac{-4.1}{0.2} =$

110. $\dfrac{-1.3}{0.05} =$

111. $\dfrac{1}{0.015} =$

112. $\dfrac{-12}{0.6} =$

113. $\dfrac{-14}{0.003} =$

114. $\dfrac{-0.3}{0.02} =$

115. Write down the number that is 0.2 units on the left of −1:_____

116. Write down the number that is 0.5 units on the left of −2:_____

117. Write down the number that is 0.3 units on the right of −1:_____

118. Write down the number that is 0.4 units on the right of −2:_____

119. Write down the number that is 0.8 units on the left of −9:_____

120. Write down the number that is 0.2 units on the left of 0:_____

121. Write down the number that is 0.9 units on the right of −9:_____

122. Write down the number that is 0.2 units on the right of −5:_____

123. Write down the number that is 0.21 units on the left of −1:_____

124. Write down the number that is 0.51 units on the left of −2:_____

125. Write down the number that is 0.34 units on the right of −1:_____

126. Write down the number that is 0.06 units on the right of –10:_____

127. Write down the number that is 0.11 units on the right of –1:_____

128. Write down the number that is 0.01 units on the right of –2:_____

129. Write down the number that is 0.34 units on the right of 9:_____

130. Write down the number that is 0.06 units on the right of 10:__10.06_____

131. Write down the number that is 0.17 units on the right of –9:_____

132. Write down the number that is 0.78 units on the left of –3:_____

133. Write down the number that is 0.01 units on the left of –7:_____

134. Write down the number that is 0.02 units on the right of –1:_____

135. Write down the number that is 0.002 units on the right of –10:__–9.998_____

136. Write down the number that is 0.111 units on the right of –1:__0.889_____

137. Write down the number that is 0.021 units on the right of –2:__–1.979_____

138. Write down the number that is 0.4 units on the right of 9:__–8.6_____

139. Write down the number that is 0.03 units on the right of 10:__–9.97_____

140. Write down the number that is 0.202 units on the right of –9:__8.798_____

141. Write down numbers that are very close to 2 on its left:__1.999__ right:__2.001__

142. Write down numbers that are very close to 1 on its left:__.999__ right:__1.001__

143. Write down numbers that are very close to 0 on its left:__–0.001__ right:__0.001__

144. Write down numbers that are very close to –1 on its left:__–1.001__ right:__–0.999__

145. Write down numbers that are very close to –7 on its left:__7.001__ right:__–6.999__

146. Write down numbers that are very close to –12 on its left:__–12.001__ right:__–11.999__

147. Write down numbers that are very close to –2 on its left:__–2.001__ right:__–1.999__

148. Write down numbers that are very close to –10 on its left:__–10.001__ right:__–9.999__

149. Write down numbers that are very close to 9 on its left:__8.999__ right:__9.001__

150. Write down numbers that are very close to 100 on its left:__99.999__ right:__100.001__

151. Write down 2 numbers between 3 and 3.1: __3.06__ , __3.07__ . Write the

same numbers as fractions: __306/100__ , __307/100__

152. Write down 2 numbers between 6.2 and 6.3: __6.26__ , __6.27__ . Write the

same numbers as fractions: __626/100__ , __627/100__

153. Write down 2 numbers between 6.2 and 6.21: __6.201__ , __6.202__ . Write

the same numbers as fractions: __6201/1000__ , __6202/1000__

154. Write down 2 numbers between –5.2 and –5.3: __-5.21__ , __-5.22__ . Write

the same numbers as fractions: __521/100__ , __522/100__

155. Write down 2 numbers between 0.25 and 0.251: __0.2501__ , __0.2502__ . Write

the same numbers as fractions: __2501/1000__ , __2502/1000__

156. Write down 2 numbers between 1.11 and 1.111: __1.102__ , __1.103__ . Write

the same numbers as fractions: __1102/1000__ , __1103/1000__

157. Write down 2 numbers between 0.21 and 0.22: __0.202__ , __0.203__ . Write

the same numbers as fractions: __202/100__ , __203/100__

158. Write down 2 numbers between 5.99 and 5.999: __5.992__ , __5.993__ . Write

the same numbers as fractions: __5992/1000__ , __5.993/1000__

159. Write down 2 numbers between 6 and 6.01: __6.001__ , __6.002__ . Write the

same numbers as fractions: __6001/1000__ , __6002/1000__

160. Write the value of each position shown on the number line:

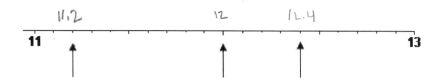

161. Write the value of each position shown on the number line:

162. Write the value of each position shown on the number line:

Batter

-0.65 → .62   → .57   → .15   -0.45

163. Circle the fractions that are greater than 1: $\dfrac{7}{6}, \dfrac{6}{7}, \dfrac{35}{34}, \dfrac{21}{7}, \dfrac{10001}{10000}$

164. A fraction will be greater than 1 if _____

165. Circle the fractions that are greater than 2: $\dfrac{50}{26}, \dfrac{60}{30}, \dfrac{35}{40}, \dfrac{20}{7}, \dfrac{20001}{10000}$

166. A fraction will be greater than 2 if _____

167. Circle the fractions that are greater than 5: $\dfrac{50}{10}, \dfrac{47}{9}, \dfrac{100}{6}, \dfrac{28}{3}, \dfrac{1201}{300}$

168. A fraction will be greater than 5 if _____

169. Circle the fractions that are smaller than $\dfrac{1}{2}$: $\dfrac{1}{3}, \dfrac{2}{3}, \dfrac{4}{9}, \dfrac{28}{29}, \dfrac{34}{60}, \dfrac{23}{51}, \dfrac{17}{32}, \dfrac{34}{67}$

170. A fraction will be smaller than $\dfrac{1}{2}$ if: D 2 wide as big as N _____

171. Circle the fractions that are smaller than $\dfrac{1}{3}$: $\dfrac{2}{7}, \dfrac{5}{9}, \dfrac{4}{11}, \dfrac{13}{29}, \dfrac{24}{75}, \dfrac{3}{11}$

172. A fraction will be smaller than $\dfrac{1}{3}$ if: D 3 times as big as N _____

Fill the blank with: <,> or =, assume a, b, n are positive constants:

173. $\dfrac{1}{2} > \dfrac{1}{3}$

174. $\dfrac{1}{3} > \dfrac{1}{4}$

175. $\dfrac{2}{5} < \dfrac{3}{7}$

176. $\dfrac{5}{8} < \dfrac{7}{11}$

177. $\dfrac{12}{7} > \dfrac{13}{8}$

178. $\dfrac{21}{8} > \dfrac{13}{5}$

179. $\dfrac{35}{8}$ __ $\dfrac{17}{4}$

183. $\dfrac{1}{n^2}$ __ $\dfrac{1}{n}$, $n \geq 1$

180. $\dfrac{a}{b}$ __ $\dfrac{a+1}{b+1}$

184. n^2 __ n , $0 \leq n \leq 1$

181. $\dfrac{a}{b-1}$ __ $\dfrac{a+1}{b+1}$

185. $\dfrac{1}{n^2}$ __ $\dfrac{1}{n}$, $0 \leq n \leq 1$

182. $\dfrac{1}{n+1}$ __ $\dfrac{1}{n}$, $n \geq 0$

186. $\dfrac{1}{a}$ __ $\dfrac{1}{b}$, $0 < a < b$

187. Indicate the location of the fractions on the number line: $-\dfrac{7}{6}, -\dfrac{6}{7}, \dfrac{17}{34}, \dfrac{-1}{7}, \dfrac{10001}{5000}$

188. Indicate the location of the fractions on the number line: $-\dfrac{1}{6}, -\dfrac{8}{7}, \dfrac{20}{9}, \dfrac{-10}{20}, \dfrac{99}{50}$

189. Indicate the location of the fractions on the number line: $-\dfrac{4}{5}, -\dfrac{3}{2}, \dfrac{5}{2}, \dfrac{9}{8}, \dfrac{100}{33}$

190. Indicate the location of the fractions on the number line: $-\dfrac{7}{5}, -\dfrac{9}{3}, \dfrac{2}{3}, \dfrac{1}{10}, -\dfrac{66}{32}$

191. Indicate the location of the fractions on the number line: $-\dfrac{7}{8}, -\dfrac{6}{13}, \dfrac{11}{21}, \dfrac{-2}{17}, \dfrac{100}{501}$

192. Indicate the location of the fractions on the number line: $-\dfrac{10}{6}, -\dfrac{8}{7}, \dfrac{181}{90}, \dfrac{-102}{200}, \dfrac{189}{60}$

193. Indicate the location of the fractions on the number line: $-\dfrac{6}{5}, -\dfrac{5}{2}, \dfrac{2}{5}, \dfrac{90}{80}, \dfrac{33}{100}$

194. Indicate the location of the fractions on the number line: $-\dfrac{12}{5}, -\dfrac{6}{3}, \dfrac{11}{6}, \dfrac{11}{10}, -\dfrac{37}{12}$

195. Indicate the location of the fractions on the number line: $-\dfrac{10}{4}, -\dfrac{2}{10}, \dfrac{64}{33}, \dfrac{21}{10}, -\dfrac{3}{1}$

Calculate:

196. $1+\dfrac{2}{3}=$

197. $\dfrac{5}{6}+\dfrac{2}{3}=$

198. $\dfrac{2}{7}-\dfrac{1}{6}=$

199. $5\cdot\dfrac{3}{8}-\dfrac{2}{12}=$

200. $\left(\dfrac{2}{14}-\dfrac{3}{7}\right)\cdot\dfrac{2}{9}=$

201. $\left(\dfrac{7}{2}-\dfrac{4}{3}\right)\cdot\dfrac{1}{5}=$

202. $\dfrac{5}{6}+\dfrac{2}{3}-6\cdot\dfrac{1}{2}=$

203. $\left(\dfrac{7}{2}-\dfrac{4}{3}\cdot\dfrac{1}{5}\right)-\dfrac{1}{5}=$

204. $2-\dfrac{3}{10}-\dfrac{4}{3}\cdot\dfrac{1}{5}=$

205. $4-\left(\dfrac{5}{6}-\dfrac{4}{3}\right)\cdot\dfrac{1}{5}=$

206. $\dfrac{1}{a}+\dfrac{1}{a}=$

207. $\dfrac{1}{d}+d=$

208. $\dfrac{1}{a}+\dfrac{a}{1}=$

209. $\dfrac{1}{b+1}+b=$

210. $\dfrac{a}{b}+\dfrac{1}{b}=$

211. $\dfrac{a}{b}+\dfrac{d}{b}=$

212. $\dfrac{a}{c}+\dfrac{d}{b}=$ $\dfrac{ab+cd}{cb}$

213. $\dfrac{a+b}{b}+\dfrac{d}{b}+2=$

214. $\dfrac{\left(\dfrac{a}{b}\right)}{b}=$

215. $\dfrac{a}{\left(\dfrac{a}{b}\right)}=$

216. $\dfrac{\left(\dfrac{b}{a}\right)}{b}=$

217. $\dfrac{\left(\dfrac{b}{a}\right)}{1}=$

218. $\dfrac{\left(\dfrac{1}{a}\right)}{b}=$

219. $\dfrac{\left(\dfrac{b}{1}\right)}{b}=$

220. $\dfrac{1}{\left(\dfrac{a}{b}\right)}=$

221. $\dfrac{\left(\dfrac{a}{b}\right)}{\left(\dfrac{a}{b}\right)}=$

222. $\dfrac{\left(\dfrac{b}{a}\right)}{\left(\dfrac{a}{b}\right)}=$

223. $\dfrac{\left(\dfrac{a}{1}\right)}{\left(\dfrac{a}{b}\right)}=$

224. $\dfrac{\left(\dfrac{a}{b}\right)}{\left(\dfrac{1}{b}\right)}=$

225. $\dfrac{\left(\dfrac{c+1}{d}\right)}{\left(\dfrac{1}{d}+d\right)}=$

226. $\dfrac{1}{\left(\dfrac{1}{d}+d\right)}+d=$

227. $\dfrac{1-d}{(d+2)}+\dfrac{2}{d}=$

228. $\dfrac{1}{d} + \dfrac{2}{d^2} + \dfrac{1}{d^3} =$

229. $\dfrac{2}{3} + \dfrac{3a}{c} - \dfrac{b}{2} =$

230. $\dfrac{\left(\dfrac{4}{b} - \dfrac{a}{7}\right)}{2} =$

231. $\dfrac{a}{c(c+1)} + \dfrac{d}{c+1} =$

232. $\dfrac{2x}{\left(\dfrac{2x+2}{3+x}\right)} + \dfrac{\left(\dfrac{x+1}{x-2}\right)}{x-3} =$

233. $\dfrac{\left(2x + \dfrac{1}{x}\right)}{\left(1 + \dfrac{1}{x}\right)} =$

234. $\dfrac{12}{2a} \times \dfrac{a+1}{6} =$

235. $\dfrac{12}{2a} \div \dfrac{a}{6} =$

236. $3 \times \dfrac{4}{3} =$

237. $3 \div \dfrac{4}{3} =$

238. $12 - \dfrac{4}{3} =$

239. $a \times \dfrac{b}{3c} =$

240. $\dfrac{b}{3a} \div 3a =$

241. $\dfrac{b}{3a} \times 3a =$

242. $\dfrac{\left(\dfrac{1}{3} + \dfrac{2}{5}\right)}{\left(\dfrac{5}{3} - \dfrac{1}{3}\right)} =$

243. $\dfrac{\left(\dfrac{b}{3c}\right)}{2} =$

244. $\dfrac{\left(\dfrac{1}{2}\right)}{2\left(\dfrac{2}{3c}\right)} =$

245. $\dfrac{\left(\dfrac{1}{2}\right)}{2} =$

246. $\dfrac{\left(\dfrac{2}{7}\right)}{3} =$

247. $\dfrac{2}{\left(\dfrac{2}{7}\right)} =$

248. $\dfrac{3}{\left(\dfrac{a}{7}\right)} =$

249. $\dfrac{6}{\left(\dfrac{8}{3}\right)} =$

250. $\dfrac{\left(\dfrac{4}{3}\right)}{\left(\dfrac{3}{4}\right)} =$

251. $\dfrac{\left(\dfrac{2}{3}\right)}{\left(\dfrac{4}{5}\right)} =$

252. $\dfrac{\left(\dfrac{2}{3}\right)}{\left(\dfrac{2}{3}\right)} =$

253. $\left(\dfrac{a}{b}\right) \cdot \left(\dfrac{c}{a}\right) =$

254. $\left(\dfrac{2}{c}\right) \cdot \left(\dfrac{c}{7}\right) =$

255. $\left(\dfrac{b+1}{3}\right) \cdot \left(\dfrac{2}{b}\right) =$

256. $\left(\dfrac{z+1}{z-2}\right) \cdot \left(\dfrac{4}{z+1}\right) =$

257. $\left(\dfrac{3a+6}{5}\right) \cdot \left(\dfrac{1}{a+2}\right) =$

258. $\left(\dfrac{2c-4}{c}\right) \cdot \left(\dfrac{2c}{4c-8}\right) =$

259. $\dfrac{1}{\left(\dfrac{2}{4}\right)} \cdot \left(\dfrac{2}{3}\right) =$

260. $\dfrac{\left(\dfrac{3}{4}\right)}{\left(\dfrac{a}{2}\right)} \cdot \left(\dfrac{2}{3}\right) =$

261. $\dfrac{\left(\dfrac{1}{a}\right)}{\left(\dfrac{2}{a}\right)} + 2 =$

262. $\dfrac{\left(x+\dfrac{1}{x}\right)}{\left(1-\dfrac{1}{x}\right)} =$

263. $\dfrac{\left(\dfrac{1}{1+x}+1\right)}{\left(x-\dfrac{2}{x}\right)}=$

264. $\dfrac{\left(\dfrac{x}{3}-2\right)}{\left(2-\dfrac{2+x}{3}\right)}=$

265. $\dfrac{2x}{\left(\dfrac{2}{3+x}\right)}+\dfrac{\left(\dfrac{2}{x}\right)}{x+3}=$

266. $\dfrac{a-b}{\left(1-\dfrac{a}{b}\right)}=$

267. $\dfrac{2}{(1-a)}+\dfrac{2}{a(1-a)}=$

268. $\dfrac{a}{(3+a)^2}+\dfrac{2}{(a+3)}=$

269. $\dfrac{1}{(1-x)^3}+\dfrac{2}{(1-x)^2}=$

270. $\dfrac{1}{(1-x)^3}+\dfrac{2}{x(1-x)^2}=$

271. $\dfrac{1}{(1-x)(2-x)}+\dfrac{2}{x(1-x)^2}=$

272. $\dfrac{2}{(1-x)x}+\dfrac{2}{x^2(1-x)^2}=$

273. $\dfrac{a^2+1}{a}-\dfrac{a+1}{a^2+a}=$

274. $\dfrac{a+x}{x}-\dfrac{y+1}{xy}+\dfrac{2}{y}=$

275. $\dfrac{a+x}{a-x} \div \dfrac{a+x}{x-a} =$

276. $\dfrac{a+x}{a^2-x^2} - \dfrac{a-x}{x-a} =$

277. $\left(\dfrac{2c-4}{c} \right) \div \left(\dfrac{4c^2+16}{c^2} \right) =$

278. $\left(\dfrac{6xy+2}{3y} \right) \div \left(\dfrac{3xy+1}{6y^5} \right) =$

279. $\left(\dfrac{x^2-z^2}{xyz} \right) + \left(\dfrac{z-x^2}{xy} \right) =$

True or False:

280. $\dfrac{a+b}{c} = \dfrac{a}{c} + \dfrac{b}{c}$

281. $\dfrac{a+b}{c+d} = \dfrac{a}{c} + \dfrac{b}{d}$

282. $\dfrac{a+b}{a} = 1 + \dfrac{b}{a}$

283. $\dfrac{a-b}{b-a} = -1$

284. $\dfrac{a}{c+d} = \dfrac{a}{c} + \dfrac{a}{d}$

285. $\dfrac{c-d}{d} = c$

286. $\dfrac{c-d}{d} = -1 + c$

287. $\dfrac{ab}{ad} = \dfrac{b}{d}$

288. $\dfrac{a(c-d)}{a} = c - d$

289. $\dfrac{ac-d}{c-d} = a$

290. $\dfrac{2a+d}{d-2a} = -1$

1.4. – EXPONENTS

Product:

$a^0 = $ ___ $a^1 = $ ___ $a^2 = $ ___ $\times$ ___

$a^3 = $ ___ $\times$ ___ $\times$ ___

$a^3 a^2 = $ _____ $= $ ___

$$a^m a^n = \underline{\hspace{2cm}}$$

Division:

$$\frac{a^5}{a^3} = \underline{\overline{\hspace{2cm}}} = \overline{\overline{\hspace{1cm}}} = \underline{\hspace{0.5cm}}$$

$$\frac{a^2}{a^5} = \underline{\overline{\hspace{2cm}}} = \overline{\overline{\hspace{1cm}}} = \underline{\hspace{0.5cm}}$$

$$\frac{a^m}{a^n} = \underline{\hspace{1cm}}$$

Power:

$(a^2)^3 = $ _____ $= $ ___

$$\left(\frac{a^2}{b}\right)^3 = \underline{\overline{\hspace{2cm}}} = \overline{\overline{\hspace{1cm}}}$$

$$(a^m)^n = \underline{\hspace{1cm}}$$

$$\left(\frac{a^m}{b^k}\right)^n = \overline{\overline{\hspace{1cm}}}$$

Radicals:

$(a^3)^{\frac{1}{2}} = $ ___ $= $ ___

$(a^4)^{\frac{1}{7}} = $ ___ $= $ ___

$$(a^m)^{\frac{1}{n}} = \underline{\hspace{1cm}} = \underline{\hspace{1cm}}$$

Exercises

Write in all possible forms and evaluate without using a calculator (follow example):

1. $4^{-1} = \dfrac{1}{4} = 0.25$

2. $10^0 = $

3. $10^1 = $

4. $10^3 = $

5. $10^{-1} = $

6. $10^{-2} = $

7. $10^{-3} = $

8. $10^{-4} = $

9. $2^0 = $

10. $2^1 = $

11. $2^{-1} = $

12. $2^{-2} = $

13. $2^{-3} = $

14. $2^{-4} = $

15. $(-1)^0 = $

16. $-1^0 = $

17. $(-1)^1 = $

18. $-1^1 = $

19. $(-1)^{-1} = $

20. $-1^2 = $

21. $(-1)^2 =$

22. $-1^2 =$

23. $(-1)^{-2} =$

24. $-1^{-2} =$

25. $(-3)^0 =$

26. $(-3)^1 =$

27. $-3^1 =$

28. $(-3)^2 =$

29. $-3^2 =$

30. $(-3)^{-1} =$

31. $-3^{-1} =$

32. $(-3)^{-2} =$

33. $-3^{-2} =$

34. $9^{\frac{1}{2}} =$

35. $4^{\frac{1}{2}} =$

36. $16^{-\frac{1}{2}} =$

37. $8^{-\frac{2}{3}} =$

38. $27^{-\frac{4}{3}} =$

39. $125^{-\frac{1}{3}} =$

40. $16^{\frac{3}{4}} =$

41. $(3^{-1})^2 =$

42. $(-8^{-3})^{\frac{2}{3}} =$

43. $(-27^{-1})^{\frac{2}{3}} =$

44. $(16^{-1})^{-\frac{3}{2}} =$

45. $\left(\dfrac{1}{2}\right)^0 =$

46. $\left(\dfrac{1}{2}\right)^1 =$

47. $\left(\dfrac{1}{2}\right)^{-1} =$

48. $\left(\dfrac{1}{2}\right)^2 =$

49. $\left(\dfrac{1}{2}\right)^{-2} =$

50. $\left(\dfrac{3}{5}\right)^0 =$

51. $\left(\dfrac{3}{4}\right)^1 =$

52. $\left(\dfrac{2}{5}\right)^{-1} =$

53. $\left(\dfrac{5}{11}\right)^2 =$

54. $\left(\dfrac{a}{b}\right)^{-1} =$

55. $\left(\dfrac{1}{b}\right)^{-1} =$

56. $b^{-1} =$

57. $\left(\dfrac{-11}{2}\right)^{-2} =$

58. $\left(\dfrac{3}{-2}\right)^1 =$

59. $\left(\dfrac{-12}{\sqrt{2}}\right)^{-1} =$

60. $\left(\dfrac{5\sqrt{2}}{11}\right)^2 =$

61. $\left(\dfrac{-2\sqrt{5}}{2}\right)^{-2} =$

62. $\left(\dfrac{3+5\sqrt{2}}{-2}\right)^2 =$

63. $\left(\dfrac{-12}{2-\sqrt{2}}\right)^{-2} =$

64. $\left(\dfrac{5+\sqrt{2}}{11}\right)^{2} =$

65. $\left(\dfrac{-2-\sqrt{5}}{2+\sqrt{2}}\right)^{-2} =$

66. $\left(\dfrac{-27}{8}\right)^{\frac{2}{3}} =$

67. $\left(\dfrac{16}{9}\right)^{\frac{3}{4}} =$

68. $\left(\dfrac{1}{2}\right)^{\frac{3}{2}} =$

69. $\left(\dfrac{9}{16}\right)^{\frac{1}{2}} =$

70. $\left(\dfrac{8}{27}\right)^{-\frac{1}{3}} =$

71. $a^{-2} =$

72. $a^{-\frac{1}{2}} =$

73. $a^{-\frac{2}{7}} =$

74. $5^{27}5^{-29} =$

75. $4^{27}2^{-49} =$

76. $9^{12}3^{-20} =$

77. $a^{7}a^{-9} =$

78. $(-125)^{\frac{2}{3}} =$

79. $\dfrac{5^{10}}{5^{2}} =$

80. $\dfrac{3^{10}}{9^{2}}3^{-2} =$

81. $\dfrac{3^{1}}{9^{\frac{1}{2}}}3^{-\frac{1}{2}} =$

82. $\dfrac{\sqrt{2}\cdot4^{2}}{2^{\frac{3}{4}}}2^{-\frac{1}{2}} =$

83. $\dfrac{a^{-1}}{a^{-2}} =$

84. $\sqrt{\dfrac{a^{-10}}{a^{-12}}} =$

85. $\sqrt{\sqrt{a}} =$

86. $\sqrt{a\sqrt{a}} =$

87. $a\sqrt{\sqrt[3]{a}} =$

88. $\dfrac{1}{\sqrt[4]{\sqrt{a}}} =$

89. $\sqrt{\sqrt{\sqrt[7]{a^{2}}}} =$

90. $\sqrt[3]{\sqrt{a\sqrt{a^{2}}}} =$

91. $\dfrac{2\sqrt{a}}{\sqrt{2a}} =$

92. $\dfrac{\sqrt{a}}{\sqrt[3]{a}} =$

93. $\dfrac{a\sqrt{a}}{\sqrt[5]{a}} =$

94. $\dfrac{\sqrt{8}\sqrt{a}}{\sqrt{2a}} =$

95. $\sqrt{\dfrac{\sqrt{a}a^{-1}}{a\sqrt{a^{-2}}}} =$

96. $\dfrac{a}{\sqrt{2a^{-1}}} =$

97. $\dfrac{\sqrt{\dfrac{1}{a}}}{\sqrt{aa^{-2}}} =$

98. $\left(\dfrac{2}{5}\right)^3 \times \left(\dfrac{5}{3}\right)^3 =$

99. $\left(\dfrac{4}{7}\right)^2 \div \left(\dfrac{9}{7}\right)^2 =$

100. $\sqrt{\left(\dfrac{7}{5}\right)^7 \div \left(\dfrac{49}{125}\right)^3} =$

101. $\left(\dfrac{2}{5}\right)^3 \cdot \left(\dfrac{3}{5}\right)^{-4} =$

102. $\left(\dfrac{4^2}{5^{-1}}\right)^3 \cdot \left(\dfrac{25^{-1}}{64}\right)^2 =$

103. $\left(\dfrac{3^{-5}}{4^2}\right)^2 \div \left(\dfrac{9^{-2}}{2^3}\right)^3 =$

104. $\left(\dfrac{5^4}{7^{-3}}\right)^2 \div \left(\dfrac{25^{-1}}{49}\right)^{-3} =$

105. $\sqrt[3]{\left(\dfrac{3}{4}\right)^5 \div \left(\dfrac{9}{64}\right)^2} =$

106. $\left(\dfrac{2^{-3}}{3^{-2}}\right)^3 \cdot \left(\dfrac{4}{27}\right)^2 =$

107. $2^{-1} + 2 =$

108. $3^{-1} - 3^{-2} =$

109. $5^{-1} - 5^{-2} =$

110. $3^{-3} + 2^{-2} =$

111. $3^{-2} + 4^{-2} =$

112. $7^{-2} + 2^{-2} =$

113. $8^{-2} - 3^{-2} =$

114. $7^{-2} - 2^{-3} =$

115. $a^{-1} + a^{-1} =$

116. $ba^{-1} + a^{-1} =$

117. $2x^{-1} + x^{-2} =$

118. $a^{-1} - ba^{-1} =$

119. $(ba)^{-1} + a^{-1} =$

120. $\dfrac{1}{x} + x^{-2} =$

121. $ba^{-1} + (ba)^{-1} =$

122. $\dfrac{a+a}{3a} =$

123. $\dfrac{2a+a}{5\sqrt{a}} =$

124. $\dfrac{a^2+a^3}{2a} =$

125. $\dfrac{4b^{-1}a^2}{2ba^{-1}} =$

126. $\dfrac{4b^{-3}}{\sqrt{2b}} =$

127. $\dfrac{9b^{-\frac{1}{2}}a^2}{27^{-1}b^{-1}a} =$

128. $\dfrac{4b^{-1}a^5a^2}{8ba^{-1}} =$

129. $\dfrac{\sqrt[4]{a^2}+\sqrt{a}}{\sqrt{2a}} =$

130. $\dfrac{b\sqrt[3]{a}+ba^{\frac{1}{3}}}{a\sqrt{b}} =$

131. $\dfrac{3^{-2}}{9^{\frac{2}{3}}}27^{\frac{5}{4}} =$

132. $\dfrac{4^{-4}\sqrt{2}}{8^{-\frac{2}{3}}}16^{\frac{3}{4}} =$

133. $\sqrt{5}\,\dfrac{25^2 5^{-1}}{25^{\frac{4}{3}}}5^{\frac{1}{4}}\sqrt[3]{5} =$

134. $\dfrac{4^{-2}2^{-4}}{16^2(\sqrt[6]{16^4})}8^{\frac{1}{4}}2^{-1} =$

135. $x\sqrt{x}\sqrt{3} =$

136. $x\sqrt{x}+\sqrt{2x} =$

137. $\dfrac{1}{x\sqrt{x}} =$

138. $\dfrac{x\sqrt[3]{x}}{\sqrt{x}} =$

139. $\dfrac{\sqrt{2x}}{x\sqrt{4x}} =$

140. $\dfrac{\sqrt{3x}}{x+x^2} =$

141. $\dfrac{\sqrt{3x}}{\sqrt[3]{3x^2}} =$

142. $\dfrac{\sqrt{25x^2}}{\sqrt[3]{5x^3}} =$

143. $s^n s^{2n} s^2 =$

144. $a^{2k}ba^3b^{2k}a =$

145. $\dfrac{3^n}{9^n}27^n =$

146. $\dfrac{3^{2n+1}}{81^{n-2}}27^{2n} =$ *foo dae*

147. $\dfrac{6^n}{8^{2n}}24^{3n} =$

148. $\dfrac{2^n}{8^{n+1}}16^{n-2} =$

149. $\dfrac{5^{-n}}{125^{2n-2}}5^{-n+2} =$

150. $\dfrac{12^{2n+1}}{48^{3n-1}}\div 36^{4n} =$

151. $\dfrac{x^{-n}}{x^{2n-2}}x^{-n+5} =$

152. $\dfrac{2x^{-n+1}}{2^2 x^{3n+2}}x^{n+5} =$

29

153. $\dfrac{2yx^{-2n+3}}{2^5 y^{-1} x^{-4n+2}} x^{-2n+1} =$

154. $\dfrac{4^2 y^2 x^{-3} z}{2^2 xz^2 y^{-1} x} x^{-2} z^2 =$

155. $\dfrac{4^2 y^2 (x^{-2} z^2)^{-2}}{(2^2 x)^3 z^2 y^{-1} x} x^{-2} z^2 =$

156. $\dfrac{4^{-2} y^3 (x^{-2} z^3)^{-1}}{(2^{-3} x)^{-3} z^{-2} y^{-1} x} xz^2 =$

157. $\left(\dfrac{a}{b^2}\right)^2 \div \left(\dfrac{a^{-1}}{b^3}\right)^{-3} \cdot \left(\dfrac{1}{b}\right)^3 =$

158. $\left(\dfrac{ab}{b^2}\right)^{-2} \div \left(\dfrac{(2ba)^{-1}}{\bullet\ b^3}\right)^{-3} \cdot \left(\dfrac{2}{b}\right)^3 =$

159. $\dfrac{a^{-2} b^n (a^{-2n} b^3)^{-1}}{(b^{-3n} a)^3 \sqrt{ab^{-1}}} =$

160. $\dfrac{a^{-2} b^n (a^{-2n} b^2)^n}{(b^{-3n} a)^n a^{-2n} b^n} =$

161. $\dfrac{3^n a^{-2} b^n (a^{-2n} b^3)^{n+1}}{(9^n b^{-2n} a)^n a^{-2n} b^{n+2}} =$

162. $\dfrac{3^n + 3^{n+1}}{3^{n-1}} =$

163. $\dfrac{4^n + 4^{n-1}}{2^{n-2}} =$

164. $\dfrac{7^{2n} + 7^{2n-1}}{7^{2n-2}} =$

165. $\dfrac{7^{3n-1} - 7^{3n}}{7^{2n-2}} =$

166. $\dfrac{3^n + 3^{n+1}}{3^{n-1} + 3^n} =$

167. $\dfrac{2^n + 2^{n-1}}{2^{n-2} + 2^{n-1}} =$

168. $\dfrac{2^n - 2^{n-1} + 2^{n-2}}{2^{n-2} + 2^{n-1} - 2^n} =$

169. $\dfrac{3^n - 3^{n-3} + 3^{n-2}}{3^{n-2} - 3^{n-1} - 3^n} =$

1.5 – ALGEBRAIC EXPRESSIONS

Expand and/or Sum and simplify as much as possible:

1. $x + x =$

2. $x - 2x =$

3. $xy + xy =$

4. $3x^2 y - xy =$

5. $x^2 + x - 5x^2 =$

6. $3xy^2 + xy - x^2 y + 7xy =$

7. $x + y - (2x - 3y) =$

8. $2(x^2 y + xy) - x(2xy - 3y) =$

9. $b(ab + b) - a(b^2 - b) =$

10. $x + \dfrac{x}{2} =$

11. $a + 2(\dfrac{a}{2} - 3a) =$

12. $2(5z^2 y^3 + 3zy^3) - 2zy(6zy^2 - 8y^2) =$

13. $2(5z^2 y^3 \cdot 3zy^3) =$

14. $b \cdot ab^3 ab =$

15. $b(ab \cdot b) \cdot a(b^2) =$

16. $x \cdot ayb^6 yxb^2 =$

17. $x^m x =$

18. $a^n x^m x^t =$

19. $\sqrt{x} + \sqrt{x} =$

20. $\sqrt{x} \cdot \sqrt{x} =$

21. $x(5 + x) =$

22. $(x + 1)^2 =$

23. $(x - 1)^2 =$

24. $(x + 2)^2 =$

25. $(x - 2)^2 =$

26. $(a + b)^2 =$

27. $(a - b)^2 =$

28. $(2a + b)^2 =$

29. $(a - 3b)^2 =$

30. $(2x + 3)^2 =$

31. $(4 - x)^2 =$

32. $(x + 2)(x - 3) =$

33. $(x - 2)(x + 2) =$

34. $(3 + x)(x - 7) =$

35. $(2x + 2)(x - 5) =$

36. $(3x - 1)(x + 2) =$

37. $(x - 1)(x + 1) =$

38. $(x - 2)(x + 2) =$

39. $(x - a)(x + a) =$

40. $\sqrt{x} \cdot \sqrt{x} \cdot \sqrt{x} \cdot \sqrt{x} =$

31

41. $\sqrt{x} + \sqrt{x} + \sqrt{x} + \sqrt{x} =$

42. $2\sqrt{x} + 3\sqrt{x} - \sqrt{x} - \sqrt{x} =$

43. $(x - \sqrt{a})(x + \sqrt{a}) =$

44. $(x + 4)(x^2 - 4x + 3) =$

45. $(x + 6)(x^5 - 6x^2 - 3x + 1) =$

46. $(x - a)(x + 2a + b) =$

47. $(\sqrt{7} - \sqrt{x})(\sqrt{7} + \sqrt{x}) =$

48. $(ax - \sqrt{b})(ax + \sqrt{b}) =$

49. $(\sqrt{a} - \sqrt{b})(\sqrt{a} + \sqrt{b}) =$

50. $(6 - \dfrac{x}{8})(6 + \dfrac{8}{x}) =$

51. $(\dfrac{1}{x} - \dfrac{x}{8})(x + \dfrac{8}{x}) =$

52. $(\sqrt{7} - \sqrt{x})(\sqrt{7} + \dfrac{1}{\sqrt{x}}) =$

53. $(2x - 3c)(2x + 3c - 1) =$

54. $x(x + 8)^2 =$

55. $(x - 6)^2 3x =$

56. $(5 - \sqrt{ab})(5 + \sqrt{ab}) =$

57. $2 - (x + 1)^2 =$

58. $(x + 3)^2 - (x + 2)^2 =$

59. $(x - 2)^2 + (x + 2)^2 =$

60. $(x - \sqrt{2})^2 =$

61. $(x - \sqrt{2})(x + \sqrt{2}) =$

62. $5(2x - \sqrt{a})(2x + \sqrt{a}) =$

63. $(\sqrt{a} - \sqrt{b})^2 =$

64. $2(x - \sqrt{10})(x + \sqrt{10}) =$

65. $(x - \dfrac{2}{x})^2 =$

66. $(x - \dfrac{2}{\sqrt{x}})^2 =$

67. $(3x - \dfrac{2}{3\sqrt{x}})^2 =$

68. $2(\sqrt{a} - \dfrac{1}{\sqrt{a}})^2 =$

69. $(\sqrt{a} - \dfrac{1}{\sqrt{a}})(-\sqrt{a} - \dfrac{1}{\sqrt{a}}) =$

70. $(2^x + 2^{-x})^2 =$

71. $(4^{2x} + 2^{-x})^2 =$

72. $(3^{2x} + 3^{-2x})^2 =$

73. $(7^x - 7)^2 =$

74. $(a^{nx} - b^{nx})^2 =$

75. $(x^2 - y^2)(x^2 + y^2) =$

76. $(x^3 - y^3)(x^3 + y^3) =$

77. $(x^n - y^n)(x^n + y^n) =$

78. $(a^x - b^x)^2 =$

79. $(a^{mx} - a^{-mx})^2 =$

80. $(a^{mx} - a^{-mx})(a^{mx} + a^{-mx}) =$

Given the following polynomials, obtain the maximum possible common factor:

1. $x - ax =$

2. $3x - x - ax =$

3. $-x + ax =$

4. $xy + 2x =$

5. $8xy - 2y =$

6. $-6x + 12xy =$

7. $12xyz + 2xy =$

8. $14xy - 2yz =$

9. $12xz + 14xyz =$

10. $xy + 4y^2 + 5y =$

11. $z - 4z^2 + 8zy =$

12. $-8x^3 - 4xyz =$

13. $-6x^4 + x^2y^2 + x^2 =$

14. $-9x^7y^3 + 3x^3y =$

15. $-90x^{10}y^5 - 3x^3y^4 =$

16. $-80x^4y^6z^8 + 8x^{12}y^4z^6 =$

17. $xyz + 2x^2y^2z^2 + 3x^3y^3z^3 =$

18. $10x^3y^2z^4 + 2x^2y^6z^4 - 5x^2y^4z^2 =$

19. $20x^{30}y^{20}z^{40} - 2x^{20}y^{60}z^{40} - 2x^{20}y^{40}z^{20} =$

20. $ax^m + x^m =$

21. $ax^{m+1} + x^m =$

22. $ax^m + x^{m-1} =$

23. $ax^m - x =$

24. $-ax^m - x^{2m} =$

25. $z^{n+1} - z^{n+2} =$

26. $ax^{m+2} + x^{m-1} =$

Given the following polynomials factor, if possible.

1. $x^2 - 6x + 9 =$

2. $x^2 - 5x + 6 =$

3. $x^2 + 4x + 10 =$

4. $-x^2 - x + 6 =$

5. $x^2 + x - 6 =$

6. $x^2 + 5x + 6 =$

7. $-x^2 + 7x - 10 =$

8. $x^2 - 6x + 12 =$

9. $x^2 + 3x + 2 =$

10. $x^2 - x - 2 =$

11. $-x^2 + 4x =$

12. $-x^2 + 4x - 10 =$

13. $x^2 + x - 2 =$

14. $x^2 + 3x + 7 =$

15. $x^2 - 3x + 2 =$

16. $x^2 - x + 7 =$

17. $x^2 + 5x + 9 =$

18. $-x^2 - 5x + 6 =$

19. $x^2 - 2xa + a^2 =$

20. $x^2 - a^2 =$

21. $c^2 - a^2 =$

22. $x^2 - x =$

23. $2x^2 - x =$

24. $2x^2 + 3x =$

25. $x^2 + 5x =$

26. $x^2 - 7x + 12 =$

27. $2x^2 - 4x =$

28. $x^2 - 7x + 10 =$

29. $x^2 - 7x + 6 =$

30. $x^2 - x - 12 =$

31. $x^2 + x - 12 =$

32. $x^2 - 3x - 10 =$

33. $x^2 - 8x - 9 =$

34. $x^2 - 1 =$

35. $x^2 + 1 =$

36. $x^2 - 2 =$

37. $x^2 - 3 =$

38. $x^2 - 4 =$

39. $-x^2 + 1 =$

40. $-x^2 + 2 =$

41. $-x^2 + 3 =$

42. $-x^2 + 4 =$

43. $-x^2 + 13 =$

44. $-x^2 + 49 =$

45. $2x^2 - 72 =$

46. $-x^2 - 2 =$

47. $5x^2 - 125 =$

48. $-x^2 + 81 =$

49. $-3x^2 + 27 =$

50. $2x^2 - 6 =$

51. $3x^2 - 1 =$

52. $-2x^2 - 3 =$

53. $5x^2 - 6 =$

54. $4x^2 - 2 =$

55. $-8x^2 - 1 =$

56. $x^2 - b =$

57. $ax^2 - b =$

58. $-ax^2 + b =$

59. $2x^2 - 4x + 2 =$

60. $3x^2 - 3x - 18 =$

61. $-4x^2 + 20x + 24 =$

62. $7x^2 + 7x - 630 =$

63. $-5x^2 + 10x + 75 =$

64. $3x^2 - 12x - 63 =$

65. $2x^2 + 2x - 112 =$

66. $2x^2 - 12x - 14 =$

67. $-5x^2 + 15x + 90 =$

68. $-3x^2 - 12x - 12 =$

69. $-2x^2 - 26x - 84 =$

70. $6x^2 + 48x + 72 =$

Conclusion:

Factoring a quadratic expression is possible only if _____ Example: _____

If _____ both factors _____ Example: _____

If _____ Example: _____

34

Factor and simplify:

1. $\dfrac{x^2 - 6x + 9}{x^2 - 7x + 12} =$

2. $\dfrac{x^2 - 5x + 6}{x^2 + x - 6} =$

3. $\dfrac{x^2 - 9}{x^2 - 7x + 12} =$

4. $\dfrac{x^2 - 1}{x^2 - 2x + 1} =$

5. $\dfrac{x^2 - 6x + 8}{x^2 - 4x + 4} =$

6. $\dfrac{x^2 - 16}{x^2 + 5x + 4} =$

7. $\dfrac{x^2 - x - 2}{x^2 + 6x + 5} =$

8. $\dfrac{3x + 9}{x^2 - 9} =$

9. $\dfrac{x^2 - 6x}{x^2 - 7x + 6} =$

10. $\dfrac{x^2 - x}{x^2 + x - 2} =$

11. $\dfrac{x^2 - 4}{x^2 + x - 2} =$

12. $\dfrac{4 - x}{x - 4} =$

13. $\dfrac{x^2 - x}{1 - x} =$

14. $\dfrac{2x - 1}{4x^2 - 4x + 1} =$

15. $\dfrac{x^2 - 2x}{x^2 - 4} =$

16. $\dfrac{4x^2 + 4x + 1}{2x^2 + 5x + 2} =$

17. $\dfrac{3x^2 + 4x + 1}{9x^2 - 1} =$

18. $\dfrac{4x^2 + 4x - 3}{2x^2 - 13x + 15} =$

19. $\dfrac{4x^2 + 4x - 3}{2x^2 + 13x + 15} =$

20. $\dfrac{5x^2 - 12x + 4}{10x^2 + 16x - 8} =$

21. $\dfrac{3x^2 - 20x - 7}{x^2 - 9x + 14} =$

22. $\dfrac{4x^2 - 2x - 20}{x^2 - 3x + 10} =$

23. $\dfrac{2x^2 - 13x + 6}{2x^2 - 14x + 12} =$

24. $\dfrac{81x^2 + 162x + 81}{x^2 - 1} =$

25. $\dfrac{4x^2 + 11x + 6}{4x^2 + 15x + 9} =$

26. $\dfrac{4x^2 + 12x + 9}{4x^2 - 9} =$

27. $\dfrac{4x^2 - 20x + 25}{2x^2 - 15x + 25} =$

28. $\dfrac{7x^2 + 2x - 5}{x^2 - 4x - 5} =$

29. $\dfrac{2x^2 + 15x + 27}{2x^2 + 3x - 27} =$

30. $\dfrac{4x^2 + 6x + 2}{2x^2 - 2} =$

1.6. – PERCENTAGES

1. A percentage is _____ we sometimes use _____ or

   _____ to represent it.

2. Write as a fraction and as a decimal:

   a. 1% = _____   h. 0.1% = _____

   b. 10% = _____   i. 0.13% = _____

   c. 89% = _____   j. 0.06% = _____

   d. 100% = _____   k. 0.072% = _____

   e. 101% = _____   l. 1.03% = _____

   f. 110% = _____   m. 7.056% = _____

   g. 200% = _____   n. 5356% = _____

A PERCENTAGE OF A QUANTITY

3. Find (write the expression and simplify it to get a final answer):

   a. 1% of 900 = _____   i. 100% of 900 = _____

   b. 2% of 900 = _____   j. 101% of 900 = _____

   c. 3% of 900 = _____   k. 110% of 900 = _____

   d. 10% of 900 = _____   l. 120% of 900 = _____

   e. 15% of 900 = _____   m. 125% of 900 = _____

   f. 20% of 900 = _____   n. 140% of 900 = _____

   g. 25% of 900 = _____   o. 200% of 900 = _____

   h. 35% of 900 = _____   p. 300% of 900 = _____

4. Find (write the expression and simplify it to get a final answer):

   a. 1% of 50 = _____   e. 20% of 110 = _____

   b. 2% of 50 = _____   f. 25% of 350 = _____

   c. 10% of 70 = _____   g. 35% of 1100 = _____

   d. 15% of 90 = _____   h. 100% of 125 = _____

i. 101% of 520 = _____   m. 140% of 9100 = _____

j. 110% of 130 = _____   n. 200% of 240 = _____

k. 120% of 122 = _____   o. 300% of 120 = _____

l. 125% of 250 = _____   p. A% of M = _____

5. Johann scored 130 out 200 in a test, find his score in percentage?

6. Given that in a group of 20 students, 3 are taller than 188cm. Write down the percentage of student shorter than 188cm_____

7. Nina scored 70 out 80 in a test, find her score in percentage?

8. Given a square with side x. Inside it a smaller square is drawn with side length of 90% of x. Find the percentage of the area that is shaded and not shaded.

9. Given a square with length side x and a circle inscribed in it. Find the percentage of the area shaded and not shaded.

10. Given the following figure. a is 40% of x and b is 40% less of y.

   a. Find the areas of both rectangles in terms of x and y.
   b. Find the percentage of the area shaded and not shaded.

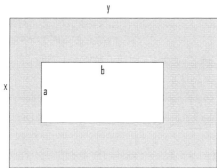

11. In a certain box of cookies there are 80 cookies of 3 colours: white, brown and black. 15% of the cookies are white, 15 cookies are brown and the rest are black.

    a. Find the percentage of brown and black cookies in the box.

    b. Dani ate 2 cookies of each colour; find the new percentages of each kind.

12. Jeff bought a car for 4000$ and sold it for 5000$, Find his benefit in percent.

13. Jessica bought a car for 4000$ and sold it for 3000$, Find her lost in percent.

14. Given the rectangle, write down the percentage of it that is shaded: _____

    Simplify the fraction:

15. Given the following square. Write down the percentage of it that is

    shaded: _____, Simplify the fraction:

16. Given the following circle, find the percentage of the circle that is shaded and not shaded. Write your answer as a fraction, decimal and percentage.

    Shaded: _____   Not Shaded: _____

17. It is known that the area shaded is 30% of 60% of the circle. Find the percentage of the circle that is shaded and not shaded. Write your answer as a fraction, decimal and percentage.

    Shaded: _____   Not Shaded: _____

18. It is known that 20% of 75% of a class of 40 students are going to the cinema. How many are going? Write your answer as a fraction and decimal.

19. It is known that 10% of 40% of a certain amount is 40 euros, find the amount.

20. It is known that 60% of 40% of a certain amount is 20 euros, find the amount.

21. Find 10% of 20% of 30% of 200: _____

22. Find 20% of 30% of 30% of 300: _____

23. Find 80% of 120% of 400: _____

24. Find 90% of 130% of 70% 500: _____

25. It is known that 20% of 20% of a certain amount is 5 euros, find the amount.

26. It is known that 10% of 30% of 5% of a certain amount is 50 euros, find the amount.

27. Given a circle with radius R cm. We know that the area shaded is 20π cm^2 and that 40% of 90% the circle is shaded. Find R in its most simplified form.

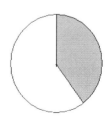

INCREASE OR DECREASE BY A PERCENTAGE

28. The price of a shirt is A $. In case the price increases by:

    a. In case the price increases by 1, state the new price in terms of A _____

    b. In case the price increases by 2%, state the new price in terms of A _____

    c. In case the price increases by 3%, state the new price in terms of A _____

    d. In case the price increases by 5%, state the new price in terms of A _____

    e. In case the price increases by 8%, state the new price in terms of A _____

    f. In case the price increases by 10%, state the new price in terms of A _____

    g. In case the price increases by 18%, state the new price in terms of A _____

    h. In case the price increases by 30%, state the new price in terms of A _____

    i. In case the price increases by 50%, state the new price in terms of A _____

    j. In case the price increases by 58%, state the new price in terms of A _____

    k. In case the price increases by 90%, state the new price in terms of A _____

    l. In case the price increases by 100%, state the new price in terms of A _____

    m. In case the price increases by 101%, state the new price in terms of A _____

    n. In case the price increases by 108%, state the new price in terms of A _____

    o. In case the price increases by 110%, state the new price in terms of A _____

    p. In case the price increases by 200%, state the new price in terms of A _____

    q. In case the price increases by 228%, state the new price in terms of A _____

    r. In case the price increases by 300%, state the new price in terms of A _____

29. The price of a shirt is A $.

    a. In case the price decreases by 1%, state the new price in terms of A _____

    b. In case the price decreases by 2%, state the new price in terms of A _____

    c. In case the price decreases by 3%, state the new price in terms of A _____

    d. In case the price decreases by 5%, state the new price in terms of A _____

e. In case the price decreases by 8%, state the new price in terms of A _____

f. In case the price decreases by 10%, state the new price in terms of A _____

g. In case the price decreases by 18%, state the new price in terms of A _____

h. In case the price decreases by 30%, state the new price in terms of A _____

i. In case the price decreases by 50%, state the new price in terms of A _____

j. In case the price decreases by 58%, state the new price in terms of A _____

k. In case the price decreases by 90%, state the new price in terms of A _____

l. In case the price decreases by 100%, state the new price in terms of A _____

m. In case the price decreases by 101%, state the new price in terms of A _____

n. In case the price decreases by 110%, state the new price in terms of A _____

30.

a. To increase an amount by 10% we multiply it by _____

b. To increase an amount by 25% we multiply it by _____

c. To increase an amount by 7.2% we multiply it by _____

d. To decrease an amount by 12% we multiply it by _____

e. To decrease an amount by 35% we multiply it by _____

f. To decrease an amount by 5.1% we multiply it by _____

g. To decrease an amount by 100% we multiply it by _____

h. To increase an amount by 100% we multiply it by _____

i. To increase an amount by 200% we multiply it by _____

j. To increase an amount by M% we multiply it by _____

k. To decrease an amount by S% we multiply it by _____

31. The price of a shirt is B $. In case the price increases by 10% and then decreases by 10% , state the new price in terms of B _____ and the overall change in the price (as a percentage).

32. The price of a shirt is C $. In case the price increases by 20% and then decreases by 30% , state the new price in terms of C _____ and the overall change in the price (as a percentage).

33. The price of a shirt is D $. In case the price decreases by 20% and then increases by 40% , state the new price in terms of D _____ and the overall change in the price (as a percentage).

34. The price of a shirt is E $. In case the price decreases by 30% and then increases by 50% , state the new price in terms of E _____ and the overall change in the price (as a percentage).

35. The price of a shirt is E $. In case the price increases every month by 4%, write the expression for the price after 80 months: _____

36. The price of a shirt is M$. In case the price decreases every month by 12%, write the expression for the price after 10 months: _____

37. The price of a shirt is M$. In case the price decreases every month by 2.5%, write the expression for the price after 10 months: _____

38. The price of a shirt is M$. The price increases by x% every month. State its price in terms of M and x after n months: _____

BIGGER OR SMALLER BY A PERCENTAGE

39. Find the percentage by which:

    a. 5 is bigger than 4: _____

    b. 4 is smaller than 5: _____

    c. 11 is bigger than 10: _____

    d. 10 is smaller than 11: _____

    e. 51 is bigger than 50 : _____

    f. 40 is smaller than 45: _____

    g. A is bigger than B: _____

    h. x is smaller than y: _____

40. Given that the long side of the <u>shaded rectangle</u> is 70% of x and that its short side is 60% of y. Find the percentage of the big rectangle that is shaded.

41. Given that the side length of the square is two thirds of the short side of the rectangle find:

    a. The area of the shapes in terms of x.

        Rectangle: _____

        Square: _____

    b. The percentage of the area of the rectangle that is shaded and not shaded.

c. The percentage by which the <u>area</u> of the square is <u>smaller</u> than the <u>area</u> of the rectangle.

d. The percentage by which the <u>perimeter</u> of the square is <u>smaller</u> than the <u>perimeter</u> of the rectangle.

42. Given the diagram in which a rectangle is located inside a square. The side length of the square is 2x. The rectangle's long side is 80% of the side of the square. The short side of the rectangles is 30% less of the side of the square. Find

a. The area of the square in terms of x.

b. The side lengths of the rectangle in terms of x written as a fraction.

2x

c. The area of the rectangle written as a fraction in terms of x.

d. Using the previous parts the percentage of the area that is not shaded.

e. The percentage by which the <u>area</u> of the square is **bigger** than the <u>area</u> of the rectangle.

f. The percentage by which the <u>perimeter</u> of the rectangle is **smaller** than the <u>perimeter</u> of the square.

2. Ricardo drives to work 40% less than Rhona. Rhona drives to work 10% more than Alex who drives 400 km per week.

    a. How many km does Rhona drive to work per week?

    b. How many km does Ricardo drive to work per week?

    c. By what percentage does Ricardo drive more or less than Alex?

RATIO AND PROPORTION

43. The ratio between 2 and 5 is the same as between _____ and a 100.

44. The ratio between 3 and 7 is the same as between _____ and 35.

45. The ratio between 2 and 12 is the same as between 6 and _____

46. The ratio 1:3:7 is the same as _____

47. Divide 120 in the ratio 2:3

48. Divide 160 in the ratio 3:4

49. Divide 180 in the ratio 2:3:4

50. Divide 360 in the ratio 2:5:8

51. Divide 30 in the ratio 1:2:3

52. The diagram representing an apartment has the scale 1:50. The dimensions of a bedroom in the diagram are 5 x 8 cm. Find the dimensions, perimeter and area of the bedroom.

53. To make a chocolate cake the ingredients needed are 2 eggs, 1 cup of sugar and 3 cups of flower. Find the ingredients needed to make a cake half as big.

54. In a certain family with 2 children the parents eat twice as much as the kids. The family ordered 600g of Pasta, find the amount of pasta each one of the family members will eat.

55. The scale of a map is 1:800000. Find the real distance represented by:

   a. 1 cm

   b. 9 cm

   c. The distance in the map that represent 10km

   d. The distance in the map that represent 50km

1.7. – TYPES OF NUMBERS

Natural Numbers (N): $N = \{\_,\_\_,\_\_,\_\_,\_\_\dots\}$

Integers (Z): $Z = \{\dots,\_\_,\_\_,\_\_,\_\_,\_\_,0,\_\_,\_\_,\_\_,\_\_,\_\_\dots\}$

Rational Numbers (Q): $Q = \{\frac{a}{b}, a,b \in Z\}$

Numbers that **can** be written as _____ being both the

numerator and the denominator _____.

Examples: $\dfrac{1}{1}, \dfrac{2}{3}, \dfrac{-7}{3}, \dfrac{4}{-1}, \dfrac{\_\_}{\_\_}, \_\_\_\_\_, \_\_\_\_\_ \dots$

Irrational Numbers (Q'): $Q' \neq \{\frac{a}{b}, a,b \in Z\}$ Numbers that _____ be written as

fractions, being both the _____ and _____ Integers.

Examples: $\sqrt{2}, \sqrt{3}.\pi \ \dots °$

Real Numbers (R): $R = Q + Q'$ (Rationals and Irrationals)

Represented in a Venn diagram:

Fill the blanks with the corresponding letter and name

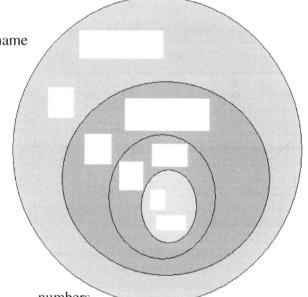

Exercises

1. Natural numbers are contained in the _____ numbers.

2. Integer numbers are contained in the _____ numbers

3. Rational numbers are contained in the _____ numbers.

4. Irrational numbers are located _____.

5. Shade the area in which the irrational numbers are located:

6. True or False:

   a. All Natural numbers are Integers: _____

   b. All Real numbers are Natural: _____

   c. All Rational numbers are Real: _____

   d. All Real numbers are Rational: _____

   e. All Integer numbers are Rational: _____

   f. All Real numbers are Irrational: _____

   g. Some Irrational numbers are Real and some are not: _____

   h. Some Irrational numbers are Integers: _____

   i. Some integers are negative: _____

   j. Some Irrationals are negative: _____

   k. Some Natural numbers are negative: _____

7. Write the value of the numbers with 10 decimal numbers (use a calculator)

   $\sqrt{2} =$ $\sqrt{3} =$

   $\sqrt{4} =$ $\sqrt{5} =$

   $\dfrac{5}{6} =$ $\dfrac{43}{27} =$

   $\dfrac{122}{90} =$ $\dfrac{158}{990} =$

   Write a conclusion: _____

8. Circle the irrational numbers:

   0.58012   0.121231234…

   0.1010010001...   0.871

   0.333…   0.227777777…

9. Fill the chart with yes or no (follow the example):

Number	Natural	Integer	Rational	Real
-2	no	yes	yes	yes
π				
$-3.121212\ldots$				
-15.16				
$\sqrt{3}$				
$-2\frac{2}{5}$				
$\sqrt[3]{8}$				
$9^{\frac{1}{3}}$				
2^{-3}				
800.0				
0				
$\frac{7}{3}$				
$-\frac{100}{50}$				
$-\frac{100}{51}$				

10. Fill the numbers column with appropriate numbers and yes or no. Follow the example.

Number	Natural	Integer	Rational	Real
	no	yes		
		no	yes	yes
	yes	yes	yes	
			no	yes
		no	yes	yes
			yes	
	no			
		yes	no	

49

11. If possible, convert the following numbers into the form: $\dfrac{n}{m}$

1. 0.333... =

2. 1.151151115... =

3. 5.3 =

4. 5.2828... =

5. –2.3535... =

6. 42.67 =

7. 12.355355... =

8. –31.44 =

9. 0.125125... =

10. 3.22332233... =

11. 1115.36 =

12. 122.53 =

13. 1.123123... =

14. 1.22565656... =

15. 1.5696969... =

16. 5.540404040... =

12. Given the following diagram:

Write the following numbers in the appropriate location in the diagram:

a. 2.2
b. −5
c. 3
d. $\dfrac{1}{3}$
e. 5^{-2}
f. $27^{-\frac{1}{3}}$
g. −3.3
h. 1.111…
i. $\dfrac{1}{\sqrt{3}}$
j. 2π
k. $1+2\pi$
l. $16^{-0.25}$
m. $\sqrt{2}+3$
n. $\dfrac{4}{2}$
o. $7^{0.5}$

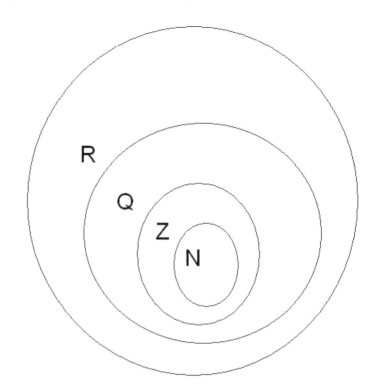

Circle the right option

13. The number −2 is:
    a. Integer and Natural.
    b. Positive
    c. Integer and Rational
    d. Natural and Real
    e. Natural and Rational
    f. None of the above

14. The number 3.41414141….. is:
    g. Integer and Natural.
    h. Natural
    i. Integer and Real
    j. Rational and Integer
    k. Rational
    l. None of the above

15. The number 3.41 is:
    m. Integer and Natural.
    n. Integer
    o. Rational and Real
    p. Integer and Real
    q. Rational and negative
    r. None of the above

16. The number $\sqrt{31}$ is:
    s. Integer and Natural.
    t. Integer
    u. Decimal
    v. Integer and Real
    w. Rational
    x. Irrational

17. The number 5 is:
    y. Natural.
    z. Integer
    aa. Real
    bb. Integer and Natural
    cc. Rational and Natural
    dd. All of the above

1.8. – ROOTS AND RATIONALIZATION

Simplify as much as possible:

1. $\sqrt{0} =$

2. $\sqrt{1} =$

3. $\sqrt{4} =$

4. $\sqrt[3]{8} =$

5. $\sqrt{100} =$

6. $\sqrt{81} =$

7. $\sqrt{121} =$

8. $\sqrt[3]{27} =$

9. $\sqrt{169} =$

10. $\sqrt[4]{16} =$

11. $\sqrt{10000} =$

12. $\sqrt[3]{64} =$

13. $\sqrt[3]{a^3} =$

14. $\sqrt{16} \cdot \sqrt{25} =$

15. $\sqrt[4]{2} \cdot \sqrt[4]{8} =$

16. $\sqrt{-1} =$

17. $\left(\sqrt{4}\right)^2 =$

18. $\sqrt[4]{81} =$

19. $\left(-\sqrt{5}\right)^2 \cdot \left(\sqrt[3]{3}\right)^3 =$

20. $\left(\sqrt{532}\right)^2 =$

21. $\left(\sqrt{a}\right)^2 \left(\sqrt[n]{a}\right)^n =$

22. $\sqrt{0.01} =$

23. $\sqrt{0.25} =$

24. $\sqrt{2.25} =$

25. $\sqrt{\dfrac{a^2}{9}} =$

26. $\sqrt{\dfrac{8}{200}} =$

27. $\sqrt{3} + \sqrt{3} =$

28. $\sqrt{2} + \sqrt{2} + \sqrt{2} =$

29. $\sqrt{2} + \sqrt{8} + \sqrt{2} =$

30. $\sqrt{4} + \sqrt{2} + \sqrt{8} =$

31. $\sqrt{9} + \sqrt{12} + \sqrt{27} =$

32. $\sqrt{50} + \sqrt{75} + \sqrt{12} =$

33. $\sqrt[3]{16} + \sqrt[3]{54} =$

34. $\sqrt[4]{32} - \sqrt[4]{162} =$

35. $\sqrt{27} + \sqrt{81} + \sqrt{48} =$

36. $\sqrt{200} + \sqrt{50} - \sqrt{18} =$

37. $\sqrt{20} + \sqrt{80} - \sqrt{125} =$

38. $\sqrt{10}\sqrt{10} =$

39. $\sqrt[3]{a} \cdot \sqrt[3]{a} \cdot \sqrt[3]{a} =$

40. $\sqrt{3}\sqrt{9}\sqrt{3} =$

41. $\dfrac{\sqrt{200}}{\sqrt{2}} -$

42. $\dfrac{\sqrt{72}}{\sqrt{2}} =$

43. $\dfrac{\sqrt{75}}{\sqrt{5}} =$

44. $\sqrt{3}\,\dfrac{\sqrt{24}}{\sqrt{2}} =$

45. $\sqrt{a}\sqrt{a} =$

46. $\sqrt{a} + \sqrt{a} =$

47. Write all the integers between $\sqrt{3}$ and $\sqrt{10}$: _____

48. Write all the integers between $\sqrt{13}$ and $\sqrt{50}$: _____

49. Write a rational number non - integer between $\sqrt{3}$ and $\sqrt{10}$: _____

50. Write all the integers between $\sqrt{24}$ and $\sqrt{80}$: _____

51. Write a rational number non - integer between $\sqrt{13}$ and $\sqrt{30}$: _____

Rationalize the denominator:

52. $\dfrac{1}{\sqrt{2}} =$

53. $\dfrac{3}{\sqrt{5}+1} =$

54. $\dfrac{-7}{\sqrt{5}-2} =$

55. $\dfrac{\sqrt{2}+3}{-5} =$

56. $\dfrac{\sqrt{2}+3}{\sqrt{6}-5} =$

57. $\dfrac{\sqrt{2}}{\sqrt{6}+\sqrt{3}} =$

58. $\dfrac{\sqrt{2}-1}{2\sqrt{5}-\sqrt{3}} =$

59. $\dfrac{-1}{2\sqrt{a}+b} =$

60. $\dfrac{3\sqrt{a}-2b}{2\sqrt{a}+\sqrt{b}} =$

Rationalize the numerator:

61. $\dfrac{\sqrt{4}}{\sqrt{5}} =$

62. $\dfrac{3-\sqrt{2}}{\sqrt{5}+1} =$

63. $\dfrac{-7}{\sqrt{5}-2} =$

64. $\dfrac{\sqrt{2}+3}{\sqrt{6}-5} =$

65. $\dfrac{\sqrt{2}}{\sqrt{x}+\sqrt{3}} =$

66. $\dfrac{\sqrt{b}-a}{2\sqrt{a}-\sqrt{3}} =$

67. $\dfrac{-3\sqrt{7}+8}{2\sqrt{5}+7} =$

68. $\dfrac{\sqrt{a}-2\sqrt{b}}{2\sqrt{a}+\sqrt{b}} =$

1.9. – INTERVAL NOTATION AND INEQUALITIES

x ∋ (a, b] or {x| a < x ≤ b} means x is between a and b, not including a and including b.

Exercises:

1. Represent the following Intervals on the real line:

a. x ∈ (2, 5]

b. x ∈ (3,6)

c. x ∈ [−5,9]

d. x ∈ [−8,−1)

e. x ∈ [−∞,−1)

f. x ∈ [−∞,6]

g. x ∈ (6, ∞]

h. {x| 7 < x < 9}

i. {x| −7 < x < −2}

j. $\{x|\ 1 < x < 2\}$

k. $\{x|\ \infty < x < 2\}$

l. $\{x|\ 1 < x < \infty\ \}$

2. Write each one of the Intervals using all types of notations:

a. $x \in (4, 5)$

b. $x \in (-\infty, 5)$

c. $x \in (4, 5)$

d. $x \in (3, \infty]$

e. $x \in\ ]-5, 9]$

f. $x \in [-8, -1[$

g. $\{x|\ 7 < x < 9\}$

h. $\{x|\ -7 < x < -2\}$

55

3. Solve the following inequalities and shade the solution on the given diagram:

a. $-x \leq 3$

b. $5 - x \leq 2$

c. $8 - 2x \leq 3$

d. $-2x \leq 4 + x$

e. $7 + x \leq x + 3$

f. $-2x \leq 2x + 1$

g. $-2x \leq 2x$

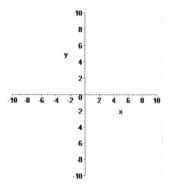

h. $-5x + 3 \le 2x - 1$

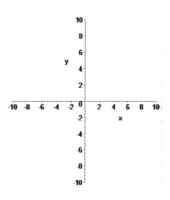

i. $7x \le 4 + 7x + 1$

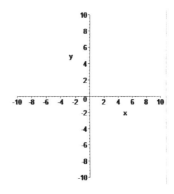

j. $\dfrac{x}{2} \le x + 1$

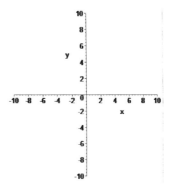

k. $\dfrac{x}{3} \le \dfrac{x}{6} + 1$

l. $\dfrac{x-4}{6} \le x-1$

m. $\dfrac{2-x}{3} \le \dfrac{x}{5}-3$

n. $\dfrac{4-2x}{5} \le \dfrac{2x}{6}-\dfrac{x}{2}$

o. $\dfrac{-2x}{5}-3 \le \dfrac{x-2}{4}-\dfrac{x-1}{2}$

p. $\dfrac{y+4}{6} \le y-1$

q. $\dfrac{2-2y}{3} \le \dfrac{y}{4}-1$

r. $\dfrac{4-y}{5} \le \dfrac{y}{2}-y$

s. $\dfrac{-2y}{5}-1 \le y-\dfrac{y-1}{2}$

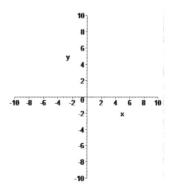

t. $-2 \le 2x \le 1$

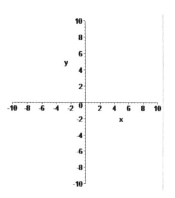

u. $-8 \le \dfrac{-6x + 3}{4} \le 7$

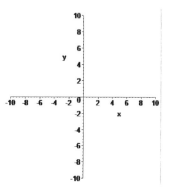

v. $-10 \le 4y + 2 \le 9$

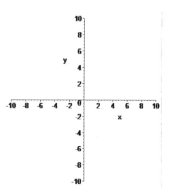

w. $0 \le \dfrac{y + 2}{3} \le 2$

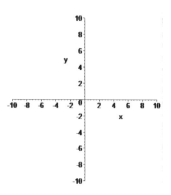

x. $-\dfrac{13}{5} \le -\dfrac{2x}{4} - x + 2 \le 0$

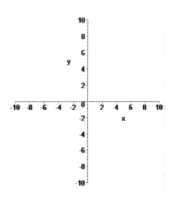

y. $0 \le 2 - \dfrac{-6x-3}{4} \le \dfrac{13}{6}$

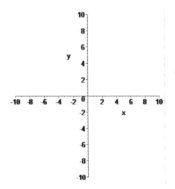

z. $-\dfrac{5}{2} \le -\dfrac{4y}{3} + y + 2 \le 3$

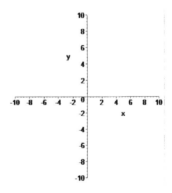

aa. $0 \le 2 - \dfrac{2y+2}{3} + y \le \dfrac{7}{6}$

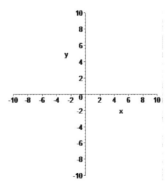

bb. $-\dfrac{12}{7} \le \dfrac{x}{2} + \dfrac{x}{3} \le 0$

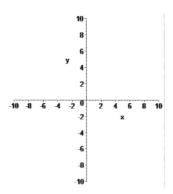

cc. $\dfrac{-7}{8} \le 2 - \dfrac{-6x+3}{4} \le \dfrac{6}{2}$

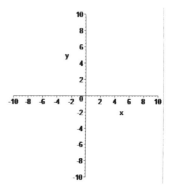

dd. $-\dfrac{10}{3} \le -\dfrac{4y+2}{5} \le \dfrac{9}{2}$

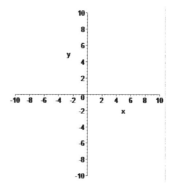

ee. $0 \le \dfrac{y+2}{3} \le \dfrac{12}{7}$

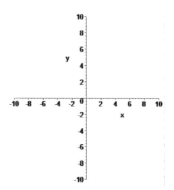

4.

    a. Solve the inequality $2x \leq 2$

    b. Solve the inequality $-x < -2$.

    c. Represent both solutions on the real line:

    d. State their intersection: _____.

5.

    a. Solve the inequality $2x - 2 \leq 2$

    b. Solve the inequality $-3x + 1 > -2$.

    c. Represent both solutions on the real line:

    d. State their intersection: _____.

6.

    a. Solve the inequality $x - 2 \leq -5$

    b. Solve the inequality $-2x + 14 \leq -2$.

    c. Represent both solutions on the real line:

    d. State their intersection: _____

7.

   a. Solve the inequality $3x - 7 \leq 2$

   b. Solve the inequality $-x < -2$.

   c. Represent both solutions on the real line:

   d. State their intersection: _____.

8.

   a. Solve the inequality $5x - 2 \leq 2$

   b. Solve the inequality $-2x + 1 > -2$.

   c. Represent both solutions on the real line:

   d. State their intersection: _____.

9.

   a. Solve the inequality $5x - 2 \leq -12$

   b. Solve the inequality $-2x - 3 \leq -2$.

   c. Represent both solutions on the real line:

   d. State their intersection: _____

1.10. – EVALUATING EXPRESSIONS

Evaluate the expression given the value of x:

1. $x = -3, \quad x^2 =$

2. $x = -3, \quad -x^2 =$

3. $x = -3, \quad x - x^2 =$

4. $x = -3, \quad -x^3 =$

5. $x = -3, \quad x^2 + x =$

6. $x = -2, \quad 2x^2 + 3x =$

7. $x = -2, \quad x^{-1} =$

8. $x = -2, \quad x^3 =$

9. $x = -3, \quad x^{-3} =$

10. $x = -9, \quad 2x^{-2} =$

11. $x = 4, \quad x^{-2} + x =$

12. $x = -2, \quad 2x^2 + \dfrac{x}{2} =$

13. $x = -2, \quad \dfrac{1}{x} + \dfrac{x}{2} =$

14. $x = 4, \quad \dfrac{1}{x-3} + \dfrac{x}{2} =$

15. $x = 10, \quad \dfrac{10}{x-5} + \dfrac{x-2}{2} =$

16. $x = -1, \quad 5x^{-3} + 2x^{-1} + 1 =$

17. $x = 3, \quad x^{-2} + x + x^2 =$

18. $x = 2, \quad x^{-3} + x^{-2} + x^{-1} + x^0 =$

19. $x = 2, \quad 2x^{-2} \cdot x^{-1} =$

20. $x = -1, \quad x^{-200} - 2x^{501} =$

21. $x = -5, \quad 5x^{-2} - x^2 =$

22. $x = -2, \quad 2^x =$

23. $x = -2, \quad 3^x =$

24. $x = -2, \quad 2^{2x+1} =$

25. $x = -1, \quad 2^{3x-1} =$

26. $x = 2, \quad 2^{\frac{3}{x}} =$

27. $x = -\dfrac{1}{2}, \quad 4^x =$

28. $x = -\dfrac{2}{3}, \quad 8^x =$

1.11. – EQUATIONS

1st Degree Equations

1. $\dfrac{x}{12} = 5$

2. $\dfrac{x}{7} + 2 = 5$

3. $\dfrac{2x}{7} + 2 = 5 - 3x$

4. $\dfrac{2x}{7} + \dfrac{2}{5} = -2x + 1$

5. $\dfrac{2x-1}{x} = 3$

6. $\dfrac{x+2}{2x} = 5$

7. $\dfrac{x-2}{2x-1} = 6$

8. $\dfrac{2x-2}{x+1} = -2$

9. $\dfrac{2x}{7} + 1 = \dfrac{-5x}{7}$

13. $\dfrac{-2}{x} = \dfrac{3}{x-2}$

10. $\dfrac{2x}{7} + 4 = \dfrac{3x}{2}$

14. $\dfrac{4}{x+1} = \dfrac{4}{x+2}$

15. $\dfrac{2}{x+1} = \dfrac{4}{x+2}$

11. $\dfrac{2}{x} - 3 = \dfrac{3}{2x}$

16. $-\dfrac{2}{2x+1} - 2 = \dfrac{4}{2x+1}$

12. $\dfrac{2}{x-2} - 3 = \dfrac{3}{x-2}$

17. $\dfrac{x}{2} - \dfrac{x}{5} = 3$

18. $\dfrac{2}{x} + \dfrac{3}{5} = 3$

19. $\dfrac{2x-7}{2} - \dfrac{3x}{5} = x$

20. $1 - \dfrac{1}{x} = 7 - \dfrac{3x+1}{x}$

21. $3 - \dfrac{2x}{x-2} = 7 - \dfrac{2x+1}{x-2}$

22. $\dfrac{2-x}{x-2} = 1$

23. $\dfrac{2-x}{x-2} = -1$

24. $\dfrac{5-7x}{3x-2} = -1 + \dfrac{5}{3x-2}$

25. $\dfrac{15-x}{3-x} = 7 - \dfrac{5x}{3-x}$

26. Write an equation with fractions, similar to previous one whose solution is 6, solve it.

27. Write an equation with fractions, similar to previous one whose solution is -5, solve it.

28. Write an equation with fractions, similar to previous one whose solution is $\dfrac{2}{3}$, solve it.

29. Write an equation with fractions, similar to previous one whose solution is $-\dfrac{3}{5}$, solve it.

30. Write an equation with fractions, similar to previous one whose solution is $-\dfrac{3}{7}$, solve it.

31. Write an equation with fractions, similar to previous one whose solution is $\dfrac{3}{4}$, solve it.

Isolate x

1. $\dfrac{4}{x} = \dfrac{a}{x+6}$

2. $\dfrac{14}{x+2} = \dfrac{a}{x+2} - a$

3. $\dfrac{2}{x+3} - a = \dfrac{a+b}{x+3}$

4. $\dfrac{5}{2x+1} - 3a = \dfrac{b}{2x+1}$

5. $\dfrac{-2x}{a+3} = \dfrac{x+2}{2a-1}$

6. $\dfrac{-5x+1}{2a} = \dfrac{bx}{3a+2}$

7. $\dfrac{a}{x+2} = \dfrac{b}{x+2} - b + 1$

8. $\dfrac{b}{2x-4} - 3 = \dfrac{b}{2x-4} - b + 1$

9. $\dfrac{1}{ax+2} = \dfrac{b}{x+a}$

10. $\dfrac{1}{ax+2} = \dfrac{b}{ax+2} - 3$

11. $3\dfrac{x}{ax+2}=3$

12. $-3\dfrac{2x}{ax+3}=b$

13. $\dfrac{2x-3}{2ax+5}=-3b$

14. $\dfrac{x}{ax+2}=\dfrac{2}{a}-3$

15. $\dfrac{bx}{x+2}=3-b$

16. $\dfrac{b+x}{x-3}=\dfrac{b}{x-3}+a$

17. $\dfrac{bx}{a}=2x+8$

18. $\dfrac{ax+b}{dx+2}=c-g$

19. $\dfrac{1}{x+2}+\dfrac{1}{b}=2$

20. $\dfrac{1-a}{x}+\dfrac{2a}{x}=2b$

21. $x - \dfrac{2+ax}{b} = 2x + 3$

22. $\dfrac{7-2ax}{x+1} = 2+b$

23. $\dfrac{3-2x}{2x-3} = a$

24. $\dfrac{2}{1-x} = \dfrac{2a}{x-1} - a$

25. $\dfrac{3}{a-2x} = \dfrac{b}{2x-a} - c$

26. Complete the RHS of the equation so its solution is a

$$xa + 1 = \underline{\hspace{2cm}}$$

27. Complete the RHS of the equation so its solution is $a - 1$

$$\dfrac{1}{xa} - a = \underline{\hspace{2cm}}$$

28. Complete the RHS of the equation so its solution is $2a$

$$x - \dfrac{1}{xa} = \underline{\hspace{2cm}}$$

29. Complete the RHS of the equation so its solution is $4a+1$

$$\dfrac{x+1}{xa} - 1 = \underline{\hspace{2cm}}$$

Quadratic equations

Given the equation $2x^2 - 5x - 3 = 0$,

    1. Solve it by factoring.

    2. Solve it by completing the square.

    3. Its discriminant is _____

Given the equation: $25x^2 - 20x + 4 = 0$,

    4. Solve it by factoring.

    5. Solve it by completing the square.

    6. Its discriminant is _____

Given the equation: $4x^2 - 4x + 2 = 0$,

7. Solve it by factoring.

8. Solve it by completing the square.

9. Its discriminant is _____

Given the equation: $ax^2 + bx + c = 0$,

10. Solve it by completing the square.

11. The equation will have 2 solutions if _____ 1 solution if _____ and

    0 solutions if _____

Practice
    a. Solve the following using the "complete to square" method.
    b. Solve the following using the quadratic formula.
    c. Write the factored equation.

1. $x^2 - 4x + 1 = 3$

2. $x^2 - 4x + 1 = -3$

3. $x^2 - 4x + 1 = -13$

4. $x^2 + 6x + 2 = 2$

5. $x^2 + 6x + 2 = -10$

6. $x^2 + 8x + 3 = -10$

7. $x^2 - 12x - 2 = 3$

8. $x^2 - 2x - 5 = 3$

9. $x^2 - 3x - 5 = 3$

10. $x^2 - 4x - 5 = 3$

11. $x^2 - 3x - 3 = -3$

12. $x^2 - 3x - 4 = -1$

13. $x^2 - 7x - 5 = 3$

14. $x^2 + x - 3 = 2$

15. $x^2 - 2x + 4 = 5$

16. $x^2 + 3x - 1 = 3$

17. $x^2 + 7x - 3 = 2$

18. $x^2 + 8x = 0$

19. $x^2 - 7x =$

20. $-x^2 + 10x + 4 = -1$

21. $2x^2 - 10x - 2 = 0$

22. $3x^2 - 9x - 6 = 0$

23. $-4x^2 - 2x - 6 = 1$

24. $2x^2 - x - 1 = 2$

25. $-5x^2 + 2x - 11 = -2$

26. $-2x^2 - 2x = 0$

27. $4x^2 - 2x = 0$

28. $-2x^2 - 3 = -5$

29. $6x^2 - 7x = 0$

30. $2x^2 - 6x = 0$

31. Write a quadratic equation whose solutions are 1 and 2

32. Write a quadratic equation whose solutions are -4 and 3

33. Write a quadratic equation whose solutions are $-\dfrac{1}{2}$ and $-\dfrac{1}{2}$

34. Write a quadratic equation whose solutions are $\dfrac{3}{7}$ and $-\dfrac{11}{2}$

35. Write a quadratic equation whose solutions are a and b

36. Write a quadratic equation whose solutions are c and 2d

3. $\;-\dfrac{2}{x^2-2x+3}=1$

Rational equations 2nd degree

1. $\;\dfrac{3}{x^2-4}=2$

4. $\;\dfrac{x}{x^2-4}=2$

2. $\;\dfrac{2}{x^2-2x+1}=1$

5. $\dfrac{x}{x-4} = 5$

6. $\dfrac{x^2}{x^2-4x} = 2$

7. $\dfrac{x^2-1}{x-5} = 2$

8. $\dfrac{x}{x-4} + \dfrac{2}{x-4} = 5$

9. $\dfrac{x}{x-4} + \dfrac{2}{x+3} = -2$

10. $\dfrac{x-1}{2x-2} - \dfrac{2x-1}{x+3} = 3$

11. $\dfrac{x}{3x+2} - \dfrac{2x-1}{2x+3} = 7$

12. $\dfrac{1}{x} + \dfrac{2}{x^2} = 3$

13. $\dfrac{2}{x^3} - \dfrac{3}{x^2} = -\dfrac{1}{x}$

14. $\dfrac{1}{x-1} + \dfrac{2}{x^2-1} = 2$

15. $\dfrac{1}{x-3} - \dfrac{2}{x^2-9} = 4$

16. $\dfrac{5}{x-2} - \dfrac{3}{x^2-4} = -2$

17. $\dfrac{2}{x^n} - \dfrac{3}{x^{n+1}} = \dfrac{5}{x^{n+2}}$

18. $\dfrac{3}{25-x^2} - \dfrac{4}{5-x} = 1$

19. Write a rational equation that has 3 as a solution. Solve the equation to check for other solutions.

20. Write a rational equation that has $\dfrac{1}{5}$ as a solution. Solve the equation to check for other solutions.

21. Write a rational equation that has $\dfrac{2}{3}$ as a solution. Solve the equation to check for other solutions.

Radical Equations

1. $\sqrt{3} = \sqrt{x}$

2. $3 = \dfrac{1}{\sqrt{x}}$

3. $1 = \sqrt{-2x}$

4. $\sqrt{x} = 1 + x$

5. $\dfrac{\sqrt{x}}{\sqrt{6}} = \dfrac{2}{\sqrt{x+1}}$

6. $8 = \dfrac{\sqrt{2x-1}}{3}$

7. $\dfrac{\sqrt{10}}{2} = \sqrt{x^2 + 1}$

8. $2 = \sqrt{x^2 + 4x}$

9. $\sqrt{8x + 2} = 0$

10. $\sqrt{5x - 2} = 6$

11. $\sqrt{5x^2 - 2} = 3$

12. $\sqrt{x^2 + 1} = -2$

13. $\sqrt{x^2 - 2} + 4 = -2$

14. $\sqrt{2x^2 - 2} + 4x = -2$

15. $\sqrt{2x-2} + 3x + 2 = -2$

16. $\sqrt{x+1} + \sqrt{x+3} = 2$

17. $\sqrt{x-1} + \sqrt{x+3} = 2$

18. $\sqrt{x-3} + \sqrt{x+3} = 3$

19. $\sqrt{5x+1} - \sqrt{3x-3} = 2$

20. $\sqrt{8x+2} - \sqrt{3x-3} = 0$

21. $\sqrt{x-1} + \sqrt{x+2} = -2$

22. $\sqrt{x+9} = x - \sqrt{2+x}$

Higher degree simple equations

1. $x^4 - 2x^2 = 0$

2. $10(2x - 3)(x^2 - 3)(x + 5)(x^3 + 2) = 0$

3. $(2x - 3)(x - 3) = 1$

4. $(6x - 7)(3x^2 - 5)(2x + 7)(2x^5 - 64)(4x^4 + 5) = 0$

5. $3x^5 - x^2 = 0$

6. $100(x - 2)^{100}(x^2 - 5)^{10} = 0$

7. $x^6 - 32x = 0$

8. $x^6 - 2x^5 + x^4 = 0$

9. $x^3 - 4x^2 + 3x = 0$

10. $2x^3 - 5x = 0$

11. $2x^3 - x^2 = 0$

12. $ax^4 - 3x = 0$

13. $ax^5 - x^2 = 0$

14. $a(x - a)^{10}(x^2 - a)^{12}(x^3 - a)^{12} = 0$

15. $x^4 - 5x^2 + 3 = -1$

16. $x^4 - 10x^2 + 3 = -6$

17. $x^6 + 3x^3 - 10 = 0$

18. $x^8 = -2x^4 - 1$

19. $x^4 - 13x^2 + 36 = 0$

20. $x^5 - 15x^3 + 54x = 0$

21. $x^5 + x^3 - 6x = 0$

22. $x^4 = 6x^2 - 5$

Rational exponent equations

1. $x^{\frac{1}{2}} = 2$

2. $x^{-1} + x^0 = a$

3. $x^{-2} = 0$

4. $2x^{\frac{2}{3}} = 3$

5. $3x^{-\frac{1}{2}} = 2$

6. $3x^{-\frac{1}{2}} = 0$

7. $ax^{-\frac{3}{7}} = 0$

8. $3x^{-\frac{6}{7}} = -2$

9. $x + x^{-\frac{1}{2}} = 0$

10. $2x - x^{\frac{2}{5}} = 0$

11. $x^{\frac{1}{3}} + 1 = 0$

12. $3x^{\frac{1}{2}} - x^2 = 0$

13. $8x^{-2} + x^{-1} = 2$

14. $5x^{\frac{4}{3}} = -1$

15. $3x^{-\frac{3}{4}} = -2$

18. $3x^{-2} = -5$

16. $x - 2x^{\frac{2}{3}} = 0$

19. $x^{\frac{1}{2}} - 2x^{\frac{1}{6}} = 0$

20. $4x^{\frac{1}{4}} - 2x^{\frac{1}{2}} = 0$

17. $2x^2 - x^{-\frac{3}{2}} = 0$

Exponential equations

1. $2^x = 2$

6. $\left(\dfrac{1}{4}\right)^{x+2} = \dfrac{1}{16}$

2. $2^{x+2} = 2^2$

7. $2^{x+2} = \dfrac{-1}{16}$

3. $\left(\dfrac{1}{32}\right)2^{3x+4} = 4$

4. $2^{-4x+1} = 8$

8. $2^{-2x+1} = 8^x$

5. $3^{-5x+3} = 9$

9. $\left(\dfrac{1}{3}\right)^{4x^2-1} = 9^{2x}$

16. $5^{x-1} = \dfrac{1}{125}$

10. $\left(\dfrac{1}{125}\right)5^{x-1} = 1$

17. $\left(\dfrac{1}{36}\right)^{2x-3} = \dfrac{1}{6}$

11. $3^{2x-5} = \dfrac{1}{3}$

18. $6^{2x-3} = -\dfrac{3}{4}$

19. $2^x = 3$

12. $3^{2x^2-5} = \dfrac{1}{27}$

20. $2^x = 0.1$

21. $5^x = 3$

22. $4^x = 0.5$

13. $\left(\dfrac{1}{5}\right)^{x-1} = -1$

23. $4^x = 0.4$

24. $1^x = 2$

14. $5^{x-1} = 5^{x(x-1)}$

25. $2^x = -2$

26. $4^x = \left(0.5\right)^{x-2}$

15. $6^{x^2-8} = 6$

87

27. $1000^{2x-1} = (0.01)^{3x-2}$

33. $6^x + 6^{x+1} = \dfrac{7}{6}$

28. $\dfrac{1}{5^x - 4} = 1$

34. $5^x + 5^{x+1} + 5^{x-1} = \dfrac{31}{5}$

29. $\dfrac{1}{5^x - 24} = 1$

35. $7^{x-1} + 7^{x-2} = \dfrac{8}{49}$

30. $\dfrac{1}{5^{3x} - 24} = 1$

36. $7^{x-1} + 7^{x-2} = \dfrac{8}{7}$

31. $\dfrac{2}{2^x - 7} = 2$

37. $2^x + 2^{x-1} + 2^{x+2} = 11$

32. $\dfrac{125}{2^{\frac{x}{3}} - 7} = 5$

38. $2^x + 2^{x-1} + 2^{x+2} = 22$

39. $5^{2x} - 6 \times 5^x = -5$

40. $3^{2x} - 4 \times 3^x - 2 = -5$

41. $5^{2x} + 4 \times 5^x - 10 = -5$

42. $8^{2x} - 9 \times 8^x + 8 = 0$

43. $2 \times 8^{2x} - 18 \times 8^x + 10 = -6$

44. $3^{2x+1} - 3^{x+2} + 81 = 0$

45. $5^{2x-1} - 6 \times 5^{x-1} = -1$

46. $3^{2x+2} - 4 \times 3^{x+2} + 27 = 0$

Systems of equations

1. One equation with 1 variable may have _____ or _____ solutions. Give examples:

2. One equation with 2 two variable may have _____ or _____ or _____ solutions. Give examples:

3. Equations of the first degree are equations in which_____ Give examples with 1,2 and 3 variables:

4. Equations of the 2nd degree are equations in which_____ Give examples with 1 and 2 variables:

5. The solution to one equation of the first degree with 2 two variable, graphically speaking, is a _____. The collection of points will form a _____.

6. Write a system of equations whose only solution is x = 1, y = 2.

7. Write a system of equations whose only solution is $x = 0, y = -\dfrac{1}{2}$.

8. Write a system of equations whose only solution is $x = -3, y = -\dfrac{3}{2}$.

9. Write a system of equations whose only solution is $x = 15, y = -6$.

10. Write a system of equations that has no solutions

11. Write a system of equations that has infinite solutions

12. Given the equations I) 2x + y = 3, II) 2y – x = 4

    a. Write a few solutions of <u>each one</u> of the equations:

        I) (__, __), (__, __), (__, __)

        II) (__, __), (__, __), (__, __)

    b. Show the solutions on the graph.

    c. Draw a conclusion:

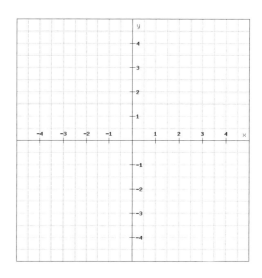

13. Given the equations I) 4x + 2y = 3, II) y + 2x = 8

    a. Write a few solutions of <u>each one</u> of the equations:

        I) _____

        II) _____

    b. Show the solutions on the graph.
    c. Draw a conclusion:

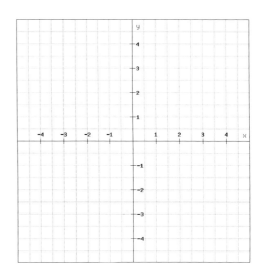

14. Given the equations I) 6x – 2y = 2, II) y – 3x = –1

    a. Write a few solutions of <u>each one</u> of the equations:

        I) _____

        II) _____

    b. Show the solutions on the graph.
    c. Draw a conclusion:

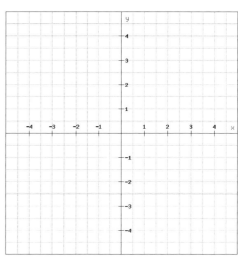

Solve:

15. $5x + 1 = 2y$
$4y + x - 3 = 0$

20. $5x + 1 = 2y$
$10y - 25x = 10$

16. $5x + 3y = 2 - 2y$
$-y + 2x - 5 = 0$

21. $2x + 1 = 2y$
$-4y + 4x + 2 = 0$

17. $5x = 2y$
$-y + 2x = 0$

22. $x + 1 = 2y$
$4y - 2x - 3 = 0$

18. $x = 2y - 7$
$4y - 2x = 0$

23. $4x = y$
$3y - 12x = 0$

19. $-5x + 1 = 2y$
$-4y + x - 3 = x$

24. $2x + 7y = 4$
$3y - 5x - 3 = 0$

25. $\dfrac{x}{2} - 1 = 5y$

   $3y + x - 2 = 0$

26. $\dfrac{x}{5} + 1 = 2y$

   $\dfrac{y}{3} + \dfrac{x}{2} - 3 = 0$

27. $\dfrac{x}{5} + 2 = 6y$

   $-3y + \dfrac{x}{10} + 1 = 0$

28. $\dfrac{x}{5} + 2 = 4y$

   $-3y + \dfrac{x}{10} + 2 = 0$

29. $\dfrac{x}{6} + 2 = \dfrac{3y}{7}$

   $\dfrac{-2y}{14} + \dfrac{x}{3} = 1$

30. $\dfrac{x}{5} + 2 = 2y$

   $-3y + \dfrac{x}{10} = -3$

31. $\begin{array}{l} x = 2y \\ -y + x^2 - 5 = 0 \end{array}$

34. $\begin{array}{l} -x^2 = 1 - 2y^2 \\ -y^2 + x^2 = 0 \end{array}$

32. $\begin{array}{l} x = 1 - y \\ -y + x^2 - 5 = 0 \end{array}$

35. $\begin{array}{l} x = 1 - y^2 \\ -y^2 + x^2 - 55 = 0 \end{array}$

33. $\begin{array}{l} x = 1 - y^2 \\ -y^2 + x^2 - 5 = 0 \end{array}$

36. $\begin{array}{l} 2x + 1 = 1 + 4y \\ -3y^2 + x^2 = 1 \end{array}$

1.12. – POLYNOMIALS

Sum, subtraction, multiplication:

1. Given the polynomials: $A = 3x + 5x^3 - 7x^{12} - 1$, $B = -3x^2 + 2x^5 - 2x^3$, $C = x^2 + x^3$
   $D = -x + 5 + 5x^4 - 4x^4 + 2x^2 - 4x^5$. Evaluate:

   a. $A + B + C + D =$

   b. $A - 2B + 3D =$

   c. $2AC =$

   d. $-3CB =$

Division: Perform the division and indicate the value of the Remainder in each case:

2. $\dfrac{x^3 + 1}{x} =$

3. Divide $-2x^3 - 5$ by $x + 1$

4. $\dfrac{2x^4 + x}{x} =$

5. $\dfrac{-2x - 5x^3 + 1}{x} =$

6. Divide $4 - x^4$ by $x - 1$

7. Divide $2x^3 + 3x - 5$ by $x - 3$

8. $\dfrac{4x^4 + x - 5}{2x - 3} =$

9. Divide $2x^3 + 4x - 7$ by $x^2 - 1$

10. Divide $5x^4 + x^3 + 2x^2 - 5$ by $-2x + 1$

11. Divide $6x^5 + 2x^4 + 2x - 5$ by $x^3 + x$

12. Divide $5x^3 + x^4 + 2x^2 - 5$ by $x^4 + 1$

13. When $x^3 - 2x + k$ is divided by $x - 2$ it leaves a remainder of 5, find k.

14. When $x^3 - 2x + k$ is divided by $x + 1$ it leaves a remainder of 0, find k.

15. When $2x^3 - x^2 + kx - 4$ is divided by $x + 2$ it leaves a remainder of 0, find k.

16. When $x^3 - x^2 + kx - 4$ is divided by $x - 1$ it leaves a remainder of 2, find k.

The Remainder Theorem

If we divide 13 by 5:

$$\frac{13}{5} = \frac{10+3}{5} = \frac{10}{5} + \frac{3}{5} = 2 + \frac{3}{5} \Rightarrow 13 = 2 \times 5 + 3$$

The same idea applies for polynomials:

$$\frac{P(Polynomial)}{D(Divisor)} = Q(quotient) + \frac{R(\text{Re}\,m\,a\,\text{in}\,der)}{D(Divisor)} \quad \text{OR} \quad P = QD + R$$

Example: If we want to divide $2x^3 - 8x^2 - 6x - 36$ by x – 1 and we are <u>only interested in the remainder</u>:

$$\frac{2x^3 - 8x^2 - 6x - 36}{x-1} = Q + \frac{R}{x-1} \quad \text{OR} \quad 2x^3 - 8x^2 - 6x - 36 = Q(x-1) + R$$

Since in an equation we can do "whatever we want" as long as we do it on both sides we can substitute x = 1 on both sides and obtain:

$$2 \times 1^3 - 8 \times 1^2 - 6 \times 1 - 36 = Q(1-1) + R$$

$$-48 = R$$

Factor Theorem

In case we obtain R = 0 we conclude that the divisor is a factor of the polynomial

In each one of the following cases write the corresponding expression and use the Remainder theorem to find the remainder:

1. $2x^3 + 2x - 15$ is divided by x – 1

    $2x^3 + 2x - 15 = Q(x - 1) + R$ Substituting x = _____ on _____ sides:

    R =

2. $-4x^4 + 3x^3 - 5x + 1$ is divided by x + 2

3. $3x^3 + 2x - 4$ is divided by x + 3

4. $3x^4 + 6x^3 - 33x^2 - 36x + 108$ is divided by x – 2

5. $-2x^4 + x^3 + x^2 - 4x - 5$ is divided by $x - 2$

6. $9x^3 + 2x - 4$ is divided by $2x - 3$

7. $x^{44} + x - 5$ is divided by $x - 1$

8. $7x^4 + 14x^3 + 14x^2 + 14x + 7$ is divided by $x + 1$

9. $4x^{4455} + x^3 - x - 5$ is divided by $x + 1$

10. $2x^3 + 3x^2 - 4x - 3$ is divided by $3x - 4$

11. In which one of the questions 1 to 10 the divisor is Also a factor of the polynomial?

Factor the following polynomials and solve the equations:

12. $2x^3 + 2x^2 - 2x - 2 = 0$

13. $2x^3 + 4x^2 + 2x + 4 = 0$

14. $+ 6x + 6 + 3x^3 + 3x^2 = 0$

15. $-4x + 12 + 2x^3 - 6x^2 = 0$

16. $x^3 - 4x^2 + 4x - 1 = 0$

17. $2x^3 - x^2 - 8x + 4 = 0$

18. $5x^3 - 8x^2 - 27x + 18 = 0$

19. $-11x^2 - x + 6 + 6x^3 = 0$

20. $4x^3 - 39x + 35 = 0$

21. $5x^3 - 8x^2 - 27x + 18 = 0$

22. $9x^3 + 18x^2 - 16x - 32 = 0$

23. $x^3 - 13x - 12 = 0$

24. $9x^3 - 32 + 18x^2 - 16x = 0$

25. $3x^3 + 6x^2 - 4x - 8 = 0$

26. $x^4 - x^3 - 12x^2 - 4x + 16 = 0$

27. $x^4 + 3x^3 - 6x - 4 = 0$

28. $6x^4 + 17x^3 + 7x^2 - 8x - 4 = 0$

29. Find the values of a and b if $6x^3 + 7x^2 + ax + b$ is divisible by $(2x - 1)$ and $(x + 1)$

30. $x^3 + ax^2 - 2x + b$ has $(x + 1)$ as a factor, and leaves a remainder of 4 when divided by $(x - 3)$. Find a and b.

31. Given that $(x - 1)$ and $(x - 2)$ are factors of $6x^4 + ax^3 - 17x^2 + bx - 4 = 0$, find a and b, and ay remaining factors.

Solutions of polynomials

1. In the equation $x^2 + 3x - 10 = 0 = (x + 5)(x - 2)$ Find:

   $x_1 \cdot x_2 = $ ____ $x_1 + x_2 = $ ____ $-\dfrac{b}{a} = $ ____ $\dfrac{c}{a} = $ ____

2. In the equation $2x^2 - 5x - 3 = 0 = (2x + 1)(x - 3)$ Find:

   $x_1 \cdot x_2 = $ ____ $x_1 + x_2 = $ ____ $-\dfrac{b}{a} = $ ____ $\dfrac{c}{a} = $ ____

3. In the equation $6x^2 - 5x - 6 = 0 = (2x + 1)(x - 3)$ Find:

   $x_1 \cdot x_2 = $ ____ $x_1 + x_2 = $ ____ $-\dfrac{b}{a} = $ ____ $\dfrac{c}{a} = $ ____

4. In the equation $x^3 - 5x^2 - 2x + 24 = 0 = (x + 2)(x - 3)(x - 4)$ Find:

   $x_1 \cdot x_2 \cdot x_3 = $ _____ $x_1 + x_2 + x_3 = $ _____ $-\dfrac{b}{a} = $ ____ $\dfrac{d}{a} = $ ____

5. In the equation $12x^3 - 4x^2 - 3x + 1 = 0 = (2x + 1)(2x - 1)(3x - 1)$ Find:

   $x_1 \cdot x_2 \cdot x_3 = $ _____ $x_1 + x_2 + x_3 = $ _____ $-\dfrac{b}{a} = $ ____ $\dfrac{d}{a} = $ ____

6. Conclusion:

   In a polynomial _____

   In a polynomial _____

   $x_1 \cdot x_2 \cdot x_3 \cdot ... x_n = $ _____ $x_1 + x_2 + x_3 + ... + x_n = $ _____

1.13. – SEQUENCES AND SERIES

Given The following sequences, write the first 3 terms and the term in the 20th position. If possible identify the pattern using text (follow example):

1. $a_n = 3n$ $a_1 = 3$ $a_2 = 6$ $a_3 = 9$ $a_{20} = 60$ Pattern: <u> add 3   </u>

2. $a_n = 3n + 1$ $a_1 =$ $a_2 =$ $a_3 =$ $a_{20} =$ Pattern: _____

3. $a_n = 3n - 5$ $a_1 =$ $a_2 =$ $a_3 =$ $a_{20} =$ Pattern: _____

4. $a_n = 2n + 1$ $a_1 =$ $a_2 =$ $a_3 =$ $a_{20} =$ Pattern: _____

5. $a_n = 2n$ $a_1 =$ $a_2 =$ $a_3 =$ $a_{20} =$ Pattern: _____

6. $a_n = 2n - 4$ $a_1 =$ $a_2 =$ $a_3 =$ $a_{20} =$ Pattern: _____

7. $a_n = -4n$ $a_1 =$ $a_2 =$ $a_3 =$ $a_{20} =$ Pattern: _____

8. $a_n = -4n + 10$ $a_1 =$ $a_2 =$ $a_3 =$ $a_{20} =$ Pattern: _____

9. $a_n = -4n - 6$ $a_1 =$ $a_2 =$ $a_3 =$ $a_{20} =$ Pattern: _____

10. $a_n = \dfrac{n}{3}$ $a_1 =$ $a_2 =$ $a_3 =$ $a_{20} =$ Pattern: _____

11. $a_n = \dfrac{n}{2}$ $a_1 =$ $a_2 =$ $a_3 =$ $a_{20} =$ Pattern: _____

12. $a_n = \dfrac{2n}{5} + 1$ $a_1 =$ $a_2 =$ $a_3 =$ $a_{20} =$ Pattern: _____

13. $a_n = \dfrac{-3n}{7} + 5$ $a_1 =$ $a_2 =$ $a_3 =$ $a_{20} =$ Pattern: _____

14. $a_n = \dfrac{n}{9} - 5$ $a_1 =$ $a_2 =$ $a_3 =$ $a_{20} =$ Pattern: _____

15. $a_n = \dfrac{n}{10} - 1$ $a_1 =$ $a_2 =$ $a_3 =$ $a_{20} =$ Pattern: _____

16. $a_n = \dfrac{3n}{4} + 2$ $a_1 =$ $a_2 =$ $a_3 =$ $a_{20} =$ Pattern: _____

17. $a_n = n^2$ $a_1 =$ $a_2 =$ $a_3 =$ $a_{20} =$ Pattern: _____

18. $a_n = n^3$ $a_1 =$ $a_2 =$ $a_3 =$ $a_{20} =$ Pattern: _____

19. $a_n = 2^n$ $a_1 =$ $a_2 =$ $a_3 =$ $a_{20} =$ Pattern: _____

20. $a_n = -2^n$ $a_1 =$ $a_2 =$ $a_3 =$ $a_{20} =$ Pattern: _____

21. $a_n = 2^{-n}$ $a_1 =$ $a_2 =$ $a_3 =$ $a_{20} =$ Pattern: _____

22. $a_n = -2^{-n}$ $a_1=$ $a_2=$ $a_3=$ $a_{20}=$ Pattern: _____

23. $a_n = (-2)^n$ $a_1=$ $a_2=$ $a_3=$ $a_{20}=$ Pattern: _____

24. $a_n = 2^{n-1}$ $a_1=$ $a_2=$ $a_3=$ $a_{20}=$ Pattern: _____

25. $a_n = 2^{n+2}$ $a_1=$ $a_2=$ $a_3=$ $a_{20}=$ Pattern: _____

26. $a_n = 3 \times 2^n$ $a_1=$ $a_2=$ $a_3=$ $a_{20}=$ Pattern: _____

27. $a_n = -5 \times 2^{n-1}$ $a_1=$ $a_2=$ $a_3=$ $a_{20}=$ Pattern: _____

28. $a_n = 5 \times 2^{1-n}$ $a_1=$ $a_2=$ $a_3=$ $a_{20}=$ Pattern: _____

29. $a_n = (-3)^{2-n}$ $a_1=$ $a_2=$ $a_3=$ $a_{20}=$ Pattern: _____

30. $a_n = 2 \times (-3)^n$ $a_1=$ $a_2=$ $a_3=$ $a_{20}=$ Pattern: _____

31. $a_n = 2 \times (-5)^{n-1}$ $a_1=$ $a_2=$ $a_3=$ $a_{20}=$ Pattern: _____

32. $a_n = (-3)^{n+1}$ $a_1=$ $a_2=$ $a_3=$ $a_{20}=$ Pattern: _____

33. $a_n = 1 + 5^{n-2}$ $a_1=$ $a_2=$ $a_3=$ $a_{20}=$ Pattern: _____

34. $a_n = 3 \times 2^n$ $a_1=$ $a_2=$ $a_3=$ $a_{20}=$ Pattern: _____

35. $a_n = -5 \times 2^{n-1}$ $a_1=$ $a_2=$ $a_3=$ $a_{20}=$ Pattern: _____

36. $a_n = 2 \times 3^n$ $a_1=$ $a_2=$ $a_3=$ $a_{20}=$ Pattern: _____

37. $a_n = 5^{n-2} + 3$ $a_1=$ $a_2=$ $a_3=$ $a_{20}=$ Pattern: _____

38. $a_n = (-3)^n$ $a_1=$ $a_2=$ $a_3=$ $a_{20}=$ Pattern: _____

39. $a_n = 2 \times (-3)^n$ $a_1=$ $a_2=$ $a_3=$ $a_{20}=$ Pattern: _____

40. $a_n = 2 \times (-5)^{n-1}$ $a_1=$ $a_2=$ $a_3=$ $a_{20}=$ Pattern: _____

41. $a_n = (-3)^{n+1}$ $a_1=$ $a_2=$ $a_3=$ $a_{20}=$ Pattern: _____

42. $a_n = 1 + 5^{n-2}$ $a_1=$ $a_2=$ $a_3=$ $a_{20}=$ Pattern: _____

43. The sequences in which the pattern is add/subtract a number are called _____

44. The sequences in which the pattern is multiply/divide (pay attention that

   dividing by a is the same as multiplying by _____) a number are called _____

45. $a_n = 2a_{n-1}$ $a_1=1$ $a_2=$ $a_3=$ $a_{20}=$ Pattern: _____

46. $a_{n+2} = a_n + a_{n+1}$ $a_1=1$ $a_2=1$ $a_3=$ $a_{20}=$ Pattern: _____

47. In the last 2 sequences the terms are given in terms of _____

48. (T/F) Arithmetic and Geometric sequences are most of the sequences that exist.

49. The terms in a convergent geometric sequence tend to _____, in a none–convergent sequence the terms tend to _____ or _____.

50. Give an example of a convergent geometric sequence:

51. Give an example of a divergent geometric sequence:

52. Give an example of a alternating convergent geometric sequence:

53. Give an example of a none alternating divergent geometric sequence:

54. A convergent geometric sequence is a sequence in which r is _____.

Arithmetic sequence (Pattern – Add a constant):

General term: $a_n = a_1 + (n-1)d$

Sum: $S_n = \dfrac{n}{2}(2a_1 + (n-1)d)$

Geometric Sequence (Pattern – multiply by a constant):

General term: $a_n = a_1 r^{n-1}$

Sum: $S_n = \dfrac{a(r^n - 1)}{r - 1}$

Convergent geometric sequence ($-1 < r < 1$): $S_\infty = \dfrac{a_1}{1-r}$

Example:

    3, 7, 11, 15…   Arithmetic sequence.
                            Pattern: add 4.
                            General term: $a_n = 3 + (n-1)4$
                            General term can be written also like this: $a_n = -1 + 4n = 4n - 1$

Given the following sequences:

a. For each one write: arithmetic, geometric convergent, geometric divergent or neither, the <u>next term</u> and their <u>general term</u> (in case they are geometric or arithmetic only).

b. Try to write the general term of the other sequences as well.

55. 1, 2, 3, 4, ___...

56. 1, 2, 4, 8, ___...

57. 1, 3, 5, 7, ___...

58. 1, 3, 9, 27, ___...

59. 4, 6, 9, 13,5, ___...

60. 4, 1, –2, –5, ___...

61. 5, 0, –4, –7, ___...

62. 10, 1000, 100000, ___...

63. 30, 10, $\dfrac{10}{3}$, $\dfrac{10}{9}$, ___...

64. 2, 10, 50, 250, ___...

65. 2, 102, 202, 302, ___...

66. 1, –1, 1, –1, ____

67. –2, 2, –2, 2, ___...

68. 3, –6, 12, –24, ___...

69. –8, 4, –2, 1, ___...

70. 5, 1, $\dfrac{1}{5}$, $\dfrac{1}{25}$, ___...

71. 100, 10, 1, $\dfrac{1}{10}$, ___..

72. $\dfrac{3}{4}$, $\dfrac{3}{8}$, $\dfrac{3}{16}$, ___...

73. 12, 11, 10, 9, ___...

74. $\dfrac{4}{9}$, $\dfrac{5}{9}$, $\dfrac{6}{9}$, ___...

75. 9, 8, 6, 5, 3, 2, ___...

76. 5, 9, 13, ___...

77. 1, $\dfrac{3}{2}$, $\dfrac{9}{4}$, $\dfrac{27}{8}$, ___...

78. 5, $-\dfrac{5}{3}$, $\dfrac{5}{9}$, $-\dfrac{5}{27}$, ___...

79. –1, –2, –3, ___ …

80. –2, 4, –8, ___ …

81. 70, 20, $\dfrac{40}{7}$, ___ …

82. 100, 10, 1, ___ …

83. 100, –10, 1, $\dfrac{-1}{10}$, ___ …

84. 3, 24, 192, ___ …

85. 90, 9, $\dfrac{9}{10}$, ___ …

86. $\dfrac{3}{2}$, $\dfrac{4}{3}$, $\dfrac{5}{4}$, ___ …

87. $\dfrac{40}{3}$, $\dfrac{20}{6}$, $\dfrac{10}{12}$, $\dfrac{5}{24}$, ___ …

88. $\dfrac{2}{3}$, $-\dfrac{4}{9}$, $\dfrac{8}{27}$, $-\dfrac{16}{81}$, ___ …

89. $-\dfrac{1}{2}$, $-\dfrac{1}{4}$, $-\dfrac{1}{8}$, $-\dfrac{1}{16}$, ___ …

90. $\dfrac{1}{7}$, $-\dfrac{1}{14}$, $\dfrac{1}{21}$, $-\dfrac{1}{28}$, ___ …

91. 8, 5, 3, 0, ___...

94. 2, –10, 50, ___...

92. $3, \dfrac{3}{4}, \dfrac{3}{16}$, ___...

95. $1, \sqrt{3}, 3, \sqrt{27}, ...$

93. $81, -9, 1, -\dfrac{1}{9}$, ___...

96. $7, \sqrt{7}, 1, \dfrac{1}{\sqrt{7}} ...$

In each one of the following sequences find the term indicated:

97. 1, 4 , 7... (a_{31})

101.　　68, –34, 17... (a_9)

98. –8, –5, –2... (a_{37})

102. 3, 14, 25... (a_9)

99. 4, –8, 16... (a_{15})

103. –4000, 1000, –250,... (a_7)

100.　　32, –8, 2... (a_{11})

104. 200, 100, 50... (a_7)

105. The 4th term of a geometric sequence is 3, the 6th term is $\dfrac{27}{4}$.

      a. Find the ratio of the sequence.
      b. Is this sequence convergent? Explain
      c. Find a_1
      d. Find a_{12}
      e. Sum the first 15 terms.

106. The 2nd term of a arithmetic sequence is –2, the 6th term is –4.

      a. Find the difference of the sequence.
      b. Find a_1
      c. Find a_{12}
      d. Sum the first 50 terms.

107. The 10th term of a geometric sequence is 5, the 14th term is $\dfrac{80}{81}$

    a. Find the ratio of the sequence.
    b. Is this sequence convergent? Explain
    c. Find a_1
    d. Find a_7
    e. Sum the first 10 terms.
    f. Sum all the terms of the sequence.

108. The 7th term of a arithmetic sequence is 120, the 16th term is 201.

    a. Find the difference of the sequence.
    b. Find a_1
    c. Find a_{12}
    d. Sum the first 50 terms.

109. All the terms in a geometric sequence are positive. The first term is 7 and the 3rd term is 28.

    a. Find the common ratio.
    b. Find the sum of the first 14 terms.

110. The fifth term of an arithmetic sequence is −20 and the twelfth term is −44.

    a. Find the common difference.
    b. Find the first term of the sequence.
    c. Calculate the eighty–seventh term.
    d. Calculate the sum of the first 150 terms.

111. Sum the following sequences:

    a. $3 + 6 + 9 + 12 + \ldots + 69 =$

    b. $6 + 14 + 22 + 30 + \ldots + 54 =$

    c. $5 + \dfrac{5}{3} + \dfrac{5}{9} + \ldots =$

    d. $1 + 2 + 3 + 4 + \ldots + 158 =$

    e. $9 + 18 + 27 + 36 + \ldots + 900 =$

    f. $80 + 20 + 5 + \ldots$

g. $100 + 97 + 94 + \ldots + 19 =$

h. $18 + 6 + 2 + \ldots =$

i. $\dfrac{2}{5} + \dfrac{6}{10} + \dfrac{18}{20} + \ldots + \dfrac{243}{80}$

j. $\dfrac{1}{3} + \dfrac{2}{9} + \dfrac{4}{27} + \ldots =$

k. $12 + 7 + 2 + \ldots - 98 =$

l. $100 + 150 + 200 + \ldots + 1000 =$

112. Consider the arithmetic series –6 + 1 + 8 + 15 + …

Find the least number of terms so that the sum of the series is greater than 10000.

113. In a theatre there are 20 seats in the first row, 23 in the 2nd, 26 in the 3rd etc. There are 40 rows in the theatre. Find the total number of seats available.

114. A ball bounces on the floor. It is released from a height of 160 cm. After the 1st bounce it reaches a height of 120 cm and 90 cm after the 2nd. If the patterns continue find:

    a. The height the ball will reach after the 6th bounce.
    b. The total distance the ball passed after a long period o time.

115. In a certain forest the current population of rabbits is 200 objects. It is know that the population increases by 20% every year.

    a. Find the population of rabbits after a year.
    b. Find the population of rabbits after 2 years.
    c. What kind of a sequence is it? State the expression for the population after n years.
    d. Find the total number of rabbits after 10 years (assuming none has died).

116. In a research it was observed that the number of defective products produced by a machine per year decreases by 10% every year (due to technological improvements). In a certain year the machine made 300 products.

    a. Find the number of defective products produced a year later.
    b. Find the number of defective products produced 2 years later.
    c. What kind of a sequence is it? State the expression for the number of errors committed after n years.
    d. Find the total number of bad products produced in the first 8 years.

117. In a certain company the pay scale follows a pattern of an arithmetic sequence (every year). This means:

    a. The salary increases by a certain % every year (True/False), explain.

    b. The salary increases by a certain amount every year (True/False), explain

118. Given the sequence: $a, a^2, a^3...$

    a. This is a _____ sequence.
    b. Write down its general term, simplified.
    c. It is known that the infinite sequence adds up to 10, find a.

119. Given the sequence: $a^{-2}, a^{-3}, a^{-4}...$

    a. This is a _____ sequence.
    b. Write down its general term, simplified.
    c. It is known that the infinite sequence adds up to $\dfrac{1}{2}$, find a.

COMPOUND INTEREST

1. 1200$ are put in account that gives 2% per year. Calculate the amount of money in the account after:

   a. 1 year.

   b. 2 years.

2. To increase an amount A by 5% it should be multiplied by _____.

3. To increase an amount A by 56% it should be multiplied by _____.

4. To decrease an amount A by 5% it should be multiplied by _____.

5. To increase an amount A by 15% it should be multiplied by _____.

6. To decrease an amount A by 12% it should be multiplied by _____.

7. To increase an amount A by 230% it should be multiplied by _____.

8. 1000$ are put in account that takes 5% commission per year. Calculate the amount of money in the account after:

   a. 1 year.

   b. 2 years.

9. 2000$ are being put in a deposit that pays 5% (per year).

a. Fill the table:

Number of Years	Interest earned at the end of the year	Amount in deposit ($)
0		2000
1	$\dfrac{5}{100}2000 = 100$	2100
2	$\dfrac{5}{100}2100 = 105$	2205
3	$\dfrac{5}{100}2205 = 110.25$	
4		
5		

b. Observe the numbers in the compound interest column: 2000, 2100, 2205… What kind of a sequence is that? Write its general term.

c. How much money will be in the account after 20 years?

d. Discuss the meaning of writing $a_n = a_1 r^{n-1}$ or writing $a_n = a_0 r^n$. Use the exercise as an example.

10. A loan of 1200$ is made at 12% per year compounded semiannually, over 5 years the debt will grow to:

    a. $\$1200(1 + 0.12)^5$
    b. $\$1200(1 + 0.06)^{10}$
    c. $\$1200(1 + 0.6)^{10}$
    d. $\$1200(1 + 0.06)^5$
    e. $\$1200(1 + 0.12)^{10}$

11. A loan of 23200$ is made at 7% per year compounded quarterly, over 6 years the debt will grow to:

    a. $\$23200(1 + 0.7)^{24}$
    b. $\$23200(1 + 0.07)^6$
    c. $\$23200(1 + 0.7)^{24}$
    d. $\$23200(1 + 0.07)^{24}$
    e. $\$23200(1 + 0.07)^{12}$

12. A loan of 20$ is made at 14% per year compounded monthly, over 8 years the debt will grow to:

    a. $\$20(1 + 0.14)^{80}$
    b. $\$20(1 + 0.01)^{96}$
    c. $\$20(1 + 0.014)^{96}$
    d. $\$20(1 + 0.01)^{12}$
    e. $\$20(1 + 0.07)^{12}$

13. A loan of X$ is made at 8% per year compounded every 4 months, over 5 years the debt will grow to:

    a. $\$X(1 + 0.08)^4$
    b. $\$X(1 + 0.02)^5$
    c. $\$X(1 + 0.08)^{15}$
    d. $\$X(1 + 0.02)^{15}$
    e. $\$X(1 + 0.8)^{15}$

14. A loan of X$ is made at i% per year compounded every m months, over n years the debt will grow to:

$$Debt = \_\_(1 + -)^{-}$$

15. Calculate the total amount owing after two years on a loan of 1500$ if the interest rate is 11% compounded

    a. Annually

    b. Semiannually

    c. Quarterly

    d. Monthly

16. How much will a client have to repay on a loan of 800$ after 2 years, if the 12% interest is compounded annually.

17. Find the compound interest **earned** by the deposit. Round to the nearest cent. $3000 at 12% compounded semiannually for 10 years

18. How many years will it take to a 100$ to double assuming interest rate is 6%. Compounded semiannually.

19. How many years will it take to a X$ to triple assuming interest rate is 7%. Compounded quarterly

20. Find the interest rate given to a certain person in case he made a deposit of 1000$ and obtained 1200$ after 3 years, compounded monthly.

21. Find the interest rate given to a certain person in case he made a deposit of 2500$ and obtained 3000$ after 10 years, compounded yearly.

SIGMA NOTATION

1. The sum $\displaystyle\sum_{k=2}^{4} 2^k$ is equal to which of the following?

   a. $2^1 + 2^2 + 2^3 + 2^4$

   b. $2^2 + 2^4$

   c. $2^2 + 3^3 + 4^4$

   d. $2^2 + 2^3 + 2^4$

2. The sum $\displaystyle\frac{1}{4}\sum_{m=2}^{4} x_m$ is equal to which of the following?

   a. $\dfrac{1}{4}x_2 + \dfrac{1}{4}x_3 + \dfrac{1}{4}x_4$

   b. $\dfrac{1}{4}x_2 + x_3 + x_4$

   c. $\dfrac{1}{2}x_2 + \dfrac{1}{3}x_3 + \dfrac{1}{4}x_4$

   d. $\dfrac{1}{4}(2+3+4)$

3. The sum $\displaystyle\sum_{j=4}^{n} \frac{j}{j+1}$ is equal to which of the following?

   a. $\dfrac{1}{2} + \dfrac{3}{4} + \dfrac{5}{6} + ... + \dfrac{n}{n+1}$

   b. $\dfrac{1}{2} + \dfrac{2}{3} + \dfrac{3}{4} + ... + \dfrac{n}{n+1}$

   c. $\dfrac{4}{5} + \dfrac{5}{6} + \dfrac{6}{7} + ... + \dfrac{n}{n+1}$

   d. $\dfrac{4}{5} + \dfrac{5}{6} + \dfrac{6}{7} + ... + \dfrac{n+4}{n+5}$

4. Write out fully what is meant by

   a. $\displaystyle\sum_{i=4}^{i=6} 2i - 1 =$

   b. $\displaystyle\sum_{i=2}^{i=5} \frac{i}{i^2 + 1} =$

   c. $\displaystyle\sum_{i=4}^{i=6} (2i - 3)^2 =$

   d. $\displaystyle\sum_{k=3}^{i=7} (2^k + \sqrt{k}) =$

   e. $\displaystyle\sum_{i=1}^{i=4} (-1)^i \times 3^{2i}$

5. Write each series using sigma notation:

    a. $4 + 9 + 16 + 25 + 36 + 49 + 64 + 81 = \displaystyle\sum_{i=\_}^{i=\_}$ _____

    b. $5 + 9 + 13 + 17 + 21 + 25 + 29 + 33\ldots = \displaystyle\sum_{i=\_}^{i=\_}$ _____

    c. $1 - \dfrac{1}{3} + \dfrac{1}{9} - \dfrac{1}{27} + \dfrac{1}{81} - \dfrac{1}{243} = \displaystyle\sum_{i=\_}^{i=\_}$ _____

6. Use sigma notation to represent $3 + 6 + 9 + 12 + \ldots$ for 28 terms. Sum the terms.

     $\displaystyle\sum_{i=\_}^{i=\_}$ _____

7. Use sigma notation to represent $-3 + 6 - 12 + 24 - 48 + \ldots$ for 35 terms. Sum the terms.

     $\displaystyle\sum_{i=\_}^{i=\_}$ _____

8. Use sigma notation to represent: $8.3 + 8.1 + 7.9 + 7.7 + \ldots + 0.9$. Sum the terms

     $\displaystyle\sum_{i=\_}^{i=\_}$ _____

9. Use sigma notation to represent: $12 + 9 + 3 + \ldots - 120$. Sum the terms

     $\displaystyle\sum_{i=\_}^{i=\_}$ _____

10. An infinite geometric series is given by $\sum_{i=1}^{\infty} 2(1-x)^i$

    a. Find the value of x for which the series has a finite sum

    b. When x = 0.5, find the minimum number of terms needed to give a sum which is greater than 1.9

11. Given the sequence x, x^2, x^3...

    a. Use sigma notation to represent the sum of its first 10 terms.

    b. Assuming its infinite and that its sum is 5 find x and write down the first three terms of the sequence.

1.14. – EQUATIONS/INEQUALITIES WITH ABSOLUTE VALUE

1. $\left|-3\right| =$ $\left|3\right| =$ $\left|-3+3\right| =$ $\left|-3-3\right| =$

2. $\left|-3\right| + 3 =$ $\left|3\right| - 4 =$ $\left|-3+5\right| + 2 =$ $\left|-3-3\right| - 3 =$

3. $\left|1-3+\left|-2\right|\right| =$ 5. $\left|-2-23\right| - \left|-12\right| =$

4. $\left|-2-3\right| + \left|-2\right| =$ 6. $2\left|1-3+\left|-2\right| +1\right| - 2 =$

7. $\left|-2-3\right|\left|-2\right| =$

8. $-\left|-12-3\right| - \left|-2-1\right| =$

9. $5 - \left|12-3+\left|1-2\right|\right| - \left|-12-10\right| + 1 =$

10. $\left|2 - \left|-12-3\right| - \left|-2-1\right|\right| =$

11. $\left|x\right| - 2\left|x\right| =$

12. $\left|x\right|\left|x\right| =$

13. An absolute value of a number represents its _____

14. $\left|x\right| = \left|-x\right|$ True / False, if false write down an example to show it

15. $\left|x+y\right| = \left|x\right| + \left|y\right|$ True / False, if false write down an example to show it

16. $-\left|x\right|$ is _____ number

17. If $x = \left|x\right|$ it means x is _____

18. If $x = -\left|x\right|$ it means x is _____

19. If x is a negative number than $-x = \left|x\right|$ True / False

20. If x is a positive number than $x = \left|x\right|$ True / False

Assuming $a \geq 0$ the following is satisfied:

I. $|x| = a$ $x = a$ OR $x = -a$
II. $|x| > a$ $x > a$ OR $x < -a$ equivalent to $x \in (-\infty, -a) \cup (a, \infty)$
III. $|x| < a$ $-a < x < a$ equivalent to $x > -a$ and $x < a$ equivalent to $x \in (-a, a)$

1. $|2x| = 5$

2. $|x| = 7$

3. $|4x| = 8$

4. $|x| = -5$

5. $|2x| = 0$

6. $|2x| = -1$

7. $|2x| = 15$

8. $|2x| < 5$

9. $|x| > 7$

10. $|4x| < 8$

11. $|x| < -5$

12. $|3x| < 0$

13. $|6x| > -1$

14. $|5x| > 0$

15. $|3x| \leq 6$

16. $|x| \geq 7$

17. $|4x| \leq 2$

18. $|x| \leq -5$

19. $|2x| < 0$

20. $|2x| \geq -1$

21. $|x| \geq 0$

22. $|2+x| = 5$

23. $|-x| = 7$

24. $|4 - x| = 8$

25. $|3 - 2x| = -5$

26. $|2 - 3x| = 0$

27. $|2 + x| = -1$

28. $|2x + 3| = 15$

29. $|4 - 2x| < 5$

30. $|-x| > 7$

31. $|4 + 2x| < 8$

32. $|x| < -5$

33. $|3 + x| < 0$

34. $|6 - 2x| > -1$

35. $|5 + x| > 0$

36. $|1 - 3x| \leq 6$

37. $|1 + x| \geq 7$

38. $|4 + x| \leq 2$

39. $|3 + 2x| \leq -5$

40. $|2 + 3x| < 0$

41. $|7 - 6x| \geq -1$

42. $|1 - x| \geq 0$

43. $|2x + 1| + 3 = 5$

44. $|7x + 21| - 5 = -5$

45. $2 - |5 - 8x| = 15$

46. $|4x + 2| = -5$

47. $|8x + 12| = 100$

48. $|2x + 1| < 2$

49. $|8 - 2x + 1| > 6$

50. $|5x - 21| + 3 > 0$

51. $|5x - 21| \geq 0$

52. $|8x + 11| - 1 > -2$

53. $|91x + 61| < -2$

54. $|8 - 3x| > 8$

55. $|18 - 6x| + 1 > 3$

56. $|1 - 6x| - 2 < 7$

57. $|8 - 5x| \leq 0$

58. $|5x - 21| > 1$

59. $|x + 11| + 1 = 5$

60. $|x + 3| - 2 \leq 5$

61. $|x + 11| = -15$

62. $|2x + 11| + 2 < 1$

63. $|3x + 11| = x$

64. $|x + 2| = 5 - x$

65. $|3x + 1| < 5x$

66. $|x - 4| = 3x$

67. $|2x - 6| \leq 5 + 2x$

68. $|2x + 4| < 2 - 3x$

69. $|2x - 2| > 11 - 2x$

70. $|7x - 16| = 5 + 12x$

71. $|2x - 6| = 21$

72. $|2x - 6| \geq 4$

73. $|3x - 6| + 1 > -4$

74. $|4x - 6| - 4 < -4x$

75. $|\frac{1}{2}x - 4| \leq 1 + x$

76. $|2x + \frac{1}{2}| > 2 - 3x$

77. $|2x - \frac{1}{2}| = 1 - 2x$

$x \in (\frac{3}{8}, \infty)$

78. $|\frac{1}{2}x - 7| \leq 3 + 2x$

79. $|\frac{x}{2} + 2| = 1 - x \qquad x = -\frac{2}{3}$

CHAPTER 2 - GEOMETRY

2.1. – INTRODUCTION TO GEOMETRY

POINTS

1. Indicate the following points on the plane: A(1,5), B(–1, 4), C(–3, –7), D(6,–5), E(–1, –1), F(2, 0),G(0,–4), H(–4, 0)

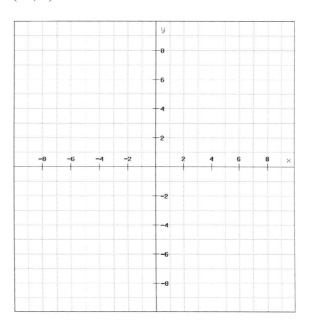

LINES

2. Indicate the following points on the plane: A(0,0), B(1, 1), C(–2, –2), D(6,6)

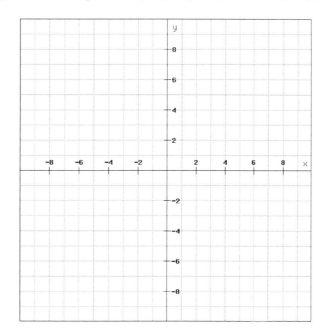

    a. What do these points have in common?

    b. Could you describe all the points that satisfy this property? How?

3. Indicate the following points on the plane: A(0,0), B(1, 2), C(–2, –4), D(4,8)

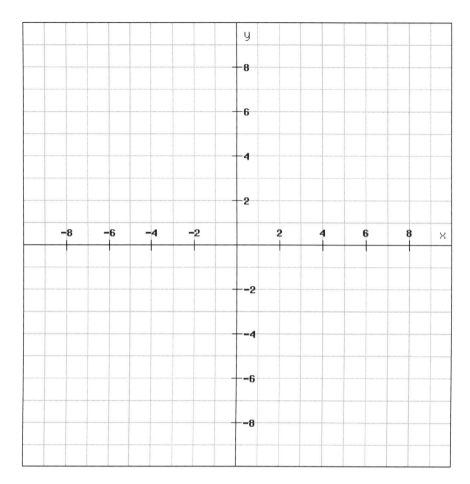

a. What do these points have in common? Use a ruler to draw the line that connects them.

b. Could you describe all the points that satisfy this property? How?

c. On the same graph sketch the following points E(0,1), F(1, 3), G(–2, –3), H(4,9)

d. What do these points have in common? Use a ruler to draw the line that connects them. What is the relation between this line and the previous line?

4. Indicate the following points on the plane: A(0, –2), B(1, 1), C(2, 4), D(–2,–8)

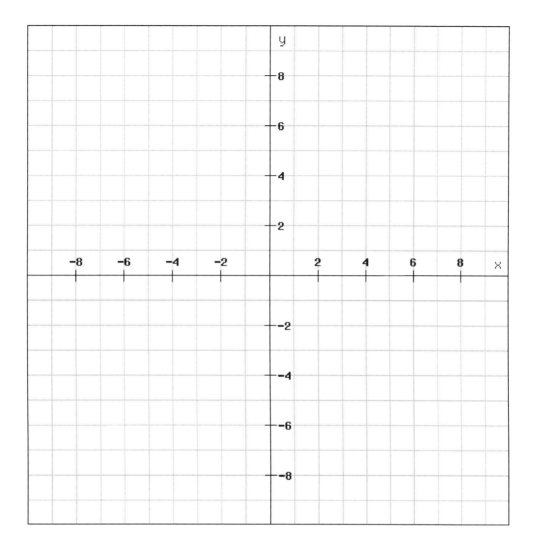

a. What do these points have in common? Use a ruler to draw the line that connects them.

b. Could you describe all the points that satisfy this property? How?

c. On the same graph sketch the following points E(0,1), F(1, 4), G(–2, –5), H(2, 7)

d. What do these points have in common? Use a ruler to draw the line that connects them. What is the relation between this line and the previous line?

2.2. – ANGLES

1. An angle is the figure formed by _____ lines called _____ that start at a common point.

   For example:

2. A straight angle is: _____

3. An acute angle is: _____

4. A right angle is: _____

5. An obtuse angle is: _____

6. Given the following diagram:

   a. CA and CB are _____

   b. The shaded angle can be called _____ or _____

7. We say that the following angle has a size of _____ degrees or ____°

8. Use the following square to sketch an angle of 45° degrees:

9. Two angles are complementary if their sum is _____

10. Two angles are supplementary if their sum is _____

11. The complementary of 20° is _____. The complementary of x° is _____

12. The supplementary of 20° is _____. The supplementary of x° is _____

13. The complementary of 42° is _____. The complementary of x° is _____

14. The supplementary of 126° is _____. The supplementary of x° is _____

15. The complementary of 81° is _____. The complementary of x° is _____

16. The supplementary of 0° is _____. The supplementary of x° is _____

17. Find all the unknown angles:

18. Find all the unknown angles:

19. Straight lines are _____ or _____

20. Given the following diagram:

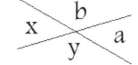

   a. The angles x and y are _____

   b. The angles x and a are _____

   c. The angles y and b are _____

21. Given the following diagram:

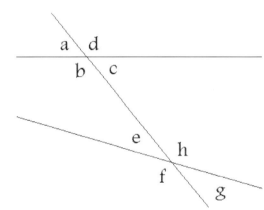

   a. The angles a and e are _____

   b. The angles b and e are _____

   c. The angles b and f are _____

   d. The angles c and e are _____

   e. The angles h and b are _____

   f. The angles e and g are _____

   g. The angles c and h are _____

   h. The angles g and h are _____

   i. The angles b and d are _____

   j. Which angle is a corresponding angle pair with g? _____

   k. Which angle is an alternate angle pair with g? _____

   l. Which angle is a co-interior angle pair with e? _____

Given the following diagram in which the transversal intersects 2 parallel lines:

m. The angles a and e are _____

n. The angles b and e are _____

o. The angles b and f are _____

p. The angles c and e are _____

q. The angles h and b are _____

r. The angles e and g are _____

s. The angles c and h are _____

22. Determine if the lines are parallel, explain why:
    Find all possible angles

    100°

    79°

23. Determine if the lines are parallel, explain why:
    Find all possible angles

    100°

    100°

24. Determine if the lines are parallel, explain why
    Find all possible angles

    50°

25. Sketch corresponding angle:

    50°

    _____

    _____

26. Sketch alternate interior angles:

    _____

    _____

27. Sketch alternate exterior angles:

_____

_____

28. Given the AB is parallel to CD, find the angles a, b, c, d, e.

29. The sum of the angles in a triangle is _____

30. The sum of the angles in a square is _____

31. The sum of the angles in a rectangle is _____

32. The sum of the angles in a quadrilateral is _____

33. The sum of the angles in a pentagon is _____

34. The sum of the angles in an hexagon is _____

35. The sum of the angles in an heptagon is _____

36. The sum of the angles in an octagon is _____

37. The sum of the angles in a shape with n sides is _____,

the reason is that _____

38. Find the regular polygons with which you can fill the floor with tiles. Explain why does this happen.

2.3. – SQUARES, RECTANGLES AND TRIANGLES

1. Indicate the following points on the plane: A(0, 6), B(6, 0), C(0, 0)

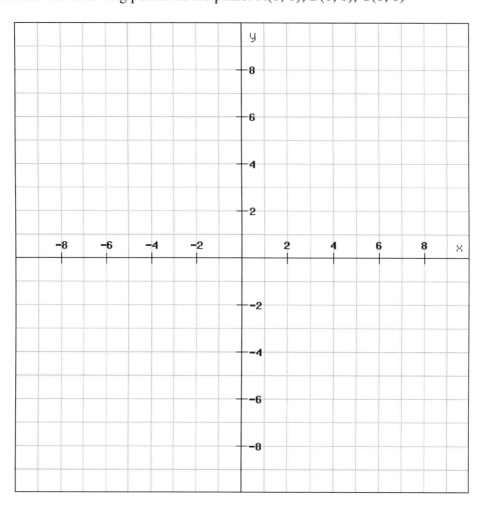

a. Use a ruler to draw the line that connects each pair of points to form a triangle.

b. Find all the angles of the triangles you can.

c. This kind of triangle is called _____ and _____

d. Write down the lengths of the 2 equal sides: _____

e. Write down the Pythagorean Theorem: _____.

This theorem is only true in _____ triangles.

f. Use P. Theorem to find the length of the third side of the triangle.

g. Add the point D(6, 6) to the graph. The form ABCD is a _____. The

area of this shape is _____

h. Use the area of the square to find the area of the triangle.

2. Indicate the following points on the plane: A(–4, 0), B(2, 6), C(8, 0)

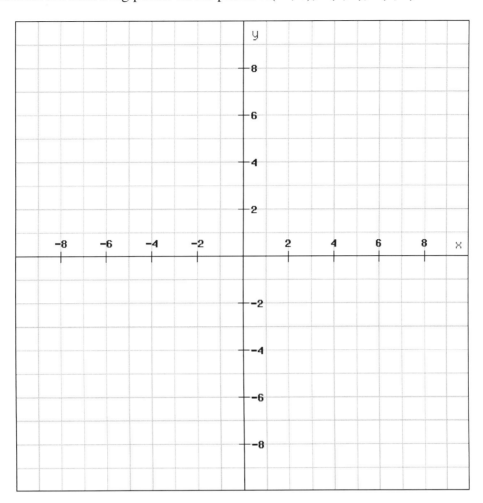

a. Use a ruler to draw the line that connects each pair of points to form a triangle.

b. This kind of triangle is called _____

c. Write down the Pythagorean Theorem: _____.

   This theorem is only true in _____ triangles.

d. Add the point D (2, 0) to the graph. The triangle ABD is _____.

e. The length of AD is _____. The Length of BD is _____. Use P. Theorem to

   find the length of AB.

f. In consequence state the length of BC:_____.

g. The perimeter of the triangle ABC is _____

h. Add the point E (–4, 6) to the graph. The shape AEBD is a _____. The area

   of this shape is ____. Use this area to find the area of the triangle ABD and ABC.

3. Indicate the following points on the plane: A(–6, 0), B(3, 6), C(5, 0)

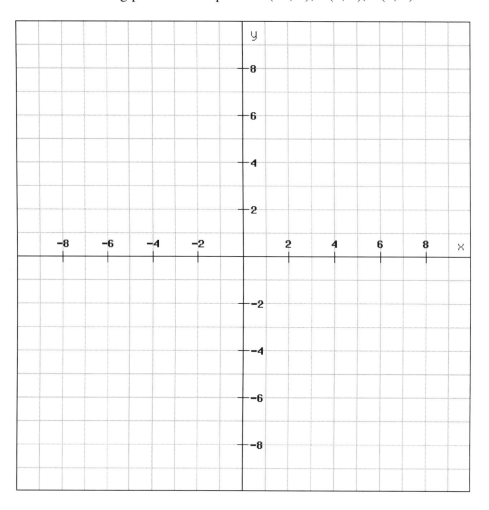

a. Use a ruler to draw the line that connects each pair of points to form a triangle.

b. Is this triangle isosceles or right angled?

c. Add the points D (–6, 6) and E (5, 6) to the graph. The shape ADEC is a _____

   The area of this shape is _____.

d. Add the point F (3, 0) to graph and use the corresponding theorem to find the

   length of AB: _____ and BC _____.

e. The perimeter of the triangle ABC is _____

f. The line BF is called the _____ of the triangle.

g. Every triangle has ____ heights. A height is a lines that starts at a _____

   and ends at _____ forming an angle of _____ with it.

h. Find the area of the triangles ABF, FBC and ABC.

4. Indicate the following points on the plane: A (−5, 0), B (5, 0), C (0, $\sqrt{75}$)

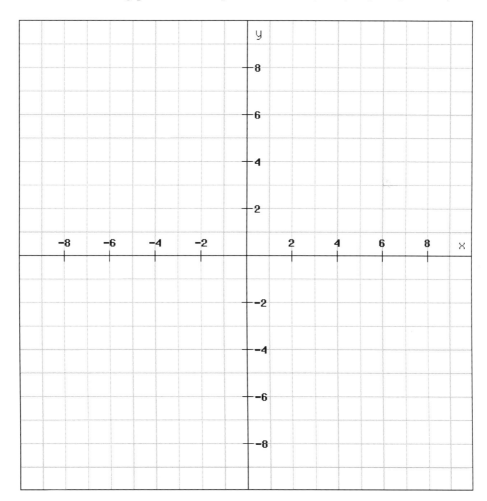

a. Use a ruler to draw the line that connects each pair of points to form a triangle.

b. Add the points D (0, 0) to the graph and use the corresponding theorem to find

length of AB: _____ and BC _____.

c. What kind of triangle is this? _____

d. What can you say about the angles of this triangle?

e. The perimeter of the triangle ABC is _____

f. Find the area of the triangle ABC.

5. Define and sketch an example, include all the known angles and lengths of sides in your example.

    a. Equilateral triangle:

    c. Right angled triangle:

    b. Isosceles triangle:

    d. Right angled and isosceles triangle:

6. The vertex angle of an isosceles triangle is 42°, find the size of its base angle.

7. The vertex angle of an isosceles triangle is 110°, find the size of its base angle.

8. The base angle of an isosceles triangle is 50°, find the size of its vertex angle.

9. The base angle of an isosceles triangle is 33°, find the size of its vertex angle.

10. Given the isosceles triangle:

    y = ___ a = ___ b = ___

11. Given the diagram, find:

x = ___ y = ___ a = ___ b = ___

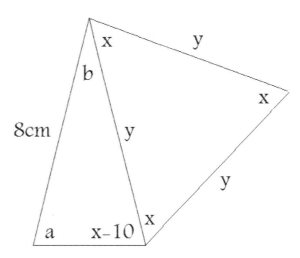

12. The base of an isosceles triangle is 10 cm, its side is 12 cm. Find its perimeter and area.

13. The base angle of an isosceles triangle is 5x + 7, the vertex angle is 2x – 2; find the size of the angles.

14. The base angle of an isosceles triangle is 9x – 10, the vertex angle is 12x – 10; find the size of the angles.

15. Given the following triangle, it is known that AB = 10cm, AD = 7cm and DC = 4cm. Angle CDB = 90°. Find:

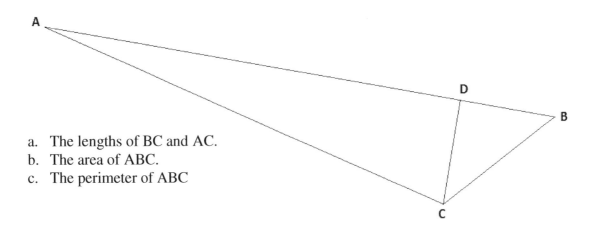

a. The lengths of BC and AC.
b. The area of ABC.
c. The perimeter of ABC

16. Given the following triangle, it is known that AC = 13cm, DB = 4cm and DC = 5cm. Angle CDB = 90°. Find:

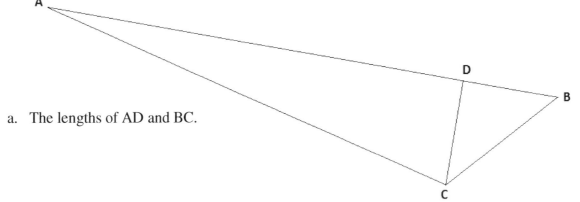

a. The lengths of AD and BC.

b. The area of DCB.

c. The perimeter of ABC

17. Given the following triangle, it is known that AC = 20cm, DB = 10cm and DC = 11 cm. Angle CDB = 90° and angle CEA = 90°. Find:

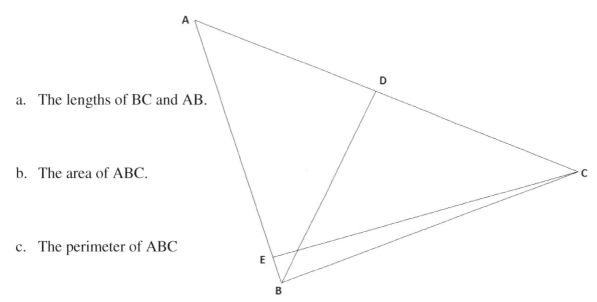

a. The lengths of BC and AB.

b. The area of ABC.

c. The perimeter of ABC

d. What do EC and BD have in common?

e. The lengths of EC, EB and AE

18. Find the perimeter and area of an isosceles right angled triangle whose <u>leg</u> is 10cm.

19. Find the perimeter and area of a right angled triangle whose sides are $6, x, 10$

20. Find the perimeter and area of a right angled triangle whose sides are $\sqrt{x}, \sqrt{x}, \dfrac{x}{2}$

21. Find the area of an isosceles right angled triangle whose <u>perimeter</u> is 20cm.

22. Find the area of an equilateral triangle whose perimeter is 30cm.

23. Given a right angled isosceles triangle whose longest side is 10 cm long.

    a. Sketch the triangle.
    b. Find the perimeter of the triangle.
    c. Find the area of the triangle.

24. Given a right angled isosceles triangle whose smallest side is X cm long.

    a. Sketch the triangle.
    b. Find the perimeter of the triangle in terms of X.
    c. Find the area of the triangle in terms of X.

25. Given an equilateral triangle whose side is 10 cm long.

    a. Sketch the triangle.
    b. Find the perimeter of the triangle.
    c. Find the area of the triangle.

26. Given an equilateral triangle whose side is X cm long.

   a. Sketch the triangle.
   b. Find the perimeter of the triangle in terms of X.
   c. Find the area of the triangle in terms of X.

27. Find the perimeter of an isosceles triangle whose base is half of its side and its area is 20 cm^2

28. Find the perimeter of an isosceles triangle whose base is a third of its side and its area is A cm^2, in terms of A.

29. Find the area of a right angled triangle in which 1 leg is 10% <u>longer</u> than the other and whose perimeter is 70cm

30. Find the area of a right angled triangle in which 1 leg is 25% <u>shorter</u> than the other and whose perimeter is 24cm

31. Given the following diagram (not to scale), BD = x cm, DC = 3BD, AD = 10 cm, AC = 20cm

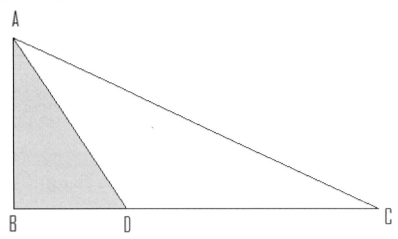

a. Write 2 equations with the given information.

b. Solve the equations to determine x.

c. Find the perimeter and area of ABC.

d. Find the perimeter and area of ABD.

e. Find the perimeter and area of ADC.

f. Determine the percentage of the area that is shaded.

30. Given the following diagram (not to scale), BD = 8 cm, AD = 17 , DC = 104 cm,

a. Find the perimeter and area of ABC

b. Find the perimeter and area of ABD.

c. Find the perimeter and area of ADC.

d. Determine the percentage of the area that is shaded.

e. Determine the percentage by which the area of ABC is bigger than ABD

f. Determine the percentage by which the area of ABC is bigger than ADC

g. Determine the percentage by which the area of ADC is bigger than ABD

h. Determine the percentage by which the area of ABD is smaller than ABC

i. Determine the percentage by which the area of ADC is smaller than ABC

j. Determine the percentage by which the area of ABD is smaller than ADC

k. Determine the percentage by which the perimeter of ABC is bigger than ABD

l. Determine the percentage by which the perimeter of ABC is bigger than ADC

m. Determine the percentage by which the perimeter of ADC is bigger than ABD

n. Determine the percentage by which the perimeter of ABD is smaller than ABC

o. Determine the percentage by which the perimeter of ADC is smaller than ABC

p. Determine the percentage by which the perimeter of ABD is smaller than ADC

2.4. – POINTS OF CONCURRENCY

1. Given the following triangle, sketch all the <u>altitudes</u> in the triangle.

   An altitude is: _____. The point where

   they meet is called "<u>orthocenter</u>". Name the point H.

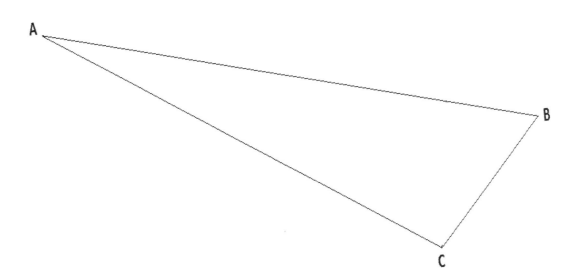

2. Given the following triangle, Sketch all the <u>perpendicular bisectors</u> in the triangle.

   The point where they meet is called <u>circumcenter</u>, it is the centre of _____

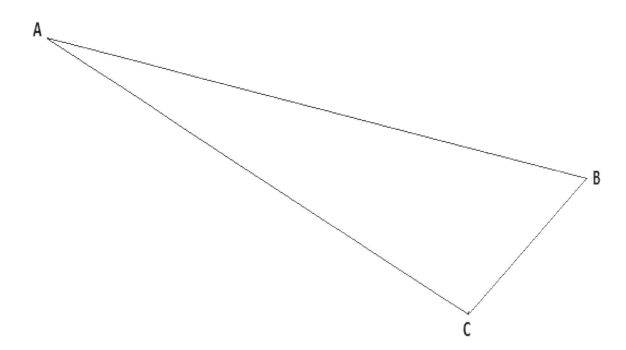

3. Given the following triangle, Sketch all the <u>angle bisectors</u> in the triangle.

   The point where they meet is called incenter, it is the centre of _____

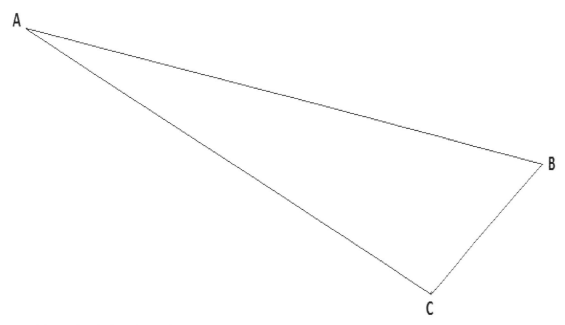

4. Given the following triangle, Sketch all the medians in the triangle.

   The point where they meet is called centroid. If the centroid is M then the following

   relations are satisfied (complete):

   $$AM = \frac{2}{3}AD \qquad\qquad BM = \qquad\qquad CM =$$

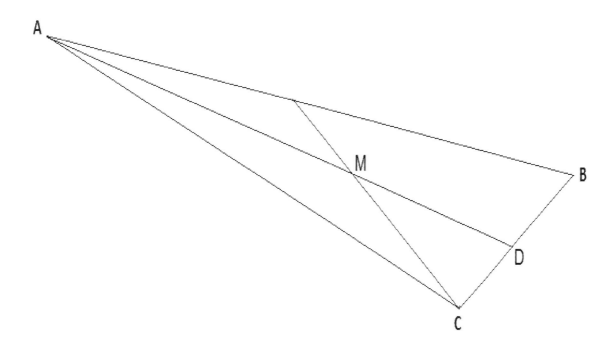

5. The Incentre is: _____

6. The Orthocentre is: _____

7. The Circumcentre is: _____

8. The Centroid is: _____

9. The Circumcentre is equidistant to _____

10. The Incentre is equidistant to _____

11. Given that the coordinates of a triangle are A(-6, 0). B(4, 0), C(2, 8)

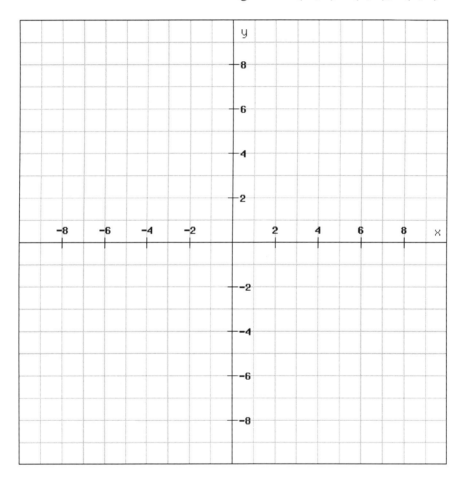

    a. Sketch the triangle.
    b. Graphically find its orthocentre.
    c. Calculate the coordinates of its orthocentre.

12. Given that the coordinates of a triangle are A(-6, 0). B(4, 0), C(2, 8)

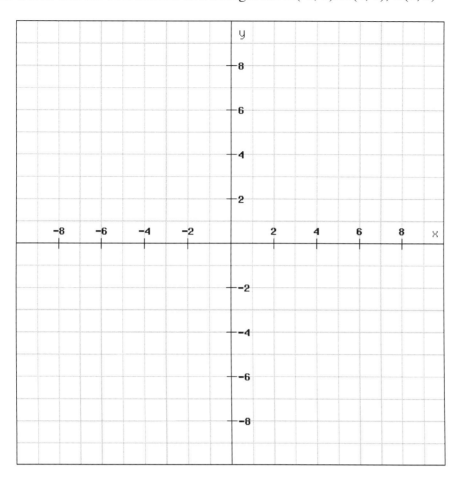

    a. Sketch the triangle.
    b. Graphically find its circumcenter.
    c. Find the points D. E, F the bisectors of AB, BC, and AC
       correspondingly.
    d. Find the slope of the lines AB, BC, find the perpendicular slopes.
    e. Use the previous part to construct 2 of the perpendicular bisectors and
       find their point of intersection which is the circumcenter

13. Given that the coordinates of a triangle are A(-6, 2). B(4, 8), C(0, -8)

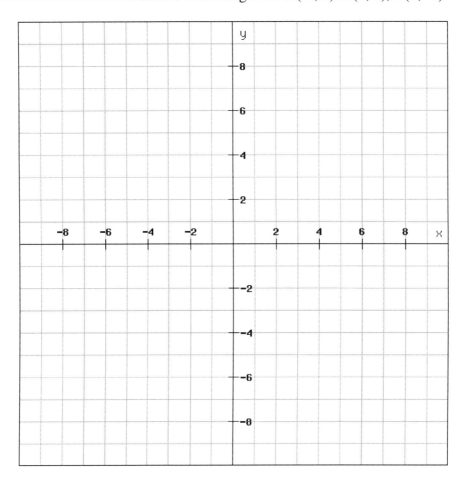

    a. Sketch the triangle.
    b. Graphically find its incentre.
    c. Find the coordinates of the incentre.

14. Given that the coordinates of a triangle are A(-6, 2). B(4, 8), C(0, -8)

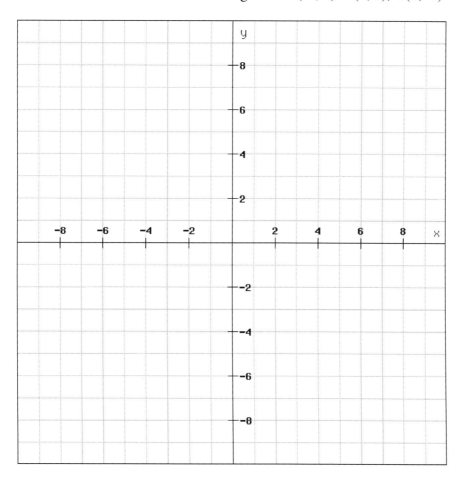

    a. Sketch the triangle.
    b. Graphically find its centroid.
    c. Calculate the coordinates of its centroid.

2.5. – CONGRUENT AND SIMILAR TRIANGLES

1. 2 triangles are similar if all of their angles are _____

2. 2 triangles are similar if <u>any</u> of the following is satisfied:

    a. 2 of their angles are _____. Sketch an example:

    b. 2 of their sides are _____ and the angles between them are _____. Sketch an example:

    c. All their sides are _____. Sketch an example:

3. All right angled triangles are similar True / False. Sketch an example to show answer:

4. Congruent triangles are similar triangles with ratio of proportionality _____

5. Similar triangles are always congruent True/False

6. congruent triangles are always Similar True/False

7. Determine if the following pair of triangles are similar, give a reason:

8. Determine if the following pair of triangles are similar, give a reason:

9. Determine if the following pair of triangles are similar, give a reason:

10. Determine if the following pair of triangles are similar, give a reason:

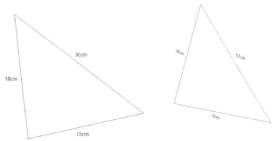

11. Determine if the following pair of triangles are similar, give a reason:

12. Determine if the following pair of triangles are similar, give a reason:

13. Given that $AB \parallel CD$, determine if the triangles ABE and CED are similar, give a reason:

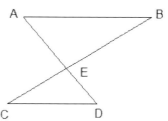

14. Given that $BC \parallel DE$, determine if the triangles ABC and ADE are similar, give a reason:

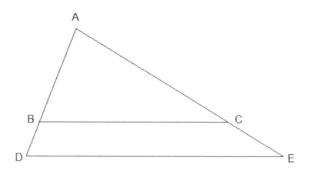

15. The shadow of a man formed by a street light on the ground is equal to twice its height. If the man is 10m away from the street light and his height is 1.80m, how high is the street light?

16. Given that $AB \parallel CD$, find ED:

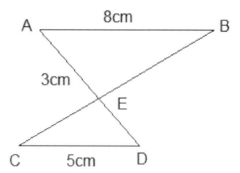

17. In the following triangle the angle BAC is a right angle. AD is an altitude from A to the BC. Show that triangles ABC, ADB and ADC are all similar. If BC = 10cm and AD = 2DC find the perimeter and area of ABD.

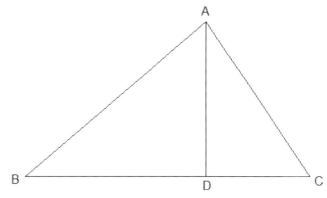

18. The following triangle AB = AC. AD is a altitude from A to the BC. Show that triangles ABD and ACD are similar. If BD = x and 2AB = 3AD, find the perimeter and area of ABC in terms of x.

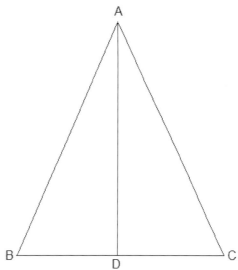

19. To measure the height of building the following operation can be performed. Jeff whose height is 180 cm puts a mirror at a distance of 22 m from a building and observed the top of the building in the mirror standing 0.4 m from it. Find the height of the building.

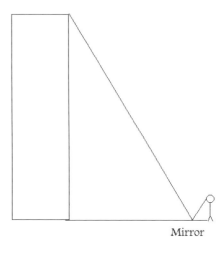

Mirror

20. Given the facade of a certain house, it is known that AC = 4m, CD = 2AC, CE = 7m DE = 3m. ABCD is a rectangle.
Find:

a. The height of the house above ground (help: lower a altitude from E).

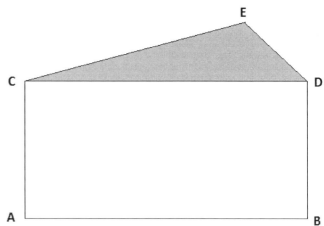

b. The area of the entire facade.

2.6. – DISTANCE AND MIDPOINT

1. Indicate the following points on the plane: A(2,3), B(6, 9), C(–3, –7), D(6,–5)

   a. Add the point (6, 3) and use Pythagorean Theorem to find the distance between the points A and B.

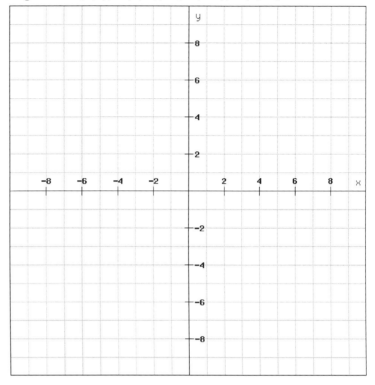

   b. Add the point (–3,–5) and use Pythagorean Theorem to find the distance between the points C and D.

   c. Find the distance AC

   d. Find the midpoint between AB (help: the midpoint x coordinate is the "average" of the x coordinates and the y coordinate is the "average" of the y coordinates)

   e. Find the midpoint between CD

   f. Find the midpoint between AC

2. Find the distance between (1, 3) and (7, –3), find the mid point.

3. Find the distance between (a, b) and (c, d), find the mid point.

4. Find a point whose distance to the point (2, 1) is 7.

5. Find a point whose distance to the point (–4, 2) is 3, can you draw a conclusion about such points in general?

6. The midpoint between the points (a, 5) and (–2, b) is (0, 0) find a and b.

7. The midpoint between the points (1+x, 2) and (–2+3x, 2 – y) is (1, 1) find x and y.

8. Given that the mid point between A(2, 5) and B is M(3, –2). Find point B.

9. Given that the mid point between A(–6, 4) and B is M(10, 0). Find point B.

10. Given that AB = BC = CD and A, B, C and D are aligned. Point A is (2, 4) and point D is (10, 10). Find points B and C.

11. Given that the distance AB = BC = CD. A, B, C, D are aligned. Point A is (–4, 8) and point B is (–2, 1). Find points C and D.

12. Given points A(3, –2), B(6, 1) and C(0, a). It is known that AC = BC, find a.

13. Given points A(–12, –8), B(–4, 7) and C(a, 0). It is known that AC = BC, find a.

2.7. – CIRCLES

1. Given the following circle:

    a. Sketch a diameter.
    b. Sketch a radius.
    c. The diameter is _____ the radius
    d. Sketch a chord smaller than the diameter
    e. Sketch a chord smaller than the radius

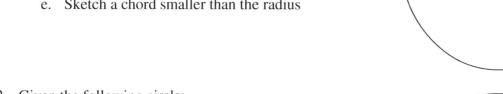

2. Given the following circle:

    a. Sketch a 60° angle.
    b. Show the corresponding minor arc/major arc
    c. Choose 3 points on the circle, connect them with chords. The triangle formed is inscribed in the circle. The circle is circumscribed about the triangle.
    d. Chords that are at the same distance from the centre are _____

3. Given the following circle:

    a. Choose 3 points on the circle, name them A, B and C. Sketch AB and BC. The angle ABC is inscribed in the circle.
    b. Choose a 4th point on the circle, name it D. Sketch AD and CD. The angle ADC is inscribed in the circle.
    c. What is your conclusion?

4. Given the following circle:

    a. Choose 3 points on the circle, name them A, B and C. Sketch AB and BC. The angle ABC is inscribed in the circle.
    b. Sketch the center of the circle; name it O. Sketch AO and CO. The angle AOC is inscribed in the circle.
    c. What is your conclusion?

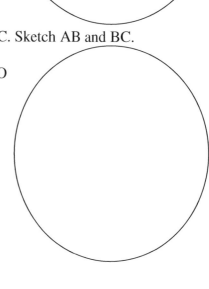

5. Given the following circle:

   a. Sketch the diameter of the circle; name it AC. Sketch a 3rd point B. Connect AB, AC and BC. The angle ABC is inscribed in the circle. Its size is: _____

   b. Choose a 4th point on the circle; name it D. Connect AD, DC. The angle ADC is inscribed in the circle. Its size is: _____

   c. What is your conclusion?

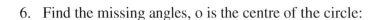

6. Find the missing angles, o is the centre of the circle:

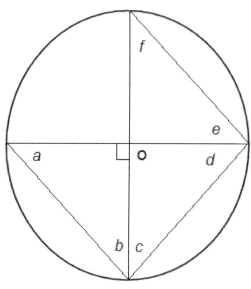

7. Find the missing angles, o is the centre of the circle:

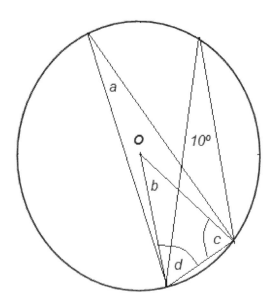

8. Find the missing angles, o is the centre of the circle:

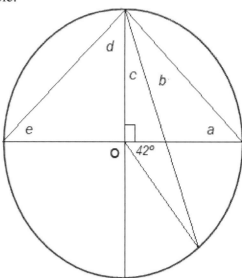

9. Find the missing angles, o is the centre of the circle:

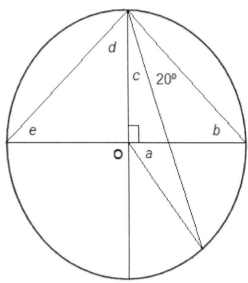

10. Find the missing angles, o is the centre of the circle:

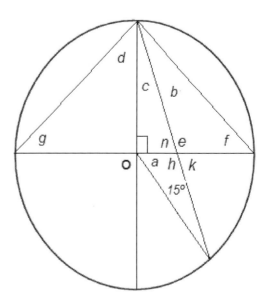

11. Given the following circle:

Sketch the diameter of the circle; name it AC. Sketch a 3rd point B. Connect AB, AC and BC. Given that the radius of the circle is 1cm and AB = 1cm find the perimeter of ABC.

12. Sketch a chord whose length is half of the diameter. In case the radius is 2cm find the area and perimeter of the triangle formed by connecting the center of the circle with the ends of the chord.

13. Given a circle with radius R, find

The Perimeter of the circle: _____

The Area of the circle: _____

14. Given a circle with radius $\dfrac{4}{\pi}$ cm, find

The Perimeter of the circle: _____

The Area of the circle: _____

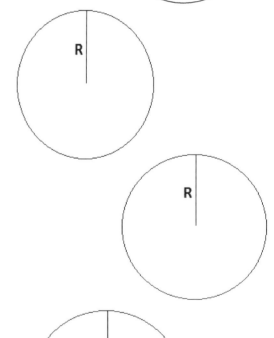

15. Given a circle with perimeter 20π cm, find

The radius of the circle: _____

The Area of the circle: _____

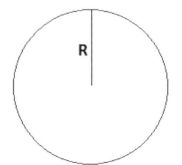

16. Given a circle with area 16π cm^2, find

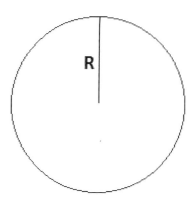

    The radius of the circle: _____

    The perimeter of the circle: _____

17. Shade 10% of the figure, find the corresponding angle. The length
Of an arc in a circle is L = _____

18. Given that R = 5 cm. Shade 20% of the figure, find the corresponding angle and
the area shaded. Find the perimeter of the shaded area.

19. Given that R = 15 cm. Shade 30% of the figure, write the corresponding angle
and find the area shaded. Find the perimeter of the shaded area.

20. Given a circle with radius 10cm:

    a.   Find the <u>percentage</u> of the area shaded.
    b.   Find the <u>size</u> of the shaded area.
    c.   Find the <u>perimeter</u> of the shaded area.

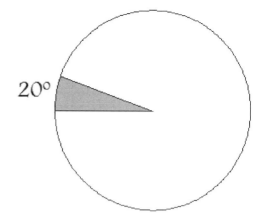

21. Given a circle with radius 10cm:

    a.   Find the <u>percentage</u> of the shaded area of the total area of the circle in terms of the angel x.
    b.   Find the <u>size</u> of the shaded area in terms of x.
    c.   Find the <u>perimeter</u> of the shaded area in terms of x.

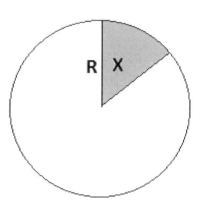

22. The length of the perimeter of a circle with radius r is _____. The

length of the arc that corresponds an angle x° is _____. In case

the angle x is measured in radians it would be _____.

The area of a circle with radius r is _____. The area of the sector

that corresponds an angle x° is _____. In case the angle x is

measured in radians it would be _____.

23. Given the circle with r = 2cm :

    a.   Show the arc corresponding an angle of 45°.
    b.   Calculate its length.
    c.   Shade the corresponding sector area.
    d.   Calculate it.

24. Given the circle with r = 3.2m:

    a. Show the arc corresponding an angle of 20º.
    b. Calculate its length.
    c. Shade the corresponding sector area.
    d. Calculate it.

25. Given the circle with r = 3m:
    a. Show the arc corresponding an angle of 18º.
    b. Calculate its length.
    c. Calculate its perimeter.
    d. Shade the corresponding sector area.
    e. Calculate it.

26. Given the circle with r = 6m:

    a. Show the arc corresponding an angle of 50º
    b. Calculate its length.
    c. Shade the corresponding sector area.
    d. Calculate it.

27. Given the following concentric circles with radii 3 cm and 5 cm correspondingly. Find the shaded area.

28. Given the following concentric circles with radii 10m and 14m correspondingly. Calculate the shaded area.

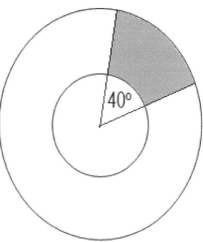

29. Given the following circle, AB is a chord on a circle with radius 10cm Calculate the shaded area.

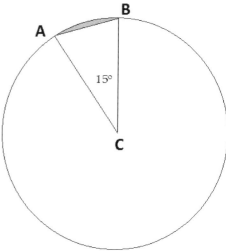

30. Given a circle with radius 8 cm. The segments AB and AC are tangent to the circle. Find the shaded area.

31. Given a circle with radius 10cm in which a square is circumscribed

    a.   Find the length of the side of the square.
    b.   Find the area of the square.
    c.   Find the area of the circle
    d.   Find the percentage of the area of the circle that the square occupies.

32. Given a circle with radius 10cm circumscribed in a square:

    a.   Find the length of the side of the square.
    b.   Find the area of the square.
    c.   Find the area of the circle
    d.   Find the percentage of the area of the square that the circle occupies.

33. On the following diagram sketch the following directions:

    a. N
    b. N30ºE
    c. N45ºE
    d. E45ºN
    e. S10ºW
    f. W80ºS
    g. W20ºN
    h. N30ºW

State a conclusion about the "uniqueness" of a direction.

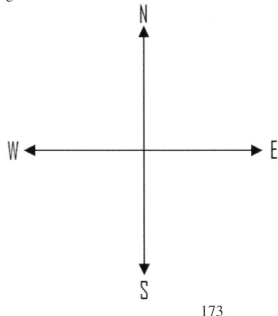

2.8. – QUADRILATERAS

1. Given the following table, fill the blank using *a, b, c, d, h, r*

	Shape	Area	Perimeter
Square			
Rectangle			
Parallelogram			
Isosceles Trapezoid			
Trapezpezoid			
Rhombus			
Kite			

2. Given the following quadrilaterals. Write the name of each one of them:

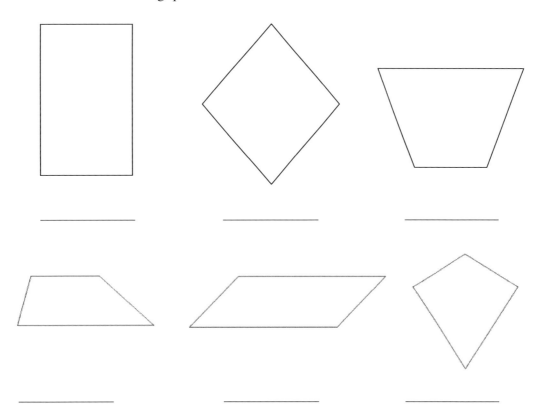

_____   _____   _____

_____   _____   _____

3. Given the following table, fill the blanks with yes or no.

	Shape (sketch)	Only 1 pair of parallel sides	2 pairs of parallel sides	1 pair of equal sides	2 pairs of equal sides	4 equal sides
Square						
Rectangle						
Parallelogram						
Isosceles Trapezoid						
Trapezoid						
Rhombus						
Kite						

4. True or False

    a. A square is also a parallelogram   True / False

    b. A square is also a rectangle   True / False

    c. A square is also a trapezoid   True / False

    d. A parallelogram is also a square   True / False

    e. A rectangle is also a square   True / False

    f. A rhombus is always a parallelogram   True / False

    g. A parallelogram is always r rhombus   True / False

    h. A parallelogram is sometimes a rhombus True / False

    i. A rhombus is always a kite   True / False

    j. All the shapes above mentioned are quadrilaterals True / False

5. Given the following table, fill the blanks with yes or no.

	Shape (Sketch diagonals as well)	Diagonals are perpendicular	Diagonals are equal	Diagonals bisect angle	Diagonals bisect each other
Square					
Rectangle					
Parallelogram					
Isosceles Trapezoid					
Trapezoid					
Rhombus					
Kite					

6. Given a square with diagonal of 4 cm, find its area and perimeter.

7. Given a square with diagonal of a cm, find its area and perimeter.

8. Given a rectangle with diagonal of 7m and one side is twice as large as the other, find its area and perimeter.

9. Given a rectangle with diagonal of 20m and one side is twice as large as the other, find its area and perimeter.

10. Given the following parallelogram. ABC is isosceles and right angled. AB = 2cm, CD = 5cm (Diagram not to scale). Find:

     a. The area and perimeter of the parallelogram
     b. The area and perimeter of ABC
     c. The area and perimeter of BCD
     d. The area and perimeter of CDE

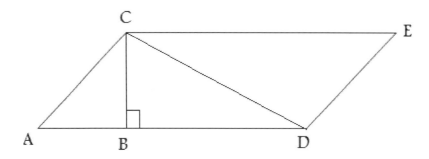

11. Given the following isosceles trapezoid. ABC is right angled. AC = 7cm, CE = 15cm and AE = 20cm (Diagram not to scale). Find:

   a. The area and perimeter of ABC and BCE
   b. The area and perimeter of the trapezoid
   c. The area and perimeter of CDE

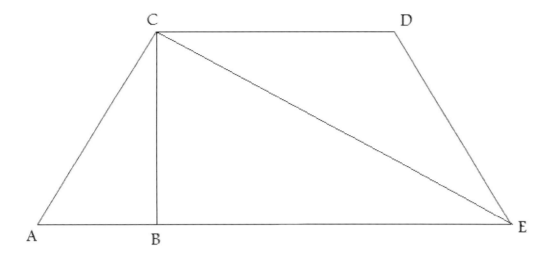

12. Given the following rhombus. BC = 6cm, AD = 18cm and find the area and perimeter the rhombus (Diagram not to scale).

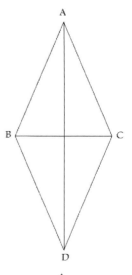

13. Given the following kite. BC = 4cm, AE = 8cm and CD = 2AC find the area and perimeter the kite (Diagram not to scale).

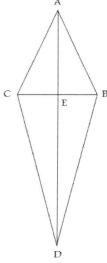

14. It is known that the perimeter of a rhombus with equal diagonals is 40cm. Find its area.

15. Find the side length of a square whose area is equal to its perimeter.

16. Find the side length of a rhombus whose area is equal to its perimeter and one of its diagonals is 5cm long.

2.9. – 3D GEOMETRY

1. Given the following table, fill the blanks

	Shape	Surface Area	Volume
Cuboid (Rectangular Prism)			
Pyramid (Square based)			
Sphere			
Cylinder			
Cone			

2. Given the following table, fill the blanks

	Shape	Surface Area	Volume
Triangular prism			
Triangle based Pyramid (Tetrahedron)			

3. Find the volume and surface area of a sphere with radius 10cm.

4. Find the volume and surface area of a sphere with radius 0.4m.

5. Find the volume of a square based pyramid with base length $2x$ cm and height is x cm.

6. Find the volume and surface area of a square based cuboid whose base length is 15 cm and height 0.1m

7. Find the volume and surface area of a cone with radius 0.4m and height 2m.

8. Find the volume and surface area of a cylinder with radius 0.4m and height 2m.

9. Given that the volume of a square based pyramid is 10 m^3 and that its height is equal to its base length, find the perimeter of its base.

10. Given that the volume of a cuboid is 10 m^3 and that the ratio between its sides is 1:2:3. Find its surface area.

11. Given that the volume of a cone is 10 m^3 and that its height is 3 times the radius of the base. Find its height.

12. Given that the volume of a sphere is 10 m^3. Find its surface area.

13. Find the volume and surface area of the following shape:

14. Find the volume and surface area of the following shape:

15. Find the volume and surface area of the following shape:

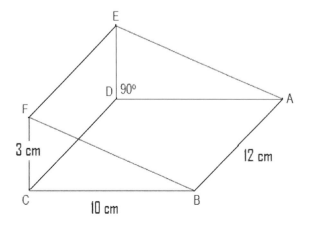

2.10. – GEOMETRIC TRANSOFRMATIONS

1. Indicate the following points on the plane: A(0,0), B(–1,6),C(4,2). Connect them to form a triangle.

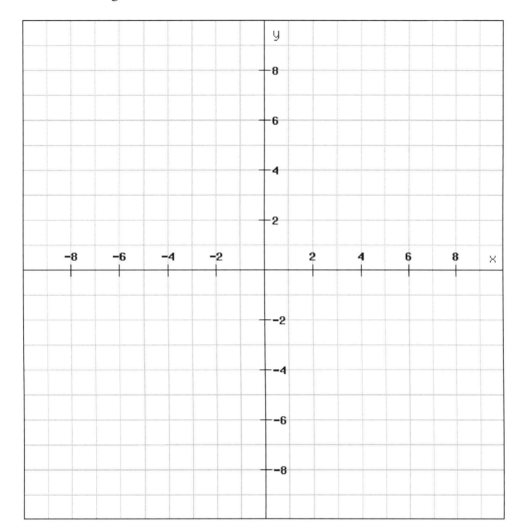

   a. Indicate the following points on the plane: A'(0,–3), B'(–1,3),C'(4,–1), Connect them to form a triangle.

   b. What can you say about the location of the 2nd triangle in comparison to the first one?

   c. This is a _____ translation.

2. Indicate the following points on the plane: A(0,0), B(−1,6),C(4,2). Connect them to form a triangle.

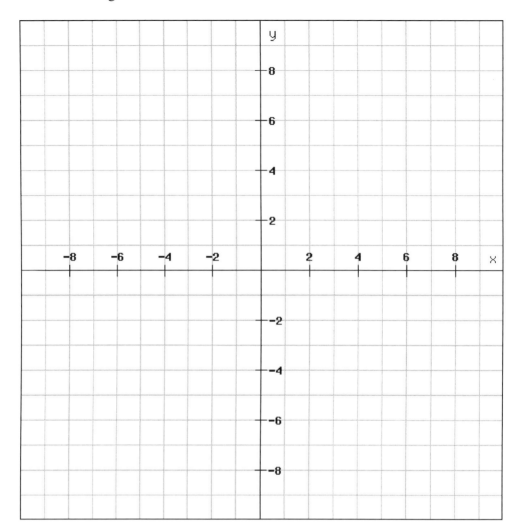

a. Indicate the following points on the plane: A'(4,0), B'(3,6),C'(8,2), Connect them to form a triangle.

b. What can you say about the location of the 2nd triangle in comparison to the first one?

c. This is a _____ translation.

3. Indicate the following points on the plane: A(0,0), B(–1,6),C(4,2). Connect them to form a triangle.

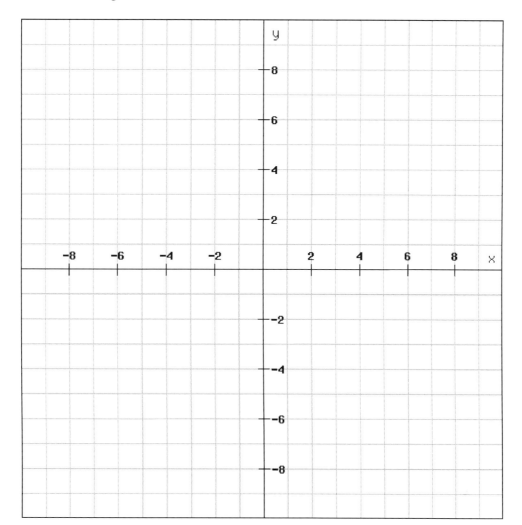

a. Indicate the following points on the plane: A'(–2,–3), B'(–3,3),C'(2,–1), Connect them to form a triangle.

b. What can you say about the location of the 2nd triangle in comparison to the first one?

c. This is a _____ and _____ translations.

4. Indicate the following points on the plane: A(1,0), B(–2,6),C(6,3). Connect them to form a triangle.

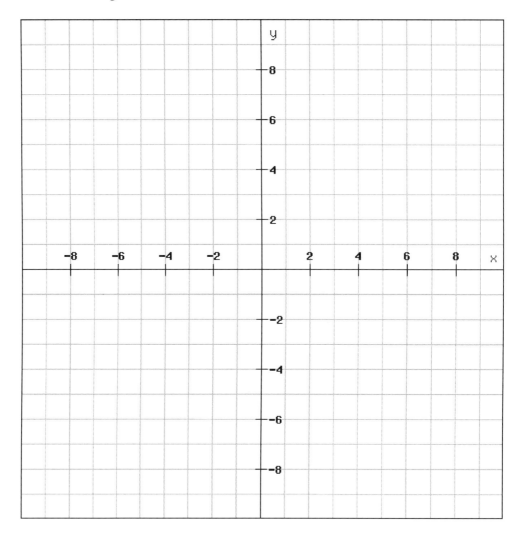

a. Indicate the following points on the plane: A'(–1,0), B'(2,6),C'(–6,3), Connect them to form a triangle.

b. What can you say about the location of the 2nd triangle in comparison to the first one?

c. This is a _____ across the y axis.

d. On changing x into _____ we are generating a _____ across the _____

5. Indicate the following points on the plane: A(1,1), B(–2,6),C(6,3). Connect them to form a triangle.

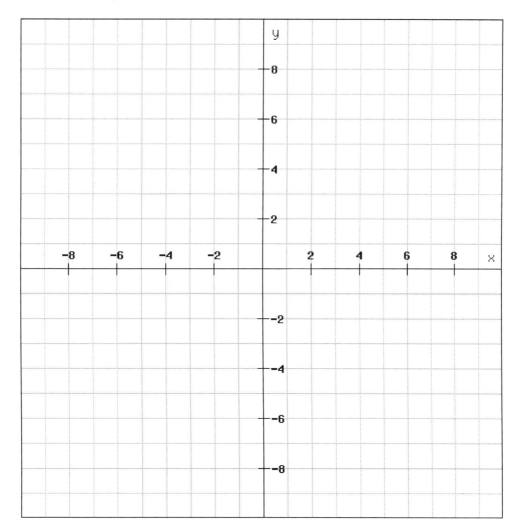

a. Indicate the following points on the plane: A'(1,–1), B'(–2,–6),C'(6,–3), Connect them to form a triangle.

b. What can you say about the location of the 2ⁿᵈ triangle in comparison to the first one?

c. This is a _____ across the x axis.

d. On changing y into _____ we are generating a _____ across the _____

6. Indicate the following points on the plane: A(–4,0), B(0,4),C(4,0), D(0, –4). Connect them to form a square.

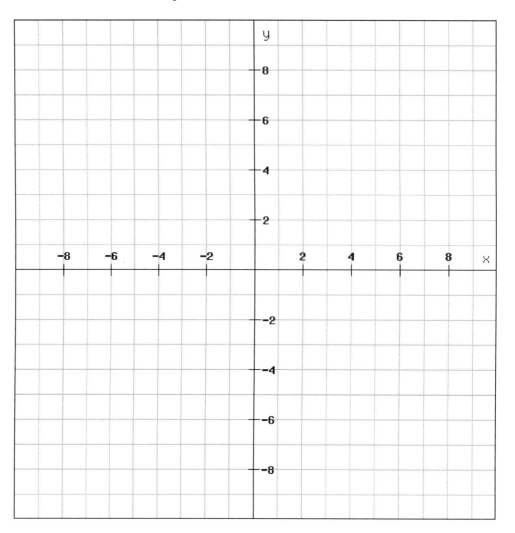

a. Indicate the following points on the plane: $\sqrt{8} \approx 2.83$

A'($-\sqrt{8}$, $\sqrt{8}$),B'($\sqrt{8}$, $\sqrt{8}$), C'($\sqrt{8}$, $-\sqrt{8}$), D'($-\sqrt{8}$, $-\sqrt{8}$) Connect them to form a square.

b. What can you say about the location of the 2nd square in comparison to the first one?

c. This is a _____ of ____ degrees.

d. Write down the coordinates of a square that is a rotation of 90° of the first one:

A'' = (__, __), B'' = (__, __), C'' = (__, __), D'' = (__, __)

Conclusions?

7. Indicate the following points on the plane: A(–5,0), B(5,0). Given also the point C(0,a)

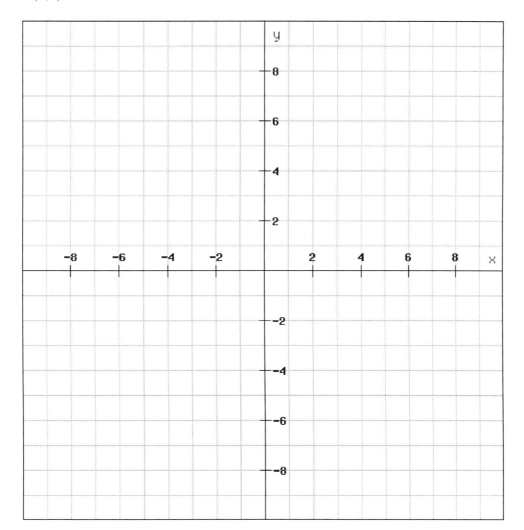

a. Show that the value of a in order to create an equilateral triangle is: $\sqrt{75}$

b. Write down the coordinates of the new points after translating the triangle 3 units left and 1 down.

A' = (__,__), B' = (__,__), C' = (__,__)

c. Write down the coordinates of the new points after rotation the triangle 30° clockwise.

A'' = (__,__), B'' = (__,__), C'' = (__,__)

d. Write down the coordinates of the new points after rotation the triangle 60° clockwise.

A''' = (__,__), B''' = (__,__), C''' = (__,__)

8. Indicate the following points on the plane: A(1,0), B(–2,5),C(4,3). Connect them to form a triangle.

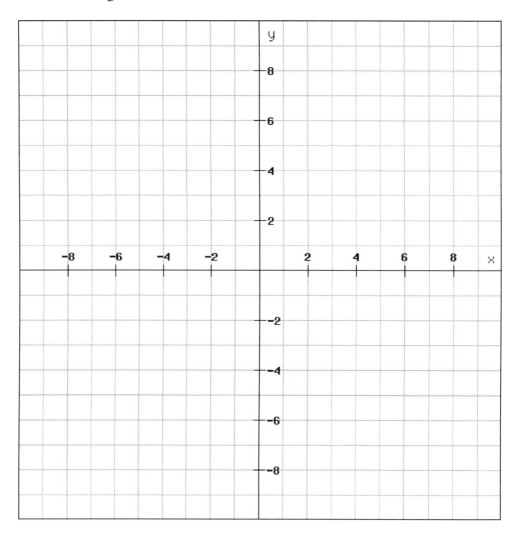

a. Indicate the following points on the plane: A'(2,0), B'(–4,10),C'(8,6), Connect them to form a triangle.

b. What can you say about the 2nd triangle in comparison to the first one?

c. This is a _____ factor _____

d. Indicate the following points on the plane: A'(0.5,0), B'(–1,2.5),C'(2,1.5), Connect them to form a triangle.

e. What can you say about the 2nd triangle in comparison to the first one?

f. This is a _____ factor _____

g. When making all sides of a shape bigger or smaller using the same factor the

shape remains _____ to the original one.

9. Indicate the following points on the plane: A(0,0), B(2, 0),C(0,–3). Connect them to form a triangle.

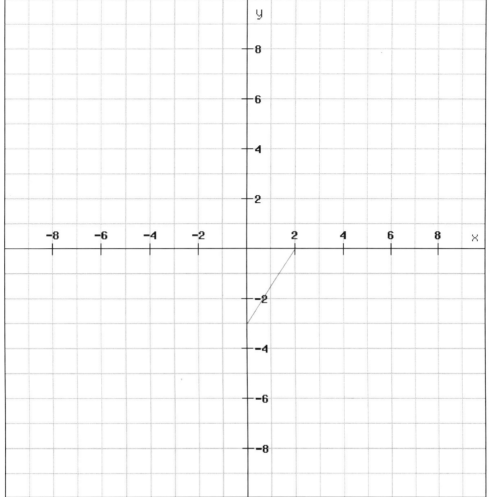

a. Indicate the points of he triangle formed if we enlarge this triangle by 3.

A' = (0, 0), B' = (6, 0), C' = (0, -9)

b. Find the relations:

$\dfrac{A'B'}{AB} = 3$ $\dfrac{A'C'}{AC} = 3$ $\dfrac{B'C'}{BC} = 3$

10. Given a triangle ABC whose sides are 3, 4 and 5 cm long.

   a. Is his a right angled triangle?
   b. Find the sides of another triangle whose sides are half the length of the sides of ABC. Is this triangle right angled?

11. Given a triangle ABC whose sides are 2, 4 and x cm long. A similar triangle has sides y, 6 and z correspondingly.

   a. Find y
   b. Find $\dfrac{z}{x}$
   c. Is it possible to find a value for x so that ABC will be right angled? If yes, find it (all possibilities).
   d. Find z in that case(s)

12. Given a rectangle ABCD whose sides are 5, and x cm long. A similar rectangle has sides y and 12 cm correspondingly. The perimeter of the 1st rectangle is 8 units longer than the perimeter of the 2nd one.

    a. Find x and y

    b. Find the area of the rectangles A_1 and A_2.

    c. Find the quotient $\dfrac{A_2}{A_1}$, conclusions?

13. Given that the area of a square is 16 times as big as the area of a different square. Find the ratio between the sides of the squares.

14. Explain the meaning of the operation "Zooming in/out" frequently used in digital imaging.

CHAPTER 3 – FUNCTIONS

3.1. – INTRODUCTION TO FUNCTIONS

1. Try to sketch an approximate graph for the height of a human, add some reasonable numbers to the graph:

Height (cm)

Age (years)

    a. Height(0) = _____, it is the Height of _____

    b. Height(t) = 100cm, t = _____

    c. Write the set of possible values for the Age: _____, this is the Domain

    d. Write the set of possible values for the Height: _____, this is the Range:

    e. This graph describes a function that shows how _____ depends on _____

2. Write the definition of a function in your own words:

3. Write 2 examples of relations that <u>are</u> functions:

4. The independent variable is usually represented in the _____

5. The dependent variable is usually represented in the _____

6. Draw a sketch of 2 functions. Can you write the mathematical expression to describe them?

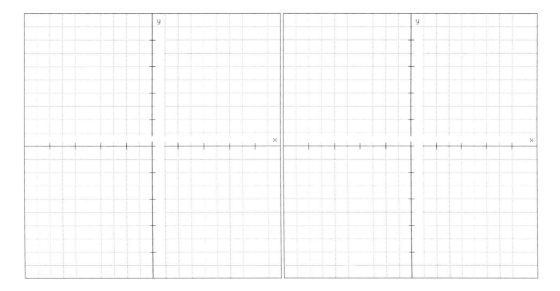

7. Write 2 examples of relations that <u>are not</u> functions:

8. Which one of the following graphs cannot represent function? Explain.

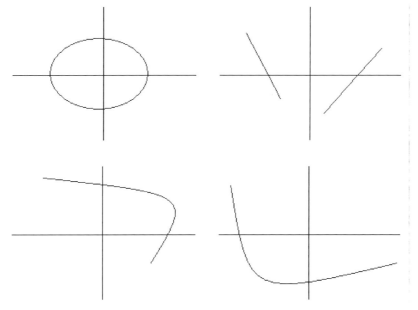

9. Draw an example of a curve that does not represent a function:

10. Draw an example of a curve that represents a function:

11. The domain of a function is the: _____

12. The Range of a function is the: _____

13. Out of the following relations circle the ones that are functions:

   a. Person's name $\rightarrow$ Person's age
   b. City $\rightarrow$ Number of habitants
   c. City $\rightarrow$ Names of habitants
   d. Family $\rightarrow$ Home Address
   e. Satellite's name $\rightarrow$ Position of satellite
   f. Time $\rightarrow$ Position of object
   g. One $\rightarrow$ One
   h. One $\rightarrow$ Many
   i. Many $\rightarrow$ One

14. Given the Weight – age curve for a human. Sketch an approximate graph:

Weight(kg)

Age (years)

a. Weight(0) = _____, it is the height of _____

b. Weight(t) = 10kg. t = _____

c. State its domain:_____

d. State its range: _____

15. Given the following function that describes the temperature in C° as a function of time (t = 0 corresponds to midnight):

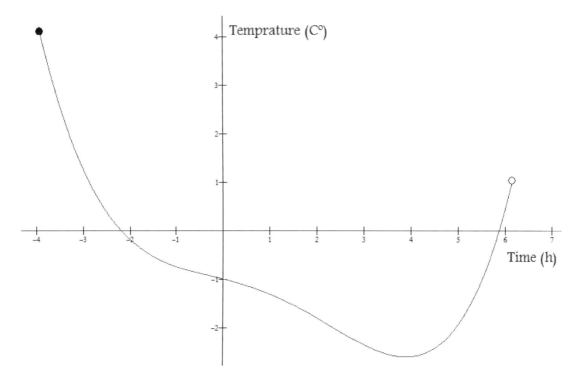

a. f(0) = _____

b. f(2) = _____ = f(__)

c. f(7) = _____

d. f(x) = 3, __x = _____

e. f(x) = 0, __x = _____

f. f(x) = –2 , __x = _____

g. State its domain: _____

h. State its range: _____

i. Function increases at: _____

j. Function decreases at: _____

k. Is this function one to one? One to many? Explain.

16. Given the function the describes the change in the benefit (%) given by a certain stock:

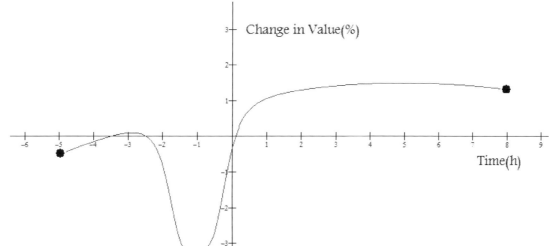

   a. f(x) = 0, _x = _____

   b. f(0) = _____ = f(__)

   c. f(−5) = _____

   d. f(1) = _____

   e. f(−2) = _____ =f(__)

   f. f(3) = _____

   g. f(x) = −2, _x = _____

   h. Is f(−2) < 0 ?

   i. Is f(−2) < f(−1) ?

   j. State its domain: _____

   k. State its range: _____

   l. Where is the function increasing? _____

   m. Where is the function decreasing? _____

   n. Where is the function stationary? _____

   o. Is this function one to one? One to many? Explain.

17. Given the following function:

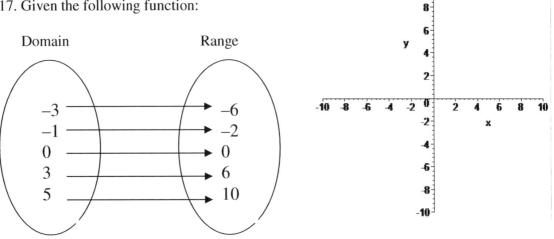

Domain   Range

-3 → -6
-1 → -2
0 → 0
3 → 6
5 → 10

a. What are the allowed values for the independent variable (The domain)?

b. What are the allowed values for the dependent variable (The range)?

c. Sketch the function on the graph.

d. Can you write a mathematical expression to express this function?

18. Given the following function:

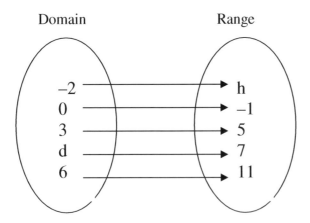

Domain   Range

-2 → h
0 → -1
3 → 5
d → 7
6 → 11

a. Can you write a mathematical expression to express this function?

b. Find h. Find d.

19. Use the graph of the gasoline consumption of a truck to answer:

    a. $f(0) =$ ____

    b. $f(50) =$ ____

    c. $f(5) =$ ____

    d. For what values of x is $f(x) = 12$

    e. Is $f(60) > f(70)$?

    f. For what values of x is $f(x) > 15$?

    g. At what positive speed is the consumption of gasoline minimum?

    h. Where is the function increasing? _____

    i. Where is the function decreasing? _____

    j. Where is the function stationary? _____

20. Functions can be represented using: _____ or _____ or _____

21. The following graph describes the concentration of a drug injected into the blood as a function of the time (in minutes) since the injection. $t = 0$ corresponds to the time of injection.

a. What is the concentration of the drug 4 hours after the injection?

b. During what period of time is the concentration increasing?

c. During what period of time is the concentration decreasing?

d. After how long is the concentration maximum?

e. When is the concentration greater than 5c?

f. When is the concentration smaller than 2c?

g. State the domain and range of the function.

22. The graph below shows the temperature in C° on a particular day as a function of time since midnight.

a. What was the temperature at 4:00 a.m.?

b. When was the temperature 0 degrees?

c. When was the temperature below freezing? (less than 0 degrees)

d. When was the temperature increasing?

e. When was the temperature decreasing?

f. State the domain and range of the function.

3.2. – LINEAR FUNCTIONS

1. Given the function: N(x) = 70. This function represents the number of heartbeats per second of a healthy man. Complete the following table:

x	−5	−4	−3	−2	−1	0	1	2	3	4	5
N(x)											

- Sketch the points of the chart on a graph (use a ruler).

- State the domain of the function: _____

- State the *y* intercept (sketched on the graph: (____, ____)

- State the *x* intercept: (____, ____)

- The function is increasing on the interval: _____

- The function is decreasing on the interval: _____

- Sketch the function of the graph used for the points initially drawn

- State the range of the function: _____

- The heartbeat rate is _____

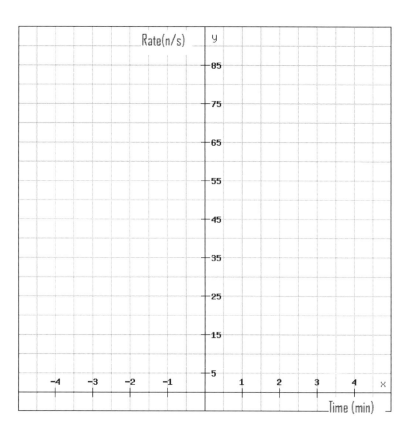

2. The position of a John in reference to his house in his afternoon walk can be modeled by the function: $D(t) = 3t - 6$, t is the time in hours and D is the position in km.

- Complete the following table:

t	−5	−4	−3	−2	−1	0	1	2	3	4	5
D(t)											

- Sketch the points of the chart on a graph (use a ruler).

- State the domain of the function: _____

- State the *y* intercept (sketched on the graph: (____, ____)

- State the *x* intercept: (____, ____)

- The function is increasing on the interval: _____

- The function is decreasing on the interval: _____

- Sketch the function of the graph used for the points initially drawn

- What is the speed of John _____How is that seen on the graph?

- State the range of the function: _____

- When was John at his house? _____

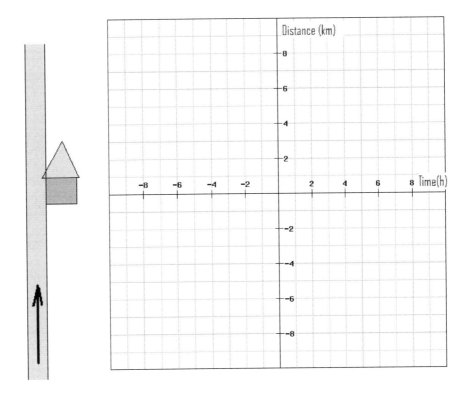

3. An elevator's behavior can be modeled by: P(t) = –2t + 5. Where P is the floor and t is time in minutes. The building has 15 floors and 3 parking levels below ground.

- Complete the following table:

t	–5	–4	–3	–2	–1	0	1	2	3	4	5
P(t)											

- Sketch the points of the chart on a graph (use a ruler).

- State the domain of the function: _____

- State the *y* intercept (sketched on the graph: (_____, _____)

- State the *x* intercept: (_____, _____)

- The function is increasing on the interval: _____

- The function is decreasing on the interval: _____

- Sketch the function of the graph used for the points initially drawn

- Describe the motion of the elevator _____. How is that seen on the graph?

- State the range of the function: _____

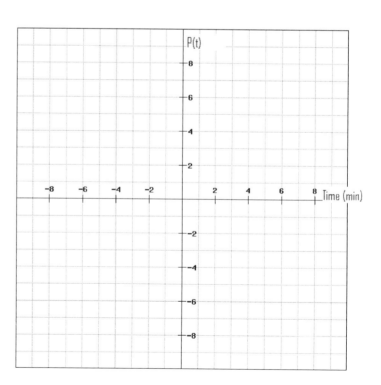

208

4. Given the function: f(x) = 4x – 3

- Complete the following table:

x	−5	−4	−3	−2	−1	0	1	2	3	4	5
f(x)											

- Sketch the points of the chart on a graph (use a ruler).

- State the domain of the function: _____

- State the y intercept (sketched on the graph: (_____, _____)

- State the x intercept: (_____, _____)

- The function is increasing on the interval: _____

- The function is decreasing on the interval: _____

- Sketch the function of the graph used for the points initially drawn

- State the range of the function: _____

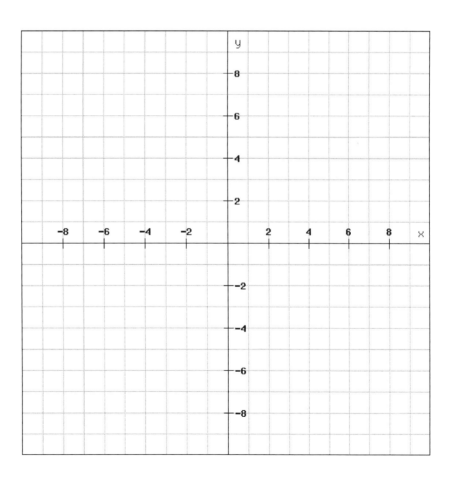

5. Given below are the equations for five different lines. Match the function with its graph.

Function	On the graph
f(x) = 20 + 2x	
g(x) = 4x + 20	
s(x) = –30 + 2x	
a(x) = 60 – x	
b(x) = – 2x + 60	

6. The general functions that describes a straight line is _____

7. We know a function is a straight line because _____

8. The y–intercept (also called vertical intercept), tells us where the line crosses the

_____. The corresponding point is of the form (,   ).

9. The x–intercept (also called horizontal intercept), tells us where the line crosses the

_____. The corresponding point is of the form (,   ).

10. If m > 0, the line _____ left to right. If _____ the line decreases left to right.

11. In case the line is horizontal m is _____ and the line is of the form _____.

12. The larger the value of m is, the _____ the graph of the line is.

13. Given the graph, write, the slope (m), b and the equation of the line:

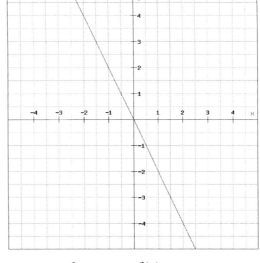

m = _____ b = _____ f(x) = _____   m = _____ b = _____ f(x) = _____

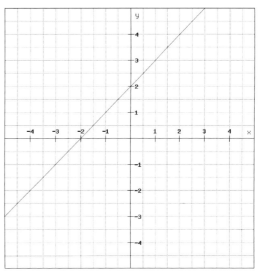

m = _____ b = _____ f(x) = _____   m = _____ b = _____ f(x) = _____

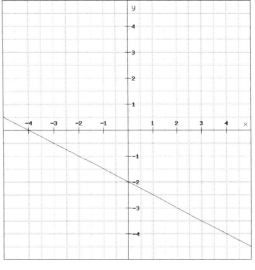

m = _____ b = _____ f(x) = _____   m = _____ b = _____ f(x) = _____

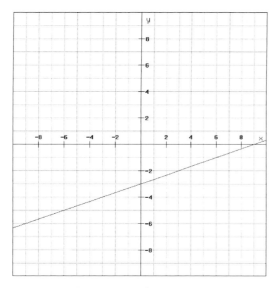

m = _____ b = _____ f(x) = _____

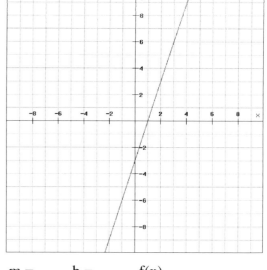

m = _____ b = _____ f(x) = _____

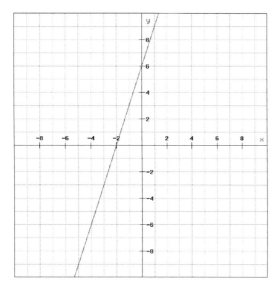

m = _____ b = _____ f(x) = _____

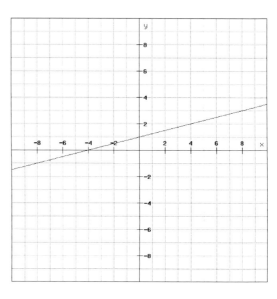

m = _____ b = _____ f(x) = _____

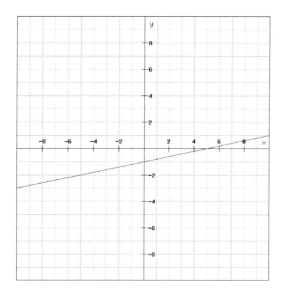

m = _____ b = _____ f(x) = _____

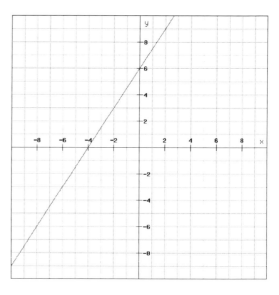

m = _____ b = _____ f(x) = _____

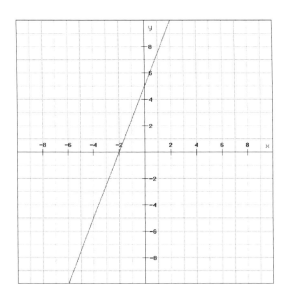

m = _____ b = _____ f(x) = _____   m = _____ b = _____ f(x) = _____

Analyze the following functions/inequlities:

1. f(x) = 1

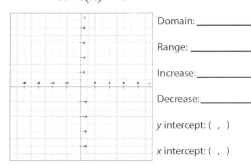

Domain:_____

Range: _____

Increase:_____

Decrease:_____

y intercept: (,)

x intercept: (,)

4. f(x) = 0

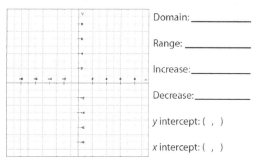

Domain:_____

Range: _____

Increase:_____

Decrease:_____

y intercept: (,)

x intercept: (,)

2. f(x) = 2

Domain:_____

Range: _____

Increase:_____

Decrease:_____

y intercept: (,)

x intercept: (,)

5. f(x) = x

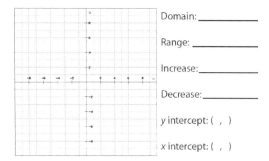

Domain:_____

Range: _____

Increase:_____

Decrease:_____

y intercept: (,)

x intercept: (,)

3. f(x) = −1

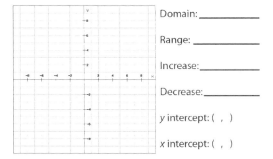

Domain:_____

Range: _____

Increase:_____

Decrease:_____

y intercept: (,)

x intercept: (,)

6. f(x) = x+1

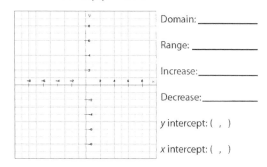

Domain:_____

Range: _____

Increase:_____

Decrease:_____

y intercept: (,)

x intercept: (,)

7.   f(x) = −x

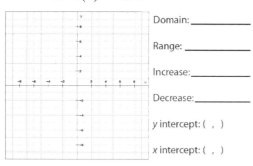

Domain: _____

Range: _____

Increase: _____

Decrease: _____

y intercept: (,)

x intercept: (,)

11. f(x) = 3 − 2x

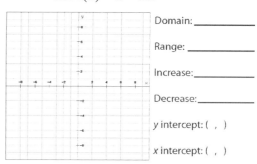

Domain: _____

Range: _____

Increase: _____

Decrease: _____

y intercept: (,)

x intercept: (,)

8.   f(x) = −x−2

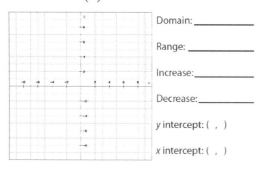

Domain: _____

Range: _____

Increase: _____

Decrease: _____

y intercept: (,)

x intercept: (,)

12. f(x) = $\dfrac{x}{3}$

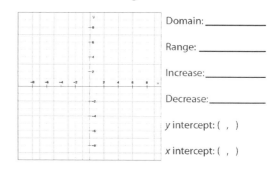

Domain: _____

Range: _____

Increase: _____

Decrease: _____

y intercept: (,)

x intercept: (,)

9.   f(x) = 2x

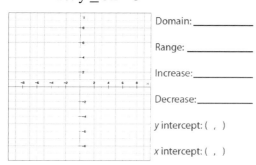

Domain: _____

Range: _____

Increase: _____

Decrease: _____

y intercept: (,)

x intercept: (,)

13. f(x) = 2x+1

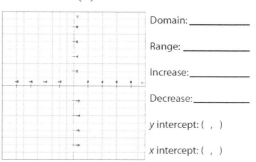

Domain: _____

Range: _____

Increase: _____

Decrease: _____

y intercept: (,)

x intercept: (,)

10. y ≤ 3x − 5

Domain: _____

Range: _____

Increase: _____

Decrease: _____

y intercept: (,)

x intercept: (,)

14. f(x) = 2x−2

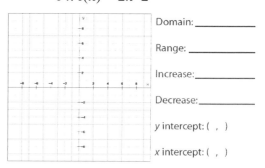

Domain: _____

Range: _____

Increase: _____

Decrease: _____

y intercept: (,)

x intercept: (,)

15. $f(x) = 3x+5$

Domain:_____

Range: _____

Increase:_____

Decrease:_____

y intercept: (,)

x intercept: (,)

19. $f(x) = -\dfrac{3}{2}x - \dfrac{3}{2}$

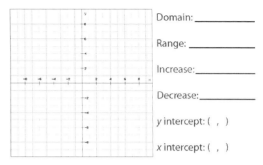

Domain:_____

Range: _____

Increase:_____

Decrease:_____

y intercept: (,)

x intercept: (,)

16. $f(x) \leq \dfrac{x}{2} - 5$

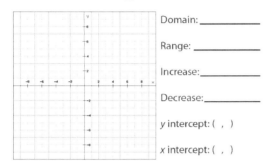

Domain:_____

Range: _____

Increase:_____

Decrease:_____

y intercept: (,)

x intercept: (,)

20. $f(x) = -\dfrac{x+3}{2}$

It is currently october 1st

Domain:_____

Range: _____

Increase:_____

Decrease:_____

y intercept: (,)

x intercept: (,)

17. $f(x) = \dfrac{x}{4} + 6$

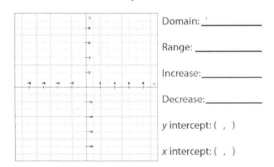

Domain:_____

Range: _____

Increase:_____

Decrease:_____

y intercept: (,)

x intercept: (,)

21. $f(x) = \dfrac{14x-1}{4}$

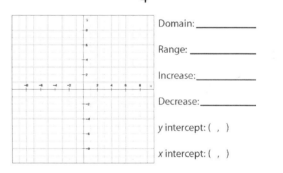

Domain:_____

Range: _____

Increase:_____

Decrease:_____

y intercept: (,)

x intercept: (,)

18. $f(x) \geq \dfrac{3x-10}{2}$

Domain:_____

Range: _____

Increase:_____

Decrease:_____

y intercept: (,)

x intercept: (,)

22. $f(x) = -\dfrac{27x-40}{15}$

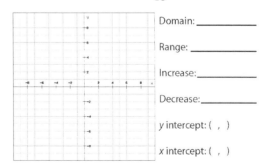

Domain:_____

Range: _____

Increase:_____

Decrease:_____

y intercept: (,)

x intercept: (,)

23. 3x + 2y = 2

Domain:_____

Range:_____

Increase:_____

Decrease:_____

y intercept: (,)

x intercept: (,)

27. y + 2x –3 ≥ 1

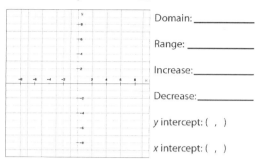

Domain:_____

Range:_____

Increase:_____

Decrease:_____

y intercept: (,)

x intercept: (,)

24. 4x– 2y –3 = 1

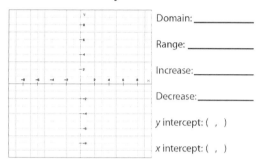

Domain:_____

Range:_____

Increase:_____

Decrease:_____

y intercept: (,)

x intercept: (,)

28. 5y + 5x = 5

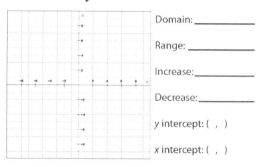

Domain:_____

Range:_____

Increase:_____

Decrease:_____

y intercept: (,)

x intercept: (,)

25. –2y + 3x = –5

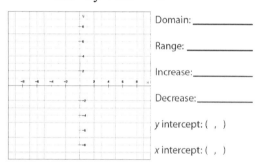

Domain:_____

Range:_____

Increase:_____

Decrease:_____

y intercept: (,)

x intercept: (,)

29. 2x – 2y –3 = 1

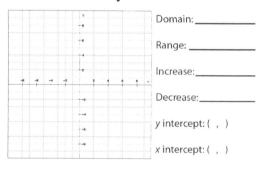

Domain:_____

Range:_____

Increase:_____

Decrease:_____

y intercept: (,)

x intercept: (,)

26. y – x ≤ 2

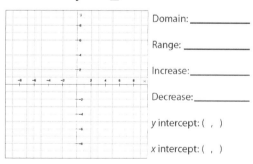

Domain:_____

Range:_____

Increase:_____

Decrease:_____

y intercept: (,)

x intercept: (,)

30. x – 2y – 150 = 0

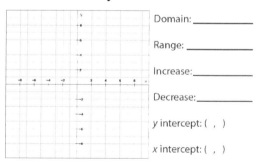

Domain:_____

Range:_____

Increase:_____

Decrease:_____

y intercept: (,)

x intercept: (,)

31. Write the equation of the line that has a slope of 2 and passes through the point (2, 4) in the forms: $y = mx + b$ and $ax + by + c = 0$, $(a, b \in Z)$

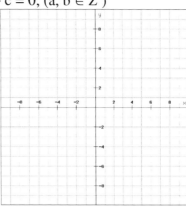

32. Write the equation of the line that has a slope of $-\dfrac{1}{2}$ and passes through the point $(-2, -3)$ in the forms: $y = mx + b$ and $ax + by + c = 0$, $(a, b \in Z)$

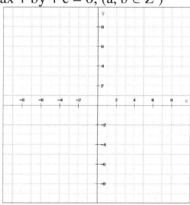

33. Write the equation of the line that has a slope of $-\dfrac{5}{2}$ and passes through the point $(-1, 2)$ in the forms: $y = mx + b$ and $ax + by + c = 0$, $(a, b \in Z)$

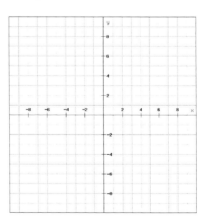

34. Find the equation of the line that passes through the points (1, 1), (2, 4), indicate its y and x intercepts and sketch it. Write its equation in the forms: y = mx + b and ax + by + c = 0, (a, b ∈ Z)

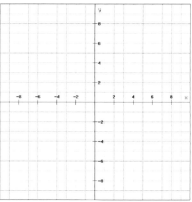

35. Find the equation of the line that passes through the points (−1, −5), (4, 3), indicate its y and x intercepts and sketch it. Write its equation in the forms: y = mx + b and ax + by + c = 0, (a, b ∈ Z)

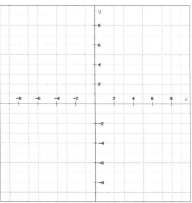

36. Find the equation of the line that passes through the points (−5, 1), (−2, 4), indicate its y and x intercepts, sketch it and write it in both formas y = mx + b and ax + by + c = 0, (a, b ∈ Z)

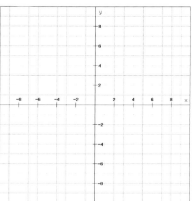

218

37. Write the equation of the line that is parallel to the line $y = 5x - 2$ and passes through the point $(-2, -1)$. Write its equation in the forms: $y = mx + b$ and $ax + by + c = 0$, $(a, b \in Z)$

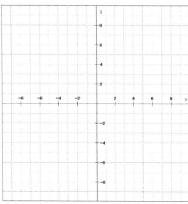

38. Write the equation of the line that is parallel to the line $y = -0.5x - 1$ and passes through the point $(-3, 6)$. Write its equation in the forms: $y = mx + b$ and $ax + by + c = 0$, $(a, b \in Z)$

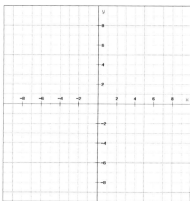

39. Sketch and write the equation of the line with a slope of $-\dfrac{1}{5}$ that passes through the point $(0,2)$.

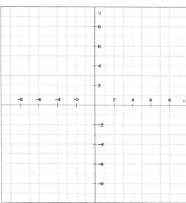

219

40. Sketch and write the equation of the lines with a slope: $1, 2, -3, -1, -\dfrac{1}{2}, -\dfrac{1}{3},$ that pass through the point (0,0).

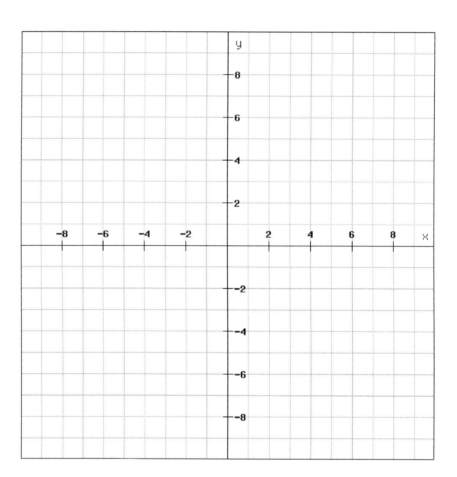

41. Sketch and write the equation of the line with a slope of –3 that passes through the point (0,–3).

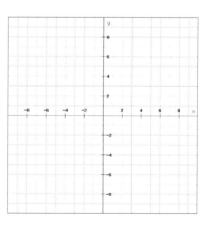

42. Sketch and write the equation of the line with a slope of 2 that passes through the point (2,0)

43. Sketch and write the equation of the line with a slope of $-\dfrac{1}{2}$ that passes through the point (–2,0)

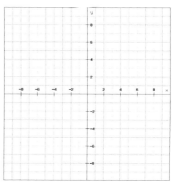

44. Sketch and write the equation of the line with a slope of 2 that passes through the point (–4,2)

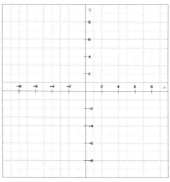

45. Find the intersection between the lines f(x) = 2x – 3 and f(x) = –5x –2

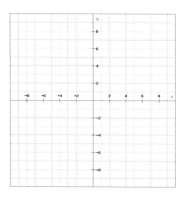

46. Find the intersection between the lines $f(x) = x - 3$ and $f(x) = x - 4$

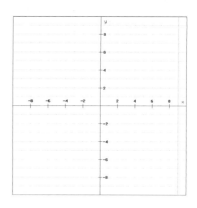

47. Find the intersection between the lines $f(x) = 2x - 3$ and $f(x) = -2x + 7$

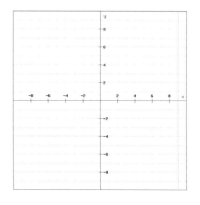

48. Find the intersection between the lines $f(x) = ax - 3$ and $f(x) = ax + 7$

49. Find the intersection between the lines $f(x) = -12x - 13$ and $f(x) = 15x + 20$.

50. Given that the lines $f(x) = 2ax - 1$ and $f(x) = 4 - 5x + 20$ do not intersect, find a.

51. Find the intersection between the lines y = 2x – 3 and 2y – 4x = – 6.

52. Given that the lines f(x) = mx – 5 and f(x) = 2x + 4 intersect at the point where x = 3, find m.

53. Given that the lines f(x) = 2x – b and f(x) = 3x + 4 intersect at the point where x = 1, find b.

54. Find the intersection between the lines 3y + 2x = 3 and 9y + 6x = 9.

55. Sketch the line $f(x) = \dfrac{-x}{2} + 3, -4 \le x < 8$

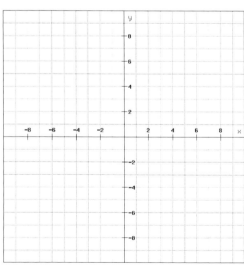

56. Given the points (1, 2) and (5, 8). Find the distance between them. Find the midpoint. Sketch to illustrate your answer.

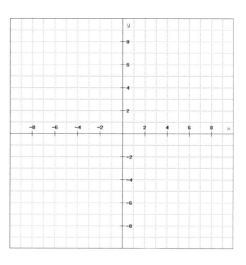

57. Given the points (–3, 2) and (5, –6). Find the distance between them. Find the midpoint. Sketch to illustrate your answer.

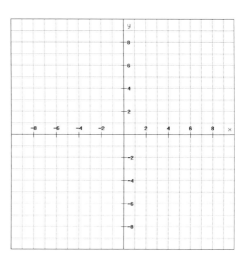

58. Given the points (–1, –6) and (–5, –1). Find the distance between them. Find the midpoint. Sketch to illustrate your answer.

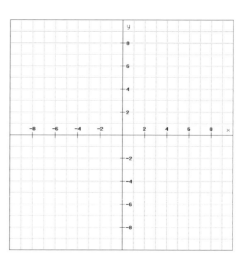

59. Given that the points $(a, -1)$ and $(5, 3)$ are 5 units away. Find a. Find the midpoint.

60. Given that the points $(1, -4)$ and $(5, c)$ are 10 units away. Find c. Find the midpoint.

61. Find the equation of all the points that are 2 units away from the origin. This

equation describes a _____

62. Find the equation of all the points that are 5 units away from the point $(2, -1)$.

This equation describes a _____

63. Given that the points $(1, -4)$ and $(5, c)$ are 10 units away. Find c. Find the midpoint.

64. Given the points $(-8, -7)$ and $(6, 2)$. Find the distance between them. Find the midpoint.

PERPENDICULAR LINES $(m \cdot m_\perp = -1)$

65. A slope perpendicular to 1 is _____, A slope perpendicular to 2 is _____

    A slope perpendicular to k is _____ A slope perpendicular to $\dfrac{a}{b}$ is _____

66. Find the equation of a line perpendicular to the line $y = 3x - 2$ that passes through the point (3, 12). Sketch to illustrate your answer.

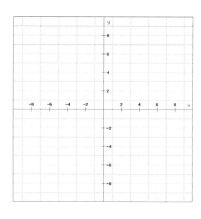

67. Find all the lines perpendicular to the line $y = -3x + 4$. Fin the ones that passes through the point (–3, 1). Sketch to illustrate your answer.

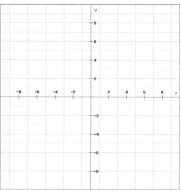

68. Find a line perpendicular to the line $y = -\dfrac{2}{5}x + 1$ that passes through the point (–1, –7). Sketch to illustrate your answer.

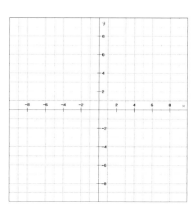

69. Given the points (–2, 5) and (4, 2).

    a. Find the equation of the line passing through them.

    b. Is the point (5, 1) on this line? Show your work.

    c. Find a perpendicular line that passes through the mid point between these points.

    d. Find all the points on the line found in c that are 0.5 units away from the point (0, 2).

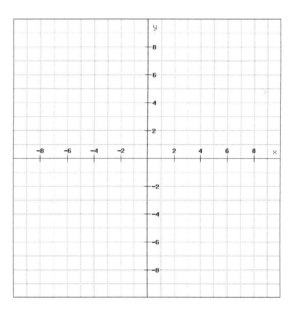

70. Find a point on the x axis that is $\sqrt{5}$ units away from the line $y = 2x + 4$

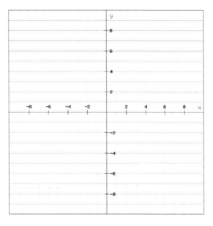

71. Find a point on the y axis that is 5 units away from the line y = 3x + 2

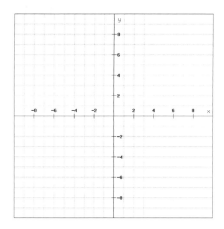

72. Given that the slope of one of the lines is 3 and that the lines are perpendicular, find the **exact** coordinates of the point of intersection of the two lines.

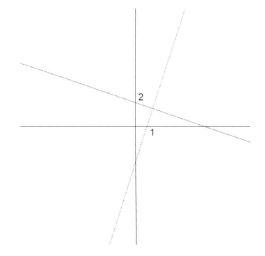

SLOPE – INTERCEPT FORM OF A LINE

73. The line $y - 3 = 2(x + 1)$ passes through the point _____ and has a slope of ____

74. The line $y + 5 = -3(x - 51)$ passes through the point _____ and has a slope of ____

75. The line $-y + 1 = (x + 3)$ passes through the point _____ and has a slope of ____

76. The line $2y + 5 = -6(x + 7)$ passes through the point _____ and has a slope of ____

77. The line $y + a = m(x + b)$ passes through the point _____ and has a slope of ____

78. The line $y - a = m(x - b)$ passes through the point _____ and has a slope of ____

79. The line $y - a = m(x + b)$ passes through the point _____ and has a slope of ____

80. Write the equation $y - 3 = 2(x + 1)$ in the explicit form

228

81. Write the equation $y + 5 = 2(x + 6)$ in the explicit form

82. Write down the equation of a line passing through the point (5, 2) with slope 1.

83. Write down the equation of a line passing through the point (–4, –3) with slope –2.

84. Write down the equation of a line passing through the point (6, 3) with slope $\dfrac{2}{3}$.

85. Write down the equation of a line passing through point (–2, –5) with slope $-\dfrac{2}{5}$.

86. Write down the equation of the line passing through points (–2, –5), (–7, –5),

87. Write down the equation of the line passing through points (–1, –3), (6, 5),

88. Write down the equation of the line passing through points (–1, 5), (7, –2),

APPLICATION

1. The price of a new toy (in US$) is C(t) = 20 – 0.5t, t given in days.

   a. Sketch the corresponding graph.

   b. What was the initial price of the toy? _____

   c. Find the price of the toy after 10 days

   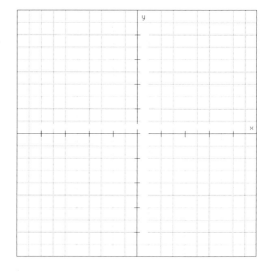

   d. What is the domain of the function, reason your answer,

   e. What is the range of the function.

   f. What is the meaning of 0.5? Does it have units? What are they?

2. On a certain planet the temperature of the soil is 10º on the surface and 0.02º wormer with every meter of depth.

   a. Write a function to describe the temperature as a function of the depth d. State its domain and range. What are the units of the slope?

   b. Find the temperature at depth of 500m

   c. Find the depth at which the temperature is 13º.

   d. Graph the function, use appropriate scale, variables and units.

3. In a factory there are 2 machines that produce a certain product. The operation cost (electricity, maintenance etc.) of Machine A is 250$ a month and the cost of production per product is 2$. The operation cost of Machine B is 200$ a month and the cost of production per product is 4$. The maximum number of products that both machines can make a month is 200.

   a. Write the functions to describe the cost C as a function of the number of products n for both machines. Indicate the domain and range of both functions. What are the units of the slope?

   b. Graph the functions, use appropriate scale, variables and units. Calculate the coordinates of important points on the graph.

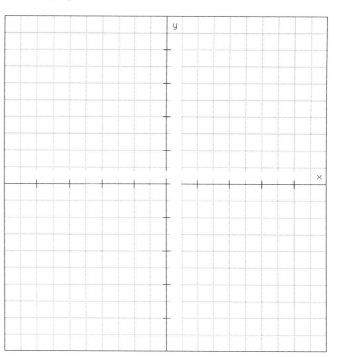

   c. Discuss in which case each machine is best.

4. A parking lot with 1200 parking spots opens at 6 am. The cars flow in a constant rate. At 10 am the parking is full.

   a. Write the function to describe the number of cars N as function of time t in hours. Indicate the domain and range of the function. What are the units of the slope?

   b. Find the number of free spots at 8:30.

   c. In case the owner needs 150 free spots at what time should he close the parking?

   d. Graph the function, use appropriate scale, variables and units.

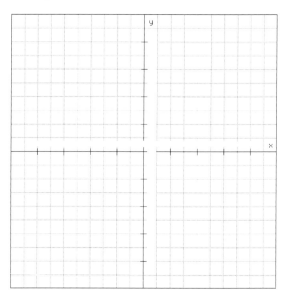

5. You need to rent a car for one day and to compare the charges of 3 different companies. Company I charges 20$ per day with additional cost of 0.20$ per mile. Company II charges 30$ per day with additional cost of 0.10$ per mile. Company III charges 60$ per day with no additional mileage charge.

    a.   Write the cost function for each one of the companies.

    b.   Sketch all 3 graphs on the same axes system.

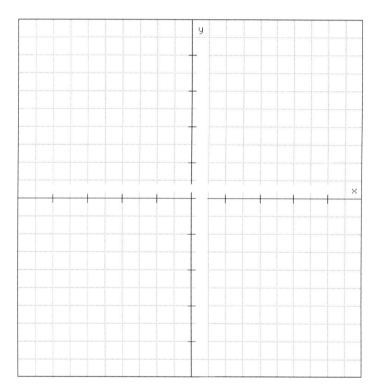

    c.   Comment on the circumstances in which renting a car from each one of the companies is best.

CHAPTER 4 - STATISTICS

4.1. – STATISTICS

In Statistics we try to obtain some conclusions by observing and/or analyzing data.

9. The set of objects that we are trying to study is called _____, the

   number of elements in the population can be _____ or _____.

10. Usually the _____ is too big and therefore we obtain a _____.

   This process is called _____.

11. We use the _____ to obtain conclusions about the _____.

Types of DATA

1. _____ data.

2. _____ data that can be divided to _____ or _____.

3. _____ can be counted while _____ data can be _____.

4. Give 3 examples of _____ data:

5. Give 3 examples of _____ _____ data:

6. Give 3 examples of _____ _____ data:

7. Given the following variables, classify them in the table:

- Eye color
- Shoe size
- Height
- Weight
- Number of cars in a parking lot
- Type of fruit

- Number of apples sold a day in a store
- Velocity of the wind
- Temperature
- Numbers of pages in a book
- Name of writer
- Number of students in a school

Categorical	Numerical Discrete	Numerical Continuous

8. In a certain class the eye color of students was studies. The following results were obtained:

Brown, Black, Brown, Blue, Brown, Black, Brown, Blue, Brown, Blue, Brown, Black, Brown, Blue.

a. How many students participated?
b. What kind of data is this?
c. Represent the information in a Bar Chart
d. Represent the information in a Pie Chart (include the %)

9. In a certain math class the following grades were obtained:

65, 72, 85, 89, 52, 71, 89, 68, 63, 76, 61, 86, 98, 79, 79, 91, 74, 89, 77, 68, 78

   a. How many students participated?
   e. What kind of data is this?
   b. Suggest a method to represent this information in a table.
   c. Use the table to create a bar graph

10. In a certain zoo the length of a certain type of animal (in meters) was studied. The following results were obtained:

1.77, 1.60, 1.89, 1.54, 1.77, 1.65, 1.86, 1.51, 1.67, 1.94, 1.73, 1.70, 1.66, 1.58

   a. How many animals participated?
   f. What kind of data is this?
   b. Suggest a method to represent this information in a table.
   c. Use the table to create a bar graph

11. In a certain group shoe size was studied and the following results obtained:

45, 36, 44, 38, 41, 42, 48, 39, 40, 42, 43, 41, 38, 45, 41, 38, 42, 44, 41, 41, 46

    a. How many students participated?
    b. What kind of data is this?
    c. Suggest a method to represent this information in a table.
    d. Use the table to create a bar graph

12. Choose a variable to collect information about in your classroom, state its kind, represent the information in a table and create a bar graph.

4.2. – MEAN, MEDIAN, MODE AND FREQUENCY DIAGRAMS

1. In a certain club the number of visitors per days was studied during 1 week and the following results obtained: 58, 79, 66, 78, 23, 66, 63

    a. State the number of elements in the set: _____

    b. What kind of data is this? _____

    c. Find its mean: _____   Find its mode: _____

    d. Write the data in an increasing order:

    e. Find its Median: _____   Q1 = _____ Q3 = _____

    f. Try to obtain the answers using technology.

2. In a certain restaurant the amount of meat (kg) consumed per day was studied and the following results obtained: 11.5, 12.2, 14.6, 15.0, 23.2, 21.2, 10.1, 13.1

    a. State the number of elements in the set: _____

    b. What kind of data is this? _____

    c. Find its mean: _____   Find its mode: _____

    d. Write the data in an increasing order:

    e. Find its Median: _____   Q1 = _____ Q3 = _____

    f. Try to obtain the answers using technology.

3. In a certain math class the number of exercises per day given for HW is the following: 5, 6, 6, 6, 4, 4, 5, 5, 4, 5, 6, 6, 7, 3, 0, 3

    a. State the number of elements in the set: _____

    b. What kind of data is this? _____

    c. Find its mean: _____   Find its mode: _____

    d. Write the data in an increasing order:

    e. Find its Median: _____   Q1 = _____ Q3 = _____

    f. Try to obtain the answers using technology.

4. In the following data: 2, 2, 3, 3, 9, 9, 9 one natural number is missing. It is known that the median with the missing number is 3. Find all the possible values of the missing number.

5. In a certain math class the following grades were obtained:

68, 79, 75, 89, 54, 81, 88, 62, 67, 75, 64, 85, 97, 77, 79, 90, 75, 89, 76, 68

    a. State the number of elements in the set: _____

    b. What kind of data is this? _____

    c. Find its mean: _____   Find its mode: _____

    d. Write the data in an increasing order:

    e. Find its Median: _____ $Q1$ = _____ $Q3$ = _____

    f. Fill the table:

Grade	Mid – Grade (M_i)	Frequency (f_i)	f_i x M_i	Cumulative Frequency (F_i)	F_i (%)
[51, 60]					
[61, 70]					
[71, 80]					
[81, 90]					
[91, 100]					.
Total					

    g. Use the table to find the mean: _____. Comment on the result compared to the previous mean obtained.

    h. Discuss the advantages and disadvantages of organizing information in a table.

    i. Is this the only possible choice for the left column of the table? Why? Discuss the advantages and disadvantages of organizing information in such a way.

j. Design a new table with a different _____

Grade	Mid – Grade (Mi)	Frequency (fi)	Fi x Mi	Cumulative Frequency (Fi)	Fi (%)

k. Use the table to find the mean: _____. Comment on the result compared to the previous mean obtained.

l. The mean of the <u>population</u> is denoted with the Greek letter mu: _____

and typically it is _____. The mean of the <u>sample</u> is denoted by

_____

m. Find the modal interval in both tables:

1st: _____ 2nd: _____

n. In general this method of organizing information is called _____

o. The 1st column is called _____ with upper interval boundary and

_____ interval boundary.

p. The 2nd column is called _____

q. On the following grid paper sketch the corresponding points.

Fi: Cumulative frequency

Variable: _____

r. This graph is called cumulative frequency curve or _____

s. Find the median using the graph: _____

t. Find the first quartile (Q_1) using the graph: $Q_1 =$ _____

u. Find the third quartile (Q_3) using the graph: $Q_3 =$ _____

v. Find P_{30} using the graph: _____ Find P_{70} using the graph: _____

w. The <u>Inter Quartile Range</u> is in general _____ in this case it is _____

x. Try to obtain the answers using technology.

6. In a certain class the following heights (in m) of students were collected:

   1.77, 1.60, 1.89, 1.54, 1.77, 1.65, 1.86, 1.51, 1.67, 1.94, 1.73, 1.70, 1.66, 1.70

   a. State the number of elements in the set: _____

   b. What kind of data is this? _____

   c. Find its mean: _____   Find its mode: _____

   d. Write the data in an increasing order:

   e. Find its Median: _____   Q1 = _____ Q3 = _____

   f. Fill the table:

Grade	Mid – Grade (Mi)	Frequency (fi)	fi x Mi	Cumulative Frequency (Fi)	Fi (%)
[1.50 – 1.60)					
[1.60 – 1.70)					
[1.70– 1.80)					
[1.80 – 1.90)					
[1.90 – 2.00)					
Total					

   g. Use the table to find the mean: _____. Comment on the result compared to the previous mean obtained.

   h. Discuss the advantages and disadvantages of organizing information in a table.

   i. Is this the only possible choice for the left column of the table? Why? Discuss the advantages and disadvantages of organizing information in such a way.

j. On the following grid paper sketch the corresponding points.

Fi: Cumulative frequency

Variable: _____

k. This graph is called cumulative frequency curve or _____

l. Find the median using the graph: _____

m. Find the first quartile (Q_1) using the graph: Q_1 = _____

n. Find the third quartile (Q_3) using the graph: Q_3 = _____

o. Find P_{30} using the graph: _____ Find P_{70} using the graph: _____

p. The Inter Quartile Range is in general _____ in this case it is_____

q. Try to obtain the answers using technology.

7. In a certain class students eye color was collected:

   Brown, Black, Brown, Blue, Brown, Blue, Green, Brown, Black, Green

   a. State the number of elements in the set: _____

   b. What kind of data is this? _____

   c. Fill the table:

Eye Color	Mid – Color (Mi)	Frequency (fi)	fi x Mi	Cumulative Frequency (Fi)	Fi (%)
Brown					
Blue					
Green					
Black					
Total					

   d. Obtain the mean: _____

   e. State the mode of the set: _____

   f. Find the modal interval: _____

   g. Find the Median using the original data: _____

   h. Find the median using the table, discuss your answer.

   i. Find the answers to all the different parts using your GDC.

   j. Represent the data in a histogram:

4.3. – PROBABILITY

Probability is the science of chance or likelihood of an event happening

If a random experiment is repeated _____ times in such a way that each of the trials is

identical and independent, where n(A) is the number of _____ event A occurred,

then: Relative frequency of event A = P(A) = $\dfrac{n(A)}{N}$ $(N \to \infty)$

Exercises

1. In an unbiased coin what is P(head) ?

    This probability is called _____.

2. Explain the difference between theoretical probability and experimental probability.

3. Throw a drawing pin and fill the table:

	Fell pointing upwards	Fell on its side	Total number of throws
Number of events			
Probability			

4. The definition of probability ("*Laplace law*")is:

    P(A) = $\dfrac{Number \text{_____}}{Total \text{_____}}$

Properties of probability

$0 \leq P(A) \leq$ ___

$P(U) =$ _____

5. Given the sentence "Good day everyone". Find the following probabilities in case the choices are being made in a random way:

    a. P(choosing a vowel) =   c. P(choosing a "e") =

    b. P(choosing a "o") =   d. P(choosing a "z") =

6. In case a student is chosen randomly in your classroom. Find the probability it's a girl.

7. Find the probability of getting a prime number sum on tossing 2 dice.

8. Find the probability of getting a sum of 17 on tossing 3 dice.

9. Find the probability of being left handed in your classroom.

10. Find the probability of obtaining a sum of 5 on tossing 2 dice.

11. Find the probability of obtaining 2 tails on tossing 2 coins.

12. Find the probability that a 2 digit number divides by 3

13. Find the probability of choosing the letter b in the word probability

14. Find the probability of choosing a number that contains the digit 7 in the first hundred numbers (1 to 100).

15. Find the probability of choosing a number that contains only even digits in the first thousand numbers (1 to 1000).

16. Knowing that the sum of 2 dice is more than 5, find the probability it's 10

CHAPTER 5

5.1. – INTERNATIONAL SYSTEM OF UNITS

1. Meter(m) is a unit of _____ Other units of _____ are: _____

2. Meter square (m^2) is a unit of _____ Other units of _____ are: _____

3. An area has units of _____A length has units of _____

4. Kilo = __ Mili = __

Convert the units, use scientific notation in at least one of each type of exercises:

5. How many metres in 2.5 km?

6. How many metres in 0.5 km?

7. How many metres^2 in $\frac{1}{3}$ km^2?

8. How many metres in 56 km?

9. How many metres in 2500 km?

10. How many km^2 in 26 m^2?

11. How many km in 75 m?

12. How many km in 1000 m?

13. How many m in $5.2 \cdot 10^7$ km?

14. How many km^2 in $5.12 \cdot 10^8$ m^2?

15. How many mm in 3.04 m?

16. How many mm^2 in 0.5 m^2?

17. How many mm^2 in 1 m^2?

18. How many mm in 2 m?

19. How many mm in 2.5 m?

20. How many mm^2 are 1.35 m^2?

21. How many cm in $\frac{1}{3}$ m?

22. How many cm^2 in 56 m^2?

23. How many cm in 3.1 km?

24. How many mm^2 in 0.5 cm^2?

25. How many cm in in 120 m?

26. How many mm^2 in 5.1 cm^2?

27. How many cm in 17 km?

28. How many m in 12392 km?

29. How many mm^2 in 5.1 m^2?

30. How many m^2 in 2.2 mm^2?

31. How many cm in 13.12 m?

32. Complete the table:

mm	cm	m	km
14			
	65		
		3	
			5
12.5			
	3.7		
		4.78	
			1.31
			0.008

mm^2	cm^2	m^2	Km^2
14			
	65		
		3	
			5
12.5			
	3.7		
		4.78	
			1.31
			0.008

5.2. – COMMON ERRORS

1. $\sqrt{A+B} = \sqrt{A} + \sqrt{B}$ True / False, Give an example to show your answer.

2. $\sqrt{A^2 + B^2} = A + B$ True / False, Give an example to show your answer.

3. $(A+B)^2 = A^2 + B^2$ True / False, if false write the correct version.

4. $(A+B)(A-B) = A^2 + B^2$ True / False, Give an example to show your answer.

5. $(A+B)(A-B) = A^2 - B^2$ True / False, if false write the correct version..

6. $(x+2)^2 = x^2 + 4x + 2$ True / False, if false write the correct version.

7. $(A-B)^2 = A^2 - B^2$ True / False, Give an example to show your answer.

8. $(2x-3)^2 = 4x^2 - 6x + 9$ True / False, if false write the correct version.

9. $(\sqrt{a} - 3)^2 = a^2 - 6a + 9$ True / False, if false write the correct version.

10. $x^2 x^3 = x^6$ True / False, if false write the correct version.

11. $(x^2)^3 = x^{(2^3)}$ True / False, if false write the correct version.

12. $\dfrac{x^{10}}{x^2} = x^5$ True / False, if false write the correct version.

13. $x^1 = 1$ True / False, if false write the correct version.

14. $x^0 = 0$ True / False, if false write the correct version.

15. $-3^2 = (-3)^2$ True / False, if false write the correct version.

16. $(4x^2) = (4x)^2$ True / False, if false write the correct version.

17. $\sqrt{7x} = 7x^{\frac{1}{2}}$ True / False, if false write the correct version.

18. $\dfrac{0}{2} = \dfrac{2}{0}$ True / False, if false write the correct version.

19. $\dfrac{14+x}{14} = x$ True / False, if false write the correct version.

20. $\dfrac{7-x}{7} = x-1$ True / False, if false write the correct version.

21. $\dfrac{a+b}{a} = 1 + \dfrac{b}{a}$ True / False, if false write the correct version.

22. $\dfrac{14+x}{14} = x + \dfrac{x}{14}$ True / False, if false write the correct version.

23. $\dfrac{1}{x+y} = \dfrac{1}{x} + \dfrac{1}{y}$ True / False, if false write the correct version.

24.   An **<u>expression</u>** and an **<u>equation</u>** is the same thing.   True / False

25. $\dfrac{\left(\dfrac{a}{b}\right)}{c} = \dfrac{a}{\left(\dfrac{b}{c}\right)}$ True / False, if false write the correct version.

26. $-a^2 = (-a)^2$ True / False, if false write the correct version.

27. $a^{-2} = (-a)^2$ True / False, if false write the correct version.

28. $a^{-2} = -a^2$ True / False, if false write the correct version.

29. $a^{-2} = -\dfrac{1}{a^2}$ True / False, if false write the correct version.

30. $a^{-2} = \dfrac{1}{a^2}$ True / False, if false write the correct version.

31. $a^{-1} = -\dfrac{1}{a}$ True / False, if false write the correct version.

32. $\dfrac{1}{2} + \dfrac{1}{3} = \dfrac{1}{2+3}$ True / False, if false write the correct version.

33. $a^{-1} + a^{-1} = a^{-2}$ True / False, if false write the correct version.

34. $a^{-1}a^{-1} = a^{-2}$ True / False, if false write the correct version.

35. $a^{-2}a^{-3} = a^{-6}$ True / False, if false write the correct version.

36. $a^{-2} + a^{-3} = a^{-5}$ True / False, if false write the correct version.

ANSWER KEY

CHAPTER 1

1.1. – ORDER OF OPERATIONS

1. $5 + 3 \cdot 2 = \underline{11}$

2. $2 \cdot 3 - (-3) = \underline{9}$

3. $-5 \cdot 5 - (-8) \cdot 2 = \underline{-9}$

4. $-2 - 5 - (-2) + 2 = \underline{-3}$

5. $(-2)(-5) - (-2) \cdot 2 = \underline{14}$

6. $25 \cdot 2 - 7 = \underline{43}$

7. $15 + 4 / 2 = \underline{17}$

8. $14 / 7 + 3 \cdot 6 = \underline{20}$

9. $5 / 5 - 30 / 2 \cdot 5 = \underline{-74}$

10. $1 + 4 / 2 - 8 / 4 \cdot 5 = \underline{-7}$

11. $20 / 4 / 2 + 4 = \underline{13/2}$

12. $12 \cdot (2 + 3) = \underline{60}$

13. $5(3 \cdot 2 / 3 \cdot 2) + 2 = \underline{22}$

14. $1 / 2 + 3 / 2 = \underline{2}$

15. $6 / 3 - 20 / 10 = \underline{0}$

16. $5(1 + 3 \cdot 2) + 2 / 2 - 8 / 4 = \underline{34}$

17. $(15 + 3) \cdot 2 - 2 = \underline{34}$

18. $0 / 5 + 3 \cdot 2 = \underline{6}$

19. $5 / 0 + 3 \cdot 2 = \underline{\text{Undefined}}$

20. $(1 + 1) \cdot (2 - 2) \cdot (4 \cdot 5 \cdot 5) = \underline{0}$

21. $(5 + 3) \cdot 2 = \underline{16}$

22. $(5 \cdot 3) \cdot 2 = \underline{30}$

23. $5 \cdot (3 \cdot 2) = \underline{30}$

24. $5 \cdot 3 \cdot 2 = \underline{30}$

25. $100 / 2^2 + 21 / 3 = \underline{32}$

26. $(2 + 1)^2 / 3 + 13 = \underline{16}$

27. $2(3^2 - 4 / 2)^2 - 1 \cdot 3 = \underline{95}$

28. $3(1 - 4 / 2^2)^2 - 4^2 / 3 = \underline{-16/3}$

29. $10(2^4 / 2 - 1^2 + 1) / 2 = \underline{40}$

30. $2 + 3(2 - 20 / 2^2)^2 - (5^2 + 3) / 2 =$

31. $5 / 0 = \underline{\text{Undefined}}$

32. $0 / 4 = \underline{0}$

33. $0 / 0 = \underline{\text{Undefined}}$

34. $(2 + 4) \cdot 5^2 - 2 / 2 = \underline{149}$

35. $-1 \cdot 5^2 - 2^2 + (-2)^{3 - 1 \cdot 2} = \underline{-31}$

36. $\left(-2^2 - 2\right)^2 \cdot (-2)^{1-1} = \underline{36}$

37. $\left(4 - 5 \cdot 2\right) / 2 - 1 = \underline{-4}$

1.2. – INTRODUCTION TO FRACTIONS

1. Given the following circle, divide it to 2 equal pieces and shade $\dfrac{1}{2}$

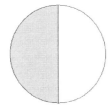

2. Given the following circle divide it to 3 equal pieces and shade $\dfrac{1}{3}$

3. Given the following circle, divide it to 4 equal pieces and shade $\dfrac{1}{4}$

4. Given the following circle, divide it to 5 equal pieces and shade $\dfrac{1}{5}$

5. Given the following circle, divide it to 6 equal pieces and shade $\dfrac{1}{6}$

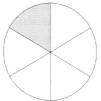

6. Given the following circle, divide it to 7 equal pieces and shade $\dfrac{1}{7}$

7. Given the following circle, divide it to 8 equal pieces and shade $\dfrac{1}{8}$

8. Given the following circle, divide it to 9 equal pieces and shade $\dfrac{1}{9}$

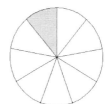

9. Given the following circle, divide it to 10 equal pieces and shade $\frac{1}{10}$

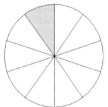

10. Given the following circle, divide it to 3 equal pieces and shade $\frac{2}{3}$

11. Given the following circle, divide it to 4 equal pieces and shade $\frac{2}{4}$

12. Given the following circle, divide it to 4 equal pieces and shade $\frac{3}{4}$

13. Given the following circle, divide it to 5 equal pieces and shade $\frac{2}{5}$

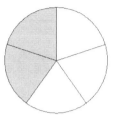

14. Given the following circle, divide it to 6 equal pieces and shade $\frac{5}{6}$

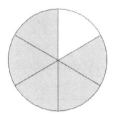

15. Given the following circle, divide it to 8 equal pieces and shade $\frac{5}{8}$

16. Given the following circle, divide it to 5 equal pieces and shade $\frac{4}{5}$

17. Given the following circle, divide it to 9 equal pieces and shade $\frac{4}{9}$

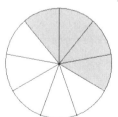

18. What fraction of the following circle is shaded: $\dfrac{5}{11}$

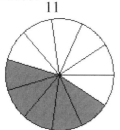

19. What fraction of the following circle is shaded: $\dfrac{2}{3}$

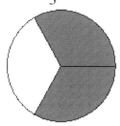

20. What fraction of the following circle is shaded: $\dfrac{5}{11}$

21. What fraction of the following circle is shaded: $\dfrac{12}{14} = \dfrac{6}{7}$

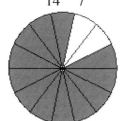

22. What fraction of the following circle is shaded: $\dfrac{7}{8}$

23. What fraction of the following circle is shaded: $\dfrac{1}{12}$

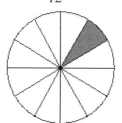

24. What fraction of the following table is shaded: $\dfrac{14}{64}$

25. What fraction of the following table is shaded: $\dfrac{6}{35}$

26. What fraction of the following table is shaded? $\dfrac{9}{24}$

255

27. What fraction is shaded? $\dfrac{5}{16}$

28. What fraction is shaded? $\dfrac{5}{12}$

29. What fraction is shaded? $\dfrac{12}{24} = \dfrac{1}{2}$

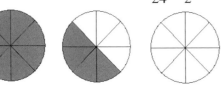

30. What fraction is shaded? $\dfrac{8}{24}$

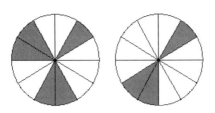

31. There were 12 cookies in the jar. John ate 5, write down the fraction of cookies john ate and the fraction that is left in the jar.

   Eaten: $\dfrac{5}{12}$, Left $\dfrac{7}{12}$

32. Lia ate 3 cookies that represented $\dfrac{3}{4}$ of the cookies in the jar. Write down the number of cookies in the jar before she ate. Make a sketch to show answer.

   4 cookies.

33. Rami ate $\dfrac{2}{5}$ of the cookies in the jar, Melissa ate $\dfrac{1}{4}$ of the cookies. Who ate more? Invent an imaginary jar with a number of cookies that will make the problem easy to solve.

   With 20 cookies the problem is solved easily:

   Rami ate more

34. How much is $\dfrac{1}{2}$ of 2? Shade to show your answer: 1

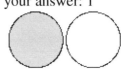

35. How much is $\dfrac{1}{3}$ of 2? Shade to show your answer: Shading a third of each gives $\dfrac{2}{3}$

36. How much is $\dfrac{1}{4}$ of 2? Shade to show your answer: Shading a quarter of each gives $\dfrac{2}{4}$

37. How much is $\frac{1}{5}$ of 2? Shade to show your answer: Shading a fifth of each gives $\frac{2}{5}$

38. How much is $\frac{1}{3}$ of 5? In 2 different ways to show your answer: $\frac{5}{3}$

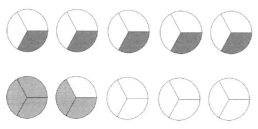

39. How much is $\frac{2}{5}$ of 4? In 2 different ways to show your answer: $\frac{8}{5}$

40. Sketch $\frac{3}{2}$ circles:

41. Sketch $\frac{5}{3}$ circles:

42. Sketch $\frac{7}{4}$ circles:

43. Sketch $\frac{8}{4}$ circles:

44. Sketch $\frac{7}{5}$ circles:

45. Sketch $\frac{8}{3}$ circles:

46. Nathan ate $\frac{2}{7}$ of the cookies in the jar, Melissa ate $\frac{1}{3}$ of the cookies.

Who ate more? Invent an imaginary jar with a number of cookies that will make the problem easy to solve. With 21 cookies the problem is easy to solve, Melissa ate more.

47. Write down the missing number(s) between 0 and 1: $\frac{1}{2}$

257

48. Write down the missing number(s)

between 0 and 1: $\dfrac{1}{3}$, $\dfrac{2}{3}$

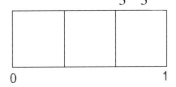

49. Write down the missing number(s)

between 0 and 1: $\dfrac{1}{4}$, $\dfrac{2}{4}$, $\dfrac{3}{4}$

50. Write down the missing number(s)

between 0 and 1: $\dfrac{1}{5}$, $\dfrac{2}{5}$, $\dfrac{3}{5}$, $\dfrac{4}{5}$

51. Write down the missing number(s)

between 0 and 1: $\dfrac{1}{6}$, $\dfrac{2}{6}$, $\dfrac{3}{6}$, $\dfrac{4}{6}$, $\dfrac{5}{6}$

52. Write down the missing number(s)

between 0 and 2: $\dfrac{1}{3}$, $\dfrac{2}{3}$, 1, $\dfrac{4}{3}$, $\dfrac{5}{3}$

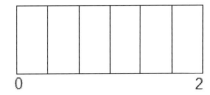

53. Write down the missing number(s)

between 0 and 2: $\dfrac{1}{4}$, $\dfrac{2}{4}$, $\dfrac{3}{4}$, 1, $\dfrac{5}{4}$, $\dfrac{6}{4}$, $\dfrac{7}{4}$

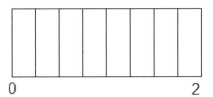

54. Write down the missing number(s) between 0 and 2:

$\dfrac{1}{5}$, $\dfrac{2}{5}$, $\dfrac{3}{5}$, $\dfrac{4}{5}$, 1, $\dfrac{6}{5}$, $\dfrac{7}{5}$, $\dfrac{8}{5}$, $\dfrac{9}{5}$

0.2, 0.4, 0.6, 0.8, 1, 1.2, 1.4, 1.6, 1.8

55. Write down the missing number(s) between 2 and 3:

$\dfrac{21}{10}$, $\dfrac{22}{10}$, $\dfrac{23}{10}$, $\dfrac{24}{10}$, $\dfrac{25}{10}$, $\dfrac{26}{10}$, $\dfrac{27}{10}$, $\dfrac{28}{10}$, $\dfrac{29}{10}$

2.1, 2.2, 2.3, 2.4, 2.5, 2.6, 2.7, 2.8, 2.9

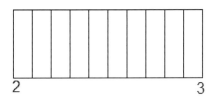

56. Write down the missing number(s) between 2 and 4:

$\dfrac{13}{6}$, $\dfrac{14}{6}$, $\dfrac{15}{6}$, $\dfrac{16}{6}$, $\dfrac{17}{6}$, 3, $\dfrac{19}{6}$, $\dfrac{20}{6}$, $\dfrac{21}{6}$, $\dfrac{22}{6}$, $\dfrac{23}{6}$

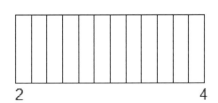

57. Write down the missing fractions(s): $-\dfrac{11}{5}=-2.2, \dfrac{3}{5}=0.6$

58. Write down the missing fractions(s): $-\dfrac{6}{5}=-1.2, \dfrac{14}{5}=2.8$

59. Write down the missing fractions(s): $-\dfrac{22}{5}=-4.4, \dfrac{17}{5}=3.4$

60. Write down the missing fractions(s): $\dfrac{1}{10}=0.1$

0   **[1/5]**

61. Write down the missing fractions(s): $\dfrac{2}{8}=0.25, \dfrac{3}{8}=0.375$

[1/8]   **[1/2]**

62. Write down the missing fractions(s): $\dfrac{7}{6}, \dfrac{8}{6}=\dfrac{4}{3}$

[1]   **[3/2]**   **[5/3]**

63. Write down the missing fractions(s): $\dfrac{15}{7}, \dfrac{16}{7}, \dfrac{17}{7}, \dfrac{18}{7}, \dfrac{19}{7}$

[13/7]   **[2]**   **[20/7]**

64. Write down the missing fractions(s): $\dfrac{28}{9}, \dfrac{29}{9}$

[26/9]   **[3]**   **[10/3]**

65. Write down the missing fractions(s): $-\dfrac{8}{9}, -\dfrac{7}{9}, -\dfrac{6}{9}, -\dfrac{5}{9}$

[-10/9]   **[-1]**   **[-4/9]**   **[-1/3]**

66. Write down the missing fractions(s): $-\dfrac{18}{5}, -\dfrac{16}{5}, -\dfrac{14}{5}, -\dfrac{12}{5}$

[-4]   **[-2]**   **[-8/5]**   **[-6/5]**

67. Write down the missing fractions(s): $\dfrac{15}{4}, \dfrac{18}{4}, \dfrac{21}{4}$

[3/4]   **[3/2]**   **[9/4]**   **[3]**   **[6]**   **[27/4]**   **[15/2]**

1.3. – DECIMALS AND FRACTIONS

Write as decimals:

1. $\frac{1}{10} = \underline{0.1}$

2. $\frac{1}{100} = \quad \underline{0.01}$

3. $\frac{1}{1000} = \quad \underline{0.001}$

4. $\frac{1}{10000} = \underline{0.0001}$

5. $\frac{2}{10} = \underline{0.2}$

6. $\frac{5}{100} = \underline{0.05}$

7. $\frac{-31}{1000} = \quad \underline{-0.031}$

8. $\frac{766}{10000} = \underline{0.0766}$

9. $\frac{55}{10} = \underline{5.5}$

10. $\frac{101}{100} = \underline{1.01}$

11. $\frac{-335}{1000} = \underline{-0.335}$

12. $\frac{20000}{10000} = \underline{2}$

13. $\frac{1}{2} = \underline{0.5}$

14. $\frac{1}{5} = \underline{0.2}$

15. $\frac{1}{4} = \underline{0.25}$

16. $\frac{1}{3} = \underline{0.333...}$

17. $\frac{1}{8} = \underline{0.125}$

18. $\frac{1}{9} = \underline{0.111...}$

19. $\frac{2}{5} = \underline{0.4}$

20. $\frac{2}{4} = \underline{0.5}$

21. $\frac{3}{5} = \underline{0.6}$

22. $\frac{4}{5} = \underline{0.8}$

23. $\frac{3}{4} = \underline{0.75}$

24. $\frac{7}{5} = \underline{1.4}$

25. $\frac{5}{4} = \underline{1.25}$

26. $\frac{9}{5} = \underline{1.6}$

27. $\frac{2}{9} = \underline{0.222...}$

28. $\frac{1}{20} = \underline{0.02}$

29. $\frac{3}{20} = \underline{0.06}$

30. $\frac{8}{5} = \underline{1.6}$

31. $\frac{18}{10} = \underline{1.8}$

Write the decimals as fractions

32. $0.3 = \frac{3}{10}$

33. $0.2 = \frac{2}{10}$

34. $0.1 = \frac{1}{10}$

35. $0.01 = \frac{1}{100}$

36. $0.02 = \frac{2}{100}$

37. $0.11 = \frac{11}{100}$

38. $0.26 = \frac{26}{100}$

39. $1.3 = \frac{13}{10}$

40. $1.42 = \frac{142}{10}$

41. $0.011 = \frac{11}{1000}$

42. $0.312 = \frac{312}{1000}$

43. $0.16 = \frac{16}{100}$

44. $1.4 = \frac{14}{10}$

45. $2.043 = \frac{2043}{1000}$

46. $43.3 = \frac{433}{10}$

47. $4.12 = \frac{412}{100}$

48. $1.302 = \frac{1302}{1000}$

49. $1.111 = \frac{1111}{1000}$

50. $102.32 = \frac{10232}{100}$

51. $2.346 = \frac{2346}{1000}$

52. Write down the fractions in different ways:

$\frac{1}{2} = \frac{2}{4} = \frac{5}{10}$ $\quad$ $\frac{1}{3} = \frac{2}{6} = \frac{10}{30}$ $\quad$ $\frac{1}{4} = \frac{2}{8} = \frac{5}{20}$ $\quad$ $\frac{7}{4} = \frac{14}{8} = \frac{70}{40}$ $\quad$ $\frac{2}{3} = \frac{4}{6} = \frac{6}{9}$ $\quad$ $\frac{11}{8} = \frac{22}{16} = \frac{55}{40}$

$$\frac{a}{b}=\frac{2a}{2b}=\frac{ka}{kb} \qquad \frac{3a}{a}=\frac{3}{1}=3 \qquad \frac{a+2}{2+a}=\frac{1}{1}=1 \qquad \frac{x}{7x}=\frac{1}{7} \qquad \frac{1+a}{a-1}=\frac{2+2a}{2a-2}$$

Fill the blank to make the fractions equal:

53. $\dfrac{a}{3}=\dfrac{2a}{6}$

54. $\dfrac{a-b}{4}=\dfrac{3a-3b}{12}$

55. $\dfrac{a}{b}=\dfrac{2a}{2b}$

56. $\dfrac{1}{a}=\dfrac{3}{3a}$

57. $\dfrac{1}{3}=\dfrac{a}{3a}$

62. $\dfrac{2a}{7x}=\dfrac{4ax}{14x^2}$

58. $\dfrac{a-b}{a-b}=1$

59. $\dfrac{2-a}{-2}=\dfrac{a-2}{2}$

60. $\dfrac{2a}{b}=\dfrac{8a}{4b}$

61. $\dfrac{x^2}{2xy}=\dfrac{2xy}{4y^2}$

Perform the operations; give the answer as a decimal and fraction:

63. $50 \cdot 0.1 = \underline{5}$

64. $85 \cdot 0.01 = \underline{0.85}$

65. $45 \cdot 0.001 = \underline{0.045}$

66. $6 \cdot 0.0001 = \underline{0.0006}$

67. $5123 \cdot 0.001 = \underline{5.123}$

68. $435 \cdot 0.01 = \underline{4.35}$

69. $15 \cdot 0.001 = \underline{0.015}$

70. $-236 \cdot 0.0001 = \underline{-0.236}$

71. $1228 \cdot 0.1 = \underline{122.8}$

72. $1085 \cdot 0.01 = \underline{10.85}$

73. $4500 \cdot 0.001 = \underline{4.5}$

74. $0.16 \cdot 0.0001 = \underline{0.000016}$

75. $12 \cdot 1.2 = \dfrac{12}{1} \cdot \dfrac{12}{10} = \dfrac{144}{10} = 1.44$

76. $25 \cdot 0.22 = \dfrac{25}{1} \cdot \dfrac{22}{100} = \dfrac{550}{100} = 5.5$

77. $2.5 \cdot 1.8 = \dfrac{25}{10} \cdot \dfrac{18}{10} = \dfrac{450}{100} = 4.5$

78. $7.2 \cdot 8.8 = \dfrac{72}{10} \cdot \dfrac{88}{10} = \dfrac{6336}{100} = 63.36$

79. $0.15 \cdot 2.01 = \dfrac{15}{100} \cdot \dfrac{201}{100} = \dfrac{3015}{10000} = 0.3105$

80. $87.5 \cdot 0.2 = \dfrac{875}{100} \cdot \dfrac{2}{10} = \dfrac{1750}{1000} = 17.5$

81. $31.5 \cdot 0.3 = \dfrac{315}{10} \cdot \dfrac{3}{10} = \dfrac{945}{100} = 9.45$

82. $0.215 \cdot 1.38 = \dfrac{215}{1000} \cdot \dfrac{138}{100} = \dfrac{29670}{100000} = 0.2967$

83. $0.5 \cdot 1.23 = \dfrac{5}{10} \cdot \dfrac{123}{100} = \dfrac{615}{1000} = 0.615$

84. $1.02 \cdot 2.5 = \dfrac{102}{100} \cdot \dfrac{25}{10} = \dfrac{2550}{1000} = 2.55$

85. $31.7 \cdot 0.18 = \dfrac{317}{10} \cdot \dfrac{18}{100} = \dfrac{5706}{1000} = 5.706$

86. $21.2 \cdot 1.13 = \dfrac{212}{10} \cdot \dfrac{113}{100} = \dfrac{23956}{1000} = 23.956$

87. $0.42 \cdot 5.56 = \dfrac{42}{100} \cdot \dfrac{556}{100} = \dfrac{23352}{10000} = 2.3352$

88. $3.1 \cdot 0.642 = \dfrac{31}{10} \cdot \dfrac{642}{1000} = \dfrac{19902}{10000} = 1.9902$

89. $13.7 \cdot 8.9 = \dfrac{137}{10} \cdot \dfrac{89}{10} = \dfrac{12192}{100} = 12.192$

90. $1.07 \cdot 0.03 = \dfrac{107}{100} \cdot \dfrac{3}{100} = \dfrac{321}{10000} = 0.0321$

Perform the operations; give the answer as a decimal and fraction:

91. $\dfrac{1}{0.1} = \underline{10}$

92. $\dfrac{5}{0.01} = \underline{500}$

93. $\dfrac{-56}{0.001} = \underline{-56000}$

94. $\dfrac{-2.3}{0.01} = \underline{-230}$

95. $\dfrac{3}{0.1} = \underline{30}$

96. $\dfrac{0.55}{0.01} = \underline{55}$

97. $\dfrac{-31.6}{0.001} = \underline{-31600}$

98. $\dfrac{0.023}{0.01} = \underline{2.3}$

99. $\dfrac{15}{0.01} = \underline{1500}$

100. $\dfrac{-215}{0.01} = \underline{-21500}$

101. $\dfrac{-45.6}{0.001} = \underline{-45600}$

102. $\dfrac{-12.3}{0.01} = \underline{-1230}$

103. $\dfrac{1}{0.02} = \dfrac{1}{\left(\dfrac{2}{100}\right)} = \left(\dfrac{100}{2}\right) = 50$

104. $\dfrac{-2}{0.03} = \dfrac{-2}{\left(\dfrac{3}{100}\right)} = \left(-\dfrac{200}{2}\right) = -100$

105. $\dfrac{-4.6}{0.05} = \dfrac{-4.6}{\left(\dfrac{5}{100}\right)} = \left(-\dfrac{460}{2}\right) = -230$

106. $\dfrac{-1.3}{0.06} = \dfrac{-1.3}{\left(\dfrac{6}{100}\right)} = \left(\dfrac{-130}{6}\right)$

107. $\dfrac{1}{0.25} = \dfrac{1}{\left(\dfrac{25}{100}\right)} = \left(\dfrac{100}{25}\right) = 4$

108. $\dfrac{-2}{0.9} = \dfrac{-2}{\left(\dfrac{9}{100}\right)} = \left(\dfrac{-200}{9}\right)$

109. $\dfrac{-4.1}{0.2} = \dfrac{-4.1}{\left(\dfrac{2}{10}\right)} = \left(\dfrac{-41}{2}\right)$

110. $\dfrac{-1.3}{0.05} = \dfrac{-1.3}{\left(\dfrac{5}{100}\right)} = \left(\dfrac{-130}{5}\right) = -26$

111. $\dfrac{1}{0.015} = \dfrac{1}{\left(\dfrac{15}{1000}\right)} = \left(\dfrac{1000}{15}\right) = \dfrac{200}{3}$

112. $\dfrac{-12}{0.6} = \dfrac{-12}{\left(\dfrac{6}{10}\right)} = \left(\dfrac{-120}{6}\right) = 20$

113. $\dfrac{-14}{0.003} = \dfrac{-14}{\left(\dfrac{3}{1000}\right)} = \left(\dfrac{-1400}{3}\right)$

114. $\dfrac{-0.3}{0.02} =$

$\dfrac{\left(-\dfrac{3}{10}\right)}{\left(\dfrac{2}{100}\right)} = \left(-\dfrac{3}{10}\right)\left(\dfrac{100}{2}\right) = -15$

115. 0.2 units on the left of -1: $\underline{-1.2}$
116. 0.5 units on the left of -2: $\underline{-2.5}$
117. 0.3 units on the right of -1: $\underline{-0.7}$
118. 0.4 units on the right of -2: $\underline{-1.6}$
119. 0.8 units on the left of -9: $\underline{-9.8}$
120. 0.2 units on the left of 0: $\underline{-0.2}$
121. 0.9 units on the right of -9: $\underline{-8.1}$
122. 0.2 units on the right of -5: $\underline{-4.8}$
123. 0.21 units on the left of -1: $\underline{-1.21}$
124. 0.51 units on the left of -2: $\underline{-1.51}$
125. 0.34 units on the right of -1: $\underline{-0.66}$
126. 0.06 units on the right of -10: $\underline{-9.94}$
127. 0.11 units on the right of -1: $\underline{-0.89}$
128. 0.01 units on the right of -2: $\underline{-1.99}$
129. 0.34 units on the right of 9: $\underline{9.34}$

130. 0.06 units on the right of 10: $\underline{10.06}$
131. 0.17 units on the right of -9: $\underline{-8.83}$
132. 0.78 units on the left of -3: $\underline{-3.78}$
133. 0.01 units on the left of -7: $\underline{-7.01}$
134. 0.02 units on the right of -1: $\underline{-0.98}$
135. 0.002 units on the right of -10: $\underline{-9.998}$
136. 0.111 units on the right of -1: $\underline{-0.889}$
137. 0.021 units on the right of -2: $\underline{-1.979}$
138. 0.4 units on the right of 9: $\underline{9.4}$
139. 0.03 units on the right of 10: $\underline{10.03}$
140. 0.202 units on the right of -9: $\underline{-8.798}$
141. Close to 2 on its left: $\underline{1.999}$ right: $\underline{2.001}$
142. Close to 1 on its left: $\underline{0.999}$ right: $\underline{1.001}$
143. Close to 0 on its left: $\underline{-0.001}$ right: $\underline{0.001}$
144. Close to -1 on its left: $\underline{-1.001}$ right: $\underline{-0.999}$

145. Close to –7 on its left: <u>–7.001</u> right: <u>–6.999</u> 148. Close to –10 on its left: <u>–10.001</u> right: <u>–9.999</u>
146. Close to –12 on its left: <u>–12.001</u> right: <u>–11.999</u> 149. Close to 9 on its left: <u>8.999</u> right: <u>9.001</u>
147. Close to –2 on its left: <u>–2.001</u> right: <u>–1.999</u> 150. Close to 100 on its left: <u>99.999</u> right: <u>100.001</u>

151. The numbers between 3 and 3.1: <u>3.01, 3.06</u>. Fractions: $\left(\dfrac{301}{100}\right), \left(\dfrac{306}{100}\right)$

152. The numbers between 6.2 and 6.3: <u>6.21, 6.25</u>. Fractions: $\left(\dfrac{621}{100}\right), \left(\dfrac{625}{100}\right)$

153. The numbers between 6.2 and 6.21: <u>6.201, 6.202</u>. Fractions: $\left(\dfrac{6201}{1000}\right), \left(\dfrac{6202}{1000}\right)$

154. The numbers between –5.2 and –5.3: <u>–5.21, –5.22</u>. Fractions: $\left(-\dfrac{521}{100}\right), \left(-\dfrac{522}{100}\right)$

155. The numbers between 0.25 and 0.251: <u>0.2501, 0.2502</u>. Fractions: $\left(\dfrac{2501}{10000}\right), \left(\dfrac{2502}{10000}\right)$

156. The numbers between 1.11 and 1.111: <u>1.1101, 1.1102</u>. Fractions: $\left(\dfrac{11101}{10000}\right), \left(\dfrac{11102}{10000}\right)$

157. The numbers between 0.21 and 0.22: <u>0.211, 0.212</u>. Fractions: $\left(\dfrac{211}{1000}\right), \left(\dfrac{212}{1000}\right)$

158. The numbers between 5.99 and 5.999: <u>5.991, 5.992</u>. Fractions: $\left(\dfrac{5991}{1000}\right), \left(\dfrac{5992}{1000}\right)$

159. The numbers between 6 and 6.01: <u>6.001, 6.002</u>. Fractions: $\left(\dfrac{6001}{1000}\right), \left(\dfrac{6002}{1000}\right)$

160. The values are: 11.2, 12, 12.4

161. The values are: 4.72, 4.77, 4.86
162. The values are: -0.62, -0.57, -0.5
163. Fractions greater than 1:
$\dfrac{7}{6}, \dfrac{35}{34}, \dfrac{21}{7}, \dfrac{10001}{10000}$
164. A fraction will be greater than 1 if <u>the numerator is greater than the denominator</u>
165. Fractions greater than 2:
$\dfrac{50}{26}, \dfrac{20}{7}, \dfrac{20001}{10000}$
166. A fraction will be greater than 2 if <u>the numerator is greater than twice the denominator</u>
167. Fractions greater than 5: $\dfrac{47}{9}, \dfrac{100}{6}, \dfrac{28}{3}$

168. A fraction will be greater than 5 if <u>the numerator is greater than 5 times the denominator</u>

169. Fractions smaller than $\dfrac{1}{2}$: $\dfrac{1}{3}, \dfrac{23}{51}$

170. A fraction will be smaller than $\dfrac{1}{2}$ if: <u>the denominator is more than twice the numerator</u>

171. Fractions smaller than $\dfrac{1}{3}$: $\dfrac{2}{7}, \dfrac{24}{75}, \dfrac{3}{11}$

172. A fraction will be smaller than $\dfrac{1}{3}$ if: <u>the denominator is more than 3 times the numerator</u>

Fill the blank with: <,> or =:

173. $\dfrac{1}{2} > \dfrac{1}{3}$

174. $\dfrac{1}{3} > \dfrac{1}{4}$

175. $\dfrac{2}{5} < \dfrac{3}{7}$

176. $\dfrac{5}{8} < \dfrac{7}{11}$

177. $\dfrac{12}{7} > \dfrac{13}{8}$

178. $\dfrac{21}{8} > \dfrac{13}{5}$

263

179. $\dfrac{35}{8} > \dfrac{17}{4}$ 　　182. $\dfrac{1}{n+1} < \dfrac{1}{n}, n \ge 0$ 　　185. $\dfrac{1}{n^2} > \dfrac{1}{n}, 0 \le n \le 1$

180. $\dfrac{a}{b} < \dfrac{a+1}{b+1}, b > a > 0$ 　183. $\dfrac{1}{n^2} < \dfrac{1}{n}, n \ge 1$ 　　186. $\dfrac{1}{a} > \dfrac{1}{b}, a < b$

181. $\dfrac{a}{b-1} > \dfrac{a+1}{b+1}, b > a > 0$ 　184. $n^2 < n, 0 \le n \le 1$

187.

188.

189.

190.

191.

192.

193.

194.

195.

$$-\frac{37}{12} \quad -\frac{12}{5} \quad -\frac{6}{3} \qquad\qquad \frac{11}{10} \quad \frac{11}{6}$$

-3 -2 -1 | 1 2 3

Calculate:

196. $1+\dfrac{2}{3}=\dfrac{5}{3}$

197. $\dfrac{5}{6}+\dfrac{2}{3}=\dfrac{10}{6}$

198. $\dfrac{2}{7}-\dfrac{1}{6}=\dfrac{5}{42}$

199. $5\cdot\dfrac{3}{8}-\dfrac{2}{12}=\dfrac{41}{24}$

200. $\left(\dfrac{2}{14}-\dfrac{3}{7}\right)\cdot\dfrac{2}{9}=\dfrac{-4}{14}\cdot\dfrac{2}{9}=\dfrac{-8}{126}$

201. $\left(\dfrac{7}{2}-\dfrac{4}{3}\right)\cdot\dfrac{1}{5}=\dfrac{13}{6}\cdot\dfrac{1}{5}=\dfrac{13}{30}$

202. $\dfrac{5}{6}+\dfrac{2}{3}=\dfrac{9}{6}$

203. $\left(\dfrac{7}{2}-\dfrac{4}{3}\cdot\dfrac{1}{5}\right)-\dfrac{1}{5}=\dfrac{67}{30}-\dfrac{6}{30}=\dfrac{61}{30}$

204. $2-\dfrac{3}{10}-\dfrac{4}{3}\cdot\dfrac{1}{5}=2-\dfrac{17}{30}=\dfrac{43}{30}$

205. $4-\left(\dfrac{5}{6}-\dfrac{4}{3}\right)\cdot\dfrac{1}{5}=4-\left(-\dfrac{1}{2}\right)\cdot\dfrac{1}{5}=\dfrac{41}{10}$

206. $\dfrac{1}{a}+\dfrac{1}{a}=\dfrac{2}{a}$

207. $\dfrac{1}{d}+d=\dfrac{1+d^2}{d}$

208. $\dfrac{1}{a}+\dfrac{a}{1}=\dfrac{1+a^2}{a}$

209. $\dfrac{1}{b+1}+b=\dfrac{1+b(b+1)}{b+1}$

210. $\dfrac{a}{b}+\dfrac{1}{b}=\dfrac{a+1}{b}$

211. $\dfrac{a}{b}+\dfrac{d}{b}=\dfrac{a+d}{b}$

212. $\dfrac{a}{c}+\dfrac{d}{b}=\dfrac{ab+cd}{cb}$

213. $\dfrac{a+b}{b}+\dfrac{d}{b}=\dfrac{a+b+d}{b}$

214. $\dfrac{\left(\dfrac{a}{b}\right)}{b}=\dfrac{a}{b^2}$

215. $\dfrac{a}{\left(\dfrac{a}{b}\right)}=b$

216. $\dfrac{\left(\dfrac{b}{a}\right)}{b}=\dfrac{1}{a}$

217. $\dfrac{\left(\dfrac{b}{a}\right)}{1}=\dfrac{b}{a}$

218. $\dfrac{\left(\dfrac{1}{a}\right)}{b}=\dfrac{1}{ab}$

219. $\dfrac{\left(\dfrac{b}{1}\right)}{b}=1$

220. $\dfrac{1}{\left(\dfrac{a}{b}\right)}=\dfrac{b}{a}$

221. $\dfrac{\left(\dfrac{a}{b}\right)}{\left(\dfrac{a}{b}\right)}=1$

222. $\dfrac{\left(\dfrac{b}{a}\right)}{\left(\dfrac{a}{b}\right)}=\dfrac{b^2}{a^2}$

223. $\dfrac{\left(\dfrac{a}{1}\right)}{\left(\dfrac{a}{b}\right)}=b$

224. $\dfrac{\left(\dfrac{a}{b}\right)}{\left(\dfrac{1}{b}\right)}=a$

225. $\dfrac{\left(\dfrac{c+1}{d}\right)}{\left(\dfrac{1}{d}+d\right)} = \dfrac{\left(\dfrac{c+1}{d}\right)}{\left(\dfrac{1+d^2}{d}\right)} = \left(\dfrac{c+1}{1+d^2}\right)$

226. $\dfrac{1}{\left(\dfrac{1}{d}+d\right)}+d =$

$\dfrac{1}{\left(\dfrac{1+d^2}{d}\right)}+d = \left(\dfrac{2d+d^3}{1+d^2}\right)$

227. $\dfrac{1-d}{(d+2)}+\dfrac{2}{d} =$

$\dfrac{d(1-d)+2(d+2)}{(d+2)d}$

228. $\dfrac{1}{d}+\dfrac{2}{d^2}+\dfrac{1}{d^3} = \dfrac{d^2+2d+1}{d^3}$

229. $\dfrac{2}{3}+\dfrac{3a}{c}-\dfrac{b}{2} = \dfrac{4c+18a-3cb}{6c}$

230. $\dfrac{\left(\dfrac{4}{b}-\dfrac{a}{7}\right)}{2} = \dfrac{\left(\dfrac{28-ab}{7b}\right)}{2} = \dfrac{28-ab}{14b}$

231. $\dfrac{a}{c(c+1)}+\dfrac{d}{c+1} = \dfrac{a+dc}{c(c+1)}$

232. $\dfrac{2x}{\left(\dfrac{2x+2}{3+x}\right)}+\dfrac{\left(\dfrac{x+1}{x-2}\right)}{x-3} =$

$\dfrac{2x(3+x)}{2x+2}+\dfrac{x+1}{(x-2)(x-3)} = \dfrac{2x(3+x)+(x+1)(x-2)}{(2x+2)(x-2)(x-3)}$

233. $\dfrac{\left(2x+\dfrac{1}{x}\right)}{\left(1+\dfrac{1}{x}\right)} = \dfrac{\left(\dfrac{2x^2+1}{x}\right)}{\left(\dfrac{x+1}{x}\right)} = \left(\dfrac{2x^2+1}{x+1}\right)$

234. $\dfrac{12}{2a}\times\dfrac{a+1}{6} = \dfrac{(a+1)}{a}$

235. $\dfrac{12}{2a}\div\dfrac{a}{6} = \dfrac{36}{2a^2}$

236. $3\times\dfrac{4}{3} = 4$

237. $3\div\dfrac{4}{3} = \dfrac{9}{4}$

238. $12-\dfrac{4}{3} = \dfrac{32}{3}$

239. $a\times\dfrac{b}{3c} = \dfrac{ab}{3c}$

240. $\dfrac{b}{3a}\div 3a = \dfrac{b}{3a^2}$

241. $\dfrac{b}{3a}\times 3a = b$

242. $\dfrac{\left(\dfrac{1}{3}+\dfrac{2}{5}\right)}{\left(\dfrac{5}{3}-\dfrac{1}{3}\right)} = \dfrac{\left(\dfrac{11}{15}\right)}{\left(\dfrac{4}{3}\right)} = \dfrac{33}{60} = \dfrac{11}{20}$

243. $\dfrac{\left(\dfrac{b}{3c}\right)}{2} = \dfrac{b}{6c}$

244. $\dfrac{\left(\dfrac{1}{2}\right)}{2\left(\dfrac{2}{3c}\right)} = \dfrac{3c}{8}$

245. $\dfrac{\left(\dfrac{1}{2}\right)}{2} = \dfrac{1}{4}$

246. $\dfrac{\left(\dfrac{2}{7}\right)}{3} = \dfrac{2}{21}$

247. $\dfrac{2}{\left(\dfrac{2}{7}\right)} = \dfrac{1}{7}$

248. $\dfrac{3}{\left(\dfrac{a}{7}\right)} = \dfrac{21}{a}$

249. $\dfrac{6}{\left(\dfrac{8}{3}\right)} = \dfrac{9}{4}$

250. $\dfrac{\left(\dfrac{4}{3}\right)}{\left(\dfrac{3}{4}\right)} = \dfrac{16}{9}$

251. $\dfrac{\left(\dfrac{2}{3}\right)}{\left(\dfrac{4}{5}\right)} = \dfrac{6}{5}$

252. $\dfrac{\left(\dfrac{2}{3}\right)}{\left(\dfrac{2}{3}\right)}=1$

253. $\left(\dfrac{a}{b}\right)\cdot\left(\dfrac{c}{a}\right)=\dfrac{c}{b}$

254. $\left(\dfrac{2}{c}\right)\cdot\left(\dfrac{c}{7}\right)=\dfrac{2}{7}$

255. $\left(\dfrac{b+1}{3}\right)\cdot\left(\dfrac{2}{b}\right)=\dfrac{2(b+1)}{3b}$

256. $\left(\dfrac{z+1}{z-2}\right)\cdot\left(\dfrac{4}{z+1}\right)=\dfrac{4}{z-2}$

257. $\left(\dfrac{3a+6}{5}\right)\cdot\left(\dfrac{1}{a+2}\right)=\dfrac{3}{5}$

258. $\left(\dfrac{2c-4}{c}\right)\cdot\left(\dfrac{2c}{4c-8}\right)=1$

259. $\dfrac{1}{\left(\dfrac{2}{4}\right)}\cdot\left(\dfrac{2}{3}\right)=\dfrac{4}{3}$

260. $\dfrac{\left(\dfrac{3}{4}\right)}{\left(\dfrac{a}{2}\right)}\cdot\left(\dfrac{2}{3}\right)=\dfrac{1}{a}$

261. $\dfrac{\left(\dfrac{1}{a}\right)}{\left(\dfrac{2}{a}\right)}+2=\dfrac{5}{2}$

262. $\dfrac{\left(x+\dfrac{1}{x}\right)}{\left(1-\dfrac{1}{x}\right)}=\dfrac{x^2+1}{x-1}$

263. $\dfrac{\left(\dfrac{1}{1+x}+1\right)}{\left(x-\dfrac{2}{x}\right)}=\dfrac{x(2+x)}{(x^2-2)(1+x)}$

264. $\dfrac{\left(\dfrac{x}{3}-2\right)}{\left(2-\dfrac{2+x}{3}\right)}=\dfrac{x-6}{4-x}$

265. $\dfrac{2x}{\left(\dfrac{2}{3+x}\right)}+\dfrac{\left(\dfrac{2}{x}\right)}{x+3}=\dfrac{(x(3+x))^2+2}{x(x+3)}$

266. $\dfrac{a-b}{\left(1-\dfrac{a}{b}\right)}=\dfrac{a-b}{\left(\dfrac{b-a}{b}\right)}=-b$

267. $\dfrac{2}{(1-a)}+\dfrac{2}{a(1-a)}=\dfrac{2(a+1)}{a(1-a)}$

268. $\dfrac{a}{(3+a)^2}+\dfrac{2}{(a+3)}=\dfrac{3a+6}{(3+a)^2}$

269. $\dfrac{1}{(1-x)^3}+\dfrac{2}{(1-x)^2}=\dfrac{3-2x}{(1-x)^3}$

270. $\dfrac{1}{(1-x)^3}+\dfrac{2}{x(1-x)^2}=\dfrac{2-x}{x(1-x)^3}$

271. $\dfrac{1}{(1-x)(2-x)}+\dfrac{2}{x(1-x)^2}=$

$=\dfrac{-x^2-x+4}{x(1-x)^2(2-x)}$

272. $\dfrac{2}{(1-x)x}+\dfrac{2}{x^2(1-x)^2}=$

$=\dfrac{-2x^2+2x+2}{x^2(1-x)^2}$

273. $\dfrac{a^2+1}{a}-\dfrac{a+1}{a^2+a}=$

$\dfrac{(a^2+1)(a+1)-(a+1)}{a(a+1)}=\dfrac{(a^2)(a+1)}{a(a+1)}=a$

274. $\dfrac{a+x}{x}-\dfrac{y+1}{xy}+\dfrac{2}{y}=\dfrac{ay+xy-y-1+2x}{xy}$

275. $\dfrac{a+x}{a-x}\div\dfrac{a+x}{x-a}=\dfrac{a+x}{a-x}\cdot\dfrac{x-a}{a+x}=-1$

276. $\dfrac{a+x}{a^2-x^2}-\dfrac{a-x}{x-a}=\dfrac{a+x+a^2-x^2}{a^2-x^2}$

277. $\left(\dfrac{2c-4}{c}\right) \div \left(\dfrac{4c^2+16}{c^2}\right) = \dfrac{2c^2-4c}{4c^2+16}$

278.
$$\left(\dfrac{6xy+2}{3y}\right) \div \left(\dfrac{3xy+1}{6y^5}\right) =$$
$$= \dfrac{(6xy+2)6y^4}{3(3xy+1)} = 4y^4$$

279.
$$\left(\dfrac{x^2-z^2}{xyz}\right) + \left(\dfrac{z-x^2}{xy}\right) =$$
$$= \dfrac{x^2-zx^2}{xyz} = \dfrac{x(1-z)}{yz}$$

True or False:

280. $\dfrac{a+b}{c} = \dfrac{a}{c} + \dfrac{b}{c}$ True

281. $\dfrac{a+b}{c+d} = \dfrac{a}{c} + \dfrac{b}{d}$ False

282. $\dfrac{a+b}{a} = 1 + \dfrac{b}{a}$ True

283. $\dfrac{a-b}{b-a} = -1$ True

284. $\dfrac{a}{c+d} = \dfrac{a}{c} + \dfrac{a}{d}$ False

285. $\dfrac{c-d}{d} = c$ False

286. $\dfrac{c-d}{d} = -1+c$ True

287. $\dfrac{ab}{ad} = \dfrac{b}{d}$ True

288. $\dfrac{a(c-d)}{a} = c-d$ True

289. $\dfrac{ac-d}{c-d} = a$ False

290. $\dfrac{2a+d}{d-2a} = -1$ False

1.4. – EXPONENTS

Product:

$a^0 = 1$

$a^1 = a$

$a^2 = a \times a$

$a^3 = a \times a \times a$

...

$a^3 a^2 = a \cdot a \cdot a \bullet a \cdot a = a^5$

$$a^m a^n = a^{m+n}$$

Division:

$\dfrac{a^5}{a^3} = \dfrac{a \cdot a \cdot a \cdot a \cdot a}{a \cdot a \cdot a} = \dfrac{a \cdot a}{1} = a^2$

$$\dfrac{a^m}{a^n} = a^{m-n}$$

$\dfrac{a^2}{a^5} = \dfrac{a \cdot a}{a \cdot a \cdot a \cdot a \cdot a} = \dfrac{1}{a \cdot a \cdot a} = \dfrac{1}{a^3} = a^{-3}$ **Power:**

$(a^2)^3 = (a^2)(a^2)(a^2) = a^6$

$$(a^m)^n = a^{mn}$$

$\left(\dfrac{a^2}{b}\right)^3 = \left(\dfrac{a^2}{b}\right)\left(\dfrac{a^2}{b}\right)\left(\dfrac{a^2}{b}\right) = \left(\dfrac{a^6}{b^3}\right)$

$$\left(\dfrac{a^m}{b^k}\right)^n = \left(\dfrac{a^{mn}}{b^{kn}}\right)$$

Radicals:

$(a^3)^{\frac{1}{2}} = a^{\frac{3}{2}} = \sqrt[2]{a^3} = \sqrt{a^3}$

$(a^4)^{\frac{1}{7}} = a^{\frac{4}{7}} = \sqrt[7]{a^4}$

$$(a^m)^{\frac{1}{n}} = a^{\frac{m}{n}} = \sqrt[n]{a^m}$$

Exercises

Write in all possible forms and evaluate without using a calculator (follow example):

1. $4^{-1} = \dfrac{1}{4} = 0.25$

2. $10^0 = \underline{1}$

3. $10^1 = \underline{10}$

4. $10^3 = \underline{1000}$

5. $10^{-1} = \dfrac{1}{10} = 0.1$

6. $10^{-2} = \dfrac{1}{100} = 0.01$

7. $10^{-3} = \dfrac{1}{1000} = 0.001$

8. $10^{-4} \ \dfrac{1}{10000} = 0.0001$

9. $2^0 = 1$

10. $2^1 = 2$

11. $2^{-1} = \dfrac{1}{2} = 0.5$

12. $2^{-2} = \dfrac{1}{2^2} = \dfrac{1}{4} = 0.25$

13. $2^{-3} = \dfrac{1}{2^3} = \dfrac{1}{8} = 0.125$

14. $2^{-4} = \dfrac{1}{2^4} = \dfrac{1}{16} = 0.0625$

15. $(-1)^0 = \underline{1}$

16. $-1^0 = -1$

17. $(-1)^1 = -1$

18. $-1^1 = -1$

19. $(-1)^{-1} = \dfrac{1}{-1} = -1$

20. $-1^2 = -1$

21. $(-1)^2 = 1$

22. $-1^2 = -1$

23. $(-1)^{-2} = \dfrac{1}{(-1)^2} = \dfrac{1}{1} = 1$

24. $-1^{-2} = -\dfrac{1}{1^2} = -\dfrac{1}{1} = -1$

25. $(-3)^0 = 1$

26. $(-3)^1 = -3$

27. $-3^1 = -3$

28. $(-3)^2 = 9$

29. $-3^2 = -9$

30. $(-3)^{-1} = \dfrac{1}{(-3)^1} = \dfrac{1}{-3} = -\dfrac{1}{3}$

31. $-3^{-1} = -\dfrac{1}{3^1} = -\dfrac{1}{3}$

32. $(-3)^{-2} = \dfrac{1}{(-3)^2} = \dfrac{1}{9}$

33. $-3^{-2} = -\dfrac{1}{3^2} = -\dfrac{1}{9}$

34. $9^{\frac{1}{2}} = \sqrt{9} = \pm 3$

35. $16^{\frac{3}{4}} = \left(2^4\right)^{\frac{3}{4}} = 2^3 = 8$

36. $(3^{-1})^2 = 3^{-2} = \dfrac{1}{3^2} = \dfrac{1}{9}$

37. $(-8^{-3})^{\frac{2}{3}}$

$(-1)^{\frac{2}{3}}\left(2^{-9}\right)^{\frac{2}{3}} = \sqrt[3]{(-1)^2}\left(2^{-6}\right) = \dfrac{1}{64}$

38. $27^{-\frac{4}{3}} = 3^{-4} = \dfrac{1}{81} =$

39. $125^{-\frac{1}{3}} = 5^{-1} = \dfrac{1}{5} =$

40. $16^{\frac{3}{4}} = 2^3 = 8 =$

41. $(3^{-1})^2 = 3^{-2} = \dfrac{1}{9} =$

42. $(-8^{-3})^{\frac{2}{3}} = (-1)^{\frac{2}{3}} \cdot (8^{-3})^{\frac{2}{3}} = 1 \cdot 8^{-2} = \dfrac{1}{64}$

43. $(-27^{-1})^{\frac{2}{3}} = (-1)^{\frac{2}{3}} \cdot (27^{-1})^{\frac{2}{3}} = 1 \cdot 3^{-2} = \dfrac{1}{9}$

44. $(16^{-1})^{-\frac{3}{2}} = (2^{-4})^{-\frac{3}{2}} = 2^6 = 64$

45. $\left(\dfrac{1}{2}\right)^0 = 1$

46. $\left(\dfrac{1}{2}\right)^1 = \dfrac{1}{2}$

47. $\left(\dfrac{1}{2}\right)^{-1} = \dfrac{1}{\left(\dfrac{1}{2}\right)} = 2$

48. $\left(\dfrac{1}{2}\right)^2 = \dfrac{1}{4}$

49. $\left(\dfrac{1}{2}\right)^{-2} = \dfrac{1}{\left(\dfrac{1}{2}\right)^2} = 4$

50. $\left(\dfrac{3}{5}\right)^0 = 1$

51. $\left(\dfrac{3}{4}\right)^1 = \dfrac{3}{4}$

52. $\left(\dfrac{2}{5}\right)^{-1} = \dfrac{1}{\left(\dfrac{2}{5}\right)} = \dfrac{5}{2}$

53. $\left(\dfrac{5}{11}\right)^2 = \dfrac{25}{121}$

54. $\left(\dfrac{a}{b}\right)^{-1} = \dfrac{1}{\left(\dfrac{a}{b}\right)} = \dfrac{b}{a}$

55. $\left(\dfrac{1}{b}\right)^{-1} = \dfrac{1}{\left(\dfrac{1}{b}\right)} = b$

56. $b^{-1} = \dfrac{1}{b}$

57. $\left(\dfrac{-11}{2}\right)^{-2} = \dfrac{4}{121}$

58. $\left(\dfrac{3}{-2}\right)^{1} = -\dfrac{3}{2}$

59. $\left(\dfrac{-12}{\sqrt{2}}\right)^{-1} = -\dfrac{\sqrt{2}}{12}$

60. $\left(\dfrac{5\sqrt{2}}{11}\right)^{2} = \dfrac{50}{121}$

61. $\left(\dfrac{-2\sqrt{5}}{2}\right)^{-2} = \dfrac{1}{5}$

62. $\left(\dfrac{3+5\sqrt{2}}{-2}\right)^{2} = \dfrac{53+30\sqrt{2}}{4}$

63. $\left(\dfrac{-12}{2-\sqrt{2}}\right)^{-2} = \dfrac{6-4\sqrt{2}}{144}$

64. $\left(\dfrac{5+\sqrt{2}}{11}\right)^{2} = \dfrac{27+10\sqrt{2}}{121}$

65. $\left(\dfrac{-2-\sqrt{5}}{2+\sqrt{2}}\right)^{-2} = \dfrac{9+4\sqrt{5}}{6+4\sqrt{2}}$

66. $\left(\dfrac{-27}{8}\right)^{\frac{2}{3}} = \dfrac{9}{4}$

67. $\left(\dfrac{16}{9}\right)^{\frac{3}{4}} = \left(\dfrac{2^4}{3^2}\right)^{\frac{3}{4}} = \dfrac{2^3}{3^{\frac{3}{2}}} = \dfrac{8}{\sqrt{27}}$

68. $\left(\dfrac{1}{2}\right)^{\frac{3}{2}} =$

69. $\left(\dfrac{9}{16}\right)^{\frac{1}{2}} =$

70. $\left(\dfrac{8}{27}\right)^{-\frac{1}{3}} =$

71. $a^{-2} =$

72. $a^{-\frac{1}{2}} =$

73. $a^{-\frac{2}{7}} =$

74. $5^{27}5^{-29} = 5^{-2} = \dfrac{1}{25}$

75. $4^{27}2^{-49} = 2^5 = 32$

76. $9^{12}3^{-20} = 3^4 = 81$

77. $a^7 a^{-9} =$

78. $(-125)^{\frac{2}{3}} =$

79. $(-125)^{\frac{2}{3}} =$

$(-1)^{\frac{2}{3}}(5^3)^{\frac{2}{3}} = \sqrt[3]{(-1)^2}\cdot 5^2 = \sqrt[3]{1}\cdot 5^2 = 25$

80. $\dfrac{5^{10}}{5^2} = 5^8$

81. $\dfrac{3^1}{9^{\frac{1}{2}}}3^{-\frac{1}{2}} = 3^{1-\frac{1}{2}-1} = 3^{-\frac{1}{2}} = \dfrac{1}{\sqrt{3}}$

82. $\dfrac{\sqrt{2}\cdot 4^2}{2^{\frac{3}{4}}}2^{-\frac{1}{2}} = 2^{\frac{1}{2}+4-\frac{1}{2}-\frac{3}{4}} = 2^{\frac{13}{4}}$

83. $\dfrac{a^{-1}}{a^{-2}} = a$

84. $\sqrt{\dfrac{a^{-10}}{a^{-12}}} = a$

85. $\sqrt{\sqrt{a}} = a^{\frac{1}{4}}$

86. $\sqrt{a\sqrt{a}} = \sqrt{a^{\frac{1}{2}+1}} = a^{\frac{3}{4}}$

87. $a\sqrt{\sqrt[3]{a}} = a^{1+\frac{1}{6}} = a^{\frac{7}{6}}$

88. $\dfrac{1}{\sqrt[4]{\sqrt{\sqrt{a}}}} = a^{-\frac{1}{16}}$

89. $\sqrt{\sqrt{\sqrt[7]{a^2}}} = a^{\frac{1}{14}}$

90. $\sqrt[3]{\sqrt{a\sqrt{a^2}}} = a^{\frac{1}{4}}$

91. $\dfrac{2\sqrt{a}}{\sqrt{2a}} = \dfrac{2}{\sqrt{2}} = \sqrt{2}$

92. $\dfrac{\sqrt{a}}{\sqrt[3]{\sqrt{a}}} = a^{\frac{1}{2}-\frac{1}{6}} = a^{\frac{1}{3}}$

93. $\dfrac{a\sqrt{a}}{\sqrt[5]{\sqrt{a}}} = a^{\frac{3}{2}-\frac{1}{10}} = a^{\frac{7}{5}}$

94. $\dfrac{\sqrt{8}\sqrt{a}}{\sqrt{2a}} = 2a^{-\frac{1}{2}}$

95. $\sqrt{\dfrac{\sqrt{a a^{-1}}}{a\sqrt{a^{-2}}}} = a^{-\frac{1}{4}}$

96. $\dfrac{a}{\sqrt{2a^{-1}}} = \dfrac{a^{\frac{3}{2}}}{\sqrt{2}}$

97. $\dfrac{\sqrt{\dfrac{1}{a}}}{\sqrt{aa^{-2}}} = a^0 = 1$

98. $\left(\dfrac{2}{5}\right)^3 \times \left(\dfrac{5}{3}\right)^3 = \dfrac{2^3 5^3}{5^3 3^3} = \dfrac{8}{27}$

99. $\left(\dfrac{4}{7}\right)^2 \div \left(\dfrac{9}{7}\right)^2 = \dfrac{2^4 7^2}{7^2 3^4} = \dfrac{16}{81}$

100. $\left(\dfrac{2}{5}\right)^3 \cdot \left(\dfrac{3}{5}\right)^{-4} = \dfrac{2^3 3^{-4}}{5^3 5^{-4}} = \dfrac{8 \cdot 5}{81} =$

$= \dfrac{40}{81}$

101. $\left(\dfrac{3}{4}\right)^5 \div \left(\dfrac{9}{64}\right)^2 = \dfrac{3^5 \cdot 2^{12}}{2^{10} 3^4} = 3 \cdot 2^2 = 12$

102. $\left(\dfrac{7}{5}\right)^7 \div \left(\dfrac{49}{125}\right)^3 = \dfrac{7^7 \cdot 5^6}{5^7 7^6} = \dfrac{7}{5}$

103. $\left(\dfrac{2^{-3}}{3^{-2}}\right)^3 \cdot \left(\dfrac{4}{27}\right)^2 = \dfrac{2^{-9} \cdot 2^4}{3^{-6} 3^6} =$

$= 2^{-5} = \dfrac{1}{32}$

104. $\left(\dfrac{4^2}{5^{-1}}\right)^3 \cdot \left(\dfrac{25^{-1}}{64}\right)^2 = \dfrac{2^{12} 5^{-4}}{5^{-3} 2^{12}} =$

$= 5^{-1} = \dfrac{1}{5}$

105. $\left(\dfrac{3^{-5}}{4^2}\right)^2 \div \left(\dfrac{9^{-2}}{2^3}\right)^3 = \dfrac{3^{-10} 2^9}{2^8 3^{-18}} =$

$= 2 \cdot 3^8$

106. $\left(\dfrac{5^4}{7^{-3}}\right)^2 \div \left(\dfrac{25^{-1}}{49}\right)^{-3} = \dfrac{5^8 5^{-6}}{7^{-6} 7^6} =$

$= 5^2 = 25$

107. $2^{-1} + 2 = \dfrac{1}{2} + 2 = \dfrac{5}{2}$

108. $3^{-1} - 3^{-2} = \dfrac{1}{3} - \dfrac{1}{9} = \dfrac{2}{9}$

109. $5^{-1} - 5^{-2} = \dfrac{1}{5} - \dfrac{1}{25} = \dfrac{4}{25}$

110. $3^{-3} + 2^{-2} = \dfrac{1}{27} + \dfrac{1}{4} = \dfrac{31}{108}$

111. $3^{-2} + 4^{-2} = \dfrac{1}{9} + \dfrac{1}{4} = \dfrac{13}{36}$

112. $7^{-2} + 2^{-2} = \dfrac{1}{49} + \dfrac{1}{4} = \dfrac{53}{196}$

113. $8^{-2} - 3^{-2} = \dfrac{1}{64} - \dfrac{1}{9} = -\dfrac{55}{576}$

114. $7^{-2} - 2^{-3} = \dfrac{1}{49} - \dfrac{1}{8} = -\dfrac{41}{392}$

115. $a^{-1} + a^{-1} = \dfrac{1}{a} + \dfrac{1}{a} = \dfrac{2}{a}$

116. $ba^{-1} + a^{-1} = \dfrac{b}{a} + \dfrac{1}{a} = \dfrac{b+1}{a}$

117. $2x^{-1} + x^{-2} = \dfrac{2}{x} + \dfrac{1}{x^2} = \dfrac{2x+1}{x^2}$

118. $a^{-1} - ba^{-1} = \dfrac{1}{a} - \dfrac{b}{a} = \dfrac{1-b}{a}$

119. $(ba)^{-1} + a^{-1} = \dfrac{1}{ab} + \dfrac{1}{a} = \dfrac{1+b}{ab}$

120. $\dfrac{1}{x} + x^{-2} = \dfrac{1}{x} + \dfrac{1}{x^2} = \dfrac{x+1}{x^2}$

121. $ba^{-1} + (ba)^{-1} = \dfrac{b}{a} + \dfrac{1}{ab} = \dfrac{b^2+1}{ab}$

122. $\dfrac{a+a}{3a} = \dfrac{2}{3}$

123. $\dfrac{2a+a}{5\sqrt{a}} = \dfrac{3}{5}a^{-\frac{1}{2}}$

124. $\dfrac{a^2+a^3}{2a} = \dfrac{a+a^2}{2}$

125. $\dfrac{4b^{-1}a^2}{2ba^{-1}} = 2a^3b^{-2}$

126. $\dfrac{4b^{-3}}{\sqrt{2b}} = 2^{\frac{3}{2}}b^{-\frac{7}{2}}$

127. $\dfrac{9b^{-\frac{1}{2}}a^2}{27^{-1}b^{-1}a} = 3^5ab^{\frac{1}{2}}$

128. $\dfrac{4b^{-1}a^5a^2}{8ba^{-1}} = 2^{-1}a^8b^{-2}$

129. $\dfrac{\sqrt[4]{a^2}+\sqrt{a}}{\sqrt{2a}} = \dfrac{2}{\sqrt{2}} = \sqrt{2}$

130. $\dfrac{b\sqrt[3]{a}+ba^{\frac{1}{3}}}{a\sqrt{b}} = \dfrac{2ba^{\frac{1}{3}}}{a\sqrt{b}} = 2\sqrt{b}a^{-\frac{2}{3}}$

131. $\dfrac{3^{-2}}{9^{\frac{2}{3}}}27^{\frac{5}{4}} = 3^{-2+\frac{15}{4}-2} = 3^{-\frac{1}{4}} = \dfrac{1}{\sqrt[4]{3}}$

132. $\dfrac{4^{-4}\sqrt{2}}{8^{-\frac{2}{3}}}16^{\frac{3}{4}} = 2^{-8+\frac{1}{2}+3+2} = 2^{-\frac{5}{2}} =$

$= \dfrac{1}{\sqrt{2^5}} = \dfrac{1}{\sqrt{32}}$

133. $\sqrt{5}\dfrac{25^2 5^{-1}}{25^{\frac{4}{3}}}5^{\frac{1}{4}}\sqrt[3]{5} = 5^{\frac{1}{2}+4-1+\frac{1}{4}+\frac{1}{3}-\frac{8}{3}} = 5^{\frac{17}{12}}$

134. $\dfrac{4^{-2}2^{-4}}{16^2(\sqrt[6]{16^4})}8^{\frac{1}{4}}2^{-1} = 2^{-4-4+\frac{3}{4}-1-8-\frac{8}{3}} = 2^{-\frac{227}{12}}$

135. $x\sqrt{x}\sqrt{3} = \sqrt{3x^{\frac{3}{2}}} = \sqrt{3x^3}$

136. $x\sqrt{x}+\sqrt{2x} = x^{\frac{3}{2}}+\sqrt{2}\cdot x^{\frac{1}{2}}$

137. $\dfrac{1}{x\sqrt{x}} = x^{-\frac{3}{2}}$

138. $\dfrac{x\sqrt[3]{x}}{\sqrt{x}} = x^{1+\frac{1}{3}-\frac{1}{2}} = x^{\frac{7}{6}} = \sqrt[6]{x^7}$

139. $\dfrac{\sqrt{2x}}{x\sqrt{4x}} = \dfrac{1}{x\sqrt{2}} = 2^{-\frac{1}{2}}x^{-1}$

140. $\dfrac{\sqrt{3x}}{x+x^2} = \dfrac{\sqrt{3x}}{x(1+x)} = \dfrac{\sqrt{3}}{\sqrt{x}(1+x)}$

141. $\dfrac{\sqrt{3x}}{\sqrt[3]{3x^2}} = 3^{\frac{1}{6}}x^{-\frac{1}{6}} = \sqrt[6]{\dfrac{3}{x}}$

142. $\dfrac{\sqrt{25x^2}}{\sqrt[3]{5x^3}} = 5^{\frac{2}{3}} = \sqrt[3]{25}$

143. $s^n s^{2n} s^2 = s^{3n+2}$

144. $a^{2k}ba^3b^{2k}a = a^{2k+4}b^{2k+1}$

145. $\dfrac{3^n}{9^n}27^n = 3^{n+3n-2n} = 3^{2n}$

146. $\dfrac{3^{2n+1}}{81^{n-2}}27^{2n} = 3^{2n+1+6n-4n+8} = 3^{4n+9}$

147. $\dfrac{6^n}{8^{2n}}24^{3n}=\dfrac{2^n3^n}{2^{6n}}2^{9n}3^{3n}=2^{4n}3^{4n}=6^{4n}$

148. $\dfrac{2^n}{8^{n+1}}16^{n-2}=2^{n+4(n-2)-3(n-1)}=2^{2n-5}$

149. $\dfrac{5^{-n}}{125^{2n-2}}5^{-n+2}=5^{-n-n+2-3(2n-2)}=5^{-8n+8}$

150. $\dfrac{12^{2n+1}}{48^{3n-1}}\div 36^{4n}=\dfrac{3^{2n+1}2^{4n+4}}{3^{3n-1}2^{12n-4}}2^{-8n}3^{-8n}=$
$=2^{-16n+8}3^{-9n+2}$

151. $\dfrac{x^{-n}}{x^{2n-2}}x^{-n+5}=x^{-4n+7}$

152. $\dfrac{2x^{-n+1}}{2^2x^{3n+2}}x^{n+5}=2^{-1}x^{-3n+4}$

153. $\dfrac{2yx^{-2n+3}}{2^5y^{-1}x^{-4n+2}}x^{-2n+1}=2^{-4}x^2y^2$

154. $\dfrac{4^2y^2x^{-3}z}{2^2xz^2y^{-1}x}x^{-2}z^2=2^2x^{-7}y^3z$

155. $\dfrac{4^2y^2(x^{-2}z^2)^{-2}}{(2^2x)^3z^2y^{-1}x}x^{-2}z^2=2^{-2}x^{-1}y^3z^{-4}$

156. $\dfrac{4^{-2}y^3(x^{-2}z^3)^{-1}}{(2^{-3}x)^{-3}z^{-2}y^{-1}x}xz^2=2^{-13}x^5y^4z$

157. $\left(\dfrac{a}{b^2}\right)^2\div\left(\dfrac{a^{-1}}{b^3}\right)^{-3}\cdot\left(\dfrac{1}{b}\right)^3=a^{-1}b^2$

158. $\left(\dfrac{ab}{b^2}\right)^{-2}\div\left(\dfrac{(2ba)^{-1}}{b^3}\right)^{-3}\cdot\left(\dfrac{2}{b}\right)^3=a^{-5}b^{-13}$

159. $\dfrac{a^{-2}b^n(a^{-2n}b^3)^{-1}}{(b^{-3n}a)^3\sqrt{ab^{-1}}}==$
$=a^{-2+2n-3-\frac{1}{2}}b^{n-3+9n+1}=a^{-\frac{11}{2}+2n}b^{10n-2}$

160. $\dfrac{a^{-2}b^n(a^{-2n}b^2)^n}{(b^{-3n}a)^na^{-2n}b^n}==$
$=a^{-2-2n^2-n+2n}b^{n+2n+3n^2-n}=a^{-2n^2+n-2}b^{3n^2+2n}$

161. $\dfrac{3^na^{-2}b^n(a^{-2n}b^3)^{n+1}}{(9^nb^{-2n}a)^na^{-2n}b^{n+2}}=$
$=3^{n-2n^2}a^{-2n^2-n-2}b^{2n^2+3n+1}$

162. $\dfrac{3^n+3^{n+1}}{3^{n-1}}=\dfrac{3^n(1+3)}{\left(3^n\cdot\dfrac{1}{3}\right)}=12$

163. $\dfrac{4^n+4^{n-1}}{2^{n-2}}=\dfrac{2^{2n}(1+\dfrac{1}{4})}{\left(2^n\cdot\dfrac{1}{4}\right)}=5\cdot 2^n$

164. $\dfrac{7^{2n}+7^{2n-1}}{7^{2n-2}}=\dfrac{7^{2n}(1+\dfrac{1}{7})}{\left(7^{2n}\cdot\dfrac{1}{49}\right)}=56$

165. $\dfrac{7^{3n-1}-7^{3n}}{7^{2n-2}}=$

$=\dfrac{7^{3n}(\dfrac{1}{7}-1)}{\left(7^{2n}\cdot\dfrac{1}{49}\right)}=-42\cdot 7^n=-6\cdot 7^{n+1}$

166. $\dfrac{3^n+3^{n+1}}{3^{n-1}+3^n}=\dfrac{3^n(1+3)}{3^n(\dfrac{1}{3}+1)}=3$

167. $\dfrac{2^n+2^{n-1}}{2^{n-2}+2^{n-1}}=\dfrac{2^n(1+\dfrac{1}{2})}{2^n(\dfrac{1}{4}+\dfrac{1}{2})}=2$

168. $\dfrac{2^n-2^{n-1}+2^{n-2}}{2^{n-2}+2^{n-1}-2^n}=\dfrac{2^n(1-\dfrac{1}{2}+\dfrac{1}{4})}{2^n(\dfrac{1}{4}+\dfrac{1}{2}-1)}=-1$

169. $\dfrac{3^n-3^{n-3}+3^{n-2}}{3^{n-2}-3^{n-1}-3^n}=\dfrac{3^n(1-\dfrac{1}{27}+\dfrac{1}{9})}{3^n(\dfrac{1}{9}-\dfrac{1}{3}-1)}=$
$=\dfrac{\left(\dfrac{29}{27}\right)}{\left(-\dfrac{33}{27}\right)}=-\dfrac{29}{33}$

1.5 – ALGEBRAIC EXPRESSIONS

Expand and/or Sum and simplify as much as possible:

1. $x + x = 2x$
2. $x - 2x = -x$
3. $xy + xy = 2xy$
4. $3x^2 y - xy = xy(3x - 1)$
5. $x^2 + x - 5x^2 = -4x^2 + x = x(-4x + 1)$
6. $3xy^2 + xy - x^2 y + 7xy =$
   $3xy^2 - x^2 y + 8xy = xy(3y - x + 8)$
7. $x + y - (2x - 3y) = -x + 4y$
8. $2(x^2 y + xy) - x(2xy - 3y) = 5xy$
9. $b(ab + b) - a(b^2 - b) = b^2 + ab =$
   $= b(b + a)$
10. $x + \dfrac{x}{2} = \dfrac{3x}{2}$
11. $a + 2(\dfrac{a}{2} - 3a) = -4a$
12. $2(5z^2 y^3 + 3zy^3) - 2zy(6zy^2 - 8y^2) =$
    $= -2z^2 y^3 + 22zy^3 = zy^3(-2z + 22)$
13. $2(5z^2 y^3 \cdot 3zy^3) = 30z^3 y^6$
14. $b \cdot ab^3 ab = a^2 b^4$
15. $b(ab \cdot b) \cdot a(b^2) = a^2 b^5$
16. $x \cdot ayb^6 yxb^2 = y^2 x^2 b^8$
17. $x^m x = x^{m+1}$
18. $a^n x^m x^t = a^n x^{m+t}$
19. $\sqrt{x} + \sqrt{x} = 2\sqrt{x}$
20. $\sqrt{x} \cdot \sqrt{x} = x$
21. $x(5 + x) = 5x + x^2$
22. $(x + 1)^2 = x^2 + 2x + 1$
23. $(x - 1)^2 = x^2 - 2x + 1$
24. $(x + 2)^2 = x^2 + 4x + 4$
25. $(x - 2)^2 = x^2 - 4x + 4$
26. $(a + b)^2 = a^2 + 2ab + b^2$
27. $(a - b)^2 = a^2 - 2ab + b^2$
28. $(2a + b)^2 = 4a^2 + 4ab + b^2$
29. $(a - 3b)^2 = a^2 - 6ab + 9b^2$
30. $(2x + 3)^2 = 4x^2 + 6x + 9$
31. $(4 - x)^2 = 16 - 8x + x^2$
32. $(x + 2)(x - 3) = x^2 - x - 6$

33. $(x - 2)(x + 2) = x^2 - 4$
34. $(3 + x)(x - 7) = x^2 - 4x - 21$
35. $(2x + 2)(x - 5) = 2x^2 - 8x - 10$
36. $(3x - 1)(x + 2) = 3x^2 + 5x - 2$
37. $(x - 1)(x + 1) = x^2 - 1$
38. $(x - 2)(x + 2) = x^2 - 4$
39. $(x - a)(x + a) = x^2 - a^2$
40. $\sqrt{x} \cdot \sqrt{x} \cdot \sqrt{x} \cdot \sqrt{x} = x^2$
41. $\sqrt{x} + \sqrt{x} + \sqrt{x} + \sqrt{x} = 4\sqrt{x}$
42. $2\sqrt{x} + 3\sqrt{x} - \sqrt{x} - \sqrt{x} = 3\sqrt{x}$
43. $(x - \sqrt{a})(x + \sqrt{a}) = x^2 - a$
44. $(x + 4)(x^2 - 4x + 3) =$
    $= x^3 - 19x + 12$
45. $(x + 6)(x^5 - 6x^2 - 3x + 1) =$
    $x^6 + 6x^5 - 6x^3 - 39x^2 - 17x + 6$
46. $(x - a)(x + 2a + b) = x^2 + ax + xb - 2a^2 - ab$
47. $(\sqrt{7} - \sqrt{x})(\sqrt{7} + \sqrt{x}) = 7 - x$
48. $(ax - \sqrt{b})(ax + \sqrt{b}) = a^2 x^2 - b$
49. $(\sqrt{a} - \sqrt{b})(\sqrt{a} + \sqrt{b}) = a - b$
50. $(6 - \dfrac{x}{8})(6 + \dfrac{8}{x}) = 35 - \dfrac{3x}{4} - \dfrac{48}{x}$
51. $(\dfrac{1}{x} - \dfrac{x}{8})(x + \dfrac{8}{x}) = \dfrac{8}{x^2} - \dfrac{x^2}{8}$
52. $(\sqrt{7} - \sqrt{x})(\sqrt{7} + \dfrac{1}{\sqrt{x}}) = 6 - \sqrt{7x} - \dfrac{\sqrt{7}}{\sqrt{x}}$
53. $(2x - 3c)(2x + 3c - 1) = 4x^2 - 2x - 9c^2 + 3c$
54. $x(x + 8)^2 = x^3 + 16x^2 + 64x$
55. $(x - 6)^2 3x = 3x^3 - 26x^2 + 108x$
56. $(5 - \sqrt{ab})(5 + \sqrt{ab}) = 25 - ab$
57. $2 - (x + 1)^2 = -x^2 - 2x + 1$
58. $(x + 3)^2 - (x + 2)^2 = 2x + 5$
59. $(x - 2)^2 + (x + 2)^2 = 2x^2 + 8$
60. $(x - \sqrt{2})^2 = x^2 - 2\sqrt{2}x + 2$
61. $(x - \sqrt{2})(x + \sqrt{2}) = x^2 - 2$
62. $5(2x - \sqrt{a})(2x + \sqrt{a}) = 20x^2 - 5a$

63. $(\sqrt{a} - \sqrt{b})^2 = a - 2\sqrt{ab} + b$

64. $2(x - \sqrt{10})(x + \sqrt{10}) = 2x^2 - 10$

65. $(x - \frac{2}{x})^2 = x^2 - 4 + 4x^{-2}$

66. $(x - \frac{2}{\sqrt{x}})^2 = x^2 - 4\sqrt{x} + 4x^{-1}$

67. $(3x - \frac{2}{3\sqrt{x}})^2 = 9x^2 - 4\sqrt{x} + \frac{4}{9x}$

68. $2(\sqrt{a} - \frac{1}{\sqrt{a}})^2 = 2a - 4 + 2a^{-1}$

69. $(\sqrt{a} - \frac{1}{\sqrt{a}})(-\sqrt{a} - \frac{1}{\sqrt{a}}) = -a + a^{-1}$

70. $(2^x + 2^{-x})^2 = 2^{2x} + 2 + 2^{-2x}$

71. $(4^{2x} + 2^{-x})^2 = 2^{8x} + 2^{3x+1} + 2^{-2x}$

72. $(3^{2x} + 3^{-2x})^2 = 3^{4x} + 2 + 3^{-4x}$

73. $(7^x - 7)^2 = 7^{2x} - 2 \cdot 7^{x+1} + 49$

74. $(a^{nx} - b^{nx})^2 = a^{2nx} - 2a^{nx}b^{nx} + b^{2nx}$

75. $(x^2 - y^2)(x^2 + y^2) = x^4 - y^4$

76. $(x^3 - y^3)(x^3 + y^3) = x^6 - y^6$

77. $(x^n - y^n)(x^n + y^n) = x^{2n} - y^{2n}$

78. $(a^x - b^x)^2 = a^{2x} - 2a^x b^x + b^{2x}$

79. $(a^{mx} - a^{-mx})^2 = a^{2mx} - 2 + b^{-2mx}$

80. $(a^{mx} - a^{-mx})(a^{mx} + a^{-mx}) = a^{2mx} - a^{-2mx}$

Given the following polynomials, obtain the maximum possible common factor:

1. $x - ax = x(1 - a)$
2. $3x - x - ax = x(2 - a)$
3. $-x + ax = x(a - 1)$
4. $xy + 2x = x(y + 2)$
5. $8xy - 2y = 2x(4y - 1)$
6. $-6x + 12xy = 6x(2y - 1)$
7. $12xyz + 2xy = 2xy(6z - 1)$
8. $14xy - 2yz = 2y(7x - z)$
9. $12xz + 14xyz = 2xz(6 + 7y)$
10. $xy + 4y^2 + 5y = y(x+4y+5)$
11. $z - 4z^2 + 8zy = z(1 - 4z + 8y)$
12. $-8x^3 - 4xyz = -4x(x^2 + yz)$
13. $-6x^4 + x^2y^2 + x^2 = x^2(-6x^2 + y^2 + 1)$
14. $-9x^7y^3 + 3x^3y = 3yx^2(-3y^2x^5 + x)$
15. $-90x^{10}y^5 - 3x^3y^4 = -3x^3y^4(-30x^7y + 1)$

16. $-80x^4y^6z^8 + 8x^{12}y^4z^6 =$
    $8x^4y^4z^6(-10x^8y^2z^2 + x^8)$
17. $xyz + 2x^2y^2z^2 + 3x^3y^3z^3 =$
    $xyz(1 + 2xyz + x^2y^2z^2)$
18. $10x^3y^2z^4 + 2x^2y^6z^4 - 5x^2y^4z^2 =$
    $x^2y^2z^2(10x z^2 + 2 z^2y^4 + 5y^2)$
19. $20x^{30}y^{20}z^{40} - 2x^{20}y^{60}z^{40} - 2x^{20}y^{40}z^{20} =$
    $2x^{20}y^{20}z^{20}(10x^2z^{20} - z^{20}y^{40} - y^{20})$
20. $ax^m + x^m = x^m(a + 1)$
21. $ax^{m+1} + x^m = x^m(ax + 1)$
22. $ax^m + x^{m-1} = x^m(a + x^{-1})$
23. $ax^m - x = x(ax^{m-1} - 1)$
24. $-ax^m - x^{2m} = -x^m(a + x^m)$
25. $z^{n+1} - z^{n+2} = z^n(z - z^2)$
26. $ax^{m+2} + x^{m-1} = x^{m-1}(ax^3 + 1)$

Given the following polynomials factor, if possible.

1. $x^2 - 6x + 9 = (x - 3)^2$
2. $x^2 - 5x + 6 = (x - 3)(x - 2)$
3. $x^2 + 4x + 10 = Not\ possible$
4. $-x^2 - x + 6 = -(x + 3)(x - 2)$
5. $x^2 + x - 6 = (x + 3)(x - 2)$
6. $x^2 + 5x + 6 = (x + 3)(x + 2)$
7. $-x^2 + 7x - 10 = -(x - 2)(x - 5)$
8. $x^2 - 6x + 12 = Not\ possible$
9. $x^2 + 3x + 2 = (x + 2)(x + 1)$
10. $x^2 - x - 2 = (x - 2)(x + 1)$
11. $-x^2 + 4x = -x(x - 4)$

12. $-x^2 + 4x - 10 = Not\ possible$
13. $x^2 + x - 2 = (x + 2)(x - 1)$
14. $x^2 + 3x + 7 = Not\ possible$
15. $x^2 - 3x + 2 = (x - 2)(x - 1)$
16. $x^2 - x + 7 = Not\ possible$
17. $x^2 + 5x + 9 = Not\ possible$
18. $-x^2 - 5x + 6 = Not\ possible$
19. $x^2 - 2xa + a^2 = (x - a)^2$
20. $x^2 - a^2 = (x - a)(x + a)$
21. $c^2 - a^2 = (c - a)(c + a)$
22. $x^2 - x = x(x - 1)$

23. $2x^2 - x = x(2x - 1)$

24. $2x^2 + 3x = x(2x + 3)$

25. $x^2 + 5x = x(x + 5)$

26. $x^2 - 7x + 12 = (x - 3)(x - 4)$

27. $2x^2 - 4x = 2x(x - 2)$

28. $x^2 - 7x + 10 = (x - 2)(x - 5)$

29. $x^2 - 7x + 6 = (x - 1)(x - 6)$

30. $x^2 - x - 12 = (x - 4)(x + 3)$

31. $x^2 + x - 12 = (x + 4)(x - 3)$

32. $x^2 - 3x - 10 = (x - 5)(x + 2)$

33. $x^2 - 8x - 9 = (x - 9)(x + 1)$

34. $x^2 - 1 = (x - 1)(x + 1)$

35. $x^2 + 1 = Not \quad possible$

36. $x^2 - 2 = (x - \sqrt{2})(x + \sqrt{2})$

37. $x^2 - 3 = (x - \sqrt{3})(x + \sqrt{3})$

38. $x^2 - 4 = (x - 2)(x + 2)$

39. $-x^2 + 1 = -(x + 1)(x - 1)$

40. $-x^2 + 2 = -(x + \sqrt{2})(x - \sqrt{2})$

41. $-x^2 + 3 = -(x + \sqrt{3})(x - \sqrt{3})$

42. $-x^2 + 4 = -(x + 2)(x - 2)$

43. $-x^2 + 13 = -(x + \sqrt{13})(x - \sqrt{13})$

44. $-x^2 + 49 = -(x + 7)(x - 7)$

45. $2x^2 - 72 = 2(x + 6)(x - 6)$

46. $-x^2 - 2 = Not \quad possible$

47. $5x^2 - 125 = 5(x - 5)(x + 5)$

48. $-x^2 + 81 = -(x + 9)(x - 9)$

49. $-3x^2 + 27 = -3(x + 3)(x - 3)$

50. $2x^2 - 6 = 2(x + \sqrt{3})(x - \sqrt{3})$

51. $3x^2 - 1 = 3(x + \sqrt{\frac{1}{3}})(x - \sqrt{\frac{1}{3}})$

52. $-2x^2 - 3 = -2(x^2 + \frac{3}{2})$

53. $5x^2 - 6 = 5(x - \sqrt{\frac{6}{5}})(x + \sqrt{\frac{6}{5}})$

54. $4x^2 - 2 = 4(x - \sqrt{\frac{1}{2}})(x + \sqrt{\frac{1}{2}})$

55. $-8x^2 - 1 = -8(x^2 + \frac{1}{8})$

56. $x^2 - b = (x + \sqrt{b})(x - \sqrt{b})$

57. $ax^2 - b = a(x + \sqrt{\frac{b}{a}})(x - \sqrt{\frac{b}{a}})$

58. $-ax^2 + b = -a(x + \sqrt{\frac{b}{a}})(x - \sqrt{\frac{b}{a}})$

59. $2x^2 - 4x + 2 = 2(x - 1)^2$

60. $3x^2 - 3x - 18 = 3(x - 3)(x + 2)$

61. $-4x^2 + 20x + 24 = -4(x - 6)(x + 1)$

62. $7x^2 + 7x - 630 = 7(x + 10)(x - 9)$

63. $-5x^2 + 10x + 75 = -5(x - 5)(x + 3)$

64. $3x^2 - 12x - 63 = 3(x - 7)(x + 3)$

65. $2x^2 + 2x - 112 = 2(x + 8)(x - 7)$

66. $2x^2 - 12x - 14 = 2(x - 7)(x + 1)$

67. $-5x^2 + 15x + 90 = -5(x - 6)(x + 3)$

68. $-3x^2 - 12x - 12 = -3(x + 2)^2$

69. $-2x^2 - 26x - 84 = -2(x + 6)(x + 7)$

70. $6x^2 + 48x + 72 = 6(x + 6)(x + 2)$

Conclusion:

Factoring a quadratic expression is possible only if <u>discriminant > 0</u> Example:
$x^2 + 5x + 6 = (x + 2)(x + 3), discri \min ant = 1 > 0$ If <u>discriminant = 0</u> both factors <u>are</u>
<u>identical</u> Example: $x^2 + 6x + 9 = (x + 3)(x + 3), discri \min ant = 0$
If <u>discriminant < 0, the quadratic expression cannot be factorized</u> Example:
$x^2 + 6x + 10, discri \min ant = -4 < 0$

Factor and simplify:

1. $\dfrac{x^2-6x+9}{x^2-7x+12}=\dfrac{(x-3)}{(x-4)}$

2. $\dfrac{x^2-5x+6}{x^2+x-6}=\dfrac{(x-3)}{(x+3)}$

3. $\dfrac{x^2-9}{x^2-7x+12}=\dfrac{(x+3)}{(x-4)}$

4. $\dfrac{x^2-1}{x^2-2x+1}=\dfrac{(x+1)}{(x-1)}$

5. $\dfrac{x^2-6x+8}{x^2-4x+4}=\dfrac{(x-4)}{(x-2)}$

6. $\dfrac{x^2-16}{x^2+5x+4}=\dfrac{(x-4)}{(x+1)}$

7. $\dfrac{x^2-x-2}{x^2+6x+5}=\dfrac{(x-2)}{(x+5)}$

8. $\dfrac{3x+9}{x^2-9}=\dfrac{3}{(x-3)}$

9. $\dfrac{x^2-6x}{x^2-7x+6}=\dfrac{x}{(x-1)}$

10. $\dfrac{x^2-x}{x^2+x-2}=\dfrac{x}{(x+2)}$

11. $\dfrac{x^2-4}{x^2+x-2}=\dfrac{(x-2)}{(x-1)}$

12. $\dfrac{4-x}{x-4}=-1$

13. $\dfrac{x^2-x}{1-x}=-x$

14. $\dfrac{2x-1}{4x^2-4x+1}=\dfrac{1}{(2x-1)}$

15. $\dfrac{x^2-2x}{x^2-4}=\dfrac{x}{(x+2)}$

16. $\dfrac{4x^2+4x+1}{2x^2+5x+2}=\dfrac{(2x+1)}{(x+2)}$

17. $\dfrac{3x^2+4x+1}{9x^2-1}=\dfrac{(3x+1)}{(3x-1)}$

18. $\dfrac{4x^2+4x-3}{2x^2-13x+15}=\dfrac{(2x-1)(2x+3)}{(x-5)(2x-3)}$

19. $\dfrac{4x^2+4x-3}{2x^2+13x+15}=\dfrac{(2x-1)}{(x+5)}$

20. $\dfrac{5x^2-12x+4}{10x^2+16x-8}=\dfrac{(x-2)}{(2x+4)}$

21. $\dfrac{3x^2-20x-7}{x^2-9x+14}=\dfrac{(3x+1)(x-7)}{(x-7)(x-2)}=\dfrac{(3x+1)}{(x-2)}$

22. $\dfrac{4x^2-2x-20}{x^2-3x+10}=\dfrac{(2x+4)(2x-5)}{(x+2)(x-5)}=\dfrac{2(2x-5)}{(x-5)}$

23. $\dfrac{2x^2-13x+6}{2x^2-14x+12}=\dfrac{(2x-1)(x-6)}{(2x-2)(x-6)}=\dfrac{(2x-1)}{(2x-2)}$

24. $\dfrac{81x^2+162x+81}{x^2-1}=\dfrac{(9x+9)^2}{(x-1)(x+1)}=\dfrac{81(x+1)}{(x-1)}$

25. $\dfrac{4x^2+11x+6}{4x^2+15x+9}=\dfrac{(4x+3)(x+2)}{(4x+3)(x+3)}=\dfrac{(x+2)}{(x+3)}$

26. $\dfrac{4x^2+12x+9}{4x^2-9}=\dfrac{(2x+3)(2x+3)}{(2x-3)(2x+3)}=\dfrac{(2x+3)}{(2x-3)}$

27. $\dfrac{4x^2-20x+25}{2x^2-15x+25}=\dfrac{(2x-5)(2x-5)}{(2x-5)(x-5)}=\dfrac{(2x-5)}{(x-5)}$

28. $\dfrac{7x^2+2x-5}{x^2-4x-5}=\dfrac{(7x-5)(x+1)}{(x-5)(x+1)}=\dfrac{(7x-5)}{(x-5)}$

29. $\dfrac{2x^2+15x+27}{2x^2+3x-27}=\dfrac{(2x+9)(x+3)}{(2x+9)(x-3)}=\dfrac{(x+3)}{(x-3)}$

30. $\dfrac{4x^2+6x+2}{2x^2-2}=\dfrac{(2x+1)(2x+2)}{2(x-1)(x+1)}=\dfrac{(2x+1)}{(x-1)}$

1.6. – PERCENTAGES

1. A percentage is <u>a way to represent a part of a whole</u> we sometimes use <u>a fraction</u> or a <u>decimal number</u> to represent it.

2. Write as a fraction and as a decimal:

   a. $1\% = \dfrac{1}{100} = 0.01$

   b. $10\% = \dfrac{10}{100} = 0.1$

   c. $89\% = \dfrac{89}{100} = 0.89$

   d. $100\% = \dfrac{100}{100} = 1$

   e. $101\% = \dfrac{101}{100} = 1.01$

   f. $110\% = \dfrac{110}{100} = 1.1$

   g. $200\% = \dfrac{200}{100} = 2$

   h. $0.1\% = \dfrac{1}{1000} = 0.001$

   i. $0.13\% = \dfrac{13}{10000} = 0.0013$

   j. $0.06\% = \dfrac{6}{10000} = 0.0006$

   k. $0.072\% = \dfrac{72}{100000} = 0.00072$

   l. $1.03\% = \dfrac{103}{10000} = 0.0103$

   m. $7.056\% = \dfrac{7056}{100000} = 0.07056$

   n. $5356\% = \dfrac{5356}{100} = 53.56$

A PERCENTAGE OF A QUANTITY

3. Find (write the expression and simplify it to get a final answer):

   a. 1% of 900 = <u>9</u>
   b. 2% of 900 = <u>18</u>
   c. 3% of 900 = <u>27</u>
   d. 10% of 900 = <u>90</u>
   e. 15% of 900 = <u>135</u>
   f. 20% of 900 = <u>180</u>
   g. 25% of 900 = <u>225</u>
   h. 35% of 900 = <u>315</u>

   i. 100% of 900 = <u>900</u>
   j. 101% of 900 = <u>909</u>
   k. 110% of 900 = <u>990</u>
   l. 120% of 900 = <u>1080</u>
   m. 125% of 900 = <u>1125</u>
   n. 140% of 900 = <u>1260</u>
   o. 200% of 900 = <u>1800</u>
   p. 300% of 900 = <u>2700</u>

4. Find (write the expression and simplify it to get a final answer):

   a. 1% of 50 = <u>0.5</u>
   b. 2% of 50 = <u>1</u>
   c. 10% of 70 = <u>7</u>
   d. 15% of 90 = <u>13.5</u>
   e. 20% of 110 = <u>22</u>
   f. 25% of 350 = <u>87.5</u>
   g. 35% of 1100 = <u>385</u>
   h. 100% of 125 = <u>125</u>
   i. 101% of 520 = <u>525.2</u>

   j. 110% of 130 = <u>143</u>
   k. 120% of 122 = <u>146.4</u>
   l. 125% of 250 = <u>312.5</u>
   m. 140% of 9100 = <u>12740</u>
   n. 200% of 240 = <u>480</u>
   o. 300% of 120 = <u>360</u>
   p. A% of M $= \dfrac{AM}{100}$

5. His score $\dfrac{130}{200} = \dfrac{65}{100} = 65\%$

6. $\dfrac{17}{20} = 0.85 = 18\%$

7. Her score $\dfrac{70}{80} = 0.875 = 87.5\%$

8. $P_{shaded} = \dfrac{\left(\dfrac{90}{100}x\right) \cdot \left(\dfrac{90}{100}x\right)}{x^2} = \dfrac{81}{100} = 81\%$

   $P_{NotShaded} = 100 - 81 = 19\%$

9.
$$P_{NotShaded} = \frac{\pi\left(\frac{x}{2}\right)^2}{x^2} = \frac{\pi}{4} \approx 0.785 = 78.5\%$$
$$P_{Shaded} = 100 - 78.5 = 21.5\%$$

10.
$$A_{Big} = xy$$
$$A_{small} = \left(\frac{40}{100}x\right)\left(\frac{60}{100}x\right) = \frac{24}{100}xy$$
$$P_{NotShaded} = \frac{\left(\frac{24}{100}xy\right)}{xy} = \frac{24}{100} = 24\%$$
$$P_{Shaded} = 100 - 24 = 76\%$$

11.
a.
$$P_{Brown} = \frac{15}{80} = 0.1875 = 18.75\%$$
$$White = \frac{15}{100} \cdot 80 = 12\,cookies$$
$$P_{Black} = \frac{80 - 12 - 15}{80} = \frac{53}{80} = 0.6625 = 66.25\%$$

b.
$$P_{Brown} = \frac{13}{78} \approx 0.167 = 16.7\%$$
$$P_{White} = \frac{10}{78} \approx 0.128 = 12.8\%$$
$$P_{Black} = \frac{51}{78} = 0.654 = 65.4\%$$

12. His benefit $\frac{1000}{4000} = \frac{25}{100} = 25\%$

13. Her lost $\frac{1000}{4000} = \frac{25}{100} = 25\%$

14. The percentage of it that is shaded: <u>50%</u>

15. The percentage of it that is shaded: $\frac{1}{8} = \frac{12.5}{100} = 12.5\%$

16. The percentage of the circle that is

Shaded: $\frac{20}{360} = \frac{1}{18} \approx 0.0556 = 0.556\%$ Not Shaded: $\frac{340}{360} = \frac{17}{18} \approx 0.944 = 9.44\%$

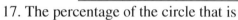

17. The percentage of the circle that is

Shaded: $\frac{30}{100} \cdot \frac{60}{100} = \frac{18}{100} = 18\%$ Not Shaded: <u>82%</u>

18. $\frac{20}{100} \cdot \frac{75}{100} 40 = \frac{600}{100} = 6$ *Students*

19. The amount. $\frac{10}{100} \cdot \frac{40}{100} x = 40$; $x = 1000$

20. The amount. $\frac{60}{100} \cdot \frac{40}{100} x = 20$; $x = \frac{2000}{24}$ *euros*

21. 10% of 20% of 30% of 200. $\frac{10}{100} \cdot \frac{20}{100} \cdot \frac{30}{100} \cdot 200 = 1.2$

22. 20% of 30% of 30% of 300. $\frac{20}{100} \cdot \frac{30}{100} \cdot \frac{30}{100} \cdot 300 = 1.8$

23. Find 80% of 120% of 400. $\frac{80}{100} \cdot \frac{120}{100} \cdot 400 = 384$

24. Find 90% of 130% of 70% 500. $\dfrac{90}{100}\cdot\dfrac{130}{100}\cdot\dfrac{70}{100}\cdot 500 = 409.5$

25. The amount. $\dfrac{20}{100}\cdot\dfrac{20}{100}x = 5$; $x = 125\,euros$

26. The amount. $\dfrac{10}{100}\cdot\dfrac{30}{100}\cdot\dfrac{5}{100}x = 50$; $x = 33333.333...euros$

27. $20\pi = \dfrac{40}{100}\cdot\dfrac{90}{100}\pi R^2$; $\sqrt{\dfrac{2000}{36}} = R$; $R \approx 7.45cm$

INCREASE OR DECREASE BY A PERCENTAGE

28. The price of a shirt is A $.

a. 1.01A
b. 1.02A
c. 1.03A
d. 1.05A
e. 1.08A
f. 1.1A
g. 1.18A
h. 1.3A
i. 1.5A
j. 1.58A
k. 1.9A
l. 2A
m. 2.01A
n. 2.08A
o. 2.1A
p. 3A
q. 3.28A
r. 4A

29. The price of a shirt is A $.

a. 0.99A
b. 0.98A
c. 0.97A
d. 0.95A
e. 0.92A
f. 0.90A
g. 0.82A
h. 0.7A
i. 0.5A
j. 0.42A
k. 0.1A
l. 0
m. Can't be it means negative price.
n. Can't be it means negative price.

30.

a. 1.1
b. 1.25
c. 1.072
d. 0.88
e. 0.65
f. 0.949
g. 0
h. 2
i. 3
j. $1+\dfrac{M}{100} = \dfrac{100+M}{100}$
k. $1-\dfrac{S}{100} = \dfrac{100-S}{100}$

31. $B\dfrac{110}{100}\cdot\dfrac{90}{100} = \dfrac{99}{100}B$, so overall change is 1% decrease.

32. $C\dfrac{120}{100}\cdot\dfrac{70}{100} = \dfrac{84}{100}C$, so overall change is 16% decrease.

33. $D\dfrac{80}{100}\cdot\dfrac{140}{100} = \dfrac{112}{100}D$, so overall change is 12% increase

34. $E\dfrac{70}{100}\cdot\dfrac{150}{100} = \dfrac{105}{100}E$, so the overall change is 5% increase.

35. $E\left(\dfrac{104}{100}\right)^{80} = E(1.04)^{80}$

36. $M\left(\dfrac{88}{100}\right)^{10} = M(0.88)^{10}$

37. $M\left(\dfrac{97.5}{100}\right)^{10} = M(0.975)^{10}$

38. $M\left(\dfrac{100+x}{100}\right)^{n} = M\left(1+\dfrac{x}{100}\right)^{n}$

BIGGER OR SMALLER BY A PERCENTAGE

39. Find the percentage by which:

a. 5 is bigger than 4:
$$\frac{5-4}{4} = \frac{1}{4} = 0.25 = 25\%$$

b. 4 is smaller than 5:
$$\frac{5-4}{5} = \frac{1}{5} = 0.2 = 20\%$$

c. 11 is bigger than 10:
$$\frac{11-10}{10} = \frac{1}{10} = 0.1 = 10\%$$

d. 10 is smaller than 11:
$$\frac{11-10}{11} = \frac{1}{11} \approx 0.091 = 9.1\%$$

e. 51 is bigger than 50 :
$$\frac{51-50}{50} = \frac{1}{50} = 0.02 = 2\%$$

f. 40 is smaller than 45:
$$\frac{45-40}{45} = \frac{5}{45} \approx 0.0889 = 8.89\%$$

g. A is bigger than B:
$$\frac{A-B}{B} = \frac{A}{B} - 1$$

h. x is smaller than y:
$$\frac{y-x}{y} = 1 - \frac{y}{x}$$

40. Given that the long side of the <u>shaded rectangle</u> is 70% of x and that its short side is 60% of y. Find the percentage of the big rectangle that is shaded.

$$P_{shaded} = \frac{\left(\frac{70}{100}x\right)\cdot\left(\frac{60}{100}y\right)}{xy} = \frac{42}{100} = 42\%$$

41. Given that the side length of the square is two thirds of the short side of the rectangle find:

a. The area of the shapes in terms of x.

Rectangle: $\underline{A = 3x^2}$ Square: $A = \left(\frac{2}{3}x\right)^2 = \frac{4}{9}x^2$

b. The percentage of the area of the rectangle that is shaded and not shaded.

$$P_{NotShaded} = \frac{\left(\frac{4}{9}x^2\right)}{3x^2} = \frac{4}{27} \approx 0.148 = 14.8\%$$

$$P_{Shaded} = \frac{\left(3x^2 - \frac{4}{9}x^2\right)}{3x^2} = \frac{\left(\frac{23}{9}x^2\right)}{3x^2} \frac{23}{27} \approx 0.852 = 85.2\%$$

c. <u>Area</u> of the square is <u>smaller</u> than the <u>area</u> of the rectangle.

$$A_{Smaller} = \frac{\left(3x^2 - \frac{4}{9}x^2\right)}{3x^2} = \frac{\left(\frac{23}{9}x^2\right)}{3x^2} \frac{23}{27} \approx 0.852 = 85.2\%$$

d. <u>Perimeter</u> of the square is <u>smaller</u> than the <u>perimeter</u> of the rectangle.

$$P_{Smaller} = \frac{\left(8x - \frac{8}{3}x\right)}{8x} = \frac{16}{24} \approx 0.667 = 66.7\%$$

42. Given the diagram in which a rectangle is located inside a square. The side length of the square is 2x. The rectangle's long side is 80% of the side of the square. The short side of the rectangles is 30% less of the side of the square.

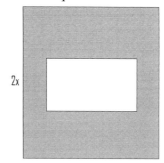

   a. The area of the square in terms of x. $A = 4x^2$

   b. Side lengths of rectangle in terms of x.
   $$a = \frac{80}{100} \cdot 2x = \frac{16x}{10} \qquad b = \frac{70}{100} \cdot 2x = \frac{14x}{10}$$

   c. Area of rectangle in terms of x.
   $$A = \frac{16x}{10} \cdot \frac{14x}{10} = \frac{224x^2}{100}$$

   d. Using the previous parts the percentage of the area that is not shaded.
   $$P_{NotShaded} = \frac{\left(\dfrac{224x^2}{100}\right)}{4x^2} = \frac{224}{400} = \frac{56}{100} = 56\%$$

   e. The <u>area</u> of the square is **bigger** than the <u>area</u> of the rectangle.
   $$A_{bigger} = \frac{\left(4x^2 - \dfrac{224x^2}{100}\right)}{\left(\dfrac{224x^2}{100}\right)} = \frac{176}{224} \approx 0.786 = 78.6\%$$

   f. <u>Perimeter</u> of the rectangle is **smaller** than the <u>perimeter</u> of the square.
   $$P_{Smaller} = \frac{8x - 6x}{8x} = \frac{1}{4} = 0.25 = 25\%$$

2. Ricardo drives to work 40% less than Rhona. Rhona drives to work 10% more than Alex who drives 400 km per week.

   a. How many km does Rhona drive to work per week?
   $$Rhona_{drives} = \frac{110}{100} \cdot 400 = 440km$$

   b. How many km does Ricardo drive to work per week?
   $$Ricardo_{drives} = \frac{60}{100} \cdot 440 = 264km$$

   c. By what percentage does Ricardo drive more or **less** than Alex?
   $$P_{less} = \frac{(400 - 264)}{400} = \frac{136}{400} = \frac{34}{100} = 34\%$$

RATIO AND PROPORTION

43. The ratio between 2 and 5 is the same as between <u>40</u> and a 100.

44. The ratio between 3 and 7 is the same as between <u>15</u> and 35.

45. The ratio between 2 and 12 is the same as between 6 and <u>36</u>

46. The ratio 1:3:7 is the same as <u>2:6:14</u>

47. Divide 120 in the ratio 2:3 $\quad \dfrac{120}{5} = 24;\qquad \dfrac{2}{3} = \dfrac{2\cdot 24}{3\cdot 24} = \dfrac{48}{72}$

48. Divide 140 in the ratio 3:4 $\quad \dfrac{140}{7} = 20;\qquad \dfrac{3}{4} = \dfrac{3\cdot 20}{4\cdot 20} = \dfrac{60}{80}$

49. Divide 180 in the ratio 2:3:4 $\dfrac{180}{9} = 20;\qquad 2:3:4 = 2\cdot 20:3\cdot 20:4\cdot 20 = 40:60:80$

50. Divide 360 in the ratio 2:5:8 $\dfrac{360}{15} = 24;\qquad 2:5:8 = 2\cdot 24:5\cdot 24:8\cdot 24 = 48:120:192$

51. Divide 30 in the ratio 1:2:3 $\dfrac{30}{6} = 5;\qquad 1:2:3 = 1\cdot 5:2\cdot 5:3\cdot 5 = 5:10:15$

52. The diagram representing an apartment has the scale 1:50. The dimensions of a bedroom in the diagram are 5 x 8 cm. Find the dimensions, perimeter and area of the bedroom.

    Dimensions: $5:8 = 5\cdot 50:8\cdot 50 = 250:400 \qquad$ *Area*: $250\cdot 400 = 100000cm^2 = 10m^2$

    Perimeter: $2(250+400) = 1300cm = 13m$

53. The ingredients needed to make a cake half as big.

    $2:1:3 = 2\cdot\dfrac{1}{2}:1\cdot\dfrac{1}{2}:3\cdot\dfrac{1}{2} = 1:\dfrac{1}{2}:\dfrac{3}{2}$

54. The amount of pasta each one of the family members will eat.

    $1:1:2:2 \qquad \dfrac{600}{6} = 100 \qquad 1\cdot 100:1\cdot 100:2\cdot 100:2\cdot 100 = 100:100:200:200$

55. The scale of a map is 1:800000. Find the real distance represented by:

    a. 1 cm $\quad 1:800000cm = 8km$

    b. 9 cm $\quad 1:800000 = 9:9\cdot 800000 = 9:7200000 = 72km$

    c. Distance in the map that represent 10km $\quad \dfrac{1000000cm}{800000} = \dfrac{10}{8} = 1.25cm$

    d. Distance in the map that represent 50km $\quad \dfrac{5000000cm}{800000} = \dfrac{50}{8} = 6.25cm$

1.7 – TYPES OF NUMBERS

Natural Numbers (N): $\mathbf{N} = \{1, 2, 3, 4...\}$

Integers (Z): $\mathbf{Z} = \{...-4, -3, -2, -1, 0, 1, 2, 3, 4...\}$

Rational Numbers (Q): $\mathbf{Q} = \{\dfrac{a}{b}, a, b \in Z\}$

Numbers that **can** be written as <u>fractions</u> being both the numerator and the denominator <u>integers</u>.

Examples: $\dfrac{1}{1}, \dfrac{2}{3}, \dfrac{-7}{3}, \dfrac{4}{-1}, \dfrac{0}{2}, 0.55, 0.121212...$

Irrational Numbers (Q'): $\mathbf{Q'} \neq \{\dfrac{a}{b}, a, b \in Z\}$ Numbers that <u>cannot</u> be written as fractions, being both the <u>numerator</u> and the <u>denominator</u> integers.

Examples: $\pi, \sqrt{2}, e ...$

Real Numbers (R): $\mathbf{R} = \mathbf{Q} + \mathbf{Q'}$ (Rationals and Irrationals)

Exercises:

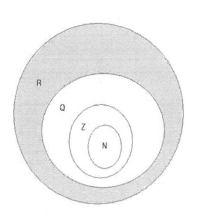

1. Natural numbers are contained in the <u>Integer</u> numbers.
2. Integer numbers are contained in the <u>Rational</u> numbers
3. Rational numbers are contained in the <u>Real</u> numbers.
4. Irrational numbers are located <u>in the outermost ring</u>.
5. Shade the area in which the irrational numbers are located:
6. True or False:
    a. All Natural numbers are Integers: <u>True</u>
    b. All Real numbers are Natural: <u>False</u>
    c. All Rational numbers are Real: <u>True</u>
    d. All Real numbers are Rational: <u>False</u>
    e. All Integer numbers are Rational: <u>True</u>
    f. All Real numbers are Irrational: <u>False</u>
    g. Some Irrational numbers are Real and some are not: <u>False</u>
    h. Some Irrational numbers are Integers: <u>False</u>
    i. Some integers are negative: <u>True</u>
    j. Some Irrationals are negative: <u>True</u>
    k. Some Natural numbers are negative: <u>False</u>
7. Write the value of the numbers with 10 decimal numbers (use a calculator)

$\sqrt{2} = 1.4142135624...$ $\qquad\qquad$ $\sqrt{3} = 1.7320508076...$

$\sqrt{4} = 2.0000000000$ $\qquad\qquad$ $\sqrt{5} = 2.2360679775...$

$\dfrac{5}{6} = 0.8333333333...$ $\qquad\qquad$ $\dfrac{43}{27} = 1.5925925925...$

$\dfrac{122}{90} = 1.3555555555...$ $\qquad\qquad$ $\dfrac{158}{990} = 0.15959595959...$

Write a conclusion: <u>Fractions can be written as decimals with repetitive pattern, there are numbers such as root of 2 in which the decimals follow no pattern or the pattern is not repetitive, these numbers are called irrational numbers.</u>

8. Circle the irrational numbers

0.58012   **0.121231234…**

0.1010010001…   0.871

0.333…   0.22777777

9. Fill the chart with yes or no (follow the example):

Number	Natural	Integer	Rational	Real
−2	no	yes	yes	yes
Π	no	no	no	yes
−3.121212….	no	no	yes	yes
−15.16	no	no	yes	yes
$\sqrt{3}$	no	no	no	yes
$-2\frac{2}{5}$	no	no	yes	yes
$\sqrt[3]{8}$	yes	yes	yes	yes

10. Fill the numbers column with appropriate numbers and yes or no. Follow the example.

Number	Natural	Integer	Rational	Real
−1	no	yes	yes	yes
0.1	no	no	yes	yes
Does not exist	yes	yes	yes	no
$\sqrt{2}$	no	no	no	yes
$\frac{1}{2}$	no	no	yes	yes
0	no	yes	yes	yes
0.333…	no	no	yes	yes
Does not exist		yes	no	

11. Convert the following numbers into the form: $\frac{n}{m}$

1. $0.333… = \frac{1}{3}$

2. $1.111… = \frac{10}{9}$

3. $5.3 = \frac{53}{10}$

4. $5.2828… = \frac{523}{99}$

5. $-2.3535… = \frac{233}{99}$

6. $42.67 = \frac{4267}{100}$

7. $12.355355… = \frac{12343}{999}$

286

8. $-31.44 = \dfrac{-3144}{100}$

9. $0.125125... = \dfrac{125}{99}$

10. $3.22332233... = \dfrac{32230}{2930}$

11. $1115.36 = \dfrac{111536}{100}$

12. $122.53 = \dfrac{12253}{100}$

13. $1.123123... = \dfrac{1122}{999}$

14. $1.22565656... = \dfrac{12134}{9900}$

15. $1.5696969... = \dfrac{1554}{990}$

16. $5.540404040... = \dfrac{5485}{990}$

12. Given the following diagram:
Write the following numbers in the appropriate location in the diagram:

a. 2.2
b. −5
c. 3
d. $\dfrac{1}{3}$
e. 5
f. −3.3
g. 1.111...
h. $\dfrac{1}{\sqrt{3}}$
i. 2π
j. $1+2\pi$
k. $\sqrt{2}+3$
l. $\dfrac{4}{2}$

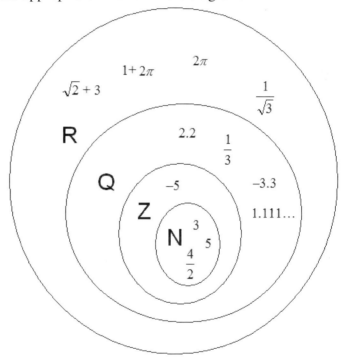

13. Circle the right option. The number −2 is:
   a. Integer and Natural.
   b. Positive
   c. **Integer and Rational**
   d. Natural and Real
   e. Natural and Rational
   f. None of the above

14. Circle the right option. The number 3.41414141..… is:

    g. Integer and Natural.

    h. Natural

    i. Integer and Real

    j. Rational and Integer

    k. Rational

    l. None of the above

15. Circle the right option. The number 3.41 is:

    m. Integer and Natural.

    n. Integer

    o. Rational and Real

    p. Integer and Real

    q. Rational and negative

    r. None of the above

16. Circle the right option. The number $\sqrt{31}$ is:

    s. Integer and Natural.

    t. Integer

    u. Decimal

    v. Integer and Real

    w. Rational

    x. Irrational

17. Circle the right option. The number 5 is:

    y. Natural.

    z. Integer

    aa. Real

    bb. Integer and Natural

    cc. Rational and Natural

    dd. All of the above

1.8 – ROOTS

Simplify as much as possible:

1. $\sqrt{0} = \underline{0}$

2. $\sqrt{1} = \underline{\pm 1}$

3. $\sqrt{4} = \underline{\pm 2}$

4. $\sqrt[3]{8} = \underline{2}$

5. $\sqrt{100} = \underline{\pm 10}$

6. $\sqrt{81} = \underline{\pm 9}$

7. $\sqrt{121} = \underline{\pm 11}$

8. $\sqrt[3]{27} = \underline{3}$

9. $\sqrt{169} = \underline{\pm 13}$

10. $\sqrt[4]{16} = \underline{\pm 2}$

11. $\sqrt{10000} = \underline{\pm 100}$

12. $\sqrt[3]{64} = \underline{4}$

13. $\sqrt[3]{a^3} = \underline{a}$

14. $\sqrt{16} \cdot \sqrt{25} = \underline{20}$

15. $\sqrt[4]{2} \cdot \sqrt[4]{8} = \underline{2}$

16. $\sqrt{-1} = \underline{not\ Real}$

17. $\left(\sqrt{4}\right)^2 = \underline{4}$

18. $\sqrt[4]{81} = \underline{\pm 3}$

19. $\left(-\sqrt{5}\right)^2 \cdot \left(\sqrt[3]{3}\right)^3 = \underline{15}$

20. $\left(\sqrt{532}\right)^2 = \underline{532}$

21. $\left(\sqrt{a}\right)^2 \left(\sqrt[n]{a}\right)^n = \underline{a^2}$

22. $\sqrt{0.01} = \sqrt{\dfrac{1}{100}} = \underline{\dfrac{1}{10}}$

23. $\sqrt{0.25} = \sqrt{\dfrac{25}{100}} = \dfrac{5}{10} = \underline{\dfrac{1}{2}}$

24. $\sqrt{2.25} = \sqrt{\dfrac{225}{100}} = \dfrac{15}{10} = \underline{\dfrac{3}{2}}$

25. $\sqrt{\dfrac{a^2}{9}} = \underline{\pm \dfrac{a}{3}}$

26. $\sqrt{\dfrac{8}{200}} = \sqrt{\dfrac{4}{100}} = \dfrac{2}{10} = \underline{\dfrac{1}{5}}$

27. $\sqrt{3} + \sqrt{3} = \underline{2\sqrt{3}}$

28. $\sqrt{2} + \sqrt{2} + \sqrt{2} = \underline{3\sqrt{2}}$

29. $\sqrt{2} + \sqrt{8} + \sqrt{2} = \underline{4\sqrt{2}}$

30. $\sqrt{4} + \sqrt{2} + \sqrt{8} = \underline{3\sqrt{2} + 2}$

31. $\sqrt{9} + \sqrt{12} + \sqrt{27} = \underline{6\sqrt{3} + 3}$

32. $\sqrt{50} + \sqrt{75} + \sqrt{12} = \underline{5\sqrt{2} + 7\sqrt{3}}$

33. $\sqrt[3]{16} + \sqrt[3]{54} = 2\sqrt[3]{2} + 3\sqrt[3]{2} = \underline{5\sqrt[3]{2}}$

34. $\sqrt[4]{32} - \sqrt[4]{162} = 2\sqrt[4]{2} - 3\sqrt[4]{2} = \underline{-\sqrt[4]{2}}$

35. $\sqrt{27} + \sqrt{81} + \sqrt{48} = \underline{7\sqrt{3} + 9}$

36. $\sqrt{200} + \sqrt{50} - \sqrt{18} = \underline{12\sqrt{2}}$

37. $\sqrt{20} + \sqrt{80} - \sqrt{125} = \underline{-\sqrt{5}}$

38. $\sqrt{10}\sqrt{10} = \underline{10}$

39. $\sqrt[3]{a} \cdot \sqrt[3]{a} \cdot \sqrt[3]{a} = \underline{a}$

40. $\sqrt{3}\sqrt{9}\sqrt{3} = \underline{9}$

41. $\dfrac{\sqrt{200}}{\sqrt{2}} = \underline{10}$

42. $\dfrac{\sqrt{72}}{\sqrt{2}} = \underline{6}$

43. $\dfrac{\sqrt{75}}{\sqrt{5}} = \underline{\sqrt{15}}$

44. $\sqrt{3}\dfrac{\sqrt{24}}{\sqrt{2}} = \underline{6}$

45. $\sqrt{a}\sqrt{a} = \underline{a}$

46. $\sqrt{a} + \sqrt{a} = \underline{2\sqrt{a}}$

47. Write all the integers between $\sqrt{3}$ and $\sqrt{10}$: $\underline{2,\ 3}$

48. Write all the integers between $\sqrt{13}$ and $\sqrt{50}$: $\underline{4,\ 5,\ 6,\ 7}$

49. Write a rational number non - integer between $\sqrt{3}$ and $\sqrt{10}$: $\underline{2.5}$

50. Write all the integers between $\sqrt{24}$ and $\sqrt{80}$: $\underline{5,\ 6,\ 7,\ 8}$

51. Write a rational number non - integer between $\sqrt{13}$ and $\sqrt{30}$: $\underline{4.5}$

Rationalize the denominator:

52. $\dfrac{1}{\sqrt{2}} = \left(\dfrac{1}{\sqrt{2}}\right)\cdot\left(\dfrac{\sqrt{2}}{\sqrt{2}}\right) = \dfrac{\sqrt{2}}{2}$

53. $\left(\dfrac{3}{\sqrt{5}+1}\right)\cdot\left(\dfrac{\sqrt{5}-1}{\sqrt{5}-1}\right) = \dfrac{3\left(\sqrt{5}-1\right)}{4}$

54. $\left(\dfrac{-7}{\sqrt{5}-2}\right)\cdot\left(\dfrac{\sqrt{5}+2}{\sqrt{5}+2}\right) = \dfrac{7\left(\sqrt{5}+2\right)}{1} = 7\left(\sqrt{5}+2\right)$

55. $\dfrac{\sqrt{2}+3}{-5}$, Denominator already rational

56. $\left(\dfrac{\sqrt{2}+3}{\sqrt{6}-5}\right)\left(\dfrac{\sqrt{6}+5}{\sqrt{6}+5}\right) = \dfrac{\left(\sqrt{2}+3\right)\left(\sqrt{6}+5\right)}{-19}$

57. $\left(\dfrac{\sqrt{2}}{\sqrt{6}+\sqrt{3}}\right)\left(\dfrac{\sqrt{6}-\sqrt{3}}{\sqrt{6}-\sqrt{3}}\right) = \dfrac{\sqrt{2}\left(\sqrt{6}-\sqrt{3}\right)}{3}$

58. $\left(\dfrac{\sqrt{2}-1}{2\sqrt{5}-\sqrt{3}}\right)\left(\dfrac{2\sqrt{5}+\sqrt{3}}{2\sqrt{5}+\sqrt{3}}\right) = \dfrac{\left(\sqrt{2}-1\right)\left(2\sqrt{5}+\sqrt{3}\right)}{17}$

59. $\left(\dfrac{-1}{2\sqrt{a}+b}\right)\cdot\left(\dfrac{2\sqrt{a}-b}{2\sqrt{a}-b}\right) = \left(\dfrac{-2\sqrt{a}+b}{4a-b^2}\right)$

60. $\left(\dfrac{3\sqrt{a}-2b}{2\sqrt{a}+\sqrt{b}}\right)\left(\dfrac{3\sqrt{a}-2b}{2\sqrt{a}-\sqrt{b}}\right) = \left(\dfrac{9a-12b\sqrt{a}+4b^2}{4a-b}\right)$

Rationalize the numerator:

61. $\dfrac{\sqrt{4}}{\sqrt{5}} = \dfrac{2}{\sqrt{5}}$

62. $\left(\dfrac{3-\sqrt{2}}{\sqrt{5}+1}\right)\cdot\left(\dfrac{3+\sqrt{2}}{3+\sqrt{2}}\right) = \dfrac{7}{\left(\sqrt{5}+1\right)\left(3+\sqrt{2}\right)}$

63. $\left(\dfrac{-7}{\sqrt{5}-2}\right)$, Numerator already rational

64. $\left(\dfrac{\sqrt{2}+3}{\sqrt{6}-5}\right)\left(\dfrac{\sqrt{2}-3}{\sqrt{2}-3}\right) = \dfrac{-7}{\left(\sqrt{6}-5\right)\left(\sqrt{2}-3\right)}$

65. $\left(\dfrac{\sqrt{2}}{\sqrt{x}+\sqrt{3}}\right)\cdot\left(\dfrac{\sqrt{2}}{\sqrt{2}}\right) = \dfrac{2}{\sqrt{2}\left(\sqrt{x}+\sqrt{3}\right)}$

66. $\left(\dfrac{\sqrt{b}-a}{2\sqrt{a}-\sqrt{3}}\right)\left(\dfrac{\sqrt{b}+a}{\sqrt{b}+a}\right) = \dfrac{b-a^2}{\left(2\sqrt{a}-\sqrt{3}\right)\left(\sqrt{b}+a\right)}$

67. $\left(\dfrac{-3\sqrt{7}+8}{2\sqrt{5}+7}\right)\left(\dfrac{-3\sqrt{7}-8}{-3\sqrt{7}-8}\right) = \dfrac{-1}{\left(2\sqrt{5}+7\right)\left(-3\sqrt{7}-8\right)}$

68. $\left(\dfrac{\sqrt{a}-2\sqrt{b}}{2\sqrt{a}+\sqrt{b}}\right)\cdot\left(\dfrac{\sqrt{a}+2\sqrt{b}}{2\sqrt{a}+\sqrt{b}}\right) = \left(\dfrac{a-4b}{4a+4\sqrt{ab}+b}\right)$

1.9 – INTERVAL NOTATION AND INEQULITIES

1. Represent the following Intervals on the real line:

   a. $x \in (2, 5]$

   b. $x \in (3,6)$

   c. $x \in [-5,9]$

   d. $x \in [-8,-1)$

   e. $x \in [-\infty,-1)$

   f. $x \in [-\infty,6]$

   g. $x \in (6, \infty]$

   h. $\{ x \mid 7 < x < 9\}$

   i. $\{ x \mid -7 < x < -2\}$

   j. $\{ x \mid 1 < x < 2\}$

   k. $\{ x \mid \infty < x < 2\}$ Not Possible

   l. $\{ x \mid 1 < x < \infty \}$

291

2. Write each one of the Intervals using all types of notations:

a. $x \in (4, 5) = 4 \leq x \leq 5$

b. $x \in (-\infty, 5) = x < 5$

c. $x \in (4, 5) = 4 < x < 5$

d. $x \in (3, \infty] = 3 < x$

e. $x \in \;]-5,9] = -5 < x \leq 9$

f. $x \in [-8,-1[\; = -8 \leq x < -1$

g. $\{ x \mid 7 < x < 9 \} = x \in (7, 9)$

h. $\{ x \mid -7 < x < -2 \} = x \in (-7, -2)$

3. Solve the following inequalities and shade the solution on the given diagram:

a. $-x \leq 3$
   $x \geq -3$

b. $5 - x \leq 2$
   $x \geq 3$

c. $8 - 2x \leq 3$
   $x \geq \dfrac{5}{2}$

d. $-2x \leq 4 + x$
   $x \geq -\dfrac{4}{3}$

e. $7 + x \leq x + 3$ Never
   $7 \leq 3$

f.
$$-2x \le 2x+1$$
$$x \ge -\frac{1}{4}$$

g.
$$-2x \le 2x$$
$$x \ge 0$$

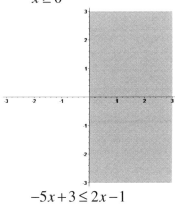

h.
$$-5x+3 \le 2x-1$$
$$x \ge \frac{4}{7}$$

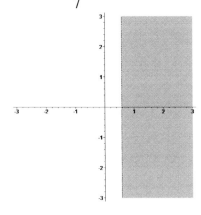

i.
$$7x \le 4+7x+1$$
$$0 \le 5, \forall x \in \mathbb{R}$$

j.
$$\frac{x}{2} \le x+1$$
$$x \ge -2$$

k.
$$\frac{x}{3} \le \frac{x}{6}+1$$
$$x \le 6$$

l.
$$\frac{x-4}{6} \le x-1$$
$$x \ge \frac{2}{5}$$

293

m.
$$\frac{2-x}{3} \le \frac{x}{5} - 3$$
$$x \ge \frac{55}{8}$$

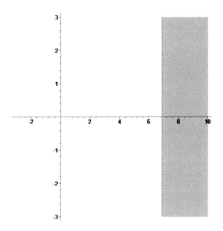

n.
$$\frac{4-2x}{5} \le \frac{2x}{6} - \frac{x}{2}$$
$$x \ge \frac{24}{7}$$

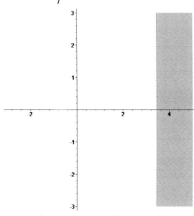

o.
$$\frac{-2x}{5} - 3 \le \frac{x-2}{4} - \frac{x-1}{2}$$
$$x \ge -20$$

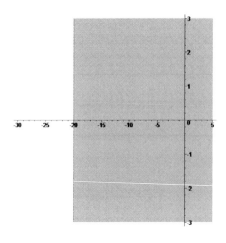

p.
$$\frac{y+4}{6} \le y-1$$
$$y \ge \frac{1}{2}$$

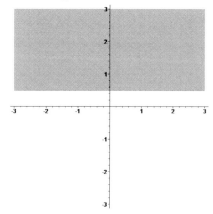

q.
$$\frac{2-2y}{3} \le \frac{y}{4} - 1$$
$$8 - 8y \le 3y - 12$$
$$\frac{20}{11} \le y$$

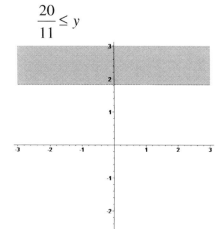

r.
$$\frac{4-y}{5} \le \frac{y}{2} - y$$
$$8 \le -3y$$
$$y \le -\frac{8}{3}$$

$$\frac{-2y}{5}-1\le y-\frac{y-1}{2}$$

s. $-4y-10\le 10y-5y+5$

$$y\ge-\frac{15}{9}$$

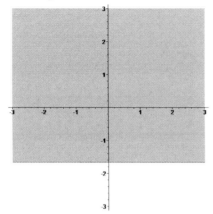

$$-2\le 2x\le 1$$

t. $-1\le x\le\frac{1}{2}$

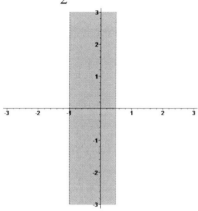

$$-8\le\frac{-6x+3}{4}\le 7$$

u. $\frac{35}{6}\ge x\ge-\frac{25}{6}$

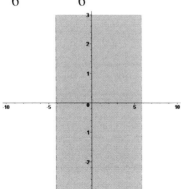

$$-10\le 4y+2\le 9$$

v. $-3\le y\le\frac{7}{4}$

$$0\le\frac{y+2}{3}\le 2$$

w. $-2\le y\le 4$

$$-\frac{13}{5}\le-\frac{2x}{4}-x+2\le 0$$

x. $-92\le-30x\le-40$

$$\frac{92}{30}\ge x\ge\frac{4}{3}$$

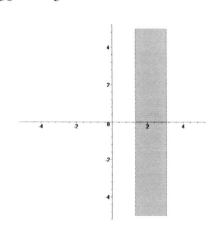

295

$$0 \leq 2 - \frac{-6x-3}{4} \leq \frac{13}{6}$$

y. $0 \leq 24 + 18x + 9 \leq 26$

$$\frac{-33}{18} \leq x \leq -\frac{7}{18}$$

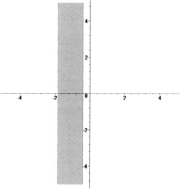

$$-\frac{5}{2} \leq -\frac{4y}{3} + y + 2 \leq 3$$

z. $-15 \leq -8y + 6y + 12 \leq 18$

$$13.5 \geq y \geq -3$$

$$0 \leq 2 - \frac{2y+2}{3} + y \leq \frac{7}{6}$$

aa. $0 \leq 12 - 4y - 4 + 6y \leq 7$

$$-4 \leq y \leq \frac{-1}{2}$$

$$-\frac{12}{7} \leq \frac{x}{2} + \frac{x}{3} \leq 0$$

bb. $-72 \leq 35x \leq 0$

$$-\frac{72}{35} \leq x \leq 0$$

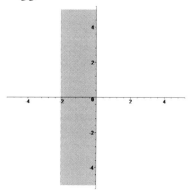

$$\frac{-7}{8} \leq 2 - \frac{-6x+3}{4} \leq \frac{6}{2}$$

cc. $-7 \leq 16 + 12x - 6 \leq 24$

$$\frac{-17}{12} \leq x \leq \frac{14}{12}$$

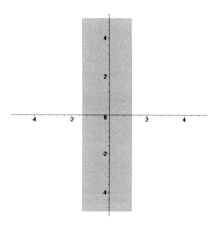

$$-\frac{10}{3} \leq -\frac{4y+2}{5} \leq \frac{9}{2}$$

dd. $-100 \leq -24y - 12 \leq 135$

$$\frac{88}{24} \geq y \geq -\frac{147}{24}$$

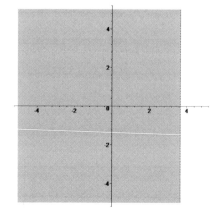

$$0 \le \frac{y+2}{3} \le \frac{12}{7}$$

ee. $0 \le 7y+14 \le 36$

$$-2 \le y \le \frac{22}{7}$$

4.

   a. Solve the inequality $2x \le 2$ $x \le 1$

   b. Solve the inequality $-x < -2$. $x \ge 2$

   c. Represent both solutions on the real line:

   d. State their intersection: <u>None</u>

5.

   a. Solve the inequality $2x - 2 \le 2$ $x \le 2$

   b. Solve the inequality $-3x + 1 > -2$. $x < 1$

   c. Represent both solutions on the real line:

   d. State their intersection: $x \in (-\infty, 1)$

6.

   a. Solve the inequality $x - 2 \le -5$ $x \le -3$

   b. Solve the inequality $-2x + 14 \le -2$. $x \ge 8$

   c. Represent both solutions on the real line:

   d. State their intersection: <u>None</u>

7.

   a. Solve the inequality $3x - 7 \le 2$ $x < 3$

   b. Solve the inequality $-x < -2$. $x > 2$

   c. Represent both solutions on the real line:

   d. State their intersection: $x \in (2, 3]$

297

8.

a. Solve the inequality $5\,x - 2 \le 2$ $x \le \dfrac{4}{5}$

b. Solve the inequality $-2\,x + 1 > -2$. $x < \dfrac{3}{2}$

c. Represent both solutions on the real line:

d. State their intersection: $x \in (-\infty, \dfrac{4}{5}]$

9.

a. Solve the inequality $5x - 2 \le -12$ $x \le -2$

b. Solve the inequality $-2x - 3 \le -2$. $x \ge -\dfrac{1}{2}$

c. Represent both solutions on the real line:

d. State their intersection: <u>None</u>

1.10. – EVALUATING EXPRESSIONS

Evaluate the expression given the value of x:

1. $x = -3$, $x^2 = 9$

2. $x = -3$, $-x^2 = -9$

3. $x = -3$, $x - x^2 = -12$

4. $x = -3$, $-x^3 = 27$

5. $x = -3$, $x^2 + x = 6$

6. $x = -2$, $2x^2 + 3x = 2$

7. $x = -2$, $x^{-1} = -\dfrac{1}{2}$

8. $x = -2$, $x^3 = -8$

9. $x = -3$, $x^{-3} = -\dfrac{1}{27}$

10. $x = -9$, $2x^{-2} = \dfrac{2}{81}$

11. $x = 4$, $x^{-2} + x = \dfrac{65}{16}$

12. $x = -2$, $2x^2 + \dfrac{x}{2} = 7$

13. $x = -2$, $\dfrac{1}{x} + \dfrac{x}{2} = -\dfrac{3}{2}$

14. $x = 4$, $\dfrac{1}{x-3} + \dfrac{x}{2} = 3$

15. $x = 10$, $\dfrac{10}{x-5} + \dfrac{x-2}{2} = 6$

16. $x = -1$, $5x^{-3} + 2x^{-1} + 1 = -6$

17. $x = 3$, $x^{-2} + x + x^2 = \dfrac{91}{9}$

18. $x = 2$, $x^{-3} + x^{-2} + x^{-1} + x^0 = \dfrac{7}{4}$

19. $x = 2$, $2x^{-2} \cdot x^{-1} = \dfrac{1}{4}$

20. $x = -1$, $x^{-200} - 2x^{501} = 3$

21. $x = -5$, $5x^{-2} - x^2 = -\dfrac{124}{5}$

22. $x = -2$, $2^x = \dfrac{1}{4}$

23. $x = -2$, $3^x = \dfrac{1}{9}$

24. $x = -2$, $2^{2x+1} = \dfrac{1}{8}$

25. $x = -1$, $2^{3x-1} = \dfrac{1}{16}$

26. $x = 2$, $2^{\frac{3}{x}} = \sqrt{8}$

27. $x = -\dfrac{1}{2}$, $4^x = \dfrac{1}{2}$

28. $x = -\dfrac{2}{3}$, $8^x = \dfrac{1}{4}$

1.11. – EQUATIONS

1st Degree (Linear Equations)

1. $\dfrac{x}{12} = 5$

   $x = 60$

2. $\dfrac{x}{7} + 2 = 5$

   $x = 21$

3. $\dfrac{2x}{7} + 2 = 5 - 3x$

   $x = \dfrac{21}{23}$

4. $\dfrac{2x}{7} + \dfrac{2}{5} = -2x + 1$

   $x = \dfrac{21}{80}$

5. $\dfrac{2x - 1}{x} = 3$

   $x = -1$

6. $\dfrac{x + 2}{2x} = 5$

   $x = \dfrac{2}{9}$

7. $\dfrac{x - 2}{2x - 1} = 6$

   $x = \dfrac{4}{11}$

8. $\dfrac{2x - 2}{x + 1} = -2$

   $x = 0$

9. $\dfrac{2x}{7} + 1 = \dfrac{-5x}{7}$

   $x = -1$

10. $\dfrac{2x}{7} + 4 = \dfrac{3x}{2}$

    $x = \dfrac{56}{17}$

11. $\dfrac{2}{x} - 3 = \dfrac{3}{2x}$

    $x = \dfrac{1}{6}$

12. $\dfrac{2}{x - 2} - 3 = \dfrac{3}{x - 2}$

    $x = \dfrac{5}{3}$

13. $\dfrac{-2}{x} = \dfrac{3}{x - 2}$

    $x = \dfrac{4}{5}$

14. $\dfrac{4}{x + 1} = \dfrac{4}{x + 2}$

    No   Solution

15. $\dfrac{2}{x + 1} = \dfrac{4}{x + 2}$

    $x = 0$

16. $-\dfrac{2}{2x + 1} - 2 = \dfrac{4}{2x + 1}$

    $x = -2$

17. $\dfrac{x}{2} - \dfrac{x}{5} = 3$

    $3x = 30$

    $x = 10$

18. $\dfrac{2}{x} + \dfrac{3}{5} = 3$

    $x = \dfrac{5}{6}$

19. $\dfrac{2x - 7}{2} - \dfrac{3x}{5} = x$

    $10x - 35 - 6x = 10x$

    $x = -\dfrac{35}{6}$

20. $1 - \dfrac{1}{x} = 7 - \dfrac{3x + 1}{x}$

    $x - 1 = 7x - 3x - 1$

    $x = 0,\, Not\ \ Valid$

    No   Solution

21. $3 - \dfrac{2x}{x - 2} = 7 - \dfrac{2x + 1}{x - 2}$

    $3x - 6 - 2x = 7x - 14 - 2x - 1$

    $x = \dfrac{9}{4}$

22. $\dfrac{2 - x}{x - 2} = 1$

    $x = 0$

23. $\dfrac{2 - x}{x - 2} = -1$

    $0 = 0,\, True\ \ \forall x \in \mathbb{R}$

24. $\dfrac{5 - 7x}{3x - 2} = -1 + \dfrac{5}{3x - 2}$

    $5 - 7x = -3x + 2 + 5$

    $x = -\dfrac{1}{2}$

25. $\dfrac{15 - x}{3 - x} = 7 - \dfrac{5x}{3 - x}$

    $x = \dfrac{6}{11}$

26. Write an equation with fractions, similar to previous one whose solution is 6, solve it.

$$\frac{x}{6} + \frac{x+1}{7} = 2$$
$$7x + 6x + 6 = 84$$
$$x = 6$$

27. Write an equation with fractions, similar to previous one whose solution is -5, solve it.

$$\frac{x}{5} - \frac{2x-5}{3} = 4$$
$$3x - 10x + 25 = 60$$
$$x = -5$$

28. Write an equation with fractions, similar to previous one whose solution is $\frac{2}{3}$, solve it.

$$\frac{3x}{2} + 6x = 5$$
$$3x + 12x = 10$$
$$x = \frac{2}{3}$$

29. Write an equation with fractions, similar to previous one whose solution is $-\frac{3}{5}$, solve it.

$$\frac{5x}{3} + 10x = -7$$
$$5x + 30x = -21$$
$$x = -\frac{3}{5}$$

30. Write an equation with fractions, similar to previous one whose solution is $-\frac{3}{7}$, solve it.

$$-\frac{14x}{3} + 7x = -1$$
$$-14x + 21x = -3$$
$$x = -\frac{3}{7}$$

31. Write an equation with fractions, similar to previous one whose solution is $\frac{3}{4}$, solve it.

$$\frac{8x}{3} + \frac{40x}{6} = 7$$
$$16x + 40x = 42$$
$$x = \frac{42}{56} = \frac{3}{4}$$

Isolate x

1. $$\frac{4}{x} = \frac{a}{x+6}$$
$$x = \frac{24}{a-4}$$

2. $$\frac{14}{x+2} = \frac{a}{x+2} - a$$
$$x = -\frac{14+a}{a}$$

3. $$\frac{2}{x+3} - a = \frac{a+b}{x+3}$$
$$x = \frac{2-b-4a}{a}$$

4. $\dfrac{5}{2x+1} - 3a = \dfrac{b}{2x+1}$

$x = \dfrac{5-b-3a}{6a}$

5. $\dfrac{-2x}{a+3} = \dfrac{x+2}{2a-1}$

$x = -\dfrac{2a+6}{5a+5}$

6. $\dfrac{-5x+1}{2a} = \dfrac{bx}{3a+2}$

$x = \dfrac{3a+2}{15a+2ab+10}$

7. $\dfrac{a}{x+2} = \dfrac{b}{x+2} - b+1$

$x = -\dfrac{a+b+2}{b+1}$

8. $\dfrac{b}{2x-4} - 3 = \dfrac{b}{2x-4} - b+1$

No Solution

9. $\dfrac{1}{ax+2} = \dfrac{b}{x+a}$

$x = \dfrac{a-2b}{ba-1}$

10. $\dfrac{1}{ax+2} = \dfrac{b}{ax+2} - 3$

$x = \dfrac{b-7}{3a}$

11. $3\dfrac{x}{ax+2} = 3$

$x = \dfrac{6}{1-3a}$

12. $-3\dfrac{2x}{ax+3} = b$

$x = -\dfrac{3b}{ab+6}$

13. $\dfrac{2x-3}{2ax+5} = -3b$

$x = \dfrac{3-15b}{6ab+2}$

14. $\dfrac{x}{ax+2} = \dfrac{2}{a} - 3$

$x = -\dfrac{4-6a}{3a^2-a}$

15. $\dfrac{bx}{x+2} = 3-b$

$x = \dfrac{6-2b}{2b-3}$

16. $\dfrac{b+x}{x-3} = \dfrac{b}{x-3} + a$

$x = \dfrac{-3a}{1-a}$

17. $\dfrac{bx}{a} = 2x+8$

$x = \dfrac{8a}{b-2a}$

18. $\dfrac{ax+b}{dx+2} = c-g$

$x = \dfrac{2g-2c+b}{dc-gd-a}$

19. $\dfrac{1}{x+2} + \dfrac{1}{b} = 2$

$x = \dfrac{3b-2}{1-2b}$

20. $\dfrac{1-a}{x} + \dfrac{2a}{x} = 2b$

$x = \dfrac{1+a}{2b}$

21. $x - \dfrac{2+ax}{b} = 2x+3$

$x = \dfrac{-3a-2}{a+b}$

22. $\dfrac{7-2ax}{x+1} = 2+b$

$x = \dfrac{5-b}{2+b+2a}$

23. $\dfrac{3-2x}{2x-3} = a$

$3-2x = 2xa - 3a$

$x = \dfrac{3+3a}{2+2a} = \dfrac{3}{2}, Not\ \ Valid$

24. $\dfrac{-2}{x-1} = \dfrac{2a}{x-1} - a$

$x = \dfrac{2+3a}{a}$

25. $\dfrac{3}{a-2x} = \dfrac{b}{2x-a} - c$

$x = \dfrac{3+b+ac}{2c}$

26. Complete RHS of the equation so solution is a

$xa+1 = a^2+1$ (plug a into x)

27. Complete RHS of the equation, solution is a - 1

$\dfrac{1}{xa} - a = \dfrac{1}{(a-1)a} - a$

(plug a - 1 into x)

28. Complete RHS of the equation so solution is $2a$

(plug $2a$ into x)

$x - \dfrac{1}{xa} = 2a - \dfrac{1}{2a^2}$

29. Complete RHS of the   (plug $4a+1$ into x)

equation so solution is

$4a+1$

$$\frac{x+1}{xa} - 1 = \frac{4a+2}{(4a+1)a} - 1$$

Quadratic equations

Given the equation $2x^2 - 5x - 3 = 0$,

1. Solve it by factoring. $(2x+1)(x-3) = 0, x_1 = -\frac{1}{2}, x_2 = 3$

2. Solve it by completing the square.

$$2x^2 - 5x - 3 = 0; \quad 2\left[x - \frac{5}{2}x - \frac{3}{2}\right] = 0; \quad 2\left[\left(x - \frac{5}{4}\right)^2 - \frac{25}{16} - \frac{3}{2}\right] = 0$$

$$2\left[\left(x - \frac{5}{4}\right)^2 - \frac{49}{16}\right] = 0; \quad \left(x - \frac{5}{4}\right)^2 - \frac{49}{16} = 0; \quad \left(x - \frac{5}{4}\right)^2 = \frac{49}{16}; \quad x - \frac{5}{4} = \pm\frac{7}{4}; \quad x_1 = -\frac{1}{2}, x_2 = 3$$

3. Its discriminant is $b^2 - 4ac = 25 + 24 = 49 > 0$

Given the equation: $25x^2 - 20x + 4 = 0$,

4. Solve it by factoring. $(5x-2)(5x-2) = 0, x_{1,2} = \frac{5}{2}$

5. Solve it by completing the square.

$$25x^2 - 20x + 4 = 0; \quad 25\left[x - \frac{4}{5}x + \frac{4}{25}\right] = 0; \quad 25\left[\left(x - \frac{2}{5}\right)^2 - \frac{4}{25} + \frac{4}{25}\right] = 0$$

$$2\left[\left(x - \frac{2}{5}\right)^2\right] = 0; \quad \left(x - \frac{2}{5}\right)^2 = 0; \quad x - \frac{2}{5} = 0; \quad x = \frac{2}{5}$$

6. Its discriminant is $b^2 - 4ac = 400 - 400 = 0$

Given the equation: $4x^2 - 4x + 2 = 0$,

7. Solve it by factoring. Cannot factor
8. Solve it by completing the square.

$$4x^2 - 4x + 2 = 0; \quad 4\left[x^2 - x + \frac{1}{2}\right] = 0; \quad 4\left[\left(x - \frac{1}{2}\right)^2 - \frac{1}{4} + \frac{1}{2}\right] = 0$$

$$4\left[\left(x - \frac{1}{2}\right)^2 + \frac{1}{4}\right] = 0; \quad \left(x - \frac{1}{2}\right)^2 + \frac{1}{4}; \quad \left(x - \frac{1}{2}\right)^2 = -\frac{1}{4}; \quad No \ Solution$$

9. Its discriminant is $b^2 - 4ac = 16 - 32 = -16 < 0$

Given the equation: $ax^2 + bx + c = 0$, n

10. Solve it by completing the square.

$$ax^2 + bx + c = 0; \quad a\left[x^2 - \frac{b}{a}x + \frac{c}{a}\right] = 0; \quad a\left[\left(x - \frac{b}{2a}\right)^2 - \frac{b^2}{4a^2} + \frac{c}{a}\right] = 0$$

$$\left(x - \frac{b}{2a}\right)^2 - \frac{b^2}{4a^2} + \frac{c}{a} = 0; \quad \left(x - \frac{b}{2a}\right)^2 = \frac{b^2 - 4ac}{4a^2}; \quad x = \frac{b}{2a} \pm \sqrt{\frac{b^2 - 4ac}{4a^2}};$$

$$x = \frac{b \pm \sqrt{b^2 - 4ac}}{2a}$$ This expression is the well known Quadratic Formula

11. The equation will have 2 solutions if <u>discriminant > 0</u> 1 solution if <u>discriminant $= 0$</u> and 0 solutions if <u>discriminant < 0</u>

Practice
a. Solve the following equations using the "complete the square method".
b. Check your answers using the quadratic formula.
c. Write the factorized expression.

1. $x^2 - 4x + 1 = 3$

$(x-2)^2 - 4 + 1 = 3$

$x = \pm\sqrt{6} + 2$

$(x - (\sqrt{6} + 2))(x - (-\sqrt{6} + 2)) = 0$

2. $x^2 - 4x + 1 = -3$

$(x-2)^2 - 4 + 1 = -3$

$x = 2$

$(x-2)(x-2) = 0$

3. $x^2 - 4x + 1 = -13$

$(x-2)^2 - 4 + 1 = -13$

No Solution

4. $x^2 + 6x + 2 = 2$

$(x+3)^2 - 9 + 2 = 2$

$x = 0, -6$

$(x)(x+6) = 0$

5. $x^2 + 6x + 2 = -10$

$(x+3)^2 - 9 + 2 = -10$

No Solution

6. $x^2 + 8x + 3 = -10$

$(x+4)^2 - 16 + 3 = -10$

$(x+4)^2 = 3$

$x = \pm\sqrt{3} - 4$

$\left(x - \left(\sqrt{3} - 4\right)\right)\left(x - \left(-\sqrt{3} - 4\right)\right) = 0$

7. $x^2 - 12x - 2 = 3$

$(x-6)^2 - 36 - 2 = 3$

$(x-6)^2 = 41$

$x = \pm\sqrt{41} + 6$

$\left(x - \left(\sqrt{41} + 6\right)\right)\left(x - \left(-\sqrt{41} + 6\right)\right) = 0$

8. $x^2 - 2x - 5 = 3$

$(x-1)^2 - 1 - 5 = 3$

$(x-1)^2 = 9$

$x = \pm 3 + 1$

$(x+2)(x-4) = 0$

9. $x^2 - 3x - 5 = 3$

$\left(x - \dfrac{3}{2}\right)^2 - \dfrac{9}{4} - 5 = 3$

$x = \dfrac{3}{2} \pm \dfrac{\sqrt{41}}{2}$

$\left(x - \left(\dfrac{3}{2} + \dfrac{\sqrt{41}}{2}\right)\right)\left(x - \left(\dfrac{3}{2} - \dfrac{\sqrt{41}}{2}\right)\right) = 0$

10. $x^2 - 4x - 5 = 3$

$(x-2)^2 - 4 - 5 = 3$

$(x-2)^2 = 12$

$x = \pm\sqrt{12} + 2$

$\left(x - \left(\sqrt{12} + 2\right)\right)\left(x - \left(-\sqrt{12} + 2\right)\right) = 0$

11. $x^2 - 3x - 3 = -3$

$\left(x - \dfrac{3}{2}\right)^2 - \dfrac{9}{4} - 3 = -3$

$x = 0, 3$

$(x)(x-3) = 0$

12. $x^2 - 3x - 4 = -1$

$\left(x - \dfrac{3}{2}\right)^2 - \dfrac{9}{4} - 4 = -1$

$x = \dfrac{3}{2} \pm \dfrac{\sqrt{21}}{2}$

$\left(x - \left(\dfrac{3}{2} + \dfrac{\sqrt{21}}{2}\right)\right)\left(x - \left(\dfrac{3}{2} - \dfrac{\sqrt{21}}{2}\right)\right) = 0$

13. $x^2 - 7x - 5 = 3$

$\left(x - \dfrac{7}{2}\right)^2 - \dfrac{49}{4} - 5 = 3$

$x = 8, -1$

$(x+1)(x-8) = 0$

14. $x^2 + x - 3 = 2$

$\left(x + \dfrac{1}{2}\right)^2 - \dfrac{1}{4} - 3 = 2$

$x = -\dfrac{1}{2} \pm \dfrac{\sqrt{21}}{2}$

$\left(x - \left(-\dfrac{1}{2} + \dfrac{\sqrt{21}}{2}\right)\right)\left(x - \left(-\dfrac{1}{2} - \dfrac{\sqrt{21}}{2}\right)\right) = 0$

15. $x^2 - 2x + 4 = 5$

$(x-1)^2 - 1 + 4 = 5$

$x = 1 \pm \sqrt{2}$

$\left(x - \left(1 + \sqrt{2}\right)\right)\left(x - \left(1 - \sqrt{2}\right)\right) = 0$

16. $x^2 + 3x - 1 = 3$

$\left(x + \dfrac{3}{2}\right)^2 - \dfrac{9}{4} - 1 = 3$

$x = 1, -4$

$(x-1)(x+4) = 0$

17. $x^2 + 7x - 3 = 2$

$\left(x + \dfrac{7}{2}\right)^2 - \dfrac{1}{4} - 3 = 2$

$x = -\dfrac{7}{2} \pm \dfrac{\sqrt{69}}{2}$

$\left(x - \left(-\dfrac{7}{2} + \dfrac{\sqrt{69}}{2}\right)\right)\left(x - \left(-\dfrac{7}{2} - \dfrac{\sqrt{69}}{2}\right)\right) = 0$

18. $x^2 + 8x = 0$

$(x+4)^2 - 16 = 0$

$x = 0, 4$

$(x)(x-4) = 0$

19. $x^2 - 7x = 0$

$\left(x - \dfrac{7}{2}\right)^2 - \dfrac{49}{4} = 0$

$x = 0, 7$

$(x)(x-7) = 0$

20. $-x^2 + 10x + 4 = -1$

$-\left((x-5)^2 - 25\right) + 4 = -1$

$(x-5)^2 = 30$

$x = 5 \pm \sqrt{30}$

$\left(x - \left(5 + \sqrt{30}\right)\right)\left(x - \left(5 - \sqrt{30}\right)\right) = 0$

21. $2x^2 - 10x - 2 = 0$

$2\left(\left(x - \dfrac{5}{2}\right)^2 - \dfrac{25}{4} - 1\right) = 0$

$x = \dfrac{5}{2} \pm \dfrac{\sqrt{29}}{2}$

$2\left(x - \left(\dfrac{5}{2} + \dfrac{\sqrt{29}}{2}\right)\right)\left(x - \left(\dfrac{5}{2} + \dfrac{\sqrt{29}}{2}\right)\right) = 0$

22. $3x^2 - 9x - 6 = 0$

$3\left(\left(x - \dfrac{3}{2}\right)^2 - \dfrac{9}{4} - 2\right) = 0$

$x = \dfrac{3}{2} \pm \dfrac{\sqrt{17}}{2}$

$3\left(x - \left(\dfrac{3}{2} + \dfrac{\sqrt{17}}{2}\right)\right)\left(x - \left(\dfrac{3}{2} - \dfrac{\sqrt{17}}{2}\right)\right) = 0$

23. $-4x^2 - 2x - 6 = 1$

$-4\left(\left(x + \dfrac{1}{4}\right)^2 - \dfrac{1}{16} + \dfrac{7}{4}\right) = 0$

$x = No \ \ Solution$

24. $2x^2 - x - 1 = 2$

$2\left(\left(x - \dfrac{1}{4}\right)^2 - \dfrac{1}{16} - \dfrac{3}{2}\right) = 0$

$x = \dfrac{1}{4} \pm \dfrac{\sqrt{13}}{4}$

$2\left(x - \left(\dfrac{1}{4} + \dfrac{\sqrt{13}}{4}\right)\right)\left(x - \left(\dfrac{1}{4} - \dfrac{\sqrt{13}}{4}\right)\right) = 0$

25. $-5x^2 + 2x - 11 = -2$

$-5\left(\left(x - \dfrac{1}{5}\right)^2 - \dfrac{1}{25} + \dfrac{9}{5}\right) = 0$

$x = No \ \ Solution$

26. $-2x^2 - 2x = 0$

$-2\left(\left(x + \dfrac{1}{2}\right)^2 - \dfrac{1}{4}\right) = 0$

$x = 0, -1$

$-2(x)(x+1) = 0$

27. $4x^2 - 2x = 0$

$4\left(\left(x - \dfrac{1}{4}\right)^2 - \dfrac{1}{16}\right) = 0$

$x = 0, \dfrac{1}{2}$

$4(x)\left(x - \dfrac{1}{2}\right) = 0$

28. $-2x^2 - 3 = -5$

$-2x^2 = -2$

$x = \pm 1$

$-2(x-1)(x+1) = 0$

29. $6x^2 - 7x = 0$

$$6\left(\left(x - \frac{7}{12}\right)^2 - \frac{49}{144}\right) = 0$$

$$x = 0, \frac{7}{6}$$

$$6(x)\left(x - \frac{7}{6}\right) = 0$$

30. $2x^2 - 6x = 0$

$$2\left(\left(x - \frac{3}{2}\right)^2 - \frac{9}{4}\right) = 0$$

$$x = 0, 3$$

$$2(x)(x - 3) = 0$$

31. Write a quadratic equation whose solutions are 1 and 2 $(x-1)(x-2) = 0$

32. Write a quadratic equation whose solutions are −4 and 3 $(x+4)(x-3) = 0$

33. Write a quadratic equation whose solutions are $-\frac{1}{2}$ and $-\frac{1}{2}$ $\left(x + \frac{1}{2}\right)^2 = 0$

34. Write a quadratic equation whose solutions are $\frac{3}{7}$ and $-\frac{11}{2}$ $(3x-7)(2x+11) = 0$
$\left(x - \frac{7}{3}\right)\left(x + \frac{11}{2}\right) = 0$ *or*

35. Write a quadratic equation whose solutions are a and b $(x-a)(x-b) = 0$

36. Write a quadratic equation whose solutions are c and 2d $(x-c)(x-2d) = 0$

Rational equations 2nd degree

1. $\dfrac{3}{x^2 - 4} = 2$
$x = \pm\dfrac{\sqrt{22}}{2}$

2. $\dfrac{2}{x^2 - 2x + 1} = 1$
$x = 1 \pm \sqrt{3}$

3. $-\dfrac{2}{x^2 - 2x + 3} = 1$
No Solution

4. $\dfrac{x}{x^2 - 4} = 2$
$x = \dfrac{1}{4} \pm \dfrac{\sqrt{65}}{4}$

5. $\dfrac{x}{x - 4} = 5$
$x = 5$

6. $\dfrac{x^2}{x^2 - 4x} = 2$
$x = 8$

7. $\dfrac{x^2 - 1}{x - 5} = 2$
No Solution

8. $\dfrac{x}{x - 4} + \dfrac{2}{x - 4} = 5$
$x = \dfrac{11}{2}$

9. $\dfrac{x}{x - 4} + \dfrac{2}{x + 3} = -2$
$x = -\dfrac{1}{2} \pm \dfrac{\sqrt{393}}{6}$

10. $\dfrac{x - 1}{2x - 2} - \dfrac{2x - 1}{x + 3} = 3$
$x = -\dfrac{13}{9}$

11. $\dfrac{x}{3x + 2} - \dfrac{2x - 1}{2x + 3} = 7$
$x = -\dfrac{89}{92} \pm \dfrac{\sqrt{561}}{92}$

12.
$$\frac{1}{x}+\frac{2}{x^2}=3$$
$$x=1,-\frac{2}{3}$$

13.
$$\frac{2}{x^3}-\frac{3}{x^2}=5$$
$$x=1,2$$

14.
$$\frac{1}{x-1}+\frac{2}{x^2-1}=2$$
$$x=\frac{1}{4}\pm\frac{\sqrt{41}}{4}$$

15.
$$\frac{1}{x-3}-\frac{2}{x^2-9}=4$$
$$x=\frac{1}{8}\pm\frac{\sqrt{593}}{8}$$

16.
$$\frac{5}{x-2}-\frac{3}{x^2-4}=-2$$
$$x=-\frac{5}{4}\pm\frac{\sqrt{33}}{4}$$

17.
$$\frac{2}{x^n}-\frac{3}{x^{n+1}}=\frac{5}{x^n}$$
$$x=-1$$

18.
$$\frac{3}{25-x^2}-\frac{4}{5-x}=1$$
$$x=2\pm\sqrt{46}$$

19. Write a rational equation that has 3 as a solution. Solve
$$\frac{3}{x}+\frac{x}{3}=2$$
$$x^2-6x+9=0$$
$$x=3$$

20. Write a rational equation that has $\frac{1}{5}$ as a solution. Solve
$$\frac{1}{5x}+\frac{2}{5x+1}=2$$
$$5x+1+10x=50x^2+10x$$
$$50x^2-5x-1=0$$
$$x_1=\frac{1}{5},x_2=-\frac{1}{10}$$

21. Write a rational equation that has $\frac{2}{3}$ as a solution. Solve
$$\frac{2}{3x}+\frac{4}{3x+2}=2$$
$$6x+4+12x=18x^2+12x$$
$$18x^2-6x-4=0$$
$$x_1=\frac{2}{3},x_2=-\frac{1}{3}$$

Radical Equations

1. $\sqrt{3}=\sqrt{x}\quad x=3$

2. $3=\frac{1}{\sqrt{x}};x=\frac{1}{9}$

3. $1=\sqrt{-2x}\quad x=-\frac{1}{2}$

4.
$$\sqrt{x}=1+x$$
$$x=1+2x+x^2$$
$$x^2+x+1=0$$
$$No\ Solution$$

5.
$$\frac{\sqrt{x}}{\sqrt{6}}=\frac{2}{\sqrt{x+1}}$$
$$\frac{x}{6}=\frac{4}{x+1}$$
$$x^2+x-24=0$$
$$x=\frac{-1\pm\sqrt{97}}{2}$$

6.
$$8=\frac{\sqrt{2x-1}}{3}$$
$$576=2x-1$$
$$x=\frac{577}{2}$$

308

$$\frac{\sqrt{10}}{2} = \sqrt{x^2 + 1}$$

7. $50 = x^2 + 1$

$x = \pm 7$

$$2 = \sqrt{x^2 + 4x}$$

$$4 = x^2 + 4x$$

8. $x^2 + 4x - 4 = 0$

$$x = \frac{-4 \pm \sqrt{32}}{2} = -2 \pm 2\sqrt{2}$$

9. $\sqrt{8x + 2} = 0$

$$x = -\frac{1}{4}$$

10. $\sqrt{5x - 2} = 6$

$$x = \frac{38}{5}$$

11. $\sqrt{5x^2 - 2} = 3$

$$x = \pm\sqrt{\frac{11}{5}}$$

12. $\sqrt{x^2 + 1} = -2$

$x = \pm\sqrt{3}$, Assuming negative root

13. $\sqrt{x^2 - 2} + 4 = -2$

$x = \pm\sqrt{38}$, Assuming negative root

14. $\sqrt{2x^2 - 2} + 4x = -2$

$$-4x - 2 = \sqrt{2x^2 - 2}$$

$$16x^2 + 16x + 4 = 2x^2 - 2$$

$$14x^2 + 16x + 6 = 0$$

$$x = \frac{-16 \pm \sqrt{negative}}{28}$$

No Solution

15. $\sqrt{2x - 2} + 3x + 2 = -2$

$$-3x - 4 = \sqrt{2x - 2}$$

$$9x^2 + 24x + 16 = 2x - 2$$

$$9x^2 + 22x + 18 = 0$$

$$x = \frac{-22 \pm \sqrt{negative}}{18}$$

No Solution

16. $\sqrt{x + 1} + \sqrt{x + 3} = 2$

$$x + 1 + x + 3 + 2\sqrt{x+1}\sqrt{x+3} = 4$$

$$\sqrt{x+1}\sqrt{x+3} = -x$$

$$x^2 + 4x + 3 = x^2$$

$$x = -\frac{3}{4}$$

17. $\sqrt{x - 1} + \sqrt{x + 3} = 2$

$$x - 1 + x + 3 + 2\sqrt{x-1}\sqrt{x+3} = 4$$

$$\sqrt{x-1}\sqrt{x+3} = 1 - x$$

$$x^2 + 2x - 3 = 1 + x^2 - 2x$$

$$x = 1$$

18. $\sqrt{x - 3} + \sqrt{x + 3} = 3$

$$x - 3 + x + 3 + 2\sqrt{x-3}\sqrt{x+3} = 9$$

$$2\sqrt{x-3}\sqrt{x+3} = 9 - 2x$$

$$4x^2 - 36 = 81 + 4x^2 - 36x$$

$$x = \frac{117}{36} = \frac{13}{4}$$

19. $\sqrt{5x + 1} - \sqrt{3x - 3} = 2$

$x = 6 \pm 2\sqrt{6}$

20. $\sqrt{8x + 2} - \sqrt{3x - 3} = 0$

$x = -1$

21. $\sqrt{x - 1} + \sqrt{x + 2} = -2$

$x = \frac{17}{16}$, Assuming negative root

22. $\sqrt{x + 9} = x - \sqrt{2 + x}$

$x = 7$

Higher degree simple equations

1. $x^4 - 2x^2 = 0$ $x = 0, \pm\sqrt{2}$

2. $10(2x - 3)(x^2 - 3)(x + 5)(x^3 + 2) = 0$ $x = \dfrac{3}{2}, \pm\sqrt{3}, -5, \sqrt[3]{-2}$

3. $(2x - 3)(x - 3) = 1$ $x = \dfrac{9}{4} \pm \dfrac{\sqrt{17}}{4}$

4. $(6x - 7)(3x^2 - 5)(2x + 7)(2x^5 - 64)(4x^4 + 5) = 0$ $x = \dfrac{7}{26}, \pm\sqrt{\dfrac{5}{3}}, -\dfrac{7}{2}, 2$

5. $3x^5 - x^2 = 0$ $x = 0, \sqrt[3]{\dfrac{1}{3}}$

6. $100(x - 2)^{100}(x^2 - 5)^{10} = 0$

    $x = 2, \pm\sqrt{5}$

7. $x^6 - 32x = 0$ $x = 0, 2$

8. $x^6 - 2x^5 + x^4 = 0$ $x = 0, 1$

9. $x^3 - 4x^2 + 3x = 0$ $x = 0, 1, 3$

10. $2x^3 - 5x = 0$ $x = 0, \pm\dfrac{\sqrt{10}}{2}$

11. $2x^3 - x^2 = 0$ $x = 0, \dfrac{1}{2}$

12. $ax^4 - 3x = 0$ $x = 0, \sqrt[3]{\dfrac{3}{a}}$

13. $ax^5 - x^2 = 0$ $x = 0, \sqrt[3]{\dfrac{1}{a}}$

14. $a(x - a)^{10}(x^2 - a)^{12}(x^3 - a)^{12} = 0$

    $x = a, \pm\sqrt{a}, \sqrt[3]{a}$

15. $x^4 - 5x^2 + 3 = -1$ $x = \pm 1, \pm 2$

16. $x^4 - 10x^2 + 3 = -6$ $x = \pm 1, \pm 3$

17. $x^6 + 3x^3 - 10 = 0$
    $x = \sqrt[3]{2}, \sqrt[3]{-5}$

18. $x^8 = -2x^4 - 1$
    No Solution

19. $x^4 - 13x^2 + 36 = 0$
    $x = \pm 2, \pm 3$

20. $x^5 - 15x^3 + 54x = 0$
    $x = 0, \pm 3, \pm\sqrt{6}$

21. $x^5 + x^3 - 6x = 0$
    $x = 0, \pm\sqrt{2}$

22. $x^4 = 6x^2 - 5$
    $x = \pm 1, \pm\sqrt{5}$

Rational exponent equations

1. $x^{\frac{1}{2}} = 2$ $x = 4$

2. $x^{-1} = a$ $x = \dfrac{1}{a}$

3. $x^{-2} = 0$ *No Solution*

4. $2x^{\frac{2}{3}} = 3$ $x = \sqrt{\dfrac{27}{8}}$

5. $3x^{-\frac{1}{2}} = 2$ $x = \sqrt{\dfrac{9}{4}}$

6. $x + x^{\frac{1}{2}} = 0$
    $x = 0, 1,$ Assuming negative root

7. $2x - x^{\frac{2}{5}} = 0$ $x = 0, \dfrac{\sqrt[3]{2}}{4}$

8. $3x^{-\frac{1}{2}} = 0$ *No Solution*

9. $ax^{-\frac{3}{7}} = 0$ *No Solution*

10. $3x^{-\frac{6}{7}} = -2$ *No Solution*

11. $x^{\frac{1}{3}}+1=0$
$x=-1$

12. $3x^{\frac{1}{2}}-x^2=0 \quad x=0, 3^{\frac{3}{5}}$

13. $8x^{-2}=2 \qquad x=2$

14. $5x^{\frac{4}{3}}=-1 \qquad No \ \ Solution$

15. $3x^{-\frac{3}{4}}=-2 \qquad No \ \ Solution$

16. $x-2x^{\frac{2}{3}}=0 \qquad x=0,8$

17. $2x^2-x^{-\frac{3}{2}}=0 \quad x=2^{-\frac{3}{8}}$

18. $3x^{-2}=-5 \qquad No \ \ Solution$

19. $x^{\frac{1}{2}}-2x^{\frac{1}{6}}=0 \quad x=0,8$

20. $4x^{\frac{1}{4}}-2x^{\frac{1}{2}}=0 \quad x=0,16$

Exponential equations

1. $2^x=2$
$x=1$

2. $2^{x+2}=2^2$
$x=0$

3. $\left(\dfrac{1}{32}\right)2^{3x+4}=4$
$x=1$

4. $2^{-4x+1}=8$
$x=-\dfrac{1}{2}$

5. $3^{-5x+3}=9$
$x=\dfrac{1}{5}$

6. $\left(\dfrac{1}{4}\right)^{x+2}=\dfrac{1}{16}$
$x=0$

7. $2^{x+2}=\dfrac{-1}{16}$
$No \ \ Solution$

8. $2^{-2x+1}=8^x$
$x=\dfrac{1}{5}$

9. $\left(\dfrac{1}{3}\right)^{4x^2-1}=9^{2x}$
$x=-\dfrac{1}{2}\pm\dfrac{\sqrt{2}}{2}$

10. $\left(\dfrac{1}{125}\right)5^{x-1}=1$
$x=4$

11. $3^{2x-5}=\dfrac{1}{3}$
$x=2$

12. $3^{2x^2-5}=\dfrac{1}{27}$
$x=\pm1$

13. $\left(\dfrac{1}{5}\right)^{x-1}=-1$
$No \ \ Solution$

14. $5^{x-1}=5^{x(x-1)}$
$x=1$

15. $6^{x^2-8}=6$
$x=\pm3$

16. $5^{x-1}=\dfrac{1}{125}$
$x=-2$

17. $\left(\dfrac{1}{36}\right)^{2x-3}=\dfrac{1}{6}$
$x=\dfrac{7}{4}$

18. $6^{2x-3}=-\dfrac{3}{4}$
$No \ \ Solution$

19. $2^x=3 \qquad x\in(1,2)$

20. $2^x=0.1 \quad x\in(-4,-3)$

21. $5^x=3 \qquad x\in(0,1)$

22. $4^x=0.5, 2^{2x}=2^{-1}$
$x=-\dfrac{1}{2}$

23. $4^x=0.4 \quad x\in(-1,0)$

24. $1^x=2 \ No \ \ Solution$

25. $2^x=-2 \ No \ \ Solution$

26. $4^x=(0.5)^{x-2}; 2^{2x}=2^{-x+2}$
$2x=-x+2; x=\dfrac{2}{3}$

27. $1000^{2x-1}=(0.01)^{3x-2}; 10^{6x-3}=10^{-6x+4}$
$6x-3=-6x+4; x=\dfrac{7}{12}$

28. $\dfrac{1}{5^x-4}=1$
$x=1$

29. $\dfrac{1}{5^x-24}=1$
$x=2$

30. $\dfrac{1}{5^{3x}-24}=1$
$x=\dfrac{2}{3}$

31. $\dfrac{2}{2^x-7}=2$
$x=3$

32. $\dfrac{125}{2^{\frac{x}{3}}-7}=5$
$x=15$

33. $6^x+6^{x+1}=\dfrac{7}{6}$
$x=-1$

34. $5^x + 5^{x+1} + 5^{x-1} = \dfrac{31}{5}$

$x = 0$

35. $7^{x-1} + 7^{x-2} = \dfrac{8}{49}$

$x = 0$

36. $7^{x-1} + 7^{x-2} = \dfrac{8}{7}$

$x = 1$

37. $2^x + 2^{x-1} + 2^{x+2} = 11$

$x = -1$

38. $2^x + 2^{x-1} + 2^{x+2} = 22$

$x = 2$

39. $5^{2x} - 6 \times 5^x = -5$

$x = 0, 1$

40. $3^{2x} - 4 \times 3^x - 2 = -5$

$x = 0, 1$

41. $5^{2x} + 4 \times 5^x - 10 = -5$

$x = 0$

42. $8^{2x} - 9 \times 8^x + 8 = 0$

$x = 0, 1$

43. $2 \times 8^{2x} - 18 \times 8^x + 10 = -6$

$x = 0, 1$

44. $3^{2x+1} - 3^{x+2} + 81 = 0$

No   Solution

45. $5^{2x-1} - 6 \times 5^{x-1} = -1$

$x = 0, 1$

46. $3^{2x+2} - 4 \times 3^{x+2} + 27 = 0$

$x = 0, 1$

Systems of equations

1. One equation with 1 variable may have <u>0</u> or 1 or <u>infinite</u> solutions. Examples:
   2x + 5 = 7 (1 solution) , x + 3 = x – 4 (0 solutions), x + 1 = x + 1 (infinite solutions)

2. One equation with 2 two variable may have <u>0</u> or <u>1</u> or <u>infinite</u> solutions. Examples:
   2x + y = 7 + y (1 solution), x + y = x + y + 5 (0 solutions) 2x + y = 1 (infinite solutions)

3. Equations of the first degree are equations in which <u>the variables are all</u> to the power of 1. Examples:
   1 variable: 3x + 1 = 5   2 variables: 3x + 7y = 15   3 variables: 3x + y – 3z = 2

4. Equations of the 2nd degree are equations <u>in which the highest power of at least one of the variables is 2</u>. Give examples with 1 and 2 variables:
   1 variable: $3x^2 + 1 = 5$ 2 variables: $3x^2 + 7y = 15$

5. The solution to one equation of the first degree with 2 two variable, graphically speaking, <u>is a point</u> The collection of points will form a <u>straight line.</u>

6. Write a system of equations whose only solution is x = 1, y = 2.
$$x + y = 3$$
$$x - y = -1$$

7. Write a system of equations whose only solution is x = 0, y = $-\dfrac{1}{2}$.
$$x - 2y = 1$$
$$x + 2y = -1$$

8. Write a system of equations whose only solution is x = –3, y = $-\dfrac{3}{2}$.
$$-x - 2y = 6$$
$$x - 2y = 0$$

9. Write a system of equations whose only solution is x = 15, y = –6.
$$x + y = 9$$
$$x + 2y = 3$$

10. Write a system of equations that has no solutions
$$x + y = 9$$
$$2x + 2y = 9$$

11. Write a system of equations that has infinite solutions
$$x + y = 1$$
$$2x + 2y = 2$$

12. Given the equations I) 2x + y = 3, II) 2y – x = 4

    a. Write a few solutions to the equations
       I) (0, 3), (1, 1), (2, -1), (-1, 5)
       II) (0, 2), (-4, 0), (-2, 1), (2, 3)
    b. Show the solutions on the graph.
    c. Draw a conclusion:
    In each one of the cases the points lie on a straight line. The lines intersect.

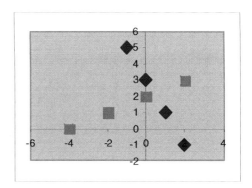

13. Given the equations I) 4x + 2y = 3, II) y + 2x = 8

    a. Write a few solutions to the equations
       I) (0, 3/2), (3/4, 0), (1, -1/2), (-1, 7/2)
       II) (0, 8), (4, 0), (1, 6), (2, 4)
    b. Show the solutions on the graph.
    c. Draw a conclusion:

    In each one of the cases the points lie on a straight line. The lines are parallel.

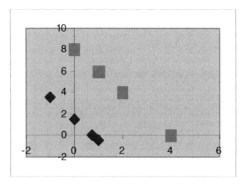

14. Given the equations I)6x – 2y = 2, II) y – 3x= –1

    a. Write a few solutions to the equations
       I) (0, -1), (1/3, 0), (1, 2), (2, 5)
       II) (0, -1), (1/3, 0), (1, 2), (2, 5)
    b. Show the solutions on the graph.
    c. Draw a conclusion: The 2 lines are identical

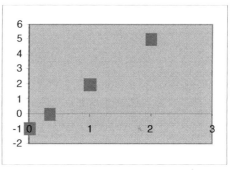

15. $5x + 1 = 2y$
    $4y + x - 3 = 0$
    $x = \dfrac{1}{11}, y = \dfrac{8}{11}$

16. $5x + 3y = 2 - 2y$
    $-y + 2x - 5 = 0$
    $x = \dfrac{9}{5}, y = -\dfrac{7}{5}$

17. $5x = 2y$
    $-y + 2x = 0$
    $x = 0, y = 0$

18. $x = 2y - 7$
    $4y - 2x = 0$

19. *No Solution*
    $-5x + 1 = 2y$
    $-4y + x - 3 = x$
    $x = \dfrac{1}{2}, y = -\dfrac{3}{4}$

20. $5x + 1 = 2y$
    $10y - 25x = 10$
    No Solution

21. $2x + 1 = 2y$
    $-4y + 4x + 2 = 0$
    $x = 0, y = \dfrac{1}{2}$

22. $x + 1 = 2y$
    $4y - 2x - 3 = 0$
    No Solution

23. $4x = y$
    $3y - 12x = 0$
    $x = 0, y = 0$

24. $2x + 7y = 4$
    $3y - 5x - 3 = 0$
    $x = -\dfrac{9}{41}, y = \dfrac{26}{41}$

25. $\dfrac{x}{2} - 1 = 5y$

$3y + x - 2 = 0$

$x - 2 = 10y$

$3y + x - 2 = 0$

$x = 2, y = 0$

26. $\dfrac{x}{5} + 1 = 2y$

$\dfrac{y}{3} + \dfrac{x}{2} - 3 = 0$

$x + 5 = 10y$

$2y + 3x - 18 = 0$

$x = \dfrac{85}{16}, y = \dfrac{33}{32}$

27. $\dfrac{x}{5} + 2 = 6y$

$-3y + \dfrac{x}{10} + 1 = 0$

$x + 10 = 30y$

$-30y + x + 10 = 0$

infinite solutions

28. $\dfrac{x}{5} + 2 = 4y$

$-3y + \dfrac{x}{10} + 2 = 0$

$x + 10 = 20y$

$-30y + x + 20 = 0$

$x = 10, y = 1$

29. $\dfrac{x}{6} + 2 = \dfrac{3y}{7}$

$\dfrac{-2y}{14} + \dfrac{x}{3} = 1$

$7x + 84 = 18y$

$-6y + 14x = 42$

$x = 6, y = 7$

30. $\dfrac{x}{5} + 2 = 2y$

$-3y + \dfrac{x}{10} = -3$

$x + 10 = 10y$

$-30y + x = -30$

$x = 0, y = 1$

31. $x = 2y$

$-y + x^2 - 5 = 0$

$x = -2, y = -1$

$x = \dfrac{5}{2}, y = \dfrac{5}{4}$

32. $x = 1 - y$

$-y + x^2 - 5 = 0$

$x = 2, y = -1$

$x = -3, y = 4$

33. $x = 1 - y^2$

$-y^2 + x^2 - 5 = 0$

$x = -3, y = 2$

$x = -3, y = -2$

34. $-x^2 = 1 - 2y^2$

$-y^2 + x^2 = 0$

$-y^2 = 1 - 2y^2$

$y = 1, x = 1;\ y = 1, x = -1$

$y = -1, x = 1;\ y = -1, x = -1$

35. $x = 1 - y^2$

$-y^2 + x^2 - 55 = 0$

Reorganize and

add equations

$x^2 + x - 56 = 0$

$x = -8, y = 3$

$x = -8, y = -3$

36. $2x + 1 = 1 + 4y$

$-3y^2 + x^2 = 1$

$y = 1, x = 2$

$y = -1, x = -2$

314

1.12. – POLYNOMIALS

<u>Sum, subtraction, multiplication</u>

1. Given the polynomials: $A = 3x + 5x^3 - 7x^{12} - 1$, $B = -3x^2 + 2x^5 - 2x^3$, $C = x^2 + x^3$
   $D = -x + 5 + 5x^4 - 4x^4 + 2x^2 - 4x^5$. Evaluate:

   a. $A + B + C + D = -7x^{12} - 2x^5 + x^4 + 4x^3 + 2x$

   b. $A - 2B + 3D = -7x^{12} - 16x^5 + 3x^4 + 9x^3 + 12x^2 + 14$

   c. $2AC = -14x^{15} - 14x^{14} + 10x^6 + 10x^5 + 6x^4 + 4x^3 - 2x^2$

   d. $-3CB = -6x^8 - 6x^7 + 6x^6 + 15x^5 + 9x^4$

<u>Division</u>

2. Divide $3x^3 + 1$ by x

   $$\frac{3x^3 + 1}{x} = 3x^2 + \frac{1}{x} (\text{Re} \, mainder : 1)$$

3. Divide $-2x^3 - 5$ by x + 1

   $$\frac{-2x^3 - 5}{x + 1} = -2x^2 + 2x - 2 + \frac{-3}{x + 1} (\text{Re} \, mainder : -3)$$

4. Divide $2x^4 + x$ by x

   $$\frac{2x^4 + x}{x} = 2x^3 + 1 (\text{Re} \, mainder : 0)$$

5. Divide $-2x - 5x^3 + 1$ by x

   $$\frac{-5x^3 - 2x + 1}{x} = -5x^4 - 2 + \frac{1}{x} (\text{Re} \, mainder : 1)$$

6. Divide $4 - x^4$ by x – 1

   $$\frac{-x^4 + 4}{x - 1} = -x^3 - x^2 - x - 1 + \frac{3}{x - 1} (\text{Re} \, mainder : 5)$$

7. Divide $2x^3 + 3x - 5$ by x – 3

   $$\frac{2x^3 + 3x - 5}{x - 3} = 2x^2 + 6x + 21 + \frac{58}{x - 3} (\text{Re} \, mainder : 58)$$

8. Divide $4x^4 + x - 5$ by 2x – 3

   $$\frac{4x^4 + x - 5}{2x - 3} = 2x^3 + 3x^2 + \frac{9}{2}x + \frac{29}{4}x + \frac{\left(\frac{67}{4}\right)}{2x - 3} (\text{Re} \, mainder : \frac{67}{4})$$

9. Divide $2x^3 + 4x - 7$ by $x^2 - 1$

   $$\frac{2x^3 + 4x - 7}{x^2 - 1} = 2x + \frac{6x - 7}{x^2 - 1} (\text{Re} \, mainder : 6x - 7)$$

10. Divide $5x^4 + x^3 + 2x^2 - 5$ by $-2x + 1$

$$\frac{5x^4 + x^3 + 2x^2 - 5}{-2x + 1} = -\frac{5}{2}x^3 - \frac{7}{4}x^2 - \frac{15}{8}x - \frac{15}{16} + \frac{\left(-\frac{65}{16}\right)}{-2x+1} \, (\text{Re} \, mainder : -\frac{65}{16})$$

11. Divide $6x^5 + 2x^4 + 2x - 5$ by $x^3 + x$

$$\frac{6x^5 + 2x^4 + 2x - 5}{x^3 + x} = 6x^2 + 2x - 6 + \frac{-2x^2 + 8x - 5}{x^3 + x} \, (\text{Re} \, mainder : -2x^2 + 8x - 5)$$

12. Divide $5x^3 + x^4 + 2x^2 - 5$ by $x^4 + 1$

$$\frac{x^4 + 5x^3 + 2x^2 - 5}{x^4 + 1} = 1 + \frac{5x^3 + 2x^2 - 6}{x^4 + 1} \, (\text{Re} \, mainder : 5x^3 + 2x^2 - 6)$$

13. When $x^3 - 2x + k$ is divided by $x - 2$ it leaves a remainder of 5, find k.
$R = P(2) = 8 - 4 + k = 5; k = 1$

14. When $x^3 - 2x + k$ is divided by $x + 1$ it leaves a remainder of 0, find k.
$R = P(-1) = -1 + 2 + k = 0; k = -1$

15. When $2x^3 - x^2 + kx - 4$ is divided by $x + 2$ it leaves a remainder of 0, find k.
$R = P(-2) = -16 - 4 - 2k - 4 = 0; k = -12$

16. When $x^3 - x^2 + kx - 4$ is divided by $x - 1$ it leaves a remainder of 2, find k.
$R = P(1) = 1 - 1 + k - 4 = 2; k = 4$

In each one of the following cases write the corresponding expression and use the Remainder theorem to find the remainder:

1. $2x^3 + 2x - 15$ is divided by $x - 1$
$2x^3 + 2x - 15 = Q(x - 1) + R$ Substituting <u>x = 1</u> on <u>both</u> sides:
$R = 2 + 2 - 15 = -11$

2. $-4x^4 + 3x^3 - 5x + 1$ is divided by $x + 2$
$-4x^4 + 3x^3 - 5x + 1 = = Q(x + 2) + R$
$R = P(-2) = -64 - 24 + 10 + 1 = -77$

3. $3x^3 + 2x - 4$ is divided by $x + 3$
$3x^3 + 2x - 4 = Q(x + 3) + R$
$R = P(-3) = -81 - 6 - 4 = -91$

4. $3x^4 + 6x^3 - 33x^2 - 36x + 108$ is divided by $x - 2$
$3x^4 + 6x^3 - 33x^2 - 36x + 108 = Q(x - 2) + R$
$R = P(2) = 48 + 48 - 132 - 72 + 108 = 0$

5. $-2x^4 + x^3 + x^2 - 4x - 5$ is divided by $x - 2$
$-2x^4 + x^3 + x^2 - 4x - 5 = Q(x - 2) + R$
$R = P(2) = -32 + 8 + 4 - 8 - 5 = -33$

6. $9x^3 + 2x - 4$ is divided by $2x - 3$

$9x^3 + 2x - 4 = Q(2x - 3) + R$

$R = P(\frac{3}{2}) = \frac{243}{8} + 3 - 4 = \frac{235}{8}$

7. $x^{44} + x - 5$ is divided by $x - 1$

$x^{44} + x - 5 = Q(x - 1) + R$

$R = P(1) = 1 + 1 - 5 = -3$

8. $7x^4 + 14x^3 + 14x^2 + 14x + 7$ is divided by $x + 1$

$7x^4 + 14x^3 + 14x^2 + 14x + 7 = Q(x + 1) + R$

$R = P(-1) = 7 - 14 + 14 - 14 + 7 = 0$

9. $4x^{4455} + x^3 - x - 5$ is divided by $x + 1$

$4x^{4455} + x^3 - x - 5 = Q(x + 1) + R$

$R = P(-1) = -4 - 1 + 1 - 5 = -9$

10. $2x^3 + 3x^2 - 4x - 3$ is divided by $3x - 4$

$2x^3 + 3x^2 - 4x - 3 = Q(3x - 4) + R$

$R = P(\frac{4}{3}) = \frac{47}{27}$

11. In which one of the questions 1 to 10 the divisor is Also a factor of the polynomial? <u>In Questions 4 and 8, the remainder is 0 so (x – 2) and (x + 1) are factors of the polynomial</u>

Factor the following polynomials and solve the equations (real solutions only):

12. $2x^3 + 2x^2 - 2x - 2 = 0$ $\qquad$ $2(x-1)(x+1)^2 = 0; x = 1, -1$

13. $2x^3 + 4x^2 + 2x + 4 = 0$ $\qquad$ $2(x+2)(x^2+1) = 0; x = -2$

14. $6x + 6 + 3x^3 + 3x^2 = 0$ $\qquad$ $3(x+1)(x^2+2) = 0; x = -1$

15. $-4x + 12 + 2x^3 - 6x^2 = 0$ $\qquad$ $2(x-3)(x-\sqrt{2})(x+\sqrt{2}) = 0; x = 3, \sqrt{2}, -\sqrt{2}$

16. $x^3 - 4x^2 + 4x - 1 = 0$

$$(x-1)\left(x - \left(\frac{3+\sqrt{5}}{2}\right)\right)\left(x - \left(\frac{3-\sqrt{5}}{2}\right)\right) = 0; x = 1, \frac{3-\sqrt{5}}{2}, \frac{3+\sqrt{5}}{2}$$

17. $2x^3 - x^2 - 8x + 4 = 0$ $\qquad$ $2(x-2)(x-\frac{1}{2})(x+2) = 0; x = 2, \frac{1}{2}, -2$

18. $5x^3 - 8x^2 - 27x + 18 = 0$ $\qquad$ $5(x-3)(x-\frac{3}{5})(x+2) = 0; x = 3, \frac{3}{5}, -2$

19. $-11x^2 - x + 6 + 6x^3 = 0$ $6(x-1)(x-\frac{3}{2})(x+\frac{2}{3}) = 0; x = 1, \frac{3}{2}, -\frac{2}{3}$

20. $4x^3 - 39x + 35 = 0$ $4(x-1)(x-\frac{5}{2})(x+\frac{7}{2}) = 0; x = 1, \frac{5}{2}, -\frac{7}{2}$

21. $5x^3 - 8x^2 - 27x + 18 = 0$ $5(x-3)(x-\frac{3}{5})(x+2) = 0; x = 3, \frac{3}{5}, -2$

22. $9x^3 + 18x^2 - 16x - 32 = 0$ $9(x+2)(x-\frac{4}{3})(x+\frac{4}{3}) = 0; x = -2, \frac{4}{3}, -\frac{4}{3}$

23. $x^3 - 13x - 12 = 0$ $2(x-4)(x+3)(x+1) = 0; x = 4, -3, -1$

24. $2x^3 + 9 - 9x^2 - 2x = 0$ $2(x-1)(x+1)(x-\frac{9}{2}) = 0; x = 1, -1, \frac{9}{2}$

25. $3x^3 + 6x^2 - 4x - 8 = 0$

$$(x+2)\left(x - \frac{2\sqrt{3}}{3}\right)\left(x + \frac{2\sqrt{3}}{3}\right) = 0; x = -2, \frac{2\sqrt{3}}{3}, -\frac{2\sqrt{3}}{3}$$

26. $x^4 - x^3 - 12x^2 - 4x + 16 = 0$ $(x-1)(x-4)(x+2)^2 = 0; x = 1, 4, -2$

27. $x^4 + 3x^3 - 6x - 4 = 0$

$$(x+2)(x+1)(x-\sqrt{2})(x+\sqrt{2}) = 0; x = -1, -2, \sqrt{2}, -\sqrt{2}$$

28. $6x^4 + 17x^3 + 7x^2 - 8x - 4 = 0$

$$(x+2)(x+1)(x-\frac{2}{3})(x+\frac{1}{2}) = 0; x = -1, -2, -\frac{1}{2}, \frac{2}{3}$$

29. The values of a and b if $6x^3 + 7x^2 + ax + b$ is divisible by $(2x - 1)$ and $(x + 1)$

$\frac{5}{2} + \frac{a}{2} + b = 0; \quad 1 - a + b = 0; \quad a = -1, b = -1$

30. $x^3 + ax^2 - 2x + b$ has $(x + 1)$ as a factor, and leaves a remainder of 4 when divided by $(x - 3)$. Find a and b.

$1 + a + b = 0; \quad -21 + 9a + b = 4; \quad a = \frac{13}{4}, b = -\frac{17}{4}$

31. Given that $(x - 1)$ and $(x - 2)$ are factors of $6x^4 + ax^3 - 17x^2 + bx - 4 = 0$, find a and b, and any remaining factors.

$-15 + a + b = 0; \quad 24 + 8a + 2b = 0; \quad a = -9, b = 24$, the remaining factors are:

$$\left(x - \left(\frac{-9 + \sqrt{129}}{12}\right)\right)\left(x - \left(\frac{-9 - \sqrt{129}}{12}\right)\right)$$

Solutions of polynomials

1. In the equation $x^2 + 3x - 10 = 0 = (x + 5)(x - 2)$ Find:

   $x_1 + x_2 = -3$ $\qquad$ $x_1 \cdot x_2 = -10$ $\qquad$ $-\dfrac{b}{a} = -3$ $\qquad$ $\dfrac{c}{a} = -10$

2. In the equation $2x^2 - 5x - 3 = 0 = (2x + 1)(x - 3)$ Find:

   $x_1 + x_2 = \dfrac{5}{2}$ $\qquad$ $x_1 \cdot x_2 = -\dfrac{3}{2}$ $\qquad$ $-\dfrac{b}{a} = \dfrac{5}{2}$ $\qquad$ $\dfrac{c}{a} = -\dfrac{3}{2}$

3. In the equation $6x^2 - 5x - 6 = 0 = (3x + 2)(2x - 3)$ Find:

   $x_1 + x_2 = \dfrac{5}{6}$ $\qquad$ $x_1 \cdot x_2 = -1$ $\qquad$ $-\dfrac{b}{a} = \dfrac{5}{6}$ $\qquad$ $\dfrac{c}{a} = -1$

4. In the equation $x^3 - 5x^2 - 2x + 24 = 0 = (x + 2)(x - 3)(x - 4)$ Find:

   $x_1 + x_2 + x_3 = 5$ $\qquad$ $x_1 \cdot x_2 \cdot x_3 = -24$ $\qquad$ $-\dfrac{b}{a} = 5$ $\qquad$ $-\dfrac{d}{a} = -24$

5. In the equation $12x^3 - 4x^2 - 3x + 1 = 0 = (2x + 1)(2x - 1)(3x - 1)$ Find:

   $x_1 + x_2 + x_3 = \dfrac{1}{3}$ $\qquad$ $x_1 \cdot x_2 \cdot x_3 = -\dfrac{1}{12}$ $\qquad$ $-\dfrac{b}{a} = \dfrac{1}{3}$ $\qquad$ $-\dfrac{d}{a} = -\dfrac{1}{12}$

6. Conclusion:

   In the polynomials of even degree:

   $x_1 + x_2 + x_3 + ... = -\dfrac{b}{a}$ $\qquad\qquad$ $x_1 \cdot x_2 \cdot x_3 \cdot ... = \dfrac{independent\ \ term}{a}$

   In the polynomials of odd degree:

   $x_1 + x_2 + x_3 + ... = -\dfrac{b}{a}$ $\qquad\qquad$ $x_1 \cdot x_2 \cdot x_3 \cdot ... = -\dfrac{independent\ \ term}{a}$

1.13. – SEQUENCES AND SERIES

Given The following sequences, write the first 3 terms and the term in the 20th position. If possible identify the pattern using text (follow example):

1. $a_n = 3n$ $a_1 = 3$ $a_2 = 6$ $a_3 = 9$ $a_{20} = 60$ Pattern: __add 3__

2. $a_n = 3n + 1$ $a_1 = 4$ $a_2 = 7$ $a_3 = 10$ $a_{20} = 61$ Pattern: __add 3__

3. $a_n = 3n - 5$ $a_1 = -5$ $a_2 = -2$ $a_3 = 1$ $a_{20} = 55$ Pattern: __add 3__

4. $a_n = 2n + 1$ $a_1 = 3$ $a_2 = 5$ $a_3 = 7$ $a_{20} = 41$ Pattern: __add 2__

5. $a_n = 2n$ $a_1 = 2$ $a_2 = 4$ $a_3 = 6$ $a_{20} = 40$ Pattern: __add 2__

6. $a_n = 2n - 4$ $a_1 = -2$ $a_2 = 0$ $a_3 = 2$ $a_{20} = 36$ Pattern: __add 2__

7. $a_n = -4n$ $a_1 = -4$ $a_2 = -8$ $a_3 = -12$ $a_{20} = -80$ Pattern: __add –4__

8. $a_n = -4n + 10$ $a_1 = 6$ $a_2 = 2$ $a_3 = -2$ $a_{20} = -70$ Pattern: __add –4__

9. $a_n = -4n - 6$ $a_1 = -10$ $a_2 = -14$ $a_3 = -18$ $a_{20} = -86$ Pattern: __add –4__

10. $a_n = \dfrac{n}{3}$ $a_1 = \dfrac{1}{3}$ $a_2 = \dfrac{2}{3}$ $a_3 = 1$ $a_{20} = \dfrac{20}{3}$ Pattern: __add $\dfrac{1}{3}$__

11. $a_n = \dfrac{n}{2}$ $a_1 = \dfrac{1}{2}$ $a_2 = 1$ $a_3 = \dfrac{3}{2}$ $a_{20} = 10$ Pattern: __add $\dfrac{1}{2}$__

12. $a_n = \dfrac{2n}{5} + 1$ $a_1 = \dfrac{7}{5}$ $a_2 = \dfrac{9}{5}$ $a_3 = \dfrac{11}{5}$ $a_{20} = 9$ Pattern: __add $\dfrac{2}{5}$__

13. $a_n = \dfrac{-3n}{7} + 5$ $a_1 = \dfrac{32}{7}$ $a_2 = \dfrac{29}{7}$ $a_3 = \dfrac{26}{7}$ $a_{20} = \dfrac{-25}{7}$ Pattern: __add $-\dfrac{3}{7}$__

14. $a_n = \dfrac{n}{9} - 5$ $a_1 = \dfrac{-44}{9}$ $a_2 = \dfrac{-43}{9}$ $a_3 = \dfrac{-42}{9}$ $a_{20} = \dfrac{-25}{9}$ Pattern: __add $\dfrac{1}{9}$__

15. $a_n = \dfrac{n}{10} - 1$ $a_1 = \dfrac{-9}{10}$ $a_2 = \dfrac{-8}{10}$ $a_3 = \dfrac{-7}{10}$ $a_{20} = 1$ Pattern: __add $\dfrac{1}{10}$__

16. $a_n = \dfrac{3n}{4} + 2$ $a_1 = \dfrac{11}{4}$ $a_2 = \dfrac{14}{4}$ $a_3 = \dfrac{17}{4}$ $a_{20} = \dfrac{68}{4}$ Pattern: __add $\dfrac{3}{4}$__

17. $a_n = n^2$ $a_1 = 1$ $a_2 = 4$ $a_3 = 9$ $a_{20} = 400$ Pattern: __different__

18. $a_n = n^3$ $a_1 = 1$ $a_2 = 8$ $a_3 = 27$ $a_{20} = 8000$ Pattern: __different__

19. $a_n = 2^n$ $a_1 = 2$ $a_2 = 4$ $a_3 = 8$ $a_{20} = 2^{20}$ Pattern: __multiply by 2__

20. $a_n = -2^n$ $a_1 = -2$ $a_2 = -4$ $a_3 = -8$ $a_{20} = -2^{20}$ Pattern: __multiply by 2__

21. $a_n = 2^{-n}$ $a_1 = \dfrac{1}{2}$ $a_2 = \dfrac{1}{4}$ $a_3 = \dfrac{1}{8}$ $a_{20} = \dfrac{1}{2^{20}}$ Pattern: __multiply by $\dfrac{1}{2}$__

22. $a_n = -2^{-n}$ $a_1 = -\dfrac{1}{2}$ $a_2 = -\dfrac{1}{4}$ $a_3 = -\dfrac{1}{8}$ $a_{20} = -\dfrac{1}{2^{20}}$ Pattern: __multiply by $\dfrac{1}{2}$__

23. $a_n = (-2)^n$ $a_1 = -2$ $a_2 = 4$ $a_3 = -8$ $a_{20} = 2^{20}$ Pattern: __multiply by –2__

24. $a_n = 2^{n-1}$ $a_1 = 1$ $a_2 = 2$ $a_3 = 4$ $a_{20} = 2^{19}$ Pattern: __multiply by 2__

25. $a_n = 2^{n+2}$ $a_1 = 8$ $a_2 = 16$ $a_3 = 32$ $a_{20} = 2^{22}$ Pattern: __multiply by 2__

26. $a_n = 3 \times 2^n$ $a_1 = 6$ $a_2 = 12$ $a_3 = 24$ $a_{20} = 3 \cdot 2^{20}$ Pattern: __multiply by 2__

27. $a_n = -5 \times 2^{n-1}$ $a_1 = -5$ $a_2 = -10$ $a_3 = -20$ $a_{20} = -5 \cdot 2^{19}$ Pattern: __multiply by 2__

28. $a_n = 5 \times 2^{1-n}$ $a_1 = 5$ $a_2 = \dfrac{5}{2}$ $a_3 = \dfrac{5}{4}$ $a_{20} = \dfrac{5}{2^{19}}$ Pattern: __multiply by $\dfrac{1}{2}$__

29. $a_n=(-3)^{2-n}$ $a_1=-3$ $a_2=1$ $a_3=-\dfrac{1}{3}$ $a_{20}=\dfrac{1}{3^{18}}$ Pattern: __multiply by $-\dfrac{1}{3}$__

30. $a_n=2\times(-3)^n$ $a_1=-6$ $a_2=18$ $a_3=-54$ $a_{20}=2\cdot3^{20}$ Pattern: __multiply by -3__

31. $a_n=2\times(-5)^{n-1}$ $a_1=2$ $a_2=-10$ $a_3=50$ $a_{20}=2\cdot(-5)^{19}$ Pattern: __multiply by -5__

32. $a_n=(-3)^{n+1}$ $a_1=9$ $a_2=-27$ $a_3=81$ $a_{20}=(-3)^{21}$ Pattern: __multiply by -3__

33. $a_n=1+5^{n-2}$ $a_1=\dfrac{6}{5}$ $a_2=2$ $a_3=6$ $a_{20}=1+5^{18}$ Pattern: __different__

34. $a_n=3\times2^n$ $a_1=6$ $a_2=12$ $a_3=24$ $a_{20}=3\cdot2^{20}$ Pattern: __multiply by 2__

35. $a_n=-5\times2^{n-1}$ $a_1=-5$ $a_2=-10$ $a_3=-20$ $a_{20}=-5\cdot2^{19}$ Pattern: __multiply by 2__

36. $a_n=2\times3^n$ $a_1=6$ $a_2=18$ $a_3=54$ $a_{20}=2\cdot3^{20}$ Pattern: __multiply by 3__

37. $a_n=5^{n-2}+3$ $a_1=\dfrac{16}{5}$ $a_2=4$ $a_3=8$ $a_{20}=3+5^{18}$ Pattern: __different__

38. $a_n=(-3)^n$ $a_1=-3$ $a_2=9$ $a_3=-27$ $a_{20}=3^{20}$ Pattern: __multiply by -3__

39. $a_n=2\times(-3)^n$ $a_1=-6$ $a_2=18$ $a_3=-54$ $a_{20}=2\cdot3^{20}$ Pattern: __multiply by -3__

40. $a_n=2\times(-5)^{n-1}$ $a_1=2$ $a_2=-10$ $a_3=50$ $a_{20}=2\cdot(-5)^{19}$ Pattern: __multiply by -5__

41. $a_n=(-3)^{n+1}$ $a_1=9$ $a_2=-27$ $a_3=81$ $a_{20}=-3^{21}$ Pattern: __multiply by -3__

42. $a_n=1+5^{n-2}$ $a_1=\dfrac{6}{5}$ $a_2=2$ $a_3=6$ $a_{20}=1+5^{18}$ Pattern: __different__

43. The sequences in which the pattern is add/subtract a number are called
   __Arithmetic__

44. The sequences in which the pattern is multiply/divide (pay attention that dividing by a is the same as multiplying by __the inverse__) a number are called
   __Geometric__

45. $a_n=2a_{n-1}$ $a_1=1$ $a_2=2$ $a_3=4$ $a_{20}=2^{19}$ Pattern: __multiply by 2__

46. $a_{n+2}=a_n+a_{n+1}$ $a_1=1$ $a_2=1$ $a_3=2$ $a_{20}=$ Pattern: __Each term is the sum of the previous 2 (Fibonacci)__

47. In the last 2 sequences the terms are given __in terms of the previous terms__

48. (T/__F__) Arithmetic and Geometric sequences are most of the sequences that exist.

49. The terms in a convergent geometric sequence tend to __a number,__ in a none–convergent sequence the terms tend to __infinity__ or __negative infinity (or alternate)__.

50. An example of a convergent geometric sequence: 200, 100, 50, 25…

51. An example of a divergent geometric sequence: 7, 21, 63, 189…

52. An example of a alternating convergent geometric sequence: 80, –40, 20, –10…

53. An example of a none alternating divergent geometric sequence: 2, 10, 50, 250...

54. A convergent geometric sequence is a sequence in which r is __between –1 and 1__

Given the following sequences:

a. For each one write: arithmetic, geometric convergent, geometric divergent or neither, the __next term__ and their __general term__ (in case they are geometric or arithmetic only).

b. Try to write the general term of the other sequences as well.

55. 1, 2, 3, 4, __5__
    $a_n=1+(n-1)1$, Arithmetic
    $a_n=n$

56. 1, 2, 4, 8, __16__
    $a_n=2^{n-1}$, Geometric

57. 1, 3, 5, 7, ___

$a_n = 1 + (n-1)2$, Arithmetic

$a_n = -1 + 2n$

58. 1, 3, 9, 27, __81__

$a_n = 3^{n-1}$, Geometric

59. 4, 6, 9, 13,5, __20.25__

$a_n = 4\left(\dfrac{3}{2}\right)^{n-1}$, Geometric

60. 4, 1, –2, –5, __–8__

$a_n = 4 + (n-1)(-3)$, Arithmetic

$a_n = 7 - 3n$

61. 5, 0, –4, –7, ___

Neither

62. 10, 1000, 100000, __10000000__

$a_n = 10 \cdot 100^{n-1}$, Geometric

63. 30, 10, $\dfrac{10}{3}$, $\dfrac{10}{9}$, $\dfrac{10}{27}$

$a_n = 30 \cdot \left(\dfrac{1}{3}\right)^{n-1}$, Geometric

64. 2, 10, 50, 250, __1250__

$a_n = 2 \cdot 5^{n-1}$, Geometric

65. 2, 102, 202, 302, __402__

$a_n = 2 + (n-1)100$, Arithmetic

$a_n = -98 + 100n$

66. 1, –1, 1, –1, __1__

$a_n = (-1)^{n-1}$, Geometric

67. –2, 2, –2, 2, __–2__

$a_n = -2(-1)^{n-1}$, Geometric

68. 3, –6, 12, –24, __48__

$a_n = 3(-2)^{n-1}$, Geometric

69. –8, 4, –2, 1, $\left(-\dfrac{1}{2}\right)$

$a_n = -8\left(-\dfrac{1}{2}\right)^{n-1}$, Geometric

70. 5, 1, $\dfrac{1}{5}$, $\dfrac{1}{25}$, $\dfrac{1}{125}$

$a_n = 5\left(\dfrac{1}{5}\right)^{n-1}$, Geometric

71. 100, 10, 1, $\dfrac{1}{10}$, $\dfrac{1}{100}$

$a_n = 100\left(\dfrac{1}{10}\right)^{n-1}$, Geometric

72. $\dfrac{3}{4}$, $\dfrac{3}{8}$, $\dfrac{3}{16}$, $\dfrac{3}{32}$

$a_n = \dfrac{3}{4}\left(\dfrac{1}{2}\right)^{n-1}$, Geometric

73. 12, 11, 10, 9, __8__

$a_n = 12 + (n-1)(-1)$, Arithmetic

$a_n = 13 - n$

74. $\dfrac{4}{9}$, $\dfrac{5}{9}$, $\dfrac{6}{9}$, $\dfrac{6}{9}$

$a_n = \dfrac{4}{9} + (n-1)\left(\dfrac{1}{9}\right)$, Arithmetic

$a_n = -98 + 100n$

75. 9, 8, 6, 5, 3, 2, ___

Neither

76. 5, 9, 13, __17__

$a_n = 5 + (n-1)4$, Arithmetic

$a_n = 1 + 4n$

77. 1, $\dfrac{3}{2}$, $\dfrac{9}{4}$, $\dfrac{27}{8}$, $\dfrac{81}{16}$

$a_n = \left(\dfrac{3}{2}\right)^{n-1}$, Geometric

78. 5, $-\dfrac{5}{3}$, $\dfrac{5}{9}$, $-\dfrac{5}{27}$, $\dfrac{5}{81}$

$a_n = 5\left(-\dfrac{1}{3}\right)^{n-1}$, Geometric

79. –1, –2, –3, __–4__

$a_n = -1 + (n-1)(-1)$, Arithmetic

$a_n = -n$

80. –2, 4, –8, __16__

$a_n = -2(-2)^{n-1}$, Geometric

81. 70, 20, $\dfrac{40}{7}$, $\dfrac{80}{14}$

$a_n = 70\left(\dfrac{2}{7}\right)^{n-1}$, Geometric

82. 100, 10, 1, $\dfrac{1}{10}$

$a_n = 100\left(\dfrac{1}{10}\right)^{n-1}$, Geometric

83. $100, -10, 1, \dfrac{-1}{10}, \dfrac{1}{100}$

$a_n = 100\left(-\dfrac{1}{10}\right)^{n-1}$, Geometric

84. $3, 24, 192, \underline{1536}$

$a_n = 3 \cdot 8^{n-1}$, Geometric

85. $90, 9, \dfrac{9}{10}, \dfrac{9}{100}$

$a_n = 90 \cdot \left(\dfrac{1}{10}\right)^{n-1}$, Geometric

86. $\dfrac{3}{2}, \dfrac{4}{3}, \dfrac{5}{4}, \dfrac{6}{5}$

Neither, General term:

$a_n = \dfrac{2+n}{1+n}$ Numerator and

denominator are arithmetic.

87. $\dfrac{40}{3}, \dfrac{20}{6}, \dfrac{10}{12}, \dfrac{5}{24}, \dfrac{5}{96}$

$a_n = \dfrac{40}{3}\left(\dfrac{1}{4}\right)^{n-1}$, Geometric

88. $\dfrac{2}{3}, -\dfrac{4}{9}, \dfrac{8}{27}, -\dfrac{16}{81}, \dfrac{32}{243}$

$a_n = \dfrac{2}{3}\left(-\dfrac{2}{3}\right)^{n-1}$, Geometric

89. $-\dfrac{1}{2}, -\dfrac{1}{4}, -\dfrac{1}{8}, -\dfrac{1}{16}, -\dfrac{1}{32}$

$a_n = -\dfrac{1}{2}\left(-\dfrac{1}{2}\right)^{n-1}$, Geometric

90. $\dfrac{1}{7}, -\dfrac{1}{14}, \dfrac{1}{21}, -\dfrac{1}{28}, \dfrac{1}{35}$

Neither, General term:

$a_n = \dfrac{1}{7n}(-1)^{n-1}$

91. $8, 5, 3, 0, \underline{\quad} \ldots$

Neither

92. $3, \dfrac{3}{4}, \dfrac{3}{16}, \dfrac{3}{64}$

$a_n = 3\left(\dfrac{1}{4}\right)^{n-1}$, Geometric

93. $81, -9, 1, -\dfrac{1}{9}, \dfrac{1}{81}$

$a_n = 81\left(-\dfrac{1}{9}\right)^{n-1}$, Geometric

94. $2, -10, 50, -250$

$a_n = 2(-5)^{n-1}$, Geometric

95. $1, \sqrt{3}, 3, \sqrt{27}, \ldots$

$a_n = 1\left(\sqrt{3}\right)^{n-1}$, Geometric

96. $7, \sqrt{7}, 1, \dfrac{1}{\sqrt{7}} \ldots$

$a_n = 7\left(\dfrac{1}{\sqrt{7}}\right)^{n-1}$, Geometric

In each one of the following sequences find the term indicated:

97. $1, 4, 7 \ldots (a_{31})$ $a_{31} = 1 + 3 \cdot 30 = 91$

98. $-8, -5, -2 \ldots (a_{37})$ $a_{37} = -8 + 3 \cdot 36 = 100$

99. $4, -8, 16 \ldots (a_{15})$ $a_{15} = 4(-2)^{14}$

100. $32, -8, 2 \ldots (a_{11})$ $a_{37} = 32\left(-\dfrac{1}{4}\right)^{10}$

101. $68, -34, 17 \ldots (a_9)$ $a_9 = 68\left(-\dfrac{1}{2}\right)^{8} = \dfrac{68}{256}$

102. $3, 14, 25 \ldots (a_9)$ $a_9 = 3 + 8 \cdot 11 = 91$

103. $-4000, 1000, -250, \ldots (a_7)$ $a_7 = -4000\left(-\dfrac{1}{4}\right)^{6} = -\dfrac{125}{128}$

104. $200, 100, 50 \ldots (a_7)$ $\qquad$ $a_7 = 200\left(\dfrac{1}{2}\right)^6 = \dfrac{200}{64}$

105. The 4th term of a geometric sequence is 3, the 6th term is $\dfrac{27}{4}$.

    a. The ratio of the sequence.

$$a_6 = a_4 r^2; \frac{27}{4} = 3r^2$$

$$r = \pm\frac{3}{2}$$

    b. Divergent $|r| > 1$

$$a_4 = a_1 r^3; 3 = \pm\left(\frac{3}{2}\right)^3 a_1$$

    c.

$$a_1 = \pm\left(\frac{8}{9}\right)$$

    d. Find a_{12}

$$a_{12} = \left(\pm\left(\frac{8}{9}\right)\right)\left(\pm\left(\frac{3}{2}\right)^{11}\right) = \frac{3^9}{2^8}$$

    e. Sum the first 15 terms.

$$S_{15} = \frac{\left(\pm\left(\frac{8}{9}\right)\right)\left(\left(\pm\left(\frac{3}{2}\right)\right)^{15} - 1\right)}{\pm\left(\frac{3}{2}\right) - 1}$$

106. The 2nd term of a arithmetic sequence is -2, the 6th term is -4.

    a. Find the difference of the sequence. $\qquad a_6 = a_2 + 4d; -4 = -2 + 4d; d = \dfrac{1}{2}$

    b. a_1 $\qquad a_2 = a_1 + d; -2 = a_1 + \dfrac{1}{2}; a_1 = -\dfrac{5}{2}$

    c. a_{12} $\qquad a_{12} = a_1 + 11d; a_{12} = -\dfrac{5}{2} + \dfrac{11}{2}; a_{12} = \dfrac{6}{2} = 3$

    d. Sum of the first 50 terms. $S_{50} = \dfrac{50}{2}\left(\dfrac{-10}{2} + \dfrac{49}{2}\right) = \dfrac{1950}{4}$

107. The 10th term of a geometric sequence is 5, the 14th term is $\dfrac{80}{81}$

    a. The ratio of the sequence. $\qquad a_{14} = a_{10} r^4; \dfrac{80}{81} = 5r^4; r = \pm\dfrac{2}{3}$

    b. a_1 $\qquad a_{10} = a_1 r^9; 5 = a_1\left(\pm\dfrac{2}{3}\right)^9; a_1 = 5\left(\pm\dfrac{3}{2}\right)^9$

    c. a_7 $\qquad a_{10} = a_7 r^3; 5 = a_7\left(\pm\dfrac{2}{3}\right)^3; a_1 = 5\left(\pm\dfrac{3}{2}\right)^3 = \pm\dfrac{135}{8}$

    d. Sum the first 10 terms. $\qquad S_{10} = \dfrac{\left(5\left(\pm\dfrac{3}{2}\right)^9\right)\left(\left(\pm\left(\dfrac{2}{3}\right)\right)^{10} - 1\right)}{\pm\left(\dfrac{2}{3}\right) - 1}$

108. The 7th term of a arithmetic sequence is 120, the 16th term is 201.

    a. The difference of the sequence. $\qquad a_{16} = a_7 + 9d; 201 = 120 + 9d; d = 9$

    b. Find a_1 $\qquad\begin{aligned} a_7 &= a_1 + 6d \\ a_1 &= 66 \end{aligned}$

    c. Find a_{12} $\qquad a_{12} = a_1 + 11d = 66 + 99 = 165$

d. Sum the first 50 terms. $S_{50} = \frac{50}{2}(132 + 49 \cdot 9) = 14325$

109. All the terms in a geometric sequence are positive. The first term is 7 and the 3rd term is 28.

$$a_3 = a_1 r^2$$

a. Find the common ratio. $28 = 7r^2$ Positive since all terms are positive.

$$r = +2$$

b. Find the sum of the first 14 terms. $S_{14} = \frac{7(2^{14} - 1)}{2 - 1} = 114681$

110. The fifth term of an arithmetic sequence is –20 and the twelfth term is –44.

$$a_{12} = a_5 + 7d$$

a. Find the common difference.

$$d = -\frac{24}{7}$$

$$a_5 = a_1 + 4d$$

b. Find the first term of the sequence. $-20 = a_1 - \frac{24}{7} \cdot 4$

$$a_1 = -\frac{44}{7}$$

c. Calculate eighty–seventh term. $a_{87} = a_1 + 86d = -\frac{44}{7} - 86 \cdot \frac{24}{7} = -\frac{2108}{7}$

d. Sum of the first 150 terms. $S_{150} = \frac{150}{2}(-\frac{88}{7} + 149 \cdot \frac{24}{7}) = \frac{261600}{7}$

111. Sum the following sequences:

a. $3 + 6 + 9 + 12 + \ldots + 69 =$ First find the number of terms:

$69 = 3 + (n - 1)3; n = 23$ $\qquad S_{23} = \frac{23}{2}(6 + 22 \cdot 3) = 828$

b. $6 + 14 + 22 + 30 + \ldots + 54 =$ First find the number of terms:

$54 = 6 + (n - 1)8; n = 7$ $\qquad S_7 = \frac{7}{2}(12 + 6 \cdot 8) = 210$

c. $5 + \frac{5}{3} + \frac{5}{9} + \ldots = S_\infty = \frac{a_1(r^\infty - 1)}{r - 1} = \frac{5\left(\left(\frac{1}{3}\right)^\infty - 1\right)}{\left(\frac{1}{3}\right) - 1} = \frac{-5}{\left(-\frac{2}{3}\right)} = -\frac{15}{2}$

Attention: $\left(\frac{1}{3}\right)^\infty \approx 0$

d. $1 + 2 + 3 + 4 + \ldots + 158 =$ First find the number of terms:

$158 = 1 + (n - 1)1; n = 158$ $\qquad S_{158} = \frac{158}{2}(2 + 157 \cdot 1) = 12561$

e. $9 + 18 + 27 + 36 + \ldots + 900 =$ First find the number of terms:

$900 = 9 + (n - 1)9; n = 100$ $\qquad S_{100} = \frac{100}{2}(18 + 99 \cdot 9) = 45450$

f. $80 + 20 + 5 + \ldots \; S_\infty = \dfrac{a_1(r^\infty - 1)}{r - 1} = \dfrac{80\left(\left(\dfrac{1}{4}\right)^\infty - 1\right)}{\left(\dfrac{1}{4}\right) - 1} = \dfrac{-80}{\left(-\dfrac{3}{4}\right)} = \dfrac{320}{3}$

Attention that $\left(\dfrac{1}{4}\right)^\infty \approx 0$

g. $100 + 97 + 94 + \ldots + 19 =$ First find the number of terms:

$19 = 100 + (n-1)(-3); n = 28$ $\qquad S_{28} = \dfrac{28}{2}(200 + 27 \cdot (-3)) = 1666$

h. $18 + 6 + 2 + \ldots =$ $\qquad S_\infty = \dfrac{a_1}{r-1} = \dfrac{18}{\left(1 - \dfrac{1}{3}\right)} = \dfrac{54}{2} = 27$

i. $\dfrac{2}{5} + \dfrac{6}{10} + \dfrac{18}{20} + \ldots + \dfrac{243}{80}$ $\qquad$ Find the number of terms:

$\dfrac{243}{80} = \dfrac{2}{5} \cdot \left(\dfrac{3}{2}\right)^{n-1}; n = 5$ $\qquad S_5 = \dfrac{\dfrac{2}{5}\left(\left(\dfrac{3}{2}\right)^5 - 1\right)}{\left(\dfrac{3}{2} - 1\right)} = \dfrac{211}{40}$

j. $\dfrac{1}{3} + \dfrac{2}{9} + \dfrac{4}{27} + \ldots = S_\infty = \dfrac{a_1}{r-1} = \dfrac{\left(\dfrac{1}{3}\right)}{\left(1 - \dfrac{2}{3}\right)} = 1$

k. $12 + 7 + 2 + \ldots - 98 =$ $\qquad$ First find the number of terms:

$-98 = 12 + (n-1)(-5); n = 23$ $\qquad S_{23} = \dfrac{23}{2}(24 + 22 \cdot (-5)) = 989$

l. $100 + 150 + 200 + \ldots + 1000 =$ First find the number of terms:

$1000 = 100 + (n-1)(50); n = 19$ $\qquad S_{19} = \dfrac{19}{2}(200 + 18 \cdot (50)) = 10450$

112. $S_n = \dfrac{n}{2}(-12 + (n-1)7) = 10000$ $\qquad$ So 55 terms are needed.

$n \approx 54.8$

113. $\qquad$ 20, 23, 26 … Arithmetic $\qquad S_{40} = \dfrac{40}{2}(40 + 39 \cdot 3) = 3140 \, seats$

114. A ball bounces on the floor. It is released from a height of 160 cm. After the 1st bounce it reaches a height of 120 cm and 90 cm after the 2nd. If the patterns continue find:

a. The height the ball will reach after the 6th bounce.

160, 120, 90, … Geometric, $r = \dfrac{120}{160} = \dfrac{90}{120} = \dfrac{3}{4}$

$a_n = 160 \cdot \left(\dfrac{3}{4}\right)^{n-1}; a_7 = 160 \cdot \left(\dfrac{3}{4}\right)^6 = \dfrac{3645}{128} \approx 28.5 cm$

Attention that a_7 corresponds to height after the 6th bounce.

b. The total distance the ball passed after a <u>long period o time</u>.

$$S_{\infty} = \frac{a_1(r^{\infty}-1)}{r-1} = \frac{160\left(\left(\frac{3}{4}\right)^{\infty}-1\right)}{\left(\frac{3}{4}\right)-1} = \frac{-160}{\left(-\frac{1}{4}\right)} = 640cm \qquad \left(\frac{3}{4}\right)^{\infty} \approx 0$$

115. In a certain forest the current population of rabbits is 200 objects. It is know that the population increases by 20% every year.

a. The population of rabbits after a year. $\quad \frac{120}{100} \cdot 200 = 240 rabbits$

b. The population of rabbits after 2 years. $\quad \frac{120}{100} \cdot 240 = 288 rabbits$

c. What kind of a sequence is it? State the expression for the population after n years. Geometric. $\quad r = \frac{120}{100} = \frac{6}{5} \qquad a_n = 200 \cdot \left(\frac{6}{5}\right)^{n-1}$

d. Find the total number of rabbits after 10 years (assuming none has died).

$$a_{11} = 200 \cdot \left(\frac{6}{5}\right)^{10} \approx 1240 rabbits$$

116. In a research it was observed that the number of defective products produced by a machine per year decreases by 10% every year (due to technological improvements). In a certain year the machine made 300 products.

a. Find the number of defective products produced a year later.

$$\frac{90}{100} \cdot 300 = 270 defective$$

b. Find the number of defective products produced 2 years later.

$$\frac{90}{100} \cdot 270 = 243 defective$$

c. What kind of a sequence is it? State the expression for the number of errors committed after n years.

Geometric. $\quad r = \frac{90}{100} = \frac{9}{10} \qquad a_n = 300 \cdot \left(\frac{9}{10}\right)^{n-1}$

d. The <u>total number</u> produced $\quad S_8 = \frac{300\left(\left(\frac{9}{10}\right)^8-1\right)}{\left(\frac{9}{10}\right)-1} \approx 1710 defective$

117. In a certain company the pay scale follows a pattern of an arithmetic sequence (every year). This means:

a. The salary increases by a certain % every year (True/**False**), explain.
<u>Since the amount of the increase is fixed, the percentage is not the same one every year. An increase by a percentage corresponds to a geometric sequence.</u>

b. The salary increases by a certain amount every year (**True**/False),
<u>Since the amount of the increase is fixed, the pattern is identical to an Arithmetic sequence.</u>

118. Given the sequence: $a, a^2, a^3 \ldots$

    a. This is a <u>geometric</u> sequence.

    b. Write down its general term, simplified. $a_n = a(a)^{n-1} = a^n$

    c. It is known that the infinite sequence adds up to 10, find a.

$$10 = \frac{a}{1-a}; \quad 10 = 11a; \quad a = \frac{10}{11}$$

119. Given the sequence: $a^{-2}, a^{-3}, a^{-4} \ldots$

    a. This is a <u>geometric</u> sequence.

    b. Write down its general term, simplified. $a_n = a^{-2}\left(a^{-1}\right)^{n-1} = a^{-1-n}$

    c. It is known that the infinite sequence adds up to $\dfrac{1}{2}$, find a

$$\frac{1}{2} = \frac{a^{-2}}{1-a^{-1}}; \quad \frac{1}{2} = \frac{\left(\frac{1}{a^2}\right)}{\left(1-\frac{1}{a}\right)}; \quad \frac{1}{2} = \frac{\left(\frac{1}{a^2}\right)}{\left(\frac{a-1}{a}\right)}; \quad \frac{1}{2} = \frac{1}{(a-1)a}; \quad a^2 - a - 2 = 0; \quad a = -1, 2$$

COMPOUND INTEREST

1. 1200\$ are put in account that gives 2% per year. Calculate the amount of money in the account after:

    a. 1 year.   <u>Amount = $1200(1.02) = 1224$ \$</u>

    b. 2 years.   <u>Amount = $1200(1.02)^2 = 1248.48$ \$</u>

2. It should be multiplied by <u>1.05</u>

3. It should be multiplied by <u>1.56</u>

4. It should be multiplied by <u>0.95</u>

5. It should be multiplied by <u>1.15</u>

6. It should be multiplied by <u>0.88</u>

7. It should be multiplied by <u>3.3</u>

8. 1000\$ are put in account that takes 5% commission per year. Calculate the amount of money in the account after:

    a. 1 year.   Amount $= 1000(0.95) = 950$ \$

    b. 2 years.   Amount $= 1000(0.95)^2 = 902.5$ \$

9. 2000$ are being put in a deposit that pays 5% (per year).

a. Fill the table:

Number of Years	Interest earned at the end of the year	Amount in deposit ($)
0		2000
1	$\frac{5}{100}2000 = 100$	2100
2	$\frac{5}{100}2100 = 105$	2205
3	$\frac{5}{100}2205 = 110.25$	2315.25
4	$\frac{5}{100}2315.25 = 115.7625$	2431.0125
5	$\frac{5}{100}2431.0125 = 121.550625$	2552.563125

b. Observe the numbers in the compound interest column: 2000, 2100, 2205... What kind of a sequence is that? Write its general term. Geometric sequence. $a_n = 2000(1.05)^{n-1}$

c. $a_{21} = 2000(1.05)^{20} \approx 5310$ $ Attention that a_{21} corresponds to "after 20 years" as a_1 corresponds to "after 0 years".

d. $a_n = 2000(1.05)^{n-1}$ means a_1 corresponds to "after 0 years" while writing $a_n = 2000(1.05)^n$ means a_1 corresponds to "after 1 year"

10. A loan of 1200$ is made at 12% per year compounded semiannually, over 5 years the debt will grow to:
   a. $\$1200(1 + 0.12)^5$
   b. $\$1200(1 + 0.06)^{10}$
   c. $\$1200(1 + 0.6)^{10}$
   d. $\$1200(1 + 0.06)^5$
   e. $\$1200(1 + 0.12)^{10}$

11. A loan of 23200$ is made at 8% per year compounded quarterly, over 6 years the debt will grow to:
   a. $\$23200(1 + 0.2)^{24}$
   b. $\$23200(1 + 0.08)^6$
   c. $\$23200(1 + 0.02)^{24}$
   d. $\$23200(1 + 0.08)^{24}$
   e. $\$23200(1 + 0.02)^6$

12. A loan of 20$ is made at 12% per year compounded monthly, over 8 years the debt will grow to:
   a. $\$20(1 + 0.12)^{80}$
   b. $\$20(1 + 0.01)^8$
   c. $\$20(1 + 0.012)^{96}$
   d. $\$20(1 + 0.01)^{96}$
   e. $\$20(1 + 0.06)^{12}$

13. A loan of X$ is made at 12% per year compounded every 4 months, over 5 years the debt will grow to:
   a. $\$X(1 + 0.12)^4$
   b. $\$X(1 + 0.3)^5$
   c. $\$X(1 + 0.12)^{15}$
   d. **$\underline{\$X(1 + 0.03)^{15}}$**
   e. $\$X(1 + 0.3)^{15}$

14. A loan of X$ is made at i% per year compounded every m months, over n years the debt will grow to:

$$Debt = X(1+\frac{i}{100})^{\frac{12n}{m}}$$

15. Calculate the total amount owing after two years on a loan of 1500$ if the interest rate is 11% compounded

   a. Annually $\quad Amount = 1500(1+\frac{11}{100})^2 \approx 1848\$$

   b. Semiannually $\quad Amount = 1500(1+\frac{11}{200})^4 \approx 1858\$$

   c. Quarterly $\quad Amount = 1500(1+\frac{11}{400})^8 \approx 1864\$$

   d. Monthly $\quad Amount = 1500(1+\frac{11}{1200})^{24} \approx 1867\$$

16. How much will a client have to repay on a loan of 800$ after 2 years, if the 12% interest is compounded annually. $\quad Amount = 800(1+\frac{12}{100})^2 = 1003.52\$$

17. Find the compound interest **earned** by the deposit. Round to the nearest cent. $3000 at 12% compounded semiannually for 10 years

$$AmountObtained = 3000(1+\frac{12}{200})^{20} \approx 9620\$$$

$$AmountEarned = 9620 - 3000 = 6620\$$$

18. How many years will it take to a 100$ to double assuming interest rate is 6%. Compounded semiannually. $200 = 100(1+\frac{6}{200})^{2n}$ So it will take 12 years.

$$n \approx 11.7$$

19. How many years will it take to a X$ to triple assuming interest rate is 7%. Compounded quarterly $3X = X(1+\frac{7}{400})^{4n}$ So it will take 16 years.

$$n \approx 15.8$$

20. Find the interest rate given to a certain person in case he made a deposit of 1000$ and obtained 1200$ after 3 years, compounded monthly.

$$1200 = 1000(1+\frac{i}{1200})^{36}$$

$$i \approx 6.09$$

21. Find the interest rate given to a certain person in case he made a deposit of 2500$ and obtained 3000$ after 10 years, compounded yearly.

$$3000 = 2500(1 + \frac{i}{100})^{10}$$

$$i \approx 1.84$$

SIGMA NOTATION

1. The sum $\sum_{k=2}^{4} 2^k$ is equal to:

   a. $2^1 + 2^2 + 2^3 + 2^4$
   b. $2^2 + 2^4$
   c. $2^2 + 3^3 + 4^4$
   d. $2^2 + 2^3 + 2^4$

2. The sum $\frac{1}{4}\sum_{m=2}^{4} x_m$ is equal to:

   a. $\frac{1}{4}x_2 + \frac{1}{4}x_3 + \frac{1}{4}x_4$
   b. $\frac{1}{4}x_2 + x_3 + x_4$
   c. $\frac{1}{2}x_2 + \frac{1}{3}x_3 + \frac{1}{4}x_4$
   d. $\frac{1}{4}(2 + 3 + 4)$

3. The sum $\sum_{j=4}^{n} \frac{j}{j+1}$ is equal to:

   a. $\frac{1}{2} + \frac{3}{4} + \frac{5}{6} + ... + \frac{n}{n+1}$
   b. $\frac{1}{2} + \frac{2}{3} + \frac{3}{4} + ... + \frac{n}{n+1}$
   c. $\frac{4}{5} + \frac{5}{6} + \frac{6}{7} + ... + \frac{n}{n+1}$
   d. $\frac{4}{5} + \frac{5}{6} + \frac{6}{7} + ... + \frac{n+4}{n+5}$

4. Write out fully what is meant by

   a. $\sum_{i=4}^{i=6} 2i - 1 = 7 + 9 + 11$

   b. $\sum_{i=2}^{i=5} \frac{i}{i^2 + 1} = \frac{2}{5} + \frac{3}{10} + \frac{4}{17} + \frac{6}{26}$

   c. $\sum_{i=4}^{i=6} (2i - 3)^2 = 25 + 49 + 81$

   d. $\sum_{k=3}^{i=7} (2^k + \sqrt{k}) = 8 + \sqrt{3} + 16 + \sqrt{4} + 32 + \sqrt{5} + 64 + \sqrt{6} + 128 + \sqrt{7}$

   e. $\sum_{i=1}^{i=4} (-1)^i \times 3^{2i} = -9 + 81 - 729 + 6561$

5. Write each series using sigma notation:

    a. $4 + 9 + 16 + 25 + 36 + 49 + 64 + 81 = \sum_{i=2}^{i=9} i^2$

    b. $5 + 9 + 13 + 17 + 21 + 25 + 29 + 33... = \sum_{i=1}^{i=\infty} 5 + (i-1)4$

    c. $1 - \dfrac{1}{3} + \dfrac{1}{9} - \dfrac{1}{27} + \dfrac{1}{81} - \dfrac{1}{243} = \sum_{i=1}^{i=6} 1 \cdot \left(-\dfrac{1}{3}\right)^{i-1}$

6. $3 + 6 + 9 + 12 + ...$ for 28 terms $= \sum_{i=1}^{i=28} 3 + (i-1)3 = \dfrac{28}{2}(6 + 27 \cdot 3) = 1218$

7. $-3 + 6 - 12 + 24 - 48 + ...$ for 35 terms $= \sum_{i=1}^{i=35} -3 \cdot (-2)^{i-1} = \dfrac{-3(2^{35} - 1)}{-2 - 1}$

8. $8.3 + 8.1 + 7.9 + 7.7 + ... + 0.9$, sum the terms, first find n, (n = 38)

$$\sum_{i=1}^{i=38} 8.3 + (i-1)(-0.2) = \dfrac{100}{2}(16.6 + 37 \cdot (-0.2)) = 1200$$

9. Use sigma notation to represent: $12 + 9 + 3 + ... -120$. Sum the terms, first find n, (n = 45)

$$\sum_{i=1}^{i=45} 12 + (i-1)(-3) = \dfrac{45}{2}(24 + 44 \cdot (-3)) = -2430$$

10. An infinite geometric series is given by $\sum_{i=1}^{\infty} 2(1-x)^i$

    a. The value of x: $-1 < (1-x) < 1; \;\; 2 > x > 0$

    b. x = 0.5, the minimum number of terms

$$\sum_{i=1}^{n} 2(0.5)^i = \dfrac{1(0.5^n - 1)}{0.5 - 1} = 1.9 \;\; n \approx 4.32 \qquad \text{So 5 terms are needed}$$

11. Given the sequence $x, x^2, x^3 ...$

    a. Use sigma notation to represent the sum of its first 10 terms. $\sum_{i=1}^{i=10} x^n$

    b. Assuming its infinite and that its sum is 5 find x and write down the first three terms of the sequence.

$$S_{\infty} = \dfrac{x}{1-x} = 5; x = \dfrac{5}{6}, a_1 = \dfrac{5}{6}, a_2 = \dfrac{25}{36}, a_3 = \dfrac{125}{216}$$

1.12. – ABSOLUTE VALUE

1. $|-3| = \underline{3}$ $|3| = \underline{3}$ $|-3+3| = \underline{0}$ $|-3-3| = \underline{6}$

2. $|-3| + 3 = \underline{6}$ $|3| - 4 = \underline{-1}$ $|-3+5| + 2 = \underline{4}$ $|-3-3| - 3 = \underline{3}$

3. $|1 - 3 + |-2|| = \underline{0}$

4. $|-2-3| + |-2| = \underline{7}$

5. $|-2-23| - |-12| = \underline{13}$

6. $2|1 - 3 + |-2| + 1| - 2 = \underline{0}$

7. $|-2-3||-2| = \underline{10}$

8. $-|-12-3| - |-2-1| = \underline{-18}$

9. $5 - |12 - 3 + |1-2|| - |-12-10| + 1 = \underline{-26}$

10. $|2 - |-12-3| - |-2-1|| = \underline{16}$

11. $|x| - 2|x| = -|x|$

12. $|x||x| = |x^2| = x^2$

13. An absolute value of a number represents <u>its distance from the origin</u>

14. $|x| = |-x|$ **True** / False, if false write down an example to show it

15. $|x + y| = |x| + |y|$ True / **False**, if false write down an example to show it

     $|2 + (-3)| \neq |2| + |-3|$

     $1 \neq 5$

16. $-|x|$ is <u>always a negative</u> number

17. If $x = |x|$ it means x is <u>positive</u>

18. If $x = -|x|$ it means x is <u>negative</u>

19. If x is a negative number than $-x = |x|$ **True** / False

20. If x is a positive number than $x = |x|$ **True** / False

1. $|2x| = 5$ $x = \pm\dfrac{5}{2}$

2. $|x| = 7$ $x = \pm 7$

3. $|4x| = 8$ $x = \pm 2$

4. $|x| = -5$ *No Solution*

5. $|2x| = 0$ $x = 0$

6. $|2x| = -1$ *No Solution*

7. $|2x| = 15$ $x = \pm\dfrac{15}{2}$

8. $|2x| < 5$ $x \in (-5, 5)$

9. $|x| > 7$ $x \in (-\infty, -7) \cup (7, \infty)$

10. $|4x| < 8$ $x \in (-2, 2)$

11. $|x| < -5$ *No Solution*

12. $|3x| < 0$ *No Solution*

13. $|6x| > -1$ $x \in \Re$

14. $|5x| > 0$ $x \in \Re, x \neq 0$

15. $|3x| < 6$ $x \in (-2, 2)$

16. $|x| \geq 7$ $x \in (-\infty, -7] \cup [7, \infty)$

17. $|4x| < 2$ $x \in (-\dfrac{1}{2}, \dfrac{1}{2})$

18. $|x| \leq -5$ *No Solution*

19. $|2x| \leq 0$ $x = 0$

20. $|2x| > -1$ $x \in \Re$

21. $|x| \geq 0$ $x \in \Re$

22. $|2 + x| = 5$ $x = 3, -7$

23. $|-x| = 7$ $x = 7, -7$

24. $|4 - x| = 8$ $\qquad x = -4, 12$

25. $|3 - 2x| = -5$ $\qquad$ *No Solution*

26. $|2 - 3x| = 0$ $\qquad x = \dfrac{3}{2}$

27. $|2 + x| = -1$ $\qquad$ *No Solution*

28. $|2x + 3| = 15$ $\qquad x = 6, -9$

29. $|4 - 2x| < 5$ $\qquad x \in (-\dfrac{1}{2}, \dfrac{9}{2})$

30. $|-x| > 7$ $\qquad x \in (-\infty, -7) \cup (7, \infty)$

31. $|4 + 2x| < 8$ $\qquad x \in (-6, 2)$

32. $|x| < -5$ $\qquad$ *No Solution*

33. $|3 + x| < 0$ $\qquad$ *No Solution*

34. $|6 - 2x| > -1$ $\qquad x \in \Re$

35. $|5 + x| > 0$ $\qquad x \in \Re, x \neq -5$

36. $|1 - 3x| \leq 6$ $\qquad x \in [-\dfrac{5}{3}, \dfrac{7}{3}]$

37. $|1 + x| \geq 7$ $\qquad x \in (-\infty, -8] \cup [6, \infty)$

38. $|4 + x| \leq 2$ $\qquad x \in [-6, -2]$

39. $|3 + 2x| \leq -5$ $\qquad$ *No Solution*

40. $|2 + 3x| < 0$ $\qquad$ *No Solution*

41. $|7 - 6x| \geq -1$ $\qquad x \in \Re$

42. $|1 - x| \geq 0$ $\qquad x \in \Re$

43. $|2x + 1| + 3 = 5$ $\qquad x = \dfrac{1}{2}, -\dfrac{3}{2}$

44. $|7x + 21| - 5 = -5$ $\qquad x = -3$

45. $2 - |5 - 8x| = 15$ $\qquad$ *No Solution*

46. $|4x + 2| = -5$ $\qquad$ *No Solution*

47. $|8x + 12| = 100$ $\qquad x = 11, -14$

48. $|2x + 1| < 2$ $\qquad x \in (-\dfrac{13}{2}, -\dfrac{9}{2})$

49. $|8 - 2x + 1| > 6$

$\qquad x \in (-\infty, \dfrac{3}{2}) \cup (\dfrac{15}{2}, \infty)$

50. $|5x - 21| > 0$ $\qquad x \in \Re, x \neq \dfrac{21}{5}$

51. $|5x - 21| \geq 0$ $\qquad x \in \Re$

52. $|8x + 11| > -2$ $\qquad x \in \Re$

53. $|91x + 61| < -2$ $\qquad$ *No Solution*

54. $|8 - 3x| > 8$

$\qquad x \in (-\infty, 0) \cup (\dfrac{16}{3}, \infty)$

55. $|18 - 6x| > 3$

$\qquad x \in (-\infty, \dfrac{5}{2}) \cup (\dfrac{7}{2}, \infty)$

56. $|1 - 6x| < 7$ $\qquad x \in (-1, \dfrac{4}{3})$

57. $|8 - 5x| \leq 0$ $\qquad x = \dfrac{8}{5}$

58. $|5x - 21| > 1$

$\qquad x \in (-\infty, 4) \cup (\dfrac{22}{5}, \infty)$

59. $|x + 11| = 5$ $\qquad x = -6, -16$

60. $|x + 3| \leq 5$ $\qquad x \in [-8, 2]$

61. $|x + 11| = -15$ $\qquad$ *No Solution*

62. $|2x + 11| + 2 < 15$ $\qquad x \in (-12, 1)$

63. $|3x + 11| = x$ $\qquad$ *No Solution*

64. $|x + 2| = 5 - x$ $\qquad x = \dfrac{3}{2}$

65. $|3x + 1| < 5x$ $\qquad x = \dfrac{1}{2}$

66. $|x - 4| = 3x$ $\qquad x = 1$

67. $|2x - 6| \leq 5 + 2x$ $\qquad x \in [\dfrac{1}{4}, \infty)$

68. $|2x + 4| < 2 - 3x$ $\qquad x \in (-\infty, -\dfrac{2}{5})$

69. $|2x - 2| > 11 - 2x$ $\qquad x \in (-\infty, \dfrac{13}{4})$

70. $|7x - 16| = 5 + 12x$ $\qquad x = \dfrac{11}{19}$

71. $|2x - 6| = 21$ $\qquad x = \dfrac{27}{2}, -\dfrac{15}{2}$

72. $|2x - 6| \geq 4$

$\qquad x \in (-\infty, 1] \cup [5, \infty)$

73. $|3x - 6| + 1 > -4$ $\qquad x \in \Re$

74. $|4x - 6| - 4 < -4x$ $\qquad$ *No Solution*

75. $|\dfrac{1}{2}x - 4| \leq 1 + x$ $\qquad x \in [2, \infty)$

76. $|2x + \dfrac{1}{2}| > 2 - 3x$ $\qquad x \in (\dfrac{3}{10}, \infty)$

77. $|2x - \dfrac{1}{2}| = 1 - 2x$ $\qquad x \in (\dfrac{3}{8}, \infty)$

78. $|\dfrac{1}{2}x - 7| \leq 3 + 2x$ $\qquad x \in [\dfrac{8}{5}, \infty)$

79. $|\dfrac{x}{2} + 2| = 1 - x$ $\qquad x = -\dfrac{2}{3}$

CHAPTER 2 - GEOMETRY

2.1. – INTRODUCTION TO GEOMETRY

POINTS

1. Indicate the following points on the plane: A(1,5), B(–1, 4), C(–3, –7), D(6,–5), E(–1, –1), F(2, 0),G(0,–4), H(–4, 0)

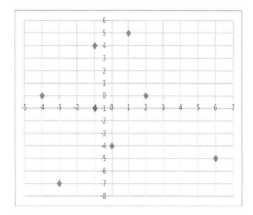

LINES

2. Indicate the following points on the plane: A(0,0), B(1, 1), C(–2, –2), D(6,6)

   a. What do these points have in common? y = x in all of them
   b. Could you describe all the points that satisfy this property? How? y = x

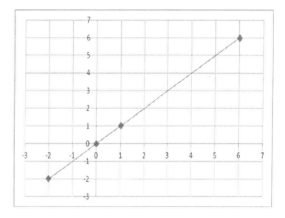

3. The points on the plane: A(0,0), B(1, 2), C(–2, –4), D(4,8)

   a. What do these points have in common?
      y = 2x in all of them
   b. Could you describe all the points that satisfy this property? How
      y = 2x in all of them
   c. The following points E(0,1), F(1, 3), G(–2, –3), H(4,9)
   d. What do these points have in common? What is the relation between this line and the previous line?
      In this line y = 2x +1. It is identical to the previous line only shifted 1 unit up.

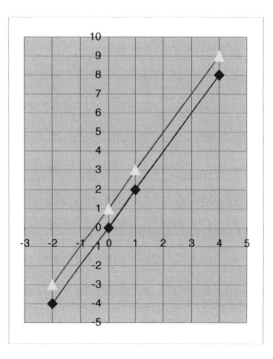

4. The points on the plane: A(0, –2), B(1, 1), C(2, 4), D(–2,–8)

   a. What do these points have in common? <u>y = 3x – 2 in all of them</u>

   b. Could you describe all the points that satisfy this property? How? <u>y = 3x – 2 in all of them</u>

   c. On the same graph sketch the following points E(0,1), F(1, 4), G(–2, –5), H(2, 7)

   d. What do these points have in common? What is the relation between this line and the previous line? <u>y = 3x + 1 in all of them, this line is the same as the other, shifted 3 units up so lines are parallel.</u>

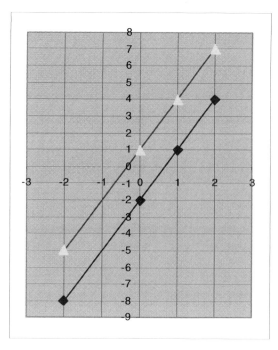

2.2. – ANGLES

1. An angle is the figure formed by <u>two</u> lines called <u>rays</u> that start at a common point.

   For example:
2. A straight angle is: <u>such that the 2 lines are aligned, we say this angle is 180º</u>
3. An acute angle is: <u>smaller than 90º</u>
4. A right angle is: <u>equal to 90º</u>
5. An obtuse angle is: <u>bigger than 90º</u>
6. Given the following diagram:
   - a. CA and CB are <u>rays</u>
   - b. The shaded angle can be called <u>acute</u> or <u>less than 90º</u>

7. We say that the following angle has a size of <u>90</u> degrees or <u>90º</u>
8. Use the following square to sketch an angle of 45º degrees:
9. Two angles are complementary if their sum is <u>90º</u>
10. Two angles are supplementary if their sum is <u>180º</u>
11. The complementary of 20º is <u>70º</u> The complementary of xº is <u>90 – xº</u>
12. The supplementary of 20º is <u>160º</u> The supplementary of xº is <u>180 – xº</u>
13. The complementary of 42º is <u>48º</u> The complementary of xº is <u>90 – xº</u>
14. The supplementary of 126º is <u>54º</u> The supplementary of xº is <u>180 – xº</u>
15. The complementary of 81º is <u>9º</u> The complementary of xº is <u>90 – xº</u>
16. The supplementary of 0º is <u>180º</u> The supplementary of xº is <u>180 – xº</u>
17. Find all the unknown angles:
    $6x = 180; x = 30º$
    Angles are 30º, 60º, 90º

18. Find all the unknown angles:
    $2x = 50; x = 25$
    Angles are 25º, 50º, y = 65º

19. Straight lines are <u>parallel</u> or 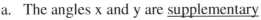 <u>intersecting</u>
Given the following diagram:
   - a. The angles x and y are <u>supplementary</u>
   - b. The angles x and a are <u>equal</u> (opposite)
   - c. The angles y and b are <u>equal</u> (opposite)

   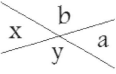

20. Given the following diagram:
   - a. The angles a and e are <u>corresponding angles</u>
   - b. The angles b and e are <u>interior angles</u>
   - c. The angles b and f are <u>corresponding angles</u>
   - d. The angles c and e are <u>alternating interior angles</u>
   - e. The angles h and b are <u>alternating interior angles</u>
   - f. The angles e and g are <u>equal</u> (opposite)
   - g. The angles c and h are <u>interior angles</u>
   - h. The angles g and h are <u>supplementary</u>
   - i. The angles b and d are <u>equal</u> (opposite)
   - j. Which angle is a corresponding angle pair with g? <u>c</u>
   - k. Which angle is an alternate angle pair with g? <u>a</u>
   - l. Which angle is a co-interior angle pair with e? <u>b</u>

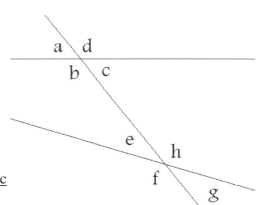

Given the following diagram in which the transversal intersects 2 parallel lines:
The angles a and e are <u>equal (corresponding angles)</u>

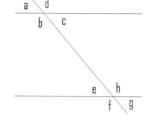

  m. The angles b and e are <u>supplementary (interior angles)</u>
  n. The angles b and f are <u>equal (corresponding angles)</u>
  o. The angles c and e are <u>equal (alternating angles)</u>
  p. The angles h and b are <u>equal (alternating angles)</u>
  q. The angles e and g are <u>equal (opposite angles)</u>
  r. The angles c and h are <u>supplementary (interior angles)</u>

21. Determine if the lines are parallel, explain why:
Find all possible angles. Lines are not parallel since the interior angles add up to 179° and not 180°.

22. Determine if the lines are parallel, explain why:
Find all possible angles. Lines are parallel since the interior angles add up to 180°.

23. Determine if the lines are parallel, explain why. Find all possible angles. Lines are parallel since the corresponding angles are equal

24. Sketch corresponding angle:

25. Sketch alternate interior angles:

26. Sketch alternate exterior angles:

27. Given the AB is parallel to CD, find the angles a, b, c, d, e.

    a = 48°, b = 132°, c = 132°, d = 42°, e = 48°

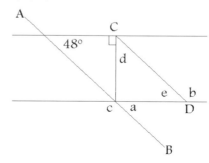

338

28. The sum of the angles in a triangle is <u>180°</u>
29. The sum of the angles in a square is <u>360°</u>
30. The sum of the angles in a rectangle is <u>360°</u>
31. The sum of the angles in a quadrilateral is <u>360°</u>
32. The sum of the angles in a pentagon is <u>540°</u>
33. The sum of the angles in an hexagon is <u>720°</u>
34. The sum of the angles in an heptagon is <u>900°</u>
35. The sum of the angles in an octagon is <u>1080°</u>
36. The sum of the angles in a shape with n sides is $180(n-2)$

    the reason is that <u>for each side added another triangle is created and therefore 180°</u>
    <u>added.</u>
37. Find the regular polygons with which you can fill the floor with tiles. Explain why does this happen.

    We can only do it using <u>equilateral triangles, squares or hexagons</u>.
    The reason is that the angle of a regular polygon with n sides is given by:

    $$\alpha = \frac{180(n-2)}{n}, \text{ for example:}$$

    Equilateral triangle n = 3, $\alpha = \frac{180(3-2)}{3} = 60°$

    Square n = 4, $\alpha = \frac{180(4-2)}{4} = 90°$

    Pentagon n = 5, $\alpha = \frac{180(5-2)}{5} = 108°$

    Hexagon n = 6, $\alpha = \frac{180(6-2)}{6} = 120°$

    Heptagon n = 7 $\alpha = \frac{180(7-2)}{7} \approx 129°$

    Octagon n = 8 $\alpha = \frac{180(8-2)}{8} = 135°$

    …

    All the rest are between 135° and 180°.

    The tile's angle must be a divisor of 360° to complete the circle at each point. The divisors of 360 are: 1,2,3,4,5,6,8,10,12,15, 18, 20, 24, 30, 36, 40, 45, **60**, 72, **90**, **120**, 180. The only ones that appear on both lists are 60, 90, 120.

2.3. – SQUARES, RECTANGLES AND TRIANGLES

1. The following points on the plane: A(0, 6), B(6, 0), C(0, 0)

   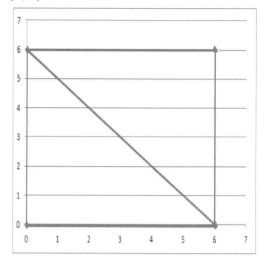

   b. Find all the angles of the triangles you can $45°, 45°, 90°$.
   c. This kind of triangle is called <u>right angled and isosceles</u>
   d. Write down the lengths of the 2 equal sides: <u>6</u>
   e. Write down the Pythagorean Theorem:
      $\underline{H^2 = a^2 + b^2}$ This theorem is only true in <u>right</u> triangles.
   f. Use P. Theorem to find the length of the third side of the triangle. $H = \sqrt{72}$
   g. Add the point D(6, 6) to the graph. The form ABCD is a <u>Rectangle</u>. The area of this shape is <u>A = 36</u>
   h. Use the area of the square to find the area of the triangle. <u>Half of it so 18.</u>

2. Indicate the following points on the plane: A(–4, 0), B(2, 6), C(8, 0)

   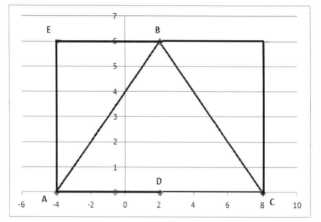

   b. This kind of triangle is called <u>isosceles</u>
   c. Write down the Pythagorean Theorem: $\underline{H^2 = a^2 + b^2}$
      This theorem is only true in <u>right angled</u> triangles.
   d. Add the point D (2, 0) to the graph. The triangle ABD is <u>right angled</u>
   e. The length of AD is <u>6</u> The Length of BD is <u>6</u> Use P. Theorem to find the length of AB. $AB = \sqrt{72}$
   f. In consequence state the length of BC: $\underline{BC = \sqrt{72}}$
   g. The perimeter of the triangle ABC is $\underline{12 + 2\sqrt{72}}$
   h. Add the point E (–4, 6) to the graph. The shape AEBD is <u>square</u>. The area of this shape is <u>36</u>. Use this area to find the area of the triangle ABD and ABC. <u>Area ABD is half so 18, ABC is twice ABD so 36</u>

3. Indicate the following points on the plane: A(–6, 0), B(3, 6), C(5, 0)

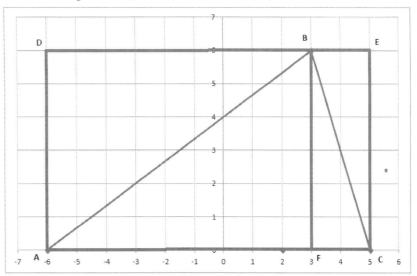

b. Is this triangle isosceles or right angled? <u>No</u>

c. The shape ADEC is a <u>rectangle.</u> The area of this shape is <u>66</u>.

d. The llength of AB: $AB = \sqrt{36+81} = \sqrt{117}$ and BC $BC = \sqrt{4+36} = \sqrt{40}$

e. The perimeter of the triangle ABC is $Perimeter = \sqrt{40} + \sqrt{117} + 11$

f. The line BF is called the <u>Height</u> of the triangle.

g. Every triangle has <u>3</u> heights. . A height is a lines that starts at a <u>vertex</u> and ends at <u>the opposite side</u> forming an angle of <u>90°</u> with it.

h. Find the area of the triangles ABF, FBC and ABC.

$$Area_{ABF} = \frac{54}{2} = 27 \_ \qquad Area_{FBC} = \frac{12}{2} = 6 \qquad Area_{ABC} = \frac{66}{2} = 33$$

4. Indicate the following points on the plane: A (–5, 0), B (5, 0), C (0, $\sqrt{75}$)

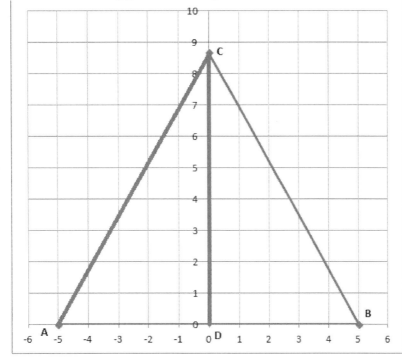

a. Done

b. Length of AB: $AB = 10$ $BC = \sqrt{25 + 75} = 10$

c. What kind of triangle is this? <u>Equilateral, all sides are equal and have a length of 10</u>

d. What can you say about the angles of this triangle<u>? All angles are equal and all are 60º</u>

e. The perimeter of the triangle ABC is <u>$Perimeter = 30$</u>

f. Find the area of the triangle ABC. $Area_{ABF} = \dfrac{base \cdot height}{2} = \dfrac{10 \cdot \sqrt{75}}{2} = 5\sqrt{75}$

The area of the triangle is half of the rectangle that can be built around it as seen in previous exercises. That is the origin of the formula provided for the area.

5. Define and sketch an example, include all the known angles and lengths of sides in your example.

a. Equilateral triangle:
<u>3 equal sides, 3 equal angles of 60º</u>

c. Right angled triangle: <u>One 90º angle</u>

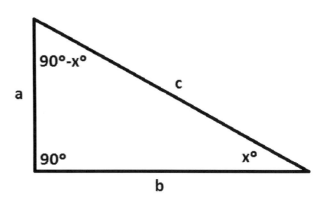

b. Isosceles triangle:
<u>2 equal sides with corresponding 2 equal angles.</u>

d. Right angled and isosceles triangle:

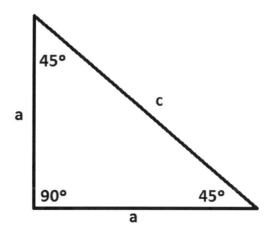

6. The vertex angle of an isosceles triangle is 42º, find the size of its base angle.
   BaseAngle $= (180 - 42)/2 = 69º$

7. The vertex angle of an isosceles triangle is 110º, find the size of its base angle.
   BaseAngle $= (180 - 110)/2 = 35º$

8. The base angle of an isosceles triangle is 50º, find the size of its vertex angle.
   VertexAngle $= 180 - 100 = 80º$

9. The base angle of an isosceles triangle is 33º, find the size of its vertex angle.
   VertexAngle $= 180 - 66 = 114º$

10. Given the isosceles triangle:

    y = <u>7cm</u>   a = <u>72º</u> b = <u>36º</u>

11. Given the diagram, find:

    x = <u>60º</u> y = <u>8cm</u> a = <u>50º</u> b = <u>80º</u>

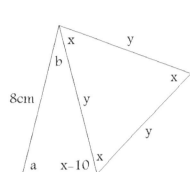

12. The base of an isosceles triangle is 10 cm, its side is 12 cm. Find its perimeter and area. *Perimeter* $= 10 + 24 = 34cm$

    $$height = \sqrt{144 - 25} = \sqrt{119} \qquad Area = \frac{10\sqrt{119}}{2} = 5\sqrt{119}cm^2$$

13. The base angle of an isosceles triangle is 5x + 7, the vertex angle is 2x – 2; find the size of the angles.
    $$Perimeter = 2(5x + 7) + 2x - 2 = 180; x = 14$$
    $$BaseAngle = 77º, VertexAngle = 26º$$

14. The base angle of an isosceles triangle is 9x – 10, the vertex angle is 12x – 10; find the size of the angles.
    $$Perimeter = 2(9x - 10) + 12x - 10 = 180; x = 7$$
    $$BaseAngle = 53º, VertexAngle = 74º$$

15. Given the following triangle, it is known that AB = 10cm, AD = 7cm and DC = 4cm. Angle CDB = 90°. Find:

   a. DB = 3cm, $BC = \sqrt{9+16} = 5cm$, $AC = \sqrt{16+49} = \sqrt{65}cm$

   b. $A_{ABC} = \dfrac{10 \cdot 4}{2} = 20cm^2$

   c. $Perimeter_{ABC} = 15 + \sqrt{65} = cm$

16. Given the following triangle, it is known that AC = 13cm, DB = 4cm and DC = 5cm. Angle CDB = 90°. Find:

   a. $AD = \sqrt{169-25} = 12cm$ $\_BC = \sqrt{16+25} = \sqrt{41}cm$

   b. $A_{DCB} = \dfrac{4 \cdot 5}{2} = 10cm^2$

   c. $Perimeter_{ABC} = 13 + 12 + 4 + \sqrt{41} = 29 + \sqrt{41}cm$

17. Given the following triangle, it is known that AC = 20cm, DB = 10cm and DC = 11 cm. Angle CDB = 90° and angle CEA = 90°. Find:

   a. $BC = \sqrt{100+121} = \sqrt{221}cm$

   $AB = \sqrt{81+100} = \sqrt{181}cm$

   b. $A_{ABC} = \dfrac{20 \cdot 10}{2} = 100cm^2$

   c. $Perimeter_{ABC} = 20 + \sqrt{181} + \sqrt{221}cm$

   d. What do EC and BD have in common?
   Both are heights of the triangle ABC.

   e. The lengths of EC, EB and

   $Area_{ABC} = \dfrac{EC \cdot AB}{2} = \dfrac{EC \cdot \sqrt{181}}{2} = 100$

   $EC = \dfrac{200}{\sqrt{181}} cm \_ EB = \sqrt{221 - \dfrac{40000}{181}} \approx 0.0743cm$

   $AE = AB - EB = \sqrt{181} - \sqrt{221 - \dfrac{40000}{181}}cm$

18. Find the perimeter and area of an isosceles right angled triangle whose <u>leg</u> is 10cm.

$$10^2 + 10^2 = z^2; z = \sqrt{200}cm \qquad P = 20 + \sqrt{200}cm \qquad A = \frac{100}{2} = 50cm^2$$

19. Find the perimeter and area of a right angled triangle whose sides are $6, x, 10$

$$6^2 + x^2 = 10^2; x = 8cm \qquad P = 24cm \qquad A = \frac{48}{2} = 24cm^2$$

20. Find the perimeter and area of a right angled triangle whose sides are $\sqrt{x}, \sqrt{x}, \frac{x}{2}$

$$x + x = \frac{x^2}{4}; x = 8cm \qquad P = 2\sqrt{8} + 4cm \qquad A = \frac{8}{2} = 4cm^2$$

21. Find the area of an isosceles right angled triangle whose <u>perimeter</u> is 20cm.
    Taking x is the legs and y as the hypotenuse:

$$x^2 + x^2 = y^2, y = \sqrt{2} \cdot x; 2x + \sqrt{2} \cdot x = 20; x = \frac{20}{2 + \sqrt{2}} \qquad A = \frac{1}{2}\left(\frac{20}{2 + \sqrt{2}}\right)^2 cm^2$$

22. Find the area of an equilateral triangle whose perimeter is 30cm.

$$3x = 30; x = 10cm \qquad h^2 + 5^2 = 10^2; h = \sqrt{75} \qquad A = \frac{10\sqrt{75}}{2} = 5\sqrt{75}cm^2$$

23. Given a right angled isosceles triangle whose longest side is 10 cm long.
    a. Sketch the triangle.
    b. Find the perimeter of the triangle.
    c. Find the area of the triangle.

$$\underline{x^2 + x^2 = 100} \qquad \underline{x = \sqrt{50}} \qquad \underline{Perimeter = 10 + 2\sqrt{50}}$$

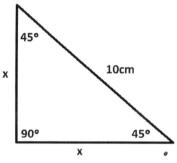

$$\underline{Area = \frac{\sqrt{50} \cdot \sqrt{50}}{2} = 25cm^2}$$

24. Given a right angled isosceles triangle whose smallest side is X cm long.

    a. Sketch the triangle.
    b. Find the perimeter of the triangle in terms of X.
    c. Find the area of the triangle in terms of X.

$$\underline{X^2 + X^2 = c^2} \qquad \underline{c = \sqrt{2}X} \qquad \underline{Perimeter = X(2 + \sqrt{2})}$$

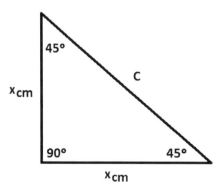

$$\underline{Area = \frac{X^2}{2} cm^2}$$

25. Given an equilateral triangle whose side is 10 cm long.

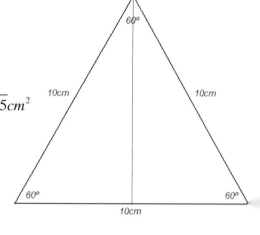

    a. Sketch the triangle.
    b. Find the perimeter of the triangle.
    c. Find the area of the triangle.

$$h^2 + 5^2 = 10^2 \,; h = \sqrt{75} \qquad P = 30cm \qquad A = \frac{10\sqrt{75}}{2} = 5\sqrt{75}\,cm^2$$

26. Given an equilateral triangle whose side is X cm long.

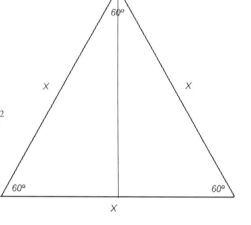

    a. Sketch the triangle.
    b. Find the perimeter of the triangle in terms of X.
    c. Find the area of the triangle in terms of X.

$$h^2 + \left(\frac{x}{2}\right)^2 = x^2 \,; h = \frac{\sqrt{3} \cdot x}{2} \qquad P = 3x\,cm \qquad A = \frac{\sqrt{3} \cdot x^2}{4}\,cm^2$$

27. Find the perimeter of an isosceles triangle whose base is half of its side and its area is 20 cm^2

$$h^2 + \left(\frac{x}{2}\right)^2 = 4x^2; \quad h = \frac{\sqrt{15}}{2}x \qquad A = \frac{\sqrt{15}x^2}{4} = 20 \qquad x = \sqrt{\frac{80}{\sqrt{15}}} \qquad P = 5\sqrt{\frac{80}{\sqrt{15}}}$$

28. Find the perimeter of an isosceles triangle whose base is a third of its side and its area is A cm^2, in terms of A.

$$h^2 + \left(\frac{x}{3}\right)^2 = 9x^2; \quad h = \frac{\sqrt{80}}{3}x \qquad A = \frac{\sqrt{80}x^2}{6} \qquad x = \sqrt{\frac{6A}{\sqrt{80}}} \qquad P = 5\sqrt{\frac{6A}{\sqrt{80}}}$$

29. Find the area of a right angled triangle in which 1 leg is 10% <u>longer</u> than the other and whose perimeter is 70cm

$$x^2 + \left(\frac{11x}{10}\right)^2 = y^2; \quad y = \frac{\sqrt{221}}{10}x \qquad P = x + \frac{11x}{10} + \frac{\sqrt{221}}{10}x = 70 \qquad x = \frac{70}{\left(1 + \frac{11}{10} + \frac{\sqrt{221}}{10}\right)}$$

$$A = \left(\frac{70}{\left(1 + \frac{11}{10} + \frac{\sqrt{221}}{10}\right)}\right) \cdot \left(\frac{70}{\left(1 + \frac{11}{10} + \frac{\sqrt{221}}{10}\right)} \cdot \frac{11}{10}\right) \cdot \frac{1}{2}\,cm^2$$

30. Find the area of a right angled triangle in which 1 leg is 25% <u>shorter</u> than the other and whose perimeter is 24cm

$$x^2 + \left(\frac{3x}{4}\right)^2 = y^2; \quad y = \frac{5}{4}x \quad P = x + \frac{3x}{4} + \frac{5x}{4} = 24 \quad x = 8$$

$$A = 8 \cdot 6 \cdot \frac{1}{2} = 24cm^2$$

31. Given the following diagram (not to scale), BD = x cm, DC = 3BD, AD = 10 cm, AC = 20cm

    a. Write 2 equations with the given information.
        $AB = y; \quad x^2 + y^2 = 10^2; \quad 16x^2 + y^2 = 20^2$

    b. Solve the equations to determine x.
        $15x^2 = 300; \quad x = \sqrt{20}cm \quad y = \sqrt{80}cm$

    c. Find the perimeter and area of ABC.
        $P = 4\sqrt{20} + \sqrt{80} + 20cm$
        $A = \dfrac{4\sqrt{20} \cdot \sqrt{80}}{2} = 80cm^2$

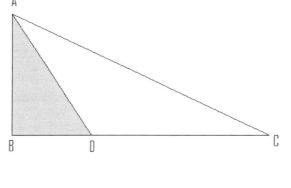

    d. Find the perimeter and area of ABD.
        $P = \sqrt{20} + \sqrt{80} + 10cm$
        $A = \dfrac{\sqrt{20} \cdot \sqrt{80}}{2} = 20cm^2$

    e. Find the perimeter and area of ADC.
        $P = 3\sqrt{20} + 30cm$
        $A = \dfrac{3\sqrt{20} \cdot \sqrt{80}}{2} = 60cm^2$

    f. Determine the percentage of the area that is shaded.
        $\dfrac{20}{80} = 0.25 = 25\%$

30. Given the following diagram (not to scale), BD = 8 cm, AD = 17 , DC = 104 cm,

    a. Find the perimeter and area of ABC
        $AB^2 + 8^2 = 17^2 \quad AB = 15cm$
        $15^2 + 112^2 = AC^2 \quad AC = 113cm$
        $P = 15 + 112 + 113 = 240cm$
        $A = \dfrac{112 \cdot 15}{2} = 840cm^2$

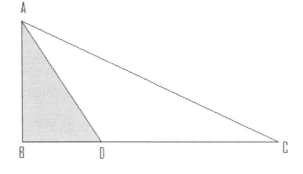

    b. Find the perimeter and area of ABD.
        $AB^2 + 8^2 = 17^2 \quad AB = 15cm$
        $P = 39cm$
        $A = \dfrac{8 \cdot 15}{2} = 60cm^2$

c. Find the perimeter and area of ADC.

$$P = 17 + 104 + 113 = 234cm$$

$$A = \frac{104 \cdot 15}{2} = 780cm^2$$

d. Determine the percentage of the area that is shaded.

$$\frac{60}{840} \approx 0.071 = 7.1\%$$

e. Determine the percentage by which the area of ABC is bigger than ABD

$$\frac{840 - 60}{60} = 13 = 1300\%$$

f. Determine the percentage by which the area of ABC is bigger than ADC

$$\frac{840 - 780}{780} \approx 0.077 = 7.7\%$$

g. Determine the percentage by which the area of ADC is bigger than ABD

$$\frac{780 - 60}{60} = 12 = 1200\%$$

h. Determine the percentage by which the area of ABD is smaller than ABC

$$\frac{840 - 60}{840} \approx 0.93 = 93\%$$

i. Determine the percentage by which the area of ADC is smaller than ABC

$$\frac{840 - 780}{840} \approx 0.071 = 7.1\%$$

j. Determine the percentage by which the area of ABD is smaller than ADC

$$\frac{780 - 60}{780} \approx 0.92 = 92\%$$

k. Determine the percentage by which the perimeter of ABC is bigger than ABD

$$\frac{240 - 39}{39} \approx 5.2 = 520\%$$

l. Determine the percentage by which the perimeter of ABC is bigger than ADC

$$\frac{240 - 234}{234} \approx 0.026 = 2.6\%$$

m. Determine the percentage by which the perimeter of ADC is bigger than ABD

$$\frac{234 - 39}{39} = 5 = 500\%$$

n. Determine the percentage by which the perimeter of ABD is smaller than ABC

$$\frac{240 - 39}{240} \approx 0.84 = 84\%$$

o. Determine the percentage by which the perimeter of ADC is smaller than ABC

$$\frac{240 - 234}{240} = 0.025 = 2.5\%$$

p. Determine the percentage by which the perimeter of ABD is smaller than ADC

$$\frac{234 - 39}{234} \approx 0.83 = 83\%$$

2.4. – POINTS OF CONCURRENCY

1. Given the following triangle, sketch all the <u>altitudes</u> in the triangle.

   An altitude is: <u>A segment for a vertex to the opposite side or its extension forming a 90° angle</u>. The point where the altitudes meet is called "<u>orthocenter</u>". Name the point H.

2. Given the following triangle, Sketch all the <u>perpendicular bisectors</u> in the triangle. The point where they meet is called <u>circumcenter</u>, it is the centre of <u>circumcircle</u>

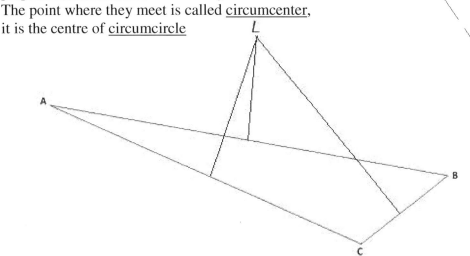

3. Given the following triangle, Sketch all the <u>angle bisectors</u> in the triangle. The point where they meet is called incenter, it is the centre of <u>inscribed circle</u>

4. Given the following triangle, Sketch all the medians in the triangle. The point where they meet is called centroid. If the centroid is M then the following relations are satisfied (complete): $AM = \dfrac{2}{3}AD \quad BM = \dfrac{2}{3}BF \quad CM = \dfrac{2}{3}CG$

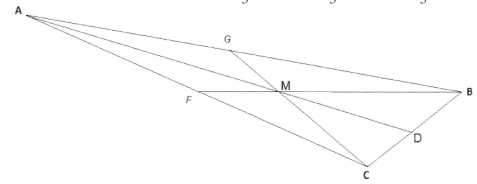

5. The Incentre is: <u>the centre of the inscribed circle, where the angle bisectors meet</u>
6. The Orthocentre is: <u>the point where the altitudes meet</u>
7. The Circumcentre is: <u>the centre of the circumcircle, where the perpendicular bisectors meet</u>
8. The Centroid is: <u>the point where the medians meet, it is also the centre of gravity of the triangle.</u>
9. The Circumcentre is equidistant <u>to the vertices of the triangle.</u>
10. The Incentre is equidistant to <u>the sides of the triangle.</u>
11. Given that the coordinates of a triangle are A(-6, 0). B(4, 0), C(2, 8)

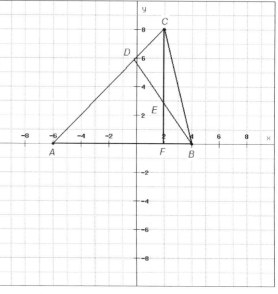

   a. Sketch the triangle.
   b. Graphically find its orthocentre.
   c. Calculate the coordinates of its orthocentre. Using Pythagorean T. and similar triangles:

$$AB = 10; CB = \sqrt{68}; AC = \sqrt{128}$$

$$DC = y; AD = \sqrt{128} - y; DB = h$$

$$y^2 + h^2 = 68$$

$$\left(\sqrt{128} - y\right)^2 + h^2 = 100$$

$$y = \sqrt{18}; h = \sqrt{50}$$

$$FB = 2; CF = 8; EF = x; CE = 8 - x, DC = \sqrt{18}$$

$$\Delta CDE \sim \Delta BFE$$

$$\frac{x}{8-x} = \frac{2}{\sqrt{18}} \qquad x = \frac{8\sqrt{2}}{3+\sqrt{2}} \qquad Orthocentre : (2, \frac{8\sqrt{2}}{3+\sqrt{2}}) \approx (2, 2.56)$$

12. Given that the coordinates of a triangle are A(-6, 0). B(4, 0), C(2, 8)

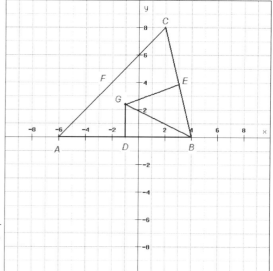

   a. Sketch the triangle.
   b. Graphically find its circumcenter.
   c. Find the points D. E, F the bisectors of AB, BC, and AC correspondingly.

$$AB = 10; CB = \sqrt{68}; AC = \sqrt{128}$$

$$D(-1,0); E(3,4); F(-2,4)$$

   d. Find the slope of the lines AB, BC, find the perpendicular slopes.

$$m_{AB} = 0; m_{BC} = -\frac{8}{2} = -4; m_{\perp AB} = vertical; m_{\perp BC} = \frac{1}{4}$$

   e. Use the previous part to construct 2 of the perpendicular bisectors and find their point of intersection which is the circumcenter

$$x = -1 \qquad y = \frac{1}{4}x + b; E(3,4); y = \frac{1}{4}x + \frac{13}{4}; Circumcentre : G(-1,3)$$

350

13. Given that the coordinates of a triangle are A(-6, 2). B(4, 8), C(0, -8)

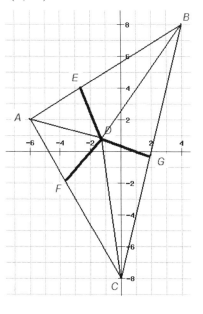

   a. Sketch the triangle.
   b. Graphically find its incentre.
   c. Find the coordinates of the incentre.
      Obtaining the point analytically extends the extension
      of this course, using the formula:

$$(x, y) = (\frac{ax_A + bx_B + cx_C}{a+b+c}, \frac{ay_A + by_B + cy_C}{a+b+c})$$

Where :

$$a = BC = \sqrt{270}$$

$$b = AC = \sqrt{136}$$

$$c = AB = \sqrt{136}$$

$$(x, y) = (\frac{-6\sqrt{270} + 4\sqrt{136} + 0}{\sqrt{270} + 2\sqrt{136}}, \frac{2\sqrt{270} + 8\sqrt{136} - 8\sqrt{136}}{\sqrt{270} + 2\sqrt{136}})$$

$$(x, y) = (\frac{-6\sqrt{270} + 4\sqrt{136}}{\sqrt{270} + 2\sqrt{136}}, \frac{2\sqrt{270}}{\sqrt{270} + 2\sqrt{136}}) \approx (-1.3, 0.83)$$

14. Given that the coordinates of a triangle are A(-6, 2). B(4, 8), C(0, -8)

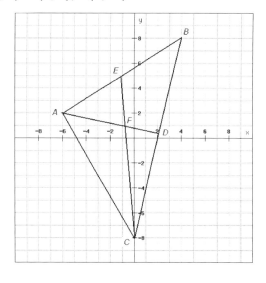

   a. Sketch the triangle.
   b. Graphically find its centroid.
   c. Calculate the coordinates of its centroid.
   Using the midpoint of a segment:

$$(x_m, y_m) = \left(\frac{x_1 + x_2}{2}, \frac{y_1 + y_2}{2}\right)$$

$$D = (2, 0) \quad E = (-1, 5)$$

Finding the equations of the medians:

$$y_{EC} = -13x - 8 \qquad y_{AD} = -\frac{1}{4}x + \frac{1}{2}$$

Finding their point of intersection:

$$-13x - 8 = -\frac{1}{4}x + \frac{1}{2}$$

$$x = -\frac{2}{3}, y = \frac{2}{3}; Centroid : (-\frac{2}{3}, \frac{2}{3})$$

2.5. – CONGRUENT AND SIMILAR TRIANGLES

1. 2 triangles are similar if all of their angles are <u>equal</u>
2. 2 triangles are similar if <u>any</u> of the following is satisfied:
   a. 2 of their angles are <u>equal (AAA)</u>. Sketch an example:

   b. 2 of their sides are <u>proportional</u> and the angles between them are <u>equal (ASA)</u>. Sketch an example:

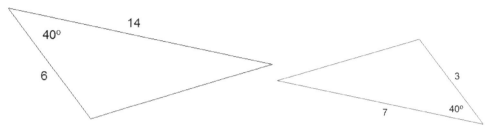

   c. All the sides are <u>proportional (SSS)</u>. Sketch an example:

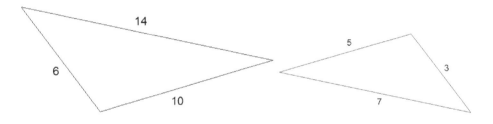

3. All right angled triangles are similar True / **False**. Sketch an example to show answer:

4. Congruent triangles are similar triangles with ratio of proportionality <u>1</u>
5. Similar triangles are always congruent True/**False**
6. congruent triangles are always Similar **True**/False
7. Determine if the following pair of triangles are similar, give a reason: <u>Similar, all angles are identical (AA)</u>
8. Determine if the following pair of triangles are similar, give a reason: <u>Not similar, no condition is satisfied</u>

9. Determine if the following pair of triangles are similar, give a reason: Not similar, no condition is satisfied

10. Determine if the following pair of triangles are similar, give a reason: Similar (SSS)

11. Determine if the following pair of triangles are similar, give a reason: Not similar, no condition is satisfied (in general for any x, y)

12. Determine if the following pair of triangles are similar, give a reason: Similar, AAA (angles are 180º/7, 360º/7, 720º/7 in both)

13. Given that $AB \parallel CD$, determine if the triangles ABE and CED are similar, give a reason: Similar, AA

14. Given that $BC \parallel DE$, determine if the triangles ABC and ADE are similar, give a reason: Similar, AA

15. The shadow of a man formed by a street light on the ground is equal to twice its height. If the man is 10m away from the street light and his height is 1.80m, how high is the street light?

$Since: \Delta ABC \sim \Delta ADE (AA)$

$$\frac{3.60}{3.60+10} = \frac{1.80}{h}$$

$h = 6.8m$

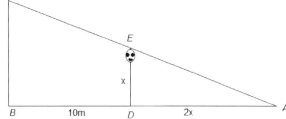

16. Given that $AB \parallel CD$, find ED:

$Since: \Delta ABE \sim \Delta DCE (AA)$

$$\frac{8}{5} = \frac{3}{ED}$$

$$ED = \frac{15}{8}$$

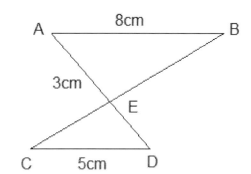

17. In the following triangle the angle BAC is a right angle. AD is an altitude from A to the BC. Show that triangles ABC, ADB and ADC are all similar. If BC = 10cm and AD = 2DC find the perimeter and area of ABD.

$Since: \Delta ABD \sim \Delta CAD (AA)$

$DC = a \quad AD = 2a$

$AC = \sqrt{5}a \quad \frac{10}{\sqrt{5}a} = \frac{\sqrt{5}a}{a}$

$a = 2 = DC \quad AD = 4$

$AC = 2\sqrt{5} \quad AB = 2AC = 4\sqrt{5}$

$Perimeter_{ABD} = 12 + 4\sqrt{5}$

$Area_{ABD} = 16$

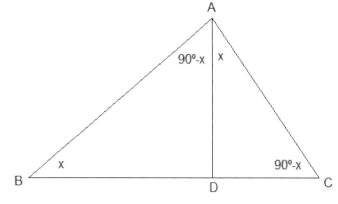

18. The following triangle AB = AC. AD is a altitude from A to the BC. Show that triangles ABD and ACD are similar. If BD = x and 2AB = 3AD, find the perimeter and area of ABC in terms of x.

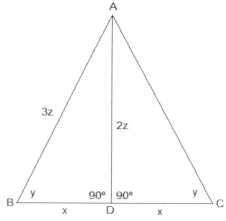

$$9z^2 = 4z^2 + x^2$$

$$z = \frac{x}{\sqrt{5}}$$

$$AD = \frac{2x}{\sqrt{5}}; AB = \frac{3x}{\sqrt{5}}$$

$$Perimeter_{ABC} = x(2 + \frac{6}{\sqrt{5}})$$

$$Area_{ABC} = \frac{2x^2}{\sqrt{5}}$$

19. To measure the height of building the following operation can be performed. Jeff whose height is 180 cm puts a mirror at a distance of 22 m from a building and observed the top of the building in the mirror standing 0.4 m from it. Find the height of the building.

$$Since: \Delta ABC \sim \Delta EDC \, (AA)$$

$$\frac{1.8}{h} = \frac{0.4}{22} \qquad h = 99m$$

20. Given the facade of a certain house, it is known that AC = 4m, CD = 2AC, CE = 7m DE = 3m. ABCD is a rectangle. Find:

a. The height of the house above ground (help: lower a altitude from E).

$$CD = 8; CF = x; FD = 8 - x; EF = y$$

Using Pythgorean theorem in CFE and DFE gives:

$$x^2 + y^2 = 49$$

$$(8 - x)^2 + y^2 = 9$$

Subtracting the equations we obtain:

$$x^2 - (8 - x)^2 = 40$$

$$16x - 64 = 40$$

$$x = \frac{104}{16} = \frac{13}{2} = 6.5cm = CF \qquad y = \sqrt{49 - \frac{169}{4}} = \sqrt{\frac{27}{4}}cm = EF$$

$$\underline{Height \ of \ façade = 4 + \sqrt{\frac{27}{4}}cm}$$

b. The area of the entire facade. $Area = 4 \cdot 8 + \dfrac{8 \cdot \sqrt{\frac{27}{4}}}{2} = 32 + 2\sqrt{27}cm^2$

2.6. – DISTANCE AND MIDPOINT

1. Indicate the following points on the plane: A(2,3), B(6, 9), C(–3, –7), D(6,–5)

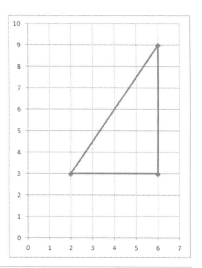

   a. Add the point (6, 3) and use Pythagorean theorem to find the distance between the points A and B.
   $$AB = \sqrt{16+36} = \sqrt{52}$$

   b. The distance between the points C and D.
   $$CD = \sqrt{81+4} = \sqrt{85}$$

   c. Distance AC
   $$AC = \sqrt{25+100} = \sqrt{125}$$

   d. Midpoint between AB
   $$Mid_{AB} = \left(\frac{2+6}{2}, \frac{3+9}{2}\right) = (4,6)$$

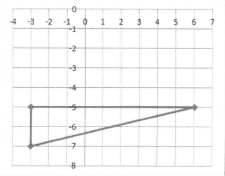

   e. Find the midpoint between CD
   $$Mid_{CD} = \left(\frac{-3+6}{2}, \frac{-7-5}{2}\right) = \left(\frac{3}{2}, -6\right)$$

   f. Find the midpoint between AC
   $$Mid_{AC} = \left(\frac{2-3}{2}, \frac{3-7}{2}\right) = \left(-\frac{1}{2}, -2\right)$$

2. Find the distance between (1, 3) and (7, –3), find the mid point.
   $$Midpoint = \left(\frac{1+7}{2}, \frac{3-3}{2}\right) = (4,0) \qquad Distance = \sqrt{(7-1)^2 + (-3-3)^2} = \sqrt{72}$$

3. Find the distance between (a, b) and (c, d), find the mid point.
   $$Midpoint = \left(\frac{a+b}{2}, \frac{c+d}{2}\right) \quad Distance = \sqrt{(c-a)^2 + (d-b)^2}$$

4. Find a point whose distance to the point (2, 1) is 7. <u>There are infinite, many solutions, for example: (a, b) is the point.</u>
   $$Distance = \sqrt{(a-2)^2 + (b-1)^2} = 7 \text{, if we choose b = 1, we obtain a = 9 so the}$$
   point is (9, 1)

5. Find a point whose distance to the point (–4, 2) is 3, can you draw a conclusion about such points in general?<u>There are infinite, the equation that describes them must be the equation of a circle. For example: (a, b) is the point.</u>
   $$Distance = \sqrt{(a+4)^2 + (b-2)^2} = 3 \text{, if we choose b = 2, we obtain a = –1 so the}$$
   point is (–1, 2)
   $$Midpoint = \left(\frac{a-2}{2}, \frac{5+b}{2}\right) = (0,0); a = 2; b = -5$$

6. The midpoint between the points (a, 5) and (–2, b) is (0, 0) find a and b.
   $$Midpoint = \left(\frac{a-2}{2}, \frac{5+b}{2}\right) = (0,0); a = 2; b = -5$$

7. The midpoint between the points (1+x, 2) and (–2+3x, 2 – y) is (1, 1) find x and y.

$$Midpo\operatorname{int} = \left(\frac{1+x-2+3x}{2},\frac{2+2-y}{2}\right) = (1,1); x = \frac{3}{4}; y = 2$$

8. Given that the mid point between A(2, 5) and B is M(3, –2). Find point B.

$$Midpo\operatorname{int} = \left(\frac{2+x}{2},\frac{5+y}{2}\right) = (3,-2); x = 4; y = -9; B(4,-9)$$

9. Given that the mid point between A(–6, 4) and B is M(10, 0). Find point B.

$$Midpo\operatorname{int} = \left(\frac{-6+x}{2},\frac{4+y}{2}\right) = (10,0); x = 26; y = -4; B(26,-4)$$

10. Given that AB = BC = CD and A, B, C and D are aligned. Point A is (2, 4) and point D is (10, 10). Find points B and C.

    In the horizontal the distance 2 to 10 is 8, divide by 3, in the vertical the distance from 4 to 10 is 6, divide by 3. Therefore: $B = (\frac{14}{3},6)$, $C = (\frac{22}{3},8)$. Can also be obtained using Pythagorean Theorem:

$$AD = \sqrt{100} = 10; B = (a,b);$$

$$AB^2 = (a-2)^2 + (b-4)^2 = \left(\frac{10}{3}\right)^2; BD^2 = (10-a)^2 + (10-b)^2 = \left(\frac{20}{3}\right)^2; a = \frac{14}{3}; b = 6$$

11. Given that the distance AB = BC = CD. A, B, C, D are aligned. Point A is (–4, 8) and point B is (–2, 1). Find points C and D.

    In the horizontal the distance -2 to -4 is 2, in the vertical the distance from 1 to 8 is 7. Therefore: $C(0,8); D(2,15)$

12. Given points A(3, –2), B(6, 1) and C(0, a). It is known that AC = BC, find a.

$$\sqrt{(0-3)^2 + (a+2)^2} = \sqrt{(0-6)^2 + (a-1)^2}$$

$$9 + a^2 + 4a + 4 = 36 + a^2 - 2a + 1$$

$$a = 4$$

13. Given points A(–12, –8), B(–4, 7) and C(a, 0). It is known that AC = BC, find a.

$$\sqrt{(a+12)^2 + (0+8)^2} = \sqrt{(a+4)^2 + (0-7)^2}$$

$$a^2 + 24a + 144 + 64 = a^2 + 8a + 16 + 49$$

$$143 = -16a$$

$$a = -\frac{143}{16}$$

2.7. – CIRCLES

1. Given the following circle:
   a. Sketch a diameter.
   b. Sketch a radius.
   c. The diameter is _____ the radius
   d. Sketch a chord smaller than the diameter
   e. Sketch a chord smaller than the radius

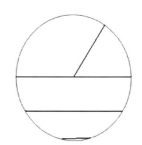

2. Given the following circle:
   a. Sketch a 60° angle.
   b. Show the corresponding minor arc/major arc
   c. Choose 3 points on the circle, connect them with chords.
      The triangle formed is inscribed in the circle. The circle is
      circumscribed about the triangle.
   d. Chords that are at the same distance from the centre are
      <u>equal</u>

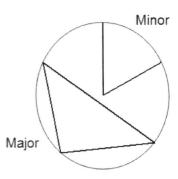

3. Given the following circle:
   a. Choose 3 points on the circle, name them A, B and C. Sketch AB
      and BC. The angle ABC is inscribed in the circle.
   b. Choose a 4th point on the circle, name it D. Sketch AD and CD.
      The angle ADC is inscribed in the circle.
   c. What is your conclusion? <u>The angles are identical</u>

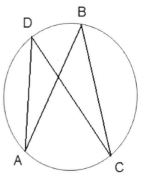

4. Given the following circle:
   a. Choose 3 points on the circle, name them A, B and C. Sketch AB
      and BC. The angle ABC is inscribed in the circle.
   b. Sketch the center of the circle; name it O. Sketch AO and CO.
      The angle AOC is a <u>central angle</u> in the circle.
   c. What is your conclusion? <u>AOC = 2ABC</u>

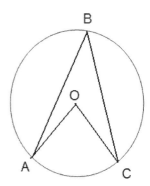

5. Given the following circle:

   a. Sketch the diameter of the circle; name it AC. Sketch a 3rd
      point B. Connect AB, AC and BC. The angle ABC is inscribed
      in the circle. Its size is: <u>90°</u>
   b. Choose a 4th point on the circle; name it D. Connect AD, DC.
      The angle ADC is inscribed in the circle. Its size is: <u>90°</u>
   c. What is your conclusion? <u>All angles supporting diameter are
      90°</u>

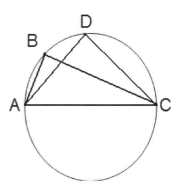

357

6. Find the missing angles, o is the centre of the circle:

$a = b = c = d = e = f = 45°$

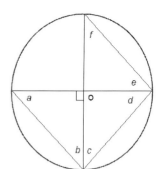

7. Find the missing angles, o is the centre of the circle:

$a = 10°$

$b = 20°$

$c = 80°$

$d = 80°$

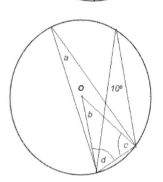

8. Find the missing angles, o is the centre of the circle:

$a = 45°$

$b = 21°$

$c = 24°$

$d = 45°$

$e = 45°$

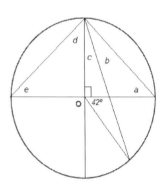

9. Find the missing angles, o is the centre of the circle:

$a = 40°$

$b = 45°$

$c = 25°$

$d = 45°$

$e = 45°$

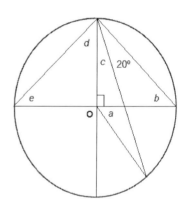

10. Find the missing angles, o is the centre of the circle:

$a = 40°$	$f = 55°$
$b = 30°$	$g = 45°$
$c = 15°$	$h = 105°$
$d = 45°$	$n = 75°$
$e = 105°$	$k = 75°$

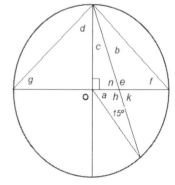

358

11. Given the following circle: Sketch the diameter of the circle; name it AC. Sketch a 3rd point B. Connect AB, AC and BC. Given that the radius of the circle is 1cm and AB = 1cm find the perimeter of ABC.

$$BC = \sqrt{4-1} = \sqrt{3}\, cm$$

$$Perimeter_{ABC} = 3 + \sqrt{3}\, cm$$

12. Sketch a chord whose length is half of the diameter. In case the radius is 2cm find the area and perimeter of the triangle formed by connecting the center of the circle with the ends of the chord.

$$OAB \quad equilateral$$

$$Perimeter_{OAB} = 3cm$$

$$Area_{OAB} = \frac{3 \cdot \left(\dfrac{\sqrt{3}}{2}\right)}{2} = \frac{3\sqrt{3}}{4}\, cm^2$$

13. Given a circle with radius R, find

The Perimeter of the circle: $Perimeter = 2\pi r$

The Area of the circle: $Area = \pi r^2$

14. Given a circle with radius $\dfrac{4}{\pi}$ cm, find

The Perimeter of the circle: $Perimeter = 10\pi \quad cm$

The Area of the circle: $Area = 25\pi \quad cm^2$

15. Given a circle with perimeter 20π cm, find

The radius of the circle: $Perimeter = 20\pi = 2\pi r; \quad r = 10cm$

The Area of the circle: $Area = 100\pi \quad cm^2$

16. Given a circle with area 16π cm^2, find

The radius of the circle: $Area = 16\pi = \pi r^2; \quad r = 4cm$

The perimeter of the circle: $Perimeter = 8\pi \quad cm$

17. Shade 10% of the figure, find the corresponding angle. The length

Of an arc in a circle is L = $\dfrac{10}{100} \cdot 2\pi r = \dfrac{\pi r}{5}$ Angle: 10% of 360º is 36º

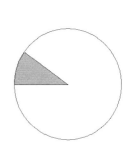

18. Given that R = 5 cm. Shade 20% of the figure, find the corresponding angle and the area shaded. Find the perimeter of the shaded area. Angle: 20% of 360º is 72º

Area shaded: 20% $of \quad \pi r^2 = 25\pi \quad is \quad \dfrac{20}{100} 25\pi = 5\pi \quad cm^2$

Perimeter of area shaded: $5 + 5 + 20\% \quad of \quad 2\pi r = 10 + \dfrac{20}{100} 2\pi 5 = 10 + 2\pi \quad cm$

19. Given that R = 15 cm. Shade 30% of the figure, write the corresponding angle and find the area shaded. Find the perimeter of the shaded area.

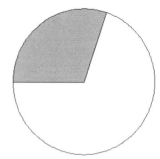

Angle: 30% of 360° is 108°

Area shaded:

$$30\% \ of \ \pi r^2 = 225\pi \ is \ \frac{30}{100}225\pi = 67.5\pi \ cm^2$$

Perimeter of area shaded:

$$10+10+30\% \ of \ 2\pi r = 20+\frac{30}{100}2\pi 15 = 20+9\pi \ cm$$

20. Given a circle with radius 10cm:

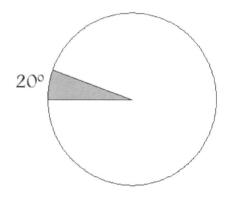

a. The percentage of the area shaded:

$$\frac{20°}{360°} = 0.0555... \approx 5.55\%$$

b. Find the size of the shaded area.

$$\frac{20}{360} \ of \ \pi r^2 = 100\pi \ is \ \frac{30}{360}100\pi = \frac{5\pi}{6} \ cm^2$$

c. Find the perimeter of the shaded area.

$$Arc = \frac{20}{360} \ of \ 2\pi r = 20\pi \ is \ \frac{30}{360}20\pi = \frac{5\pi}{3} \ cm$$

$$Perimeter \ area \ shaded = Arc + 2R = \frac{5\pi}{3} + 20 \ cm$$

21. Given a circle with radius 10cm:

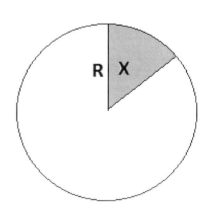

a. The percentage of the shaded area of the total area of the circle in terms of the angle x. $\dfrac{x°}{360°} = \dfrac{100x°}{360°}\%$

b. Find the size of the shaded area in terms of x.

$$\frac{x°}{360°} \cdot 100\pi = \frac{5\pi x}{18} \ cm^2$$

c. Find the perimeter of the shaded area in terms of x.

$$Arc = \frac{x°}{360°} \cdot 20\pi = \frac{\pi x}{18} \ cm$$

$$Perimeter = Arc + 2R = \frac{\pi x}{18} + 20 \ cm$$

22. The length of the perimeter of a circle with radius r is $\underline{2\pi r}$ The length of the arc that corresponds an angle x° is $\dfrac{x°}{360°}2\pi r$ In case the angle x is measured in radians it

would be $\dfrac{x}{2\pi}2\pi r = xr$ .The area of a circle with radius r is $\underline{\pi r^2}$ The area of the

sector that corresponds an angle x° is $\dfrac{x°}{360}\pi r^2$ .In case the angle x is measured in

radians it would be $\dfrac{x}{2\pi}\pi r^2 = \dfrac{xr^2}{2}$

23. Given the circle with r = 2cm :

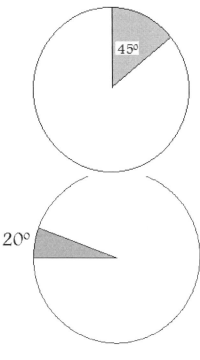

  a. Show the arc corresponding an angle of 45°.
  b. Calculate its length. $\dfrac{45°}{360°}2\pi 2 = \dfrac{\pi}{2}cm$
  c. Shade the corresponding sector area.
  d. Calculate it. $\dfrac{45°}{360°}\pi 4 = \dfrac{\pi}{2}cm^2$

24. Given the circle with r = 3.2m:

  a. Show the arc corresponding an angle of 20°.
  b. Calculate its length. $\dfrac{20°}{360°}2\pi(3.2) = \dfrac{6.4\pi}{18}cm$
  c. Shade the corresponding sector area.
  d. Calculate it. $\dfrac{20°}{360°}\pi(3.2)^2 = \dfrac{10.24\pi}{18}cm^2$

25. Given the circle with r = 3m:

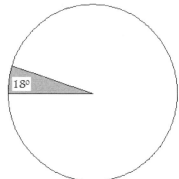

  a. The arc corresponding an angle of $\dfrac{\pi}{10}rad$. $\dfrac{\pi}{10}rad = 18°$
  b. Calculate its length. $\dfrac{3\pi}{10}cm$
  c. Calculate its perimeter. $\dfrac{3\pi}{10}+6cm$
  d. Shade the corresponding sector area.
  e. Calculate it. $\dfrac{9\pi}{20}$

26. Given the circle with r = 6m:
  a. Shade the arc corresponding an angle of 1 radian (approx 57°)
  b. Calculate its length. $xr = 6m$
  c. Shade the corresponding sector area.
  d. Calculate it. $= 158m^2$

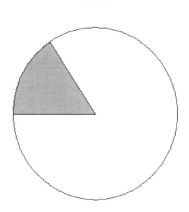

27. Given the following concentric circles with radii 3 cm and 5 cm correspondingly. Find the shaded area. $A_{shaded} = \pi(25-9) = 16\pi$ cm^2

28. Given the following concentric circles with radii 10m and 14m correspondingly. Calculate the shaded area.

$$A_{shaded} = \frac{40°}{360°}\pi(196-100) = \frac{96}{9}\pi \ cm^2$$

29. Given the following circle, AB is a chord on a circle with radius 10cm Calculate the shaded area.

$$A_{shaded} = A_{sector} - A_{triangle} = \frac{100\pi}{24} - 50\sin\left(\frac{\pi}{12}\right) \ cm^2 \approx 0.149 \ cm^2$$

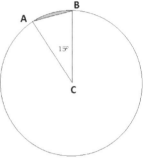

30. Given a circle with radius 8 cm. The segments AB and AC are tangent to the circle. Find the shaded area.

$$A_{shaded} = A_{sector} - A_{shaded} = \frac{A_{square} - A_{circle}}{4} = \frac{256-64\pi}{4} \approx 13.7 \ cm^2$$

31. Given a circle with radius 10cm in which a square is circumscribed

a. Find the length of the side of the square.
   Since CD = 2R = 10cm and EC = ED = x
   Using Pythagorean theorem:
   $2x^2 = 400; \ x = \sqrt{200} = EC = ED$

b. Find the area of the square.
   $Area_{square} = \sqrt{200}\sqrt{200} = 200cm^2$

c. Find the area of the circle
   $Area_{circle} = 100\pi \ cm^2$

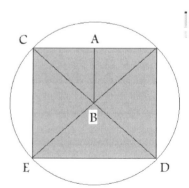

d. Find the percentage of the area of the circle that the square occupies.
   $$\frac{Area_{square}}{Area_{circle}} = \frac{200}{100\pi} = \frac{2}{\pi} \approx 0.637 \approx 64\%$$

32. Given a circle with radius 10cm circumscribed in a square:

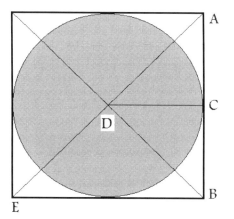

    a. Find the length of the side of the square.
      <u>2R = 20 cm</u>
      Find the area of the square.
      <u>Area = 400 cm^2</u>

    b. Find the area of the circle
      <u>$Area_{circle} = 100\pi \ \ cm^2$</u>

    c. Find the percentage of the area of the square that the circle occupies.
$$\underline{\frac{Area_{circle}}{Area_{square}} = \frac{100\pi}{400} = \frac{\pi}{4} \approx 0.785 \approx 79\%}$$

33. On the following diagram sketch the following directions:

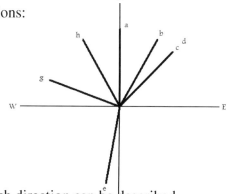

    a. N
    b. N30°E
    c. N45°E
    d. E45°N
    e. S10°W
    f. W80°S
    g. W20°N
    h. N30°W

State a conclusion about the "uniqueness" of a direction. <u>Each direction can be described in more than one way as can be seen</u>

2.8. – QUADRILATERAS

1. Given the following table, fill the blank using *a, b, c, d, h, r*

	Shape	Area	Perimeter
Square		$A = a^2$	$P = 4a$
Rectangle		$A = ab$	$P = 2(a+b)$
Parallelogram		$A = ah$	$P = 2(a+b)$
Isosceles Trapezoid		$A = \dfrac{h}{2}(a+c)$	$P = a + 2b + c$
Trapezpezoid		$A = \dfrac{h}{2}(a+b)$	$P = a + b + c + d$
Rhombus		$A = \dfrac{dr}{2}$	$P = 4a$
Kite		$A = \dfrac{dr}{2}$	$P = 2(a+b)$

2. Given the following quadrilaterals. Write the name of each one of them:

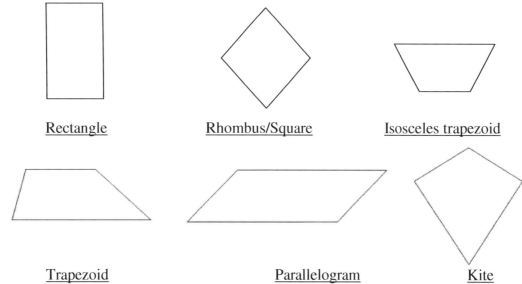

Rectangle   Rhombus/Square   Isosceles trapezoid

Trapezoid   Parallelogram   Kite

3. Given the following table, fill the blanks with yes or no.

	Shape (sketch)	Only 1 pair of parallel sides	2 pairs of parallel sides	1 pair of equal sides	2 pairs of equal sides	4 equal sides
Square		No	Yes	No	No	Yes
Rectangle		No	Yes	No	Yes	No
Parallelogram		No	Yes	No	Yes	No
Isosceles Trapezoid		Yes	No	Yes	No	No
Trapezpezoid		Yes	No	No	No	No
Rhombus		No	Yes	No	No	Yes
Kite		No	No	No	No	No

4. True or False
   a. A square is also a parallelogram **True** / False
   b. A square is also a rectangle **True** / False
   c. A square is also a trapezoid **True** / False
   d. A parallelogram is also a square True / **False**
   e. A rectangle is also a square True / **False**
   f. A rhombus is always a parallelogram **True** / False
   g. A parallelogram is always r rhombus True / **False**
   h. A parallelogram is sometimes a rhombus **True** / False
   i. A rhombus is always a kite **True** / False
   j. All the shapes above mentioned are quadrilaterals **True** / False

5. Given the following table, fill the blanks with yes or no.

	Shape (Sketch diagonals as well)	Diagonals are perpendicular	Diagonals are equal	Diagonals bisect angle	Diagonals bisect each other
Square		Yes	Yes	Yes	Yes
Rectangle		No	Yes	No	Yes
Paralleogram		No	Yes	No	Yes
Isosceles Trapezoid		No	Yes	No	No
Trapezpezoid		No	No	No	No
Rhombus		Yes	Yes	Yes	Yes
Kite		Yes	No	No	No

6. Given a square with diagonal of 4 cm, find its area and perimeter.

$x^2 + x^2 = 16; x = \sqrt{8}; Area = 8cm^2 \quad Perimeter = 4\sqrt{8}cm$

7. Given a square with diagonal of a cm, find its area and perimeter.

$x^2 + x^2 = a^2; x = \dfrac{\sqrt{a}}{2}; Area = \dfrac{a}{4}cm^2 \quad Perimeter = 2\sqrt{a}cm$

8. Given a rectangle with diagonal of 7m and one side is twice as large as the other, find its area and perimeter.

$x^2 + (2x)^2 = 7^2; x = \dfrac{7}{\sqrt{5}}; Area = \dfrac{49}{5}cm^2 \quad Perimeter = \dfrac{28}{\sqrt{5}}cm$

9. Given a rectangle with diagonal of 20m and one side is twice as large as the other, find its area and perimeter.

$x^2 + (2x)^2 = 20^2; x = \dfrac{20}{\sqrt{5}}; Area = \dfrac{400}{5}cm^2 \quad Perimeter = \dfrac{80}{\sqrt{5}}cm$

10. Given the following parallelogram. ABC is isosceles and right angled. AB = 2cm, CD = 5cm (Diagram not to scale). Find:

a. The area and perimeter of the parallelogram
$$2^2 + BD^2 = 5^2; BD = \sqrt{21}; Area = 2(2+\sqrt{21})cm^2$$
$$2^2 + 2^2 = AC^2; AC = \sqrt{8}; Perimeter = 2(2+\sqrt{21}+\sqrt{8})cm$$

b. The area and perimeter of ABC
$$Area = \frac{2 \cdot 2}{2} = 2cm^2 \qquad Perimeter = 4+\sqrt{8}cm$$

c. The area and perimeter of BCD
$$Area = \frac{\sqrt{21} \cdot 2}{2} = \sqrt{21}cm^2 \qquad Perimeter = 7+\sqrt{21}cm$$

d. The area and perimeter of CDE
$$Area = 2(2+\sqrt{21})-2-\sqrt{21} = 2+\sqrt{21}cm^2 \qquad Perimeter = 7+\sqrt{21}+\sqrt{8}cm$$

11. Given the following isosceles trapezoid. ABC is right angled. AC = 7cm, CE = 15cm and AE = 20cm (Diagram not to scale). Find:

a. The area and perimeter of ABC and BCE
$$CB = h; AB = x; BE = 20 - x$$
$$x^2 + h^2 = 7^2; \qquad (20-x)^2 + h^2 = 15^2$$
$$x = \frac{28}{5} = 5.6cm; \qquad h = \frac{21}{5} = 4.1cm$$
$$Area_{ABC} = \frac{1}{2} \cdot \frac{28}{5} \cdot \frac{21}{5} = \frac{294}{25} = 11.76cm^2; Perimeter_{ABC} = 7 + \frac{28}{5} + \frac{21}{5} = \frac{84}{5} = 16.8cm$$
$$Area_{BCE} = \frac{1}{2} \cdot \frac{82}{5} \cdot \frac{21}{5} = \frac{861}{25} = 34.44cm^2; Perimeter_{BCE} = 15 + \frac{82}{5} + \frac{21}{5} = \frac{853}{50} = 17.06cm$$

b. The area and perimeter of the trapezoid
$$Area_{ACDE} = \frac{21}{5} \cdot \frac{(20+11.8)}{2} = 66.78cm^2; Perimeter_{ACDE} = 20+11.8+14 = 45.8cm$$

c. The area and perimeter of CDE
$$Area_{CDE} = 66.78-16.8-17.06 = 32.94cm^2; Perimeter_{CDE} = 15+11.8+7 = 33.8cm$$

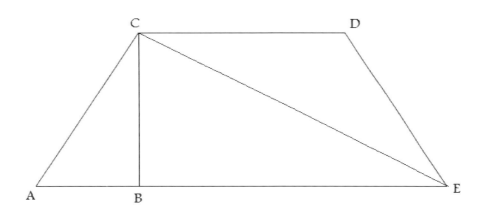

12. Given the following rhombus. BC = 6cm, AD = 18cm and find the area and perimeter the rhombus (Diagram not to scale).

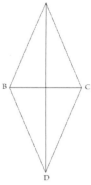

$$Area_{ABC} = \frac{6 \cdot 18}{2} = 54cm^2$$

$$3^2 + 9^2 = AB^2; AB = \sqrt{90}$$

$$Perimeter = 4\sqrt{90}cm$$

13. Given the following kite. BC = 4cm, AE = 8cm and CD = 2AC find the area and perimeter the kite (Diagram not to scale).

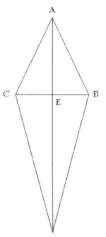

$$2^2 + 8^2 = AC^2; AC = \sqrt{68}; CD = 2\sqrt{68}$$

$$Perimeter = 6\sqrt{68}cm$$

$$2^2 + ED^2 = \left(2\sqrt{68}\right)^2; ED = \sqrt{268}$$

$$Area_{ABC} = \frac{4 \cdot (8 + \sqrt{268})}{2} = 2 \cdot (8 + \sqrt{268})cm^2$$

14. It is known that the perimeter of a rhombus with equal diagonals is 40cm. Find its area. Rhombus with equal diagonals is a square.

$$x = \frac{40}{4} = 10cm; \qquad Area = 100cm^2$$

15. Find the side length of a square whose area is equal to its perimeter.

$$x^2 = 4x \qquad x = 0cm \qquad or \qquad x = 4cm$$

16. Find the side length of a rhombus whose area is equal to its perimeter and one of its diagonals is 5cm long.

$$\frac{5d}{2} = 4\sqrt{\left(\frac{5}{2}\right)^2 + \left(\frac{d}{2}\right)^2} \qquad \frac{25d^2}{4} = 16\left(\left(\frac{5}{2}\right)^2 + \left(\frac{d}{2}\right)^2\right)$$

$$\frac{25d^2}{4} = \frac{400}{4} + \frac{16d^2}{4} \qquad 9d^2 = 400 \qquad d = \frac{20}{3}$$

The diagonals are 5 and $\frac{20}{3}$

$$Side = \sqrt{\left(\frac{5}{2}\right)^2 + \left(\frac{20}{6}\right)^2} = \sqrt{\left(\frac{25}{4}\right) + \left(\frac{400}{36}\right)} = \sqrt{\left(\frac{625}{36}\right)} = \frac{25}{6}cm$$

2.9. – 3D GEOMETRY

1. Given the following table, fill the blanks

	Shape	Surface Area	Volume
Cuboid (Rectangular Prism)		$S = 2(ab + bc + ac)$	$V = abc$
Pyramid (Square based)		$S = a^2 + 4A$ $A = Area\ \ Side$	$V = \dfrac{a^2 h}{3}$
Sphere		$S = 4\pi r^2$	$V = \dfrac{4}{3}\pi r^3$
Cylinder		$S = 2\pi rh$	$V = \pi r^2 h$
Cone		$S = \pi rL + \pi r^2$	$V = \dfrac{\pi r^2 h}{3}$

2. Given the following table, fill the blanks

	Shape	Surface Area	Volume
Triangular prism		$A = 2ac + ab + 2S$	$V = Sa$
Triangle based Pyramid (Tetrahedron)		$S = A_{base} + A_{triangles}$	$S = \dfrac{A_{base} \cdot h}{3}$

3. Find the volume and surface area of a sphere with radius 10cm.

$$A = 400\pi cm^2 \qquad V = \frac{4000}{3}\pi cm^3$$

4. Find the volume and surface area of a sphere with radius <u>0.4m = 40cm</u>.

$$A = 1600\pi cm^2 \qquad V = \frac{64000}{3}\pi cm^3$$

5. Find the volume of a square based pyramid with base length $2x$ cm and height is x cm. $V = \frac{4x^3}{3} cm^3$

6. Find the volume and surface area of a square based cuboid whose base length is 15 cm and height 0.1m

$$V = 15^2 \cdot 0.1 = 22.5 cm^3 \qquad A = 2 \cdot 15^2 + 4 \cdot 15 \cdot 0.1 = 456 cm^2$$

7. Find the volume and surface area of a cone with radius 0.4m and height 2m.

$$V = \frac{\pi \cdot 40^2 \cdot 200}{3} = \frac{320000\pi}{3} cm^3$$

$$L = \sqrt{20^2 + 200^2} \qquad A = \pi \cdot 20^2 + \pi \cdot 20\sqrt{40400} cm^2$$

8. Find the volume and surface area of a cylinder with radius 0.4m and height 2m.

$$V = \pi \cdot 20^2 \cdot 200 = 80000\pi cm^3 \qquad A = 2\pi \cdot 40^2 + 2\pi \cdot 40 \cdot 200 = 19200\pi cm^2$$

9. Given that the volume of a square based pyramid is 10 m^3 and that its height is equal to its base length, find the perimeter of its base.

$$V = \frac{x^3}{3} = 10m^3; x = \sqrt[3]{30}; P = 4\sqrt[3]{30}m$$

10. Given that the volume of a cuboid is 10 m^3 and that the ratio between its sides is 1:2:3. Find its surface area.

$$V = x \cdot 2x \cdot 3x = 10m^3; x = \sqrt[3]{\frac{5}{3}}; A = 2\left(\frac{5}{3}\right)^{\frac{2}{3}} + 4\left(\frac{5}{3}\right)^{\frac{2}{3}} + 12\left(\frac{5}{3}\right)^{\frac{2}{3}} = 18\left(\frac{5}{3}\right)^{\frac{2}{3}} cm^2$$

11. Given that the volume of a cone is 10 m^3 and that its height is 3 times the radius of the base. Find its height.

$$V = \frac{\pi \cdot R^2 \cdot 3R}{3} = 10m^3; R = \sqrt[3]{\frac{10}{\pi}}; height = 3\sqrt[3]{\frac{10}{\pi}}m$$

12. Given that the volume of a sphere is 10 m^3. Find its surface area.

$$V = \frac{4\pi R^3}{3}m^3 = 10; R = \sqrt[3]{\frac{30}{4\pi}}; A = 4\pi\left(\frac{30}{4\pi}\right)^{\frac{2}{3}}$$

13. Find the volume and surface area of the following shape:

$$V = \frac{4\pi\left(\frac{5}{2}\right)^3}{3} + \pi 5^2 \cdot 15 = \frac{125\pi}{6} + 375\pi cm^3$$

$$A = 4\pi\left(\frac{5}{2}\right)^2 + 2\pi 5^2 + 2\pi \cdot 5 \cdot 15 = 25\pi + 50\pi + 150\pi = 225\pi cm^2$$

14. Find the volume and surface area of the following shape:

$$V = \frac{\pi 4^2 \cdot 12}{3} + \pi 4^2 \cdot 10 = 64\pi + 160\pi = 224\pi cm^3$$

$$L = \sqrt{12^2 + 4^2} = \sqrt{160}$$

$$A = \pi 4^2 + 2\pi 4 \cdot 10 + \pi \cdot 4 \cdot \sqrt{160} = 96\pi + \pi \cdot 4 \cdot \sqrt{160} cm^2$$

15. Find the volume and surface area of the following shape:

$$V = \frac{3 \cdot 10}{2} \cdot 12 = 180 cm^3$$

$$L = \sqrt{10^2 + 3^2} = \sqrt{109}$$

$$A = \frac{3 \cdot 10}{2} \cdot 2 + 12 \cdot \sqrt{109} + 10 \cdot 12 + 3 \cdot 12 = 186 + 12 \cdot \sqrt{109} cm^2$$

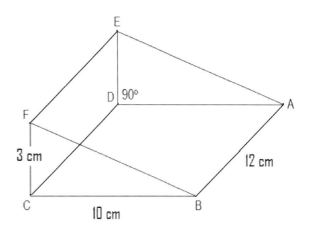

2.10. – GEOMETRIC TRANSOFRMATIONS

1. The points on the plane: A(0,0), B(–1,6),C(4,2). Connect them to form a triangle.

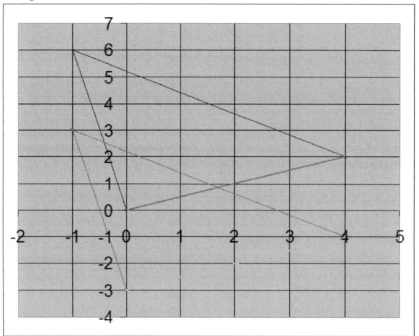

b. What can you say about the location of the 2nd triangle in comparison to the first one? <u>It is shifted 3 units down</u>

c. This is a <u>vertical</u> translation.

2. The points on the plane: A(0,0), B(–1,6),C(4,2). Connect them to form a triangle.

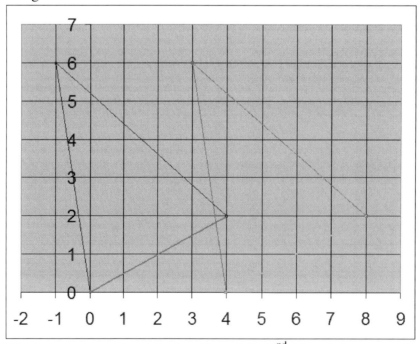

b. What can you say about the location of the 2nd triangle in comparison to the first one? <u>It is shifted 4 units to the right</u>

c. This is a <u>horizontal</u> translation.

3. Indicate the following points on the plane: A(0,0), B(–1,6),C(4,2). Connect them to form a triangle.

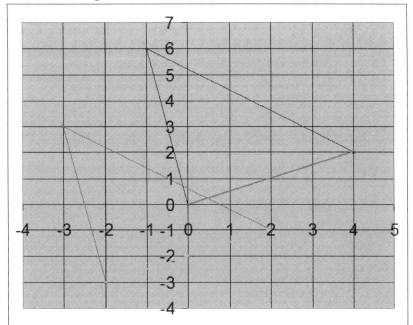

b. What can you say about the location of the 2nd triangle in comparison to the first one? <u>It is shifted 2 units to the left and 3 down</u>

c. This is a <u>horizontal</u> and <u>vertical</u> translations.

4. Indicate the following points on the plane: A(1,0), B(–2,6),C(6,3). Connect them to form a triangle.

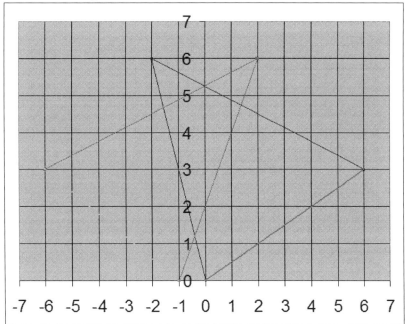

a. What can you say about the location of the 2nd triangle in comparison to the first one? <u>It is reflected.</u>

b. This is a <u>Reflection</u> across the y axis.

c. On changing x into <u>–x</u> we are generating a <u>Reflection</u> across the <u>y axis</u>

5. Indicate the following points on the plane: A(1,1), B(–2,6),C(6,3). Connect them to form a triangle.

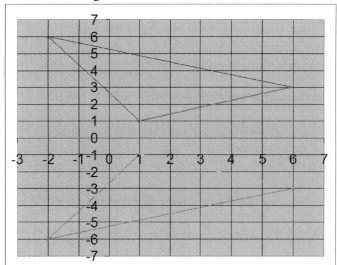

b. What can you say about the location of the 2nd triangle in comparison to the first one?

c. This is a <u>Reflection</u> about the x axis.

d. On changing y into <u>–y</u> we are generating a <u>Reflection</u> across the <u>x axis</u>

6. Indicate the following points on the plane: A(–4,0), B(0,4),C(4,0), D(0, –4). Connect them to form a square.

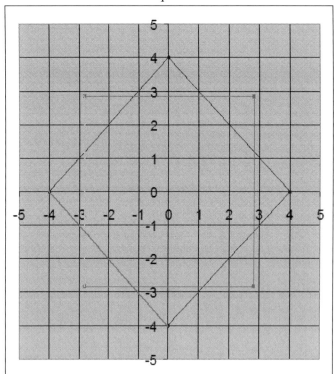

b. What can you say about the location of the 2nd square in comparison to the first one? <u>It is rotated 45° clockwise</u>

c. This is a <u>Rotation</u> of <u>45° clockwise</u> degrees.

d. Write down the coordinates of a square that is a rotation of 90° of the first one:
A'' = (4,0), B'' = (0, –4), C'' = (–4, 0), D'' = (0, 4)
Conclusions? <u>Same coordinates, Squares remain invariant under 90° rotation</u>

7. Indicate the following points on the plane: A(–5,0), B(5,0). Given also the point C(0,a)

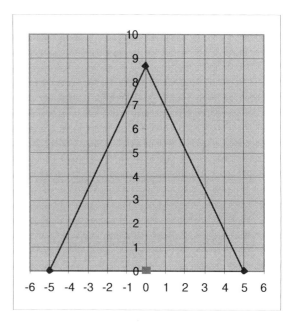

a. The value of a in order to create an equilateral triangle is: $\sqrt{75}$
   Side of triangle is 10. Using Pythagorean T. $a = \sqrt{100-25} = \sqrt{75}$

b. The coordinates of the new points after translating the triangle 3 units left and 1 down. A' = (–8, –1), B' = (2,–1), C' = (–3, $\sqrt{75}$ –1)

c. The coordinates of the points after rotation the triangle 30° clockwise.
$$A'' = \left(-5\frac{\sqrt{3}}{2}, \frac{5}{2}\right), B'' = \left(5\frac{\sqrt{3}}{2}, -\frac{5}{2}\right),$$
$$C'' = \left(\frac{5}{2}, 5\frac{\sqrt{3}}{2}\right)$$

d. The coordinates of the new points after rotation the triangle 60° clockwise.
   Same coordinates, equilateral triangle remains invariant under 60° rotation

8. Indicate the following points on the plane: A(1,0), B(–2,5),C(4,3). Connect them to form a triangle.

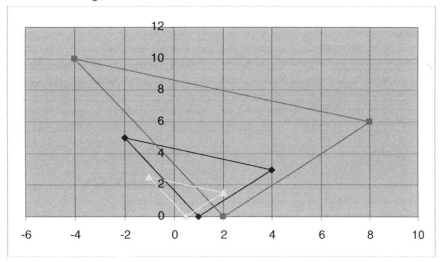

a. Indicate the following points on the plane: A'(2,0), B'(–4,10),C'(8,6), Connect them to form a triangle.
b. The 2nd triangle in comparison to the first one? Similar, just bigger
c. This is a dilation factor 2
d. Indicate the following points on the plane: A'(0.5,0), B'(–1,2.5),C'(2,1.5), Connect them to form a triangle.
e. The 3rd triangle in comparison to the first one? Similar, just smaller
f. This is a dilation factor 1/2
g. When making all sides of a shape bigger or smaller using the same factor the shape remains similar to the original one.

9. Indicate the following points on the plane: A(0,0), B(2, 0),C(0,–3). Connect them to form a triangle.

   a. The points are: A' = (0,0), B' = (6, 0), C' = (0, –9)

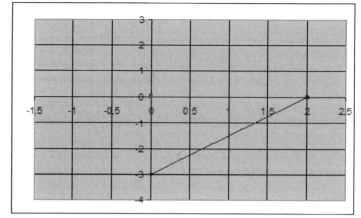

   b. The relations:

$$\frac{A'B'}{AB}=3$$

$$\frac{A'C'}{AC}=3$$

$$\frac{B'C'}{BC}=3$$

10. Given a triangle ABC whose sides are 3, 4 and 5 cm long.
   a. Is his a right angled triangle? <u>Yes: 25 = 16 + 9</u>
   b. The sides of another triangle whose sides are half the length of the sides of ABC are: <u>2.5, 2, 1.5</u>. Is this triangle right angled? <u>Yes 6.25 = 4 + 2.25</u>

11. Given a triangle ABC whose sides are 2, 4 and x cm long. A similar triangle has sides y, 6 and z correspondingly.

   a. $\dfrac{6}{4}=\dfrac{y}{2}; y=3$

   b. $\dfrac{z}{x}=\dfrac{3}{2}$

   c. A value for x so that ABC will be right angled?
$$4+16=x^2; x_1=\sqrt{20}$$
$$x^2+2=4; x_2=\sqrt{2}$$

   d. Find z in that case(s): $z_1=\dfrac{3}{2}x=\dfrac{3}{2}\sqrt{20}; z_2=\dfrac{3}{2}x=\dfrac{3}{2}\sqrt{2}$

12. Given a rectangle ABCD whose sides are 8, and x cm long. A similar rectangle has sides y and 16 cm correspondingly. The perimeter of the 2nd rectangle is 3 times as large as the perimeter of the first one.

   a. $\dfrac{8}{y}=\dfrac{x}{16}; xy=128$ $3(16+2x)=2y+32; y=8+3x$ $x=\dfrac{16}{3}, y=24$

   b. The area of the rectangles A_1 and A_2. $A_1=\dfrac{128}{3}$ $A_2=384$

   c. The quotient $\dfrac{A_2}{A_1}=\dfrac{384}{\left(\dfrac{128}{3}\right)}=9$, <u>the quotient between the areas is equal to</u>

   <u>the quotient between the sides squared.</u>

13. Given that the area of a square is 16 times as big as the area of a different square. Find the ratio between the sides of the squares.

$$\frac{A_2}{A_1}=16=\left(\frac{a_1}{a_2}\right)^2; \frac{a_1}{a_2}=4$$

14. Explain the meaning of the operation "Zooming in/out" frequently used in digital imaging. <u>Zoom means create a similar image by multiplying the distance between any 2 points by a constant. If the constant is great than 1 than we "zoom in", if the constant is between 0 and 1, we "zoom out".</u>

CHAPTER 3 – FUNCTIONS

3.1. – INTRODUCTION TO FUNCTIONS

1. Try to sketch an approximate graph for the height of a human, add some reasonable numbers to the graph:

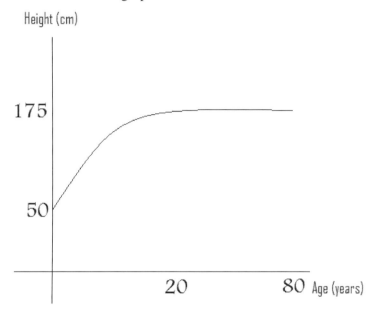

a. Height(0) = 50cm it is the Height of <u>a new born baby</u>
b. Height(t) = 100cm, t = <u>2 years</u>
c. Write the set of possible values for the Age: $Age \in [0,80]$ this is the Domain
d. Write the set of possible values for the Height: $Height \in [50,175]$ this is the Range:
e. This graph describes a function that shows how <u>height</u> depends on <u>age</u>

2. Write the definition of a function in your own words:
<u>A one to one or many to one relation between "things" (variables),</u>

3. Write 2 examples of relations that <u>are</u> functions:
<u>Day of the week</u> $\rightarrow$ <u>color of my shirt</u>

<u>Word</u> $\rightarrow$ <u>First letter of word</u>

<u>Time</u> $\rightarrow$ <u>Temperature</u>

4. The independent variable is usually represented in the <u>horizontal axis</u>
5. The dependent variable is usually represented in the <u>vertical axis</u>

6. Draw a sketch of 2 functions. Can you write the mathematical expression to describe them?

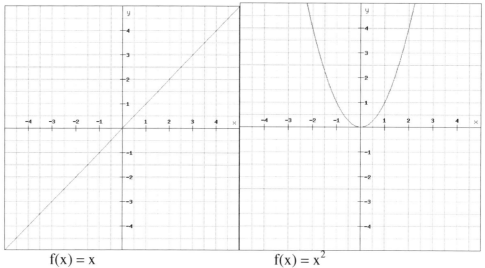

$f(x) = x$ $f(x) = x^2$

7. Write 2 examples of relations that <u>are not</u> functions:
   <u>Name of person</u> $\rightarrow$ <u>Personal information</u>   (one to many)
   <u>Name of City</u> $\rightarrow$ <u>Names of habitants</u>   (one to many)

8. Which one of the following graphs cannot represent function? Explain.

   2 y values for a certain x value.

Not a function

Not a function

9. Draw an example of a curve that does not represent a function:

10. Draw an example of a curve that represents a function:

11. The domain of a function is the: <u>The set of allowed values of the independent variable ("what x can be")</u>

12. The Range of a function is the: <u>The set of allowed values of the dependent variable ("what y can be")</u>

13. Out of the following relations circle the ones that are functions:

    a. **Person's name → Person's age**

    b. **City → Number of habitants**

    c. City → Names of habitants

    d. **Family → Home Address**

    e. **Satellite's name → Position of satellite**

    f. **Time → Position of object**

    g. **One → One**

    h. One → Many

    i. **Many → One**

14. Given the Weight – age curve for a human. Sketch an approximate graph:

    a. Weight(0) = <u>3kg</u> it is the <u>weight of new born baby</u>

    b. Weight(t) = 10kg. t = <u>3years</u>

    c. State its domain: $Age \in [0,80]$

    d. State its range: $\underline{Weight \in [3,75]}$

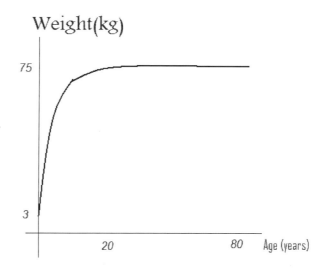

15. Given the following function that describes the temperature in C° as a function of time (t = 0 corresponds to midnight):

    a. f(0) = <u>–1</u>

    b. f(2) = <u>–1.5</u> = f(<u>5</u>)

    c. f(7) = <u>out of domain</u>

    d. f(x) = 3, x = <u>–3.7</u>

    e. f(x) = 0, <u>x = –2.2, 5.8</u>

    f. f(x) = –2 , <u>x = 2.8, 4.7</u>

    g. State its domain: $x \in [-4,6)$

    h. State its range: $\underline{f(x) \in [-3,4]}$

    i. Function increases at: $x \in (4,6)$

    j. Function decreases at: $\underline{x \in (-4,4)}$

    k. Is this function one to one? Many to one? Explain. Explain. Many to one, some y values have 2 different corresponding x values.

379

16. Given the function the describes the change in the benefit (%) given by a certain stock:

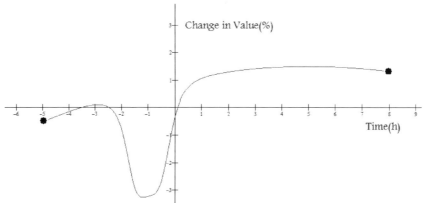

a. $f(x) = 0$, x = −2.5, −3.5, 0.2
b. $f(0) = $ −0.5 = f(−2.2)
c. $f(−5) = $ −0.6
d. $f(1) = $ 1
e. $f(−2) = $ −1 = f(−0.2)
f. $f(3) = $ 1.4
g. $f(x) = −2$, x = −0.5, −1.5
h. Is f(−2) < 0 ? yes
i. Is f(−2) < f(−1) ? No
j. Domain: $x \in [−5, 8]$

k. State its range: $f(x) \in [−3.2, 1.5]$
l. Where is the function increasing
    $x \in (−5, −3) \cup (−1.2, 5)$
m. Where is the function decreasing?
    $x \in (−3, −1.2) \cup (5, 8)$
n. Where is the function stationary?
    x = −3, −1.2
o. Is this function one to one? No, it is many to one

17. Given the following function:

Domain   Range

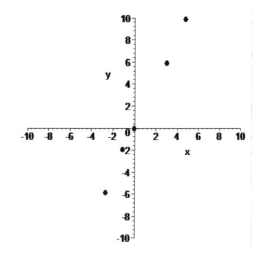

a. Allowed values for independent variable: $\{−3, −1, 0, 3, 5\}$

b. Allowed values for dependent variable: $\{−6, −2, 0, 6, 10\}$

c. Sketch the function on the graph.

d. A mathematical expression to express function: f(x) = 2x

18. Given the following function:

Domain   Range

-2   → h
0   → -1
3   → 5
d   → 7
6   → 11

a. A mathematical expression to express this function: $\underline{f(x) = 2x - 1}$
b. Find h. Find d. $\underline{h = -5, d = 4}$

19. Use the graph of the gasoline consumption of a truck to answer:

a. $f(0) = \underline{0}$
b. $f(50) = \underline{12.5}$
c. $f(5) = \underline{2.5}$
d. For what values of x is $f(x) = 12$, $\underline{x = 33, 84, 116}$
e. Is $f(60) > f(70)$? $\underline{\text{Yes}}$
f. For what values of x is $f(x) > 15$? $\underline{,x > 135}$
g. At what positive speed is the consumption of gasoline minimum? $\underline{100}$
h. Where is the function increasing? $\underline{x \in (0,50) \cup (100,145)}$
i. Where is the function decreasing? $\underline{x \in (50,100) \; x \in (50,100)}$
j. Where is the function stationary? $\underline{x = 100}$

20. Functions can be represented using: <u>graphs</u> or <u>expressions</u> or <u>lists/tables</u>

21. The following graph describes the concentration of a drug injected into the blood as a function of the time (in minutes) since the injection. $t = 0$ corresponds to the time of injection.

a. What is the concentration of the drug 4 minutes after the injection? 4c
b. During what period of time is the concentration increasing? $t \in (0, 2.2)$
c. During what period of time is the concentration decreasing? $t \in (2.2, 16)$
d. After how long is the concentration maximum? 2.2 min
e. When is the concentration greater than 5c? $t \in (1.2, 3.6)$
f. When is the concentration smaller than 2c? $t \in (0,1) \cup (5.5, 16)$
g. State the domain and range of the function.   Domain: $t \in [0, 16]$

Range: $f(t) \in [0, 11]$

22. The graph below shows the temperature in C° on a particular day as a function of time since midnight.

a. What was the temperature at 4:00 a.m.? 0.1
b. When was the temperature 0 degrees? 3:55 am, 7:55 am, 11:50 am
c. When was the temperature below freezing? (less than 0 degrees)
   $t \in (11, 3:55) \cup (11:50, 16)$
d. When was the temperature increasing? $t \in (23, 5:05) \cup (7:55, 10:35)$
e. When was the temperature decreasing? $t \in (5:05, 7:55) \cup (10:35, 16)$
f. State the domain and range of the function. Domain: $t \in [11pm, 16pm]$

Range: $f(t) \in [-5.5, 0.5]$

3.2. – LINEAR FUNCTIONS

1. Given the function: N(x) = 70. This function represents the number of heartbeats per second of a healthy man. Complete the following table:

x	−5	−4	−3	−2	−1	0	1	2	3	4	5
N(x)	70	70	70	70	70	70	70	70	70	70	70

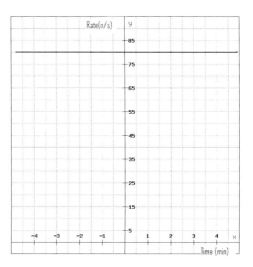

- Sketch the points of the chart on a graph (use a ruler).
- The domain of the function: $x \in \mathbb{R}$
- The y intercept : (0, 70)
- State the x intercept: None
- The function is increasing on the interval: Never
- The function is decreasing on the interval: Never
- Sketch the function of the graph used for the points initially drawn
- The range of the function: $f(x) \in \{70\}$
- The heartbeat rate is 70 beats per minute

2. The position of a John in reference to his house in his afternoon walk can be modeled by the function: D(t) = 3t − 6, t is the time in hours and D is the distance in km.

t	−5	−4	−3	−2	−1	0	1	2	3	4	5
D(t)	−21	−18	−15	−12	−9	−6	−3	0	3	6	9

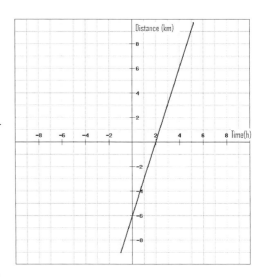

- Sketch the points of the chart on a graph (use a ruler).
- The domain of the function: $t \in \mathbb{R}$
- The y intercept: (0, −6)
- The x intercept: (2, 0)
- The function is increasing on the interval: $t \in \mathbb{R}$
- The function is decreasing on the interval: Never
- Sketch the function of the graph used for the points initially drawn
- What is the speed of John 3 km/h. How is that seen on the graph? It is the slope of the line
- State the range of the function: $f(t) \in \mathbb{R}$
- When was John at his house? At instant 2 hours

3. An elevator's behavior can be modeled by: P(t) = –2t + 5. Where P is the floor and t is time in minutes. The building has 15 floors and 3 Parking levels below ground.

t	–5	–4	–3	–2	–1	0	1	2	3	4	5
P(t)	15	13	11	9	7	5	3	1	–1	–3	No

- Sketch the points of the chart on a graph (use a ruler).
- State the domain of the function:
  $t \in [-5, 4]$
- The y intercept : (0, 5)
- The x intercept: (2.5, 0)
- The function is increasing on the interval: Never
- The function is decreasing on the interval:
  $t \in (-5, 4)$
- Sketch the function of the graph used for the points initially drawn
- Describe the motion of the elevator The elevator is descending How is that seen on the graph? The negative slope of the line, y values are decreasing with time
- State the range of the function: $f(t) \in [-3, 15]$

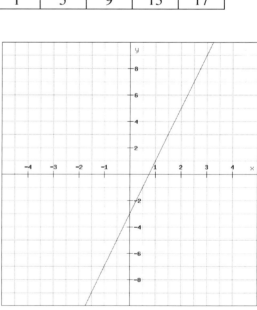

4. Given the function: f(x) = 4x – 3

x	–5	–4	–3	–2	–1	0	1	2	3	4	5
f(x)	–23	–19	–15	–11	–7	–3	1	5	9	13	17

- Sketch the points of the chart on a graph (use a ruler).
- The domain of the function: $x \in R$
- The y intercept: (0, –3)
- The x intercept: $\left(\dfrac{3}{4}, 0\right)$
- The function is increasing on the interval:
  $x \in R$
- The function is decreasing on the interval:
  Never
- Sketch the function of the graph used for the points initially drawn
- State the range of the function: $f(x) \in R$

5. Given below are the equations for five different lines. Match the function with its graph.

Function	On the graph
$f(x) = 20 + 2x$	**B**
$g(x) = 4x + 20$	**C**
$s(x) = -30 + 2x$	**A**
$a(x) = 60 - x$	**D**
$b(x) = -2x + 60$	**E**

6. The general functions that describes a straight line is <u>$f(x) = mx + b$</u>
7. We know a function is a straight line because <u>x is to the power of 1 only</u>
8. The y–intercept (also called vertical intercept), tells us where the line crosses the <u>y axis</u>. The corresponding point is of the form <u>(0 , b)</u>.
9. The x–intercept (also called horizontal intercept), tells us where the line crosses the <u>x axis</u>. The corresponding point is of the form (p , 0).
10. If m > 0, the line <u>increases</u> left to right. If <u>m < 0</u> the line decreases left to right.
11. In case the line is horizontal m is <u>zero</u> and the line is of the form <u>$f(x) = b$</u>
12. The larger the value of m is, the <u>steeper</u> the graph of the line is.

13. Given the graph, write, the slope (m), b and the equation of the line:

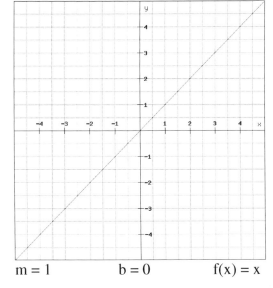

m = 1   b = 0   f(x) = x

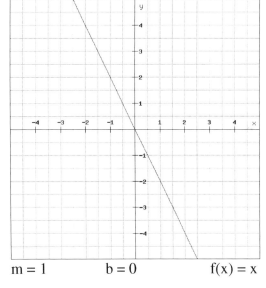

m = 1   b = 0   f(x) = x

385

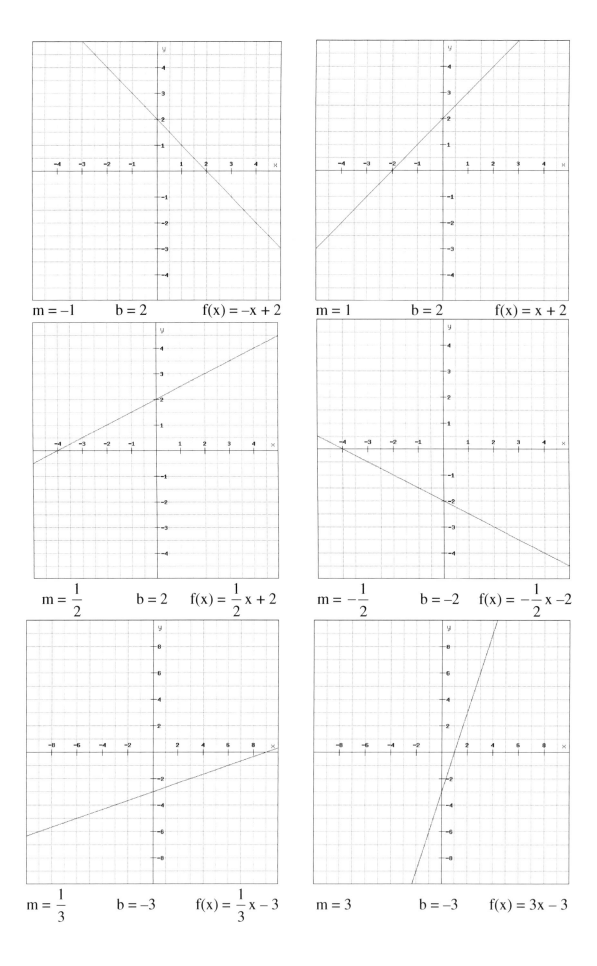

$m = -1$ $b = 2$ $f(x) = -x + 2$

$m = 1$ $b = 2$ $f(x) = x + 2$

$m = \dfrac{1}{2}$ $b = 2$ $f(x) = \dfrac{1}{2}x + 2$

$m = -\dfrac{1}{2}$ $b = -2$ $f(x) = -\dfrac{1}{2}x - 2$

$m = \dfrac{1}{3}$ $b = -3$ $f(x) = \dfrac{1}{3}x - 3$

$m = 3$ $b = -3$ $f(x) = 3x - 3$

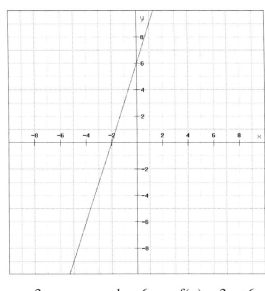

$m = 3$ $b = 6$ $f(x) = 3x + 6$

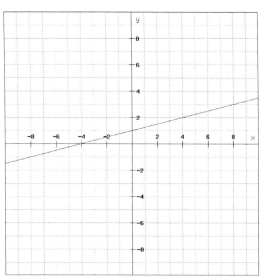

$m = \dfrac{1}{4}$ $b = 1$ $f(x) = \dfrac{1}{4}x + 1$

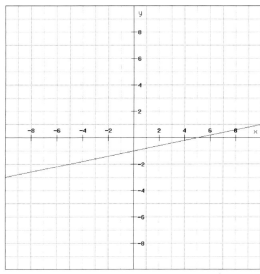

$m = \dfrac{1}{5}$ $b = -1$ $f(x) = \dfrac{1}{5}x - 1$

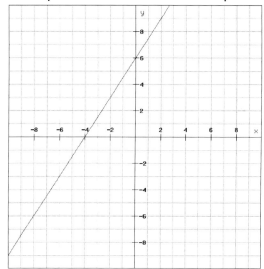

$m = \dfrac{3}{2}$ $b = 6$ $f(x) = \dfrac{3}{2}x + 6$

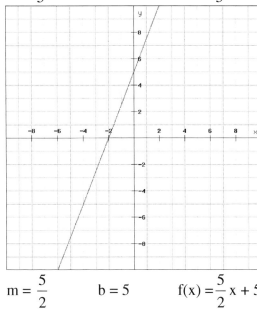

$m = \dfrac{5}{2}$ $b = 5$ $f(x) = \dfrac{5}{2}x + 5$

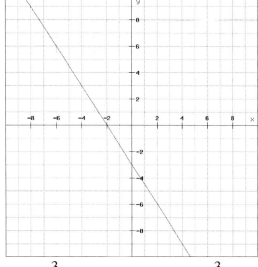

$m = -\dfrac{3}{2}$ $b = -3$ $f(x) = -\dfrac{3}{2}x - 3$

Analyze the following functions/inequlities:

1. f(x) = 1

Domain: _____ $x \in R$ _____

Range: _____ $f(x) \in \{1\}$ _____

Increase: _____ Never _____

Decrease: _____ Never _____

y intercept: $(0,1)$

x intercept: None

2. f(x) = 2

Domain: _____ $x \in R$ _____

Range: _____ $f(x) \in \{2\}$ _____

Increase: _____ Never _____

Decrease: _____ Never _____

y intercept: $(0,2)$

x intercept: None

3. f(x) = −1

Domain: _____ $x \in R$ _____

Range: _____ $f(x) \in \{-1\}$ _____

Increase: _____ Never _____

Decrease: _____ Never _____

y intercept: $(0,-1)$

x intercept: None

4. f(x) = 0

Domain: _____ $x \in R$ _____

Range: _____ $f(x) \in \{0\}$ _____

Increase: _____ Never _____

Decrease: _____ Never _____

y intercept: $(0,0)$

x intercept: None

5. f(x) = x

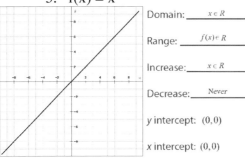

Domain: _____ $x \in R$ _____

Range: _____ $f(x) \in R$ _____

Increase: _____ $x \in R$ _____

Decrease: _____ Never _____

y intercept: $(0,0)$

x intercept: $(0,0)$

6. f(x) = x+1

Domain: _____ $x \in R$ _____

Range: _____ $f(x) \in R$ _____

Increase: _____ $x \in R$ _____

Decrease: _____ Never _____

y intercept: $(0,1)$

x intercept: $(-1,0)$

7. f(x) = −x

Domain: _____ $x \in R$ _____

Range: _____ $f(x) \in R$ _____

Increase: _____ Never _____

Decrease: _____ $x \in R$ _____

y intercept: $(0,0)$

x intercept: $(0,0)$

8. f(x) = − x − 2

Domain: _____ $x \in R$ _____

Range: _____ $f(x) \in R$ _____

Increase: _____ Never _____

Decrease: _____ $x \in R$ _____

y intercept: $(0,-2)$

x intercept: $(-2,0)$

9. f(x) = 2x

Domain: _____ $x \in R$ _____

Range: _____ $f(x) \in R$ _____

Increase: _____ $x \in R$ _____

Decrease: _____ Never _____

y intercept: $(0,0)$

x intercept: $(0,0)$

10. $y \leq 3x - 5$

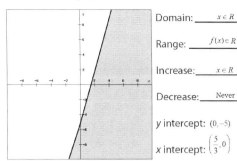

Domain: _____ $x \in R$ _____

Range: _____ $f(x) \in R$ _____

Increase: _____ $x \in R$ _____

Decrease: _____ Never _____

y intercept: $(0, -5)$

x intercept: $\left(\frac{5}{3}, 0\right)$

11. $f(x) = 3 - 2x$

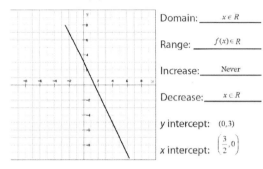

Domain: _____ $x \in R$ _____

Range: _____ $f(x) \in R$ _____

Increase: _____ Never _____

Decrease: _____ $x \in R$ _____

y intercept: $(0, 3)$

x intercept: $\left(\frac{3}{2}, 0\right)$

12. $f(x) = \dfrac{x}{3}$

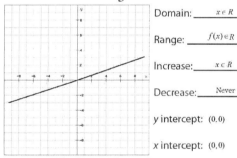

Domain: _____ $x \in R$ _____

Range: _____ $f(x) \in R$ _____

Increase: _____ $x \in R$ _____

Decrease: _____ Never _____

y intercept: $(0, 0)$

x intercept: $(0, 0)$

13. $f(x) = 2x + 1$

Domain: _____ $x \in R$ _____

Range: _____ $f(x) \in R$ _____

Increase: _____ $x \in R$ _____

Decrease: _____ Never _____

y intercept: $(0, 1)$

x intercept: $\left(-\frac{1}{2}, 0\right)$

14. $f(x) = 2x - 2$

Domain: _____ $x \in R$ _____

Range: _____ $f(x) \in R$ _____

Increase: _____ $x \in R$ _____

Decrease: _____ Never _____

y intercept: $(0, -2)$

x intercept: $(1, 0)$

15. $f(x) = 3x + 5$

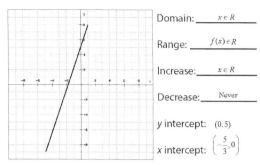

Domain: _____ $x \in R$ _____

Range: _____ $f(x) \in R$ _____

Increase: _____ $x \in R$ _____

Decrease: _____ Never _____

y intercept: $(0, 5)$

x intercept: $\left(-\frac{5}{3}, 0\right)$

16. $f(x) \leq \dfrac{x}{2} - 5$

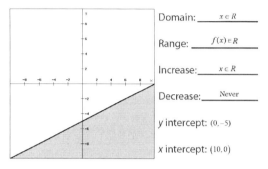

Domain: _____ $x \in R$ _____

Range: _____ $f(x) \in R$ _____

Increase: _____ $x \in R$ _____

Decrease: _____ Never _____

y intercept: $(0, -5)$

x intercept: $(10, 0)$

17. $f(x) = \dfrac{x}{4} + 6$

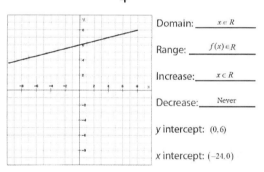

Domain: _____ $x \in R$ _____

Range: _____ $f(x) \in R$ _____

Increase: _____ $x \in R$ _____

Decrease: _____ Never _____

y intercept: $(0, 6)$

x intercept: $(-24, 0)$

18. $f(x) \geq \dfrac{3x - 10}{2} = \dfrac{3x}{2} - 5$

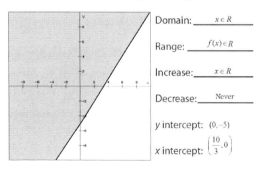

Domain: _____ $x \in R$ _____

Range: _____ $f(x) \in R$ _____

Increase: _____ $x \in R$ _____

Decrease: _____ Never _____

y intercept: $(0, -5)$

x intercept: $\left(\frac{10}{3}, 0\right)$

19. $f(x) = -\frac{3}{2}x - \frac{3}{2}$

Domain: ___$x \in R$___

Range: ___$f(x) \in R$___

Increase: ___Never___

Decrease: ___$x \in R$___

y intercept: $\left(0, -\frac{3}{2}\right)$

x intercept: $(-1, 0)$

20. $f(x) = -\frac{1}{2}x - \frac{3}{2}$

Domain: ___$x \in R$___

Range: ___$f(x) \in R$___

Increase: ___Never___

Decrease: ___$x \in R$___

y intercept: $\left(0, -\frac{3}{2}\right)$

x intercept: $(-3, 0)$

21. $f(x) = \frac{7}{2}x - \frac{1}{4}$

Domain: ___$x \in R$___

Range: ___$f(x) \in R$___

Increase: ___$x \in R$___

Decrease: ___Never___

y intercept: $\left(0, -\frac{1}{4}\right)$

x intercept: $\left(\frac{1}{14}, 0\right)$

22. $f(x) = -\frac{9}{5}x + \frac{8}{3}$

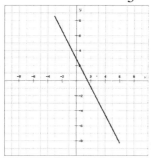

Domain: ___$x \in R$___

Range: ___$f(x) \in R$___

Increase: ___Never___

Decrease: ___$x \in R$___

y intercept: $\left(0, \frac{8}{3}\right)$

x intercept: $\left(\frac{40}{27}, 0\right)$

23. $3x + 2y = 2$

Domain: ___$x \in R$___

Range: ___$f(x) \in R$___

Increase: ___Never___

Decrease: ___$x \in R$___

y intercept: $(0, 1)$

x intercept: $\left(\frac{2}{3}, 0\right)$

24. $4x - 2y - 3 = 1$

Domain: ___$x \in R$___

Range: ___$f(x) \in R$___

Increase: ___$x \in R$___

Decrease: ___Never___

y intercept: $(0, -2)$

x intercept: $(1, 0)$

25. $-2y + 3x = -5$

Domain: ___$x \in R$___

Range: ___$f(x) \in R$___

Increase: ___$x \in R$___

Decrease: ___Never___

y intercept: $\left(0, \frac{5}{2}\right)$

x intercept: $\left(-\frac{5}{3}, 0\right)$

26. $y - x \leq 2$

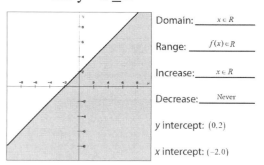

Domain: ___$x \in R$___

Range: ___$f(x) \in R$___

Increase: ___$x \in R$___

Decrease: ___Never___

y intercept: $(0, 2)$

x intercept: $(-2, 0)$

27. $y + 2x - 3 \geq 1$

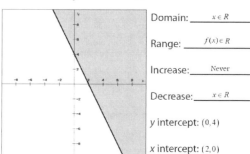

Domain: ___$x \in R$___

Range: ___$f(x) \in R$___

Increase: ___Never___

Decrease: ___$x \in R$___

y intercept: $(0, 4)$

x intercept: $(2, 0)$

28. 5y + 5x = 5

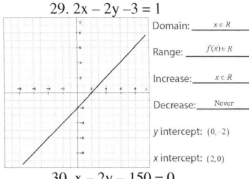

Domain: $x \in R$

Range: $f(x) \in R$

Increase: Never

Decrease: $x \in R$

y intercept: (0,1)

x intercept: (1,0)

29. 2x – 2y –3 = 1

Domain: $x \in R$

Range: $f(x) \in R$

Increase: $x \in R$

Decrease: Never

y intercept: (0, –2)

x intercept: (2,0)

30. x – 2y – 150 = 0

Cannot be seen on this graph

Domain: $x \in R$

Range: $f(x) \in R$

Increase: $x \in R$

Decrease: Never

y intercept: (0, –75)

x intercept: (150,0)

31. $y = 2x; 2x - y = 0$

32. $y = \dfrac{1}{2}x - 2; x - 2y - 4 = 0$

33. $y = -\dfrac{5}{2}x - \dfrac{1}{2}; 5x + 2y + 1 = 0$

34. $y = 3x - 2; 3x - y - 2 = 0$

35. $y = \dfrac{8}{5}x - \dfrac{17}{5}; 8x - y - 17 = 0$

36. $y = x + 6; -x + y - 6 = 0$

37. $y = 5x + 9; -5x + y - 9 = 0$

38. $y = -\dfrac{1}{2}x + \dfrac{9}{2}; x + 2y - 9 = 0$

39. $y = -\dfrac{1}{5}x + 2; x + 5y - 10 = 0$

40. $y = x; y = 2x; y = -3x; y = -x; y = -\dfrac{1}{2}x; y = -\dfrac{1}{3}x$

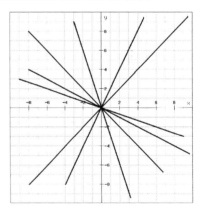

41. $y = -3x - 3$

42. $y = 2x - 4$

43. $y = -\dfrac{1}{2}x - 1$

44. $y = 2x + 10$

45. $2x - 3 = -5x - 2 \qquad x = \dfrac{1}{7} \qquad \left(\dfrac{1}{7}, -\dfrac{19}{7}\right)$

46. No intersection, lines are parallel.

47. $\left(\dfrac{7}{2}, 4\right)$

48. No intersection, lines are parallel.

49. $-12x - 13 = 15x + 20$ $\quad x = -\dfrac{33}{27}$ $\quad \left(-\dfrac{33}{27}, \dfrac{5}{3}\right)$

50. $2a = -5; a = \dfrac{-5}{2}$

51. The same line, all the points of the line are the intersection.

52. $3m - 5 = 10; m = 5$

53. $2 - b = 7; b = -5$

54. The same line, all the points of the line are the intersection.

55. Sketch the line $f(x) = \dfrac{-x}{2} + 3, -4 \le x < 8$

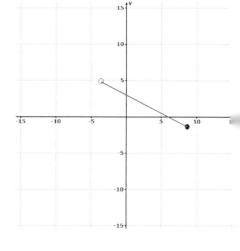

DISTANCE AND MIDPOINT BETWEEN 2 POINTS

56. Distance $= \sqrt{16 + 36} = \sqrt{52}$
    Midpoint $= (3, 5)$

57. Distance $= \sqrt{64 + 64} = \sqrt{128}$
    Midpoint $= (1, -4)$

58. Distance $= \sqrt{16 + 25} = \sqrt{41}$
    Midpoint $= \left(-3, -\dfrac{7}{2}\right)$

59. Distance $= \sqrt{(a-5)^2 + 16} = 5; a_1 = 2; a_1 = 8$
    Midpoint$(1) = \left(\dfrac{7}{2}, 1\right)$; Midpoint$(2) = \left(\dfrac{13}{2}, 1\right)$

60. Distance $= \sqrt{(c+4)^2 + 16} = 10; a_1 = -4 + 2\sqrt{21}; a_2 = -4 - 2\sqrt{21}$
    Midpoint$(1) - \left(3, -4 + \sqrt{21}\right)$; Midpoint$(2) = \left(3, -4 - \sqrt{21}\right)$

61. This equation describes a <u>circle</u> $x^2 + y^2 = 4$

62. This equation describes a <u>circle</u> $(x-2)^2 + (y+1)^2 = 25$

63. $c^2 = 100; c = \pm 10$ Midpoint $= (0, \pm 5)$

64. Distance $= \sqrt{196 + 49} = \sqrt{245}$ Midpoint $= \left(-1, -\dfrac{5}{2}\right)$

PERPENDICULAR LINES $(m \cdot m_\perp = -1)$

65. A slope perpendicular to 1 is $\underline{-1}$. A slope perpendicular to 2 is $\underline{-\dfrac{1}{2}}$

A slope perpendicular to k is $\underline{-\dfrac{1}{k}}$ A slope perpendicular to $\dfrac{a}{b}$ is $\underline{-\dfrac{b}{a}}$

66. $\underline{y = -\dfrac{1}{3}x + 13}$

67. $\underline{y = \dfrac{1}{3}x + b}$ $\underline{y = \dfrac{1}{3}x + 2}$

68. $\underline{y = \dfrac{5}{2}x - \dfrac{9}{2}}$

69. Given the points (–2, 5) and (4, 2).

a. $\underline{f(x) = -\dfrac{1}{2}x + 4}$

b. $\underline{\text{No: } f(5) = -\dfrac{5}{2} + 4 = \dfrac{3}{2} \neq 1}$

c. $\underline{f(x) = 2x + b}$ $\underline{Midpo\text{int} : (1, \dfrac{7}{2})}$ $\underline{f(x) = 2x + \dfrac{3}{2}}$

d. $\text{Points} : (x, 2x + \dfrac{3}{2})$ $d = \dfrac{1}{2} = \sqrt{(0-x)^2 + \left(2 - \left(2x + \dfrac{3}{2}\right)\right)^2}$

$\underline{x_1 = 0 \quad x_2 = \dfrac{5}{2}}$ Points are: $(0, \dfrac{3}{2}), (\dfrac{5}{2}, \dfrac{13}{2})$

70. Find a point on the x axis that is $\sqrt{5}$ units away from the line y = 2x + 4

$\text{Points} : (a, 0), (x, 2x + 4)$

$\text{distance} = 5 = \sqrt{(a-x)^2 + (0 - (2x + 4))^2}$

$Perpendicular \quad Slopes : -\dfrac{1}{2} = -\dfrac{2x+4}{a-x},$

Solving system for a: $(\dfrac{1}{2}, 0), (-\dfrac{9}{2}, 0)$

71. Find a point on the y axis that is 5 units away from the line y = 3x + 2

$\text{Points} : (0, a), (x, 3x + 2)$

$\text{distance} = 5 = \sqrt{(0-x)^2 + (a - (3x+2))^2}$

$Perpendicular \quad Slopes : -\dfrac{1}{3} = \dfrac{3x+2-a}{x},$

Solving system for a: $a \approx 14.65$

72. Given that the slope of one of the lines is 3 and that the lines are perpendicular, find the **exact** coordinates of the point of intersection of the two lines.

Increasing line (plug (1,0): $y = 3x - 3$

Decreasing line: $y = -\dfrac{1}{3}x + 2$

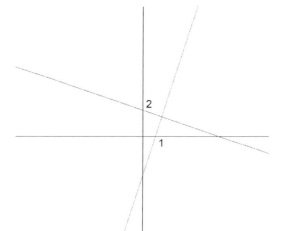

$$3x - 3 = -\dfrac{1}{3}x + 2$$

Intersection: $x = \dfrac{3}{2}$ $\left(\dfrac{3}{2}, \dfrac{1}{2}\right)$

SLOPE – INTERCEPT FORM OF A LINE

73. The line $y - 3 = 2(x + 1)$ passes through the point _____ and has a slope of ___
74. The line $y + 5 = -3(x - 51)$ passes through the point _____ and has a slope of ___
75. The line $-y + 1 = (x + 3)$ passes through the point _____ and has a slope of ___
76. The line $2y + 5 = -6(x + 7)$ passes through the point _____ and has a slope of ___
77. The line $y + a = m(x + b)$ passes through the point _____ and has a slope of ___
78. The line $y - a = m(x - b)$ passes through the point _____ and has a slope of ___
79. The line $y - a = m(x + b)$ passes through the point _____ and has a slope of ___
80. Write the equation $y - 3 = 2(x + 1)$ in the explicit form
81. Write the equation $y + 5 = 2(x + 6)$ in the explicit form
82. Write down the equation of a line passing through the point (5, 2) with slope 1.
83. Write down the equation of a line passing through the point (–4, –3) with slope –2.
84. Write down the equation of a line passing through the point (6, 3) with slope $\dfrac{2}{3}$.
85. Write down the equation of a line passing through point (–2, –5) with slope $-\dfrac{2}{5}$.
86. Write down the equation of the line passing through points (–2, –5), (–7, 5),
87. Write down the equation of the line passing through points (–1, –3), (6, 5),
88. Write down the equation of the line passing through points (–1, 5), (7, –2),

APPLICATION

1. The price of a new toy (in US$) is C(t) = 20 – 0.5t, t given in days.
   a. Sketch the corresponding graph.
   b. What was the initial price of the toy?   <u>20$</u>
   c. Find the price of the toy after 10 days   <u>15$</u>
   d. What is the domain of the function, argument the answer, <u>$t \in [0,40]$</u> Price cannot be negative.
   e. What is the range of the function? <u>$C \in [0,20]$</u>
   f. What is the meaning of 0.5? Does it have units? What are they? 0.5 <u>$\$ / day$</u>, it is the daily reduction of the price.

2. On a certain planet the temperature of the soil is 10° on the surface and 0.02° wormer with every meter of depth.

   a. Write a function to describe the temperature as a function of the depth d. State its domain and range. What are the units of the slope?
      T(d) = 10 + 0.02d
      Units of slope: C°/m
   b. Find the temperature at depth of 500m
      T(500) = 10 + 100 =110°
   c. Find the depth at which the temperature is 13°.
      13 = 10 + 0.02d
      d = 150m
   d. Graph the function, use appropriate scale, variables and units.

3. In a factory there are 2 machines that produce a certain product. The operation cost (electricity, maintenance etc.) of Machine A is 250$ a month and the cost of production per product is 2$. The operation cost of Machine B is 200$ a month and the cost of production per product is 4$. The maximum number of products that both machines can make a month is 200.

   a. Write the functions to describe the cost C as a function of the number of products n for both machines. Indicate the domain and range of both functions. What are the units of the slope?
      C1(n) = 250 + 2n   C2(n) = 200 + 4n
      Domain: $n \in [0,200]$ Domain: $n \in [0,200]$
      Range: $C1 \in [250,650]$ Range:
      $C2 \in [200,1000]$
   b. Graph the functions, use appropriate scale, variables and units. Calculate the coordinates of important points on the graph.
      250 + 2n = 200 + 4n
      n = 25, C1(25) = C2(25) = 300$
   c. Discuss in which case each machine is best.
      If $0 \le n \le 25$ Machine 1, If $25 \le n \le 200$ Machine 2

4. A parking lot with 1200 parking spots opens at 6 am. The cars flow in a constant rate. At 10 am the parking is full.

a. Write the function to describe the number of cars N as function of time t in hours. Indicate the domain and range of the function. What are the units of the slope?

$$N(t) = \frac{t-6}{4} \cdot 1200 = 300t - 1800$$

Domain: $t \in [6,10]$ Range:
$N(t) \in [0,1200]$

b. Find the number of free spots at 8:30.

$$N(8.5) = \frac{8.5-6}{4} \cdot 1200 = 750 \text{ cars, so } 450$$

free spots

c. In case the owner needs 150 free spots at what time should he close the parking?

$$N(t) = \frac{t-6}{4} \cdot 1200 = 1050 \quad \text{At 9 :30}$$

$t = 9.5$

d. Graph the function, use appropriate scale, variables and units.

5. You need to rent a car for one day and to compare the charges of 3 different companies. Company I charges 20$ per day with additional cost of 0.20$ per mile. Company II charges 30$ per day with additional cost of 0.10$ per mile. Company III charges 60$ per day with no additional mileage charge.

a. Write the cost function for each one of the companies.

$C_I = 20 + 0.2x$

$C_{II} = 30 + 0.1x$

$\underline{C_{III} = 70}$

b. Sketch all 3 graphs on the same axes system.

c. Comment on the circumstances in which renting a car from each one of the companies is best.
The black line represent the cheapest price:
It is important to find the intersection points between: lines I, II and lines II, III.
I, II: (100, 40)
II, III (400, 70)

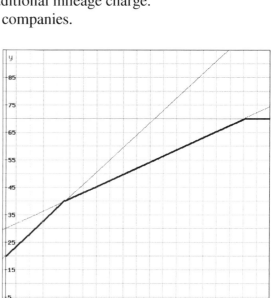

If we travel less than 100 miles Company I is best.
If we travel between 100 and 400 miles Company II is best.
If we travel more than 400 miles Company III is best.

CHAPTER 4 - STATISTICS

4.1. – STATISTICS

1. The set of objects that we are trying to study is called <u>population</u>. the number of elements in the population can be <u>finite</u> or <u>infinite</u>.
2. Usually the <u>population</u> is too big and therefore we obtain a <u>sample</u>. This process is called <u>sampling</u>.
3. We use the <u>sample</u> to obtain conclusions about the <u>population</u>.

Types of DATA

1. <u>Categorical</u> data.
2. <u>Numerical</u> data that can be divided to <u>continuous</u> or <u>discrete</u>.
3. <u>Numerical discrete</u> can be counted while <u>numerical continuous</u> data can be <u>measured</u>.
4. Give 3 examples of <u>Categorical</u> data:
   <u>Eye color (blue, green, brown etc.)</u>
   <u>Favorite food (meat, pasta, ice cream etc.)</u>
   <u>Preferred website (whatever.com, whatsup.com etc.)</u>
5. Give 3 examples of <u>numerical discrete</u> data:
   <u>Number of students in a classroom</u>
   <u>Shoe size</u>
   <u>Number of rabbits in the forest</u>
6. Give 3 examples of <u>numerical continuous</u> data:
   <u>Height of people</u>
   <u>Amount of energy in a laser beam</u>
   <u>CO_2 level in the atmosphere</u>
7. Given the following variables, classify them in the table:

Categorical	Numerical Discrete	Numerical Continuous
Eye color	Shoe size	Height
Type of fruit	Number of cars in a parking lot	Weight
Name of writer	Number of apples sold a day in a store	Velocity of the wind
	Numbers of pages in a book	Temperature
	Number of students in a school	

8. In a certain class the eye color of students was studied.
   a. How many students participated?   <u>14</u>
   b. Represent the information in a Bar Chart

   c. Represent the information in a Pie Chart

9. In a certain math class the following grades were obtained:

65, 72, 85, 89, 52, 71, 89, 68, 63, 76, 61, 86, 98, 79, 79, 91, 74, 89, 77, 68, 78

a. How many students participated? 21
b. What kind of data is this? Numerical discrete
c. Suggest a method to represent this information in a table. By grouping

d. Use the table to create a bar graph

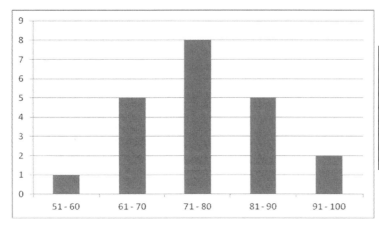

Grade	Number of students
51 - 60	1
61 - 70	5
71 - 80	8
81 - 90	5
91 - 100	2

10. In a certain zoo the length of a certain type of animal (in meters) was studied.

a. How many animals participated? 14
b. Represent the information in a Bar Chart. In this case we must choose Intervals

[1.50, 1.60)	3
[1.60, 1.70)	4
[1.70, 1.80)	4
[1.80, 1.90)	2
[1.90, 2.00)	1

Wider or narrower intervals could have been chosen

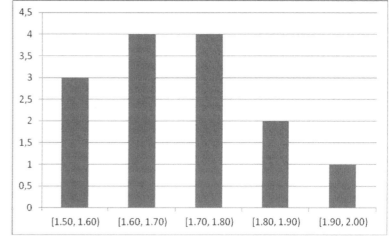

c. Represent the information in a Pie Chart

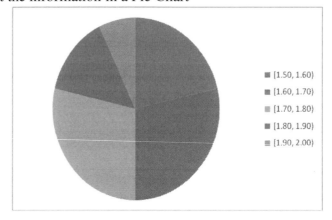

398

11. In a certain group shoe size was studied and the following results obtained:

45, 36, 44, 38, 41, 42, 48, 39, 40, 42, 43, 41, 38, 45, 41, 38, 42, 44, 41, 41, 46

   a. How many students participated? <u>21</u>
   b. What kind of data is this? <u>Numerical discrete</u>
   c. Suggest a method to represent this information in a table. <u>By grouping</u>
   d. Use the table to create a bar graph

Shoe size	Number of people
[36, 38]	4
[39, 41]	7
[42, 44]	6
[45, 47]	3
[48, 50]	1

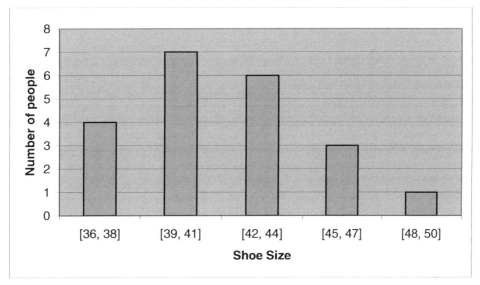

12. Choose a variable to collect information about in your classroom, state its kind, represent the information in a table and create a bar graph.

4.2. – MEAN, MEDIAN, MODE AND FREQUENCY DIAGRAMS

1. In a certain club the number of visitors per days was studied during 1 week and the following results obtained: 58, 79, 66, 78, 23, 66, 63

    a. State the number of elements in the set: <u>7</u>
    b. What kind of data is this? <u>Numerical discrete</u>
    c. Find its mean: $\mu = \dfrac{433}{7} \approx 61.9$ Find its mode: <u>66</u>
    d. Write the data in an increasing order: 23, 58, 63, 66, 66, 78, 79
    e. Find its Median: 66 (4th term)   Q1 = <u>58</u>   Q3 = <u>78</u>

2. In a certain restaurant the amount of meat (kg) consumed per day was studied and the following results obtained: 11.5, 12.2, 14.6, 15.0, 23.2, 21.2, 10.1, 13.1

    a. State the number of elements in the set: <u>8</u>
    b. What kind of data is this? <u>Numerical continuous</u>
    c. Find its mean: $\mu = \dfrac{120}{9} \approx 13.3 kg$ Find its mode: <u>None</u>
    d. Write the data in an increasing order:
        10.1. 11.5, 12.2, 13.1, 14.6, 15.0, 21.2, 23.2
    e. Find its Median: $M = \dfrac{13.1+14.6}{2} = 13.85 kg$ Q1 =

    $\dfrac{11.5+12.2}{2} = 11.85 kg$ Q3 = $\dfrac{15.0+21.2}{2} = 18.1 kg$
    f. Try to obtain the answers using technology.

3. In a certain math class the number of exercises per day given for HW is the following: 5, 6, 6, 6, 4, 4, 5, 5, 4, 5, 6, 6, 7, 3, 0, 3

    a. State the number of elements in the set: <u>16</u>
    b. What kind of data is this? <u>Numerical discrete</u>
    c. Find its mean: $\mu = \dfrac{75}{16} \approx 4.7$ Find its mode: <u>6</u>
    d. Write the data in an increasing order:
        0, 3, 3, 4, 4, 4, 5, 5, 5, 5, 6, 6, 6, 6, 6, 7
    e. Find its Median: 5   Q1 = <u>4</u>   Q3 = <u>6</u>
    f. Try to obtain the answers using technology.

4. In the following data: 2, 2, 3, 3, 9, 9, 9 one natural number is missing. It is known that the median with the missing number is 3. Find all the possible values of the missing number.

5. In a certain math class the following grades were obtained:

68, 79, 75, 89, 54, 81, 88, 62, 67, 75, 64, 85, 97, 77, 79, 90, 75, 89, 76, 68

    a. State the number of elements in the set: 20
    b. What kind of data is this? Numerical discrete

    c. Find its mean: $\mu = \dfrac{1538}{20} \approx 76.9$ Find its mode: 75

    d. Write the data in an increasing order:
       54, 62, 64, 67, 68, 68, 75, 75, 75, 76, 77, 79, 79, 81, 85, 88, 89, 89, 90, 97

    e. Find its Median: $M = \dfrac{76+77}{2} = 76.5$ Q1 = 68   Q3 = 86.5

    f. Fill the table:

Grade	Mid – Grade (Mi)	Frequency (fi)	fi x Mi	Cumulative Frequency (Fi)	Fi (%)
[51, 60]	55.5	1	55.5	1	5
[61, 70]	65.5	5	327.5	6	30
[71, 80]	75.5	7	528.5	13	65
[81, 90]	85.5	6	513	19	95
[91, 100]	95.5	1	95.5	20	100
Total		20	1520		

    g. Use the table to find the mean: $\mu = \dfrac{1520}{20} = 76$ Comment on the result compared to the previous mean obtained. Since the data was grouped the mean obtained is very similar but not identical to previous one.

    h. Discuss the advantages and disadvantages of organizing information in a table. The big advantage is that the data is much easier to read and understand, analyze. The disadvantage is that some accuracy is lost.

    i. Is this the only possible choice for the left column of the table? Why? Discuss the advantages and disadvantages of organizing information in such a way.
    No it is not the only possibility. Narrower or wider intervals can be chosen. Narrower interval implies higher accuracy but information may be harder to understand and/or analyze. It also implies more work. Wider interval implies lower level of accuracy but information may be easier to understand and/or analyze. It also implies less work.

j. Design a new table with a different interval

Grade	Mid – Grade (Mi)	Frequency (fi)	fi · Mi	Cumulative Frequency (Fi)	Fi (%)
[51, 55]	53	1	53	1	5
[56, 60]	58	0	0	1	5
[61, 65]	63	2	126	3	15
[66, 70]	68	3	204	6	30
[71, 75]	73	3	219	9	45
[76, 80]	78	4	312	13	65
[81, 85]	83	2	166	15	75
[86, 90]	88	4	352	19	95
[91, 95]	93	0	0	19	95
[96, 100]	98	1	98	20	100
Total		20	1530		

k. Use the table to find the mean: $\mu = \dfrac{1530}{20} = 76.5$ Comment on the result compared to the previous mean obtained. <u>Since more intervals are used the result is more accurate.</u>

l. The mean of the <u>population</u> is denoted with the Greek letter mu: μ and typically it is <u>unknown</u> The mean of the <u>sample</u> is denoted by $\overline{x}$

m. Find the modal interval in both tables: 1st: [71, 80] 2nd: [76, 80], [86, 90]

n. In general this method of organizing information is called <u>grouping</u>

o. The 1st column is called <u>class</u> with upper interval boundary and <u>lower</u> interval boundary.

p. The 2nd column is called <u>Mid - Class</u>

q. On the following grid paper sketch the corresponding points.

OGIVE

r. This graph is called cumulative frequency curve or <u>Ogive</u>

s. Find the median using the graph: ~ 72

t. Find the first quartile (Q_1) using the graph: Q_1 = ~ 64

u. Find the third quartile (Q_3) using the graph: Q_3 = ~ 79

v. Find P_{30} using the graph: ~ 67 Find P_{70} using the graph: ~ 78

w. The <u>Inter Quartile Range</u> is in general $Q_3 - Q_1$ in this case <u>86.5–68= 18.5</u>

x. Try to obtain the answers using technology.

6. In a certain class the following heights (in m) of students were collected:

1.77, 1.60, 1.89, 1.54, 1.77, 1.65, 1.86, 1.51, 1.67, 1.94, 1.73, 1.70, 1.66, 1.70
   a. State the number of elements in the set: 14
   b. What kind of data is this? Numerical continuous
   c. Find its mean: $\mu = \dfrac{23.99}{14} \approx 1.71m$ Find its mode: 1.70, 1.77 (bimodal)
   d. Write the data in an increasing order:
      1.51, 1.54, 1.60, 1.65, 1.66, 1.67, 1.70, 1.70, 1.73, 1.77, 1.77, 1.86, 1.89, 1.94
   e. Find its Median: $M = 1.70m$ Q1 = 1.65m   Q3 = 1.77m
   f. Fill the table:

Grade	Mid – Grade (Mi)	Frequency (fi)	fi x Mi	Cumulative Frequency (Fi)	Fi (%)
[1.50, 1.60)	1.55	2	3.1	2	15.4
[1.60, 1.70)	1.65	4	6.6	6	46.2
[1.70, 1.80)	1.75	5	8.75	10	76.9
[1.80, 1.90)	1.85	2	3.7	12	92.3
[1.90, 2.00)	1.95	1	1.95	13	100
Total		14	24.1		

   g. Use the table to find the mean: $\mu = \dfrac{24.1}{14} \approx 1.72m$. Comment on the result compared to the previous mean obtained. Since the data was grouped the mean obtained is very similar but not identical to previous one.
   h. Discuss the advantages and disadvantages of organizing information in a table. The big advantage is that the data is much easier to read and understand, analyze. The disadvantage is that some accuracy is lost Is this the only possible choice for the left column of the table? Why? Discuss the advantages and disadvantages of organizing information in such a way. No it is not the only possibility. Narrower or wider intervals can be chosen. Narrower interval implies higher accuracy but information may be harder to understand and/or analyze. It also implies more work.
   Wider interval implies lower level of accuracy but information may be easier to understand and/or analyze. It also implies less work.
   i. On the following grid paper sketch the corresponding points.

OGIVE

Height (m)

j. This graph is called cumulative frequency curve or <u>Ogive</u>
k. Find the median using the graph: $\sim 1.66m$
l. Find the first quartile (Q_1) using the graph: $Q_1 = \sim 1.58m$
m. Find the third quartile (Q_3) using the graph: $Q_3 = \sim 1.74m$
n. Find P_{20} using the graph: $\sim 1.67m$ Find P_{70} using the graph: $\sim 1.73m$
o. The <u>Inter Quartile Range</u> is in general $Q_3 - Q_1$ in this case <u>1.815 − 1.625</u>
   = 0.190m
p. Try to obtain the answers using technology.

7. In a certain class students eye color was collected:

   Brown, Black, Brown, Blue, Brown, Blue, Green, Brown, Black, Green

   a. State the number of elements in the set: <u>10</u>
   b. What kind of data is this? <u>Categorical</u>
   c. Fill the table:

Eye Color	Mid – Color (Mi)	Frequency (fi)	fi x Mi	Cumulative Frequency (Fi)	Fi (%)
Brown	N/A	4	N/A	N/A	N/A
Blue	N/A	2	N/A	N/A	N/A
Green	N/A	2	N/A	N/A	N/A
Black	N/A	2	N/A	N/A	N/A
Total	N/A	10	N/A	N/A	N/A

   d. Obtain the mean: <u>N/A</u>
   e. State the mode of the set: <u>Brown</u>

f. Find the modal interval: <u>N/A</u>
g. Find the Median using the original data: <u>N/A</u>
h. Find the median using the table, discuss your answer. <u>N/A</u>
i. Find the answers to all the different parts using your GDC.
j. Represent the data in a histogram:

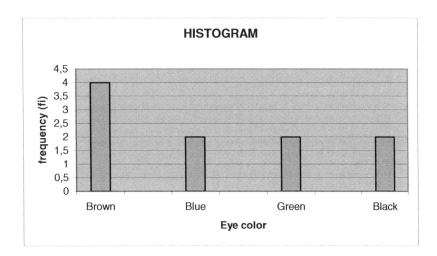

4.3. – PROBABILITY

Probability is the science of chance or likelihood of an event happening
If a random experiment is repeated <u>n</u> times in such a way that each of the trials is
identical and independent, where n(A) is the number of <u>times</u> event A occurred, then:

$$\text{Relative frequency of event A} = P(A) = \frac{n(A)}{N} \quad (N \to \infty)$$

Exercises

1. In an unbiased coin what is P(head) ? <u>0.5</u>
   This probability is called <u>"theoretical probability"</u>

2. Explain the difference between theoretical probability and "experimental"
   probability.
   <u>Theoretical probability is calculated, predicted. "experimental" probability is</u>
   <u>measured in an experiment. The probability for head is theoretically 0.5, we</u>
   <u>would need to repeat an experiment an infinite number of times to make sure it</u>
   <u>is. In reality the coin has some small probability to lend on its thin side (more</u>
   <u>than 0) so it is not really 0.5 for head…</u>

3. Throw a drawing pin at least 15 times and fill the table:
   <u>This experiment should be done in class</u>

4. The definition of probability is:
   $$P(A) = \frac{\text{Number of times A ocurred}}{\text{Total numberof times experiment repeated}}$$

Properties of probability $0 \leq P(A) \leq 1$ $P(U) = 1$

5. Given the sentence "Good morning everyone". Find the following
   probabilities in case the choices are being made in a random way:

   a. $P(\text{choosing a vowel}) = \frac{8}{19}$ c. $P(\text{choosing a "e"}) = \frac{3}{19}$

   b. $P(\text{choosing a "o"}) = \frac{4}{19}$ d. $P(\text{choosing a "z"}) = 0$

6. In case a student is chosen randomly in your classroom. Find the probability
   it´s a girl. <u>This should be done in class</u>

7. Find the probability of getting a prime number sum on tossing 2 dice.
   $$\frac{1+2+4+6+2}{36} = \frac{15}{36}$$

8. Find the probability of getting a sum of 17 on tossing 3 dice. $\frac{3}{216}$

9. Probability of being left handed in classroom. <u>This should be done in class</u>

10. Find the probability of obtaining a sum of 5 on tossing 2 dice. $\frac{4}{36}$

11. Find the probability of obtaining 2 tails on tossing 2 coins. $\dfrac{1}{4}$

12. Find the probability that a 2 digit number divides by 3 $\dfrac{30}{90}$

13. Find the probability of choosing the letter b in the word probability $\dfrac{2}{11}$

14. Find the probability of choosing a number that contains the digit 7 in the first hundred numbers (1 to 100). $\dfrac{19}{100}$ (17, 27, ….97, and 70, 71..79, without repeating 77.)

15. Find the probability of choosing a number that contains only even digits in the first thousand numbers (1 to 1000).

$$\left(\dfrac{\dfrac{50}{100}\cdot 5 + \dfrac{25}{100}\cdot 90 + \dfrac{12.5}{100}\cdot 1000}{1000} \right) = 0.15$$

16. Knowing that the sum of 2 dice is more than 5, find the probability it's 10 $\dfrac{3}{26}$ (26 sums are > 5 out of which 3 add up to 10)

CHAPTER 5

5.1. – INTERNATIONAL SYSTEM OF UNITS

1. Meter (m) is a unit of <u>length/distance</u> Other units of <u>length/distance</u> are: <u>mile</u>.

2. Meter square (m^2) is a unit of <u>area</u> Other units of <u>area</u> are: <u>mile^2</u>

3. An area has units of m^2 A length has units of <u>m</u>

4. Kilo = <u>1000</u> Mili = $\dfrac{1}{1000}$

Convert the units, use scientific notation in at least one of each type of exercises:

5. How many metres in 2.5 km?

   <u>2500m</u>

6. How many metres in 0.5 km?

   <u>500m</u>

7. How many metres^2 in $\dfrac{1}{3}$ km^2?

   $\dfrac{1000000}{3} m^2$

   Ffg

8. How many metres in 56 km?

   <u>56000m</u>

9. How many metres in 2500 km?

   <u>2500000m</u>

10. How many km^2 in 26 m^2?

    $\dfrac{26}{1000000} km^2 = 0.000026 km^2$

11. How many km in 75 m?

    <u>0.075km</u>

12. How many km in 1000 m?

    <u>1km</u>

13. How many m in $5.2 \cdot 10^7$ km?

    $5.2 \cdot 10^{10} m$

14. How many km^2 in $5.12 \cdot 10^8$ m^2?

    $\dfrac{5.12 \cdot 10^8}{10^6} = 512 km^2$

15. How many mm in 3.04 m?

    <u>3040mm</u>

16. How many mm^2 in 0.5 m^2?

    $0.5 m^2 = 0.5 \cdot 10^6 mm^2 = 5 \cdot 10^5 mm^2$

17. How many mm^2 in 1 m^2?

    $1 m^2 = 10^6 mm^2$

18. How many mm in 2 m?

    <u>2000mm</u>

19. How many mm in 2.5 m?

    <u>2500mm</u>

20. How many mm^2 are 1.35 m^2?

    $1.35 m^2 = 1.35 \cdot 10^6 mm^2$

21. How many cm in $\frac{1}{3}$ m?

 33.3cm

22. How many cm^2 in 56 m^2?

 $56m^2 = 56 \cdot 10^4 cm^2 = 5.6 \cdot 10^5 cm^2$

23. How many cm in 3.1 km?

 310000cm

24. How many mm^2 in 0.5 cm^2?

 $0.5cm^2 = 0.5 \cdot 10^2 mm^2 = 50mm^2$

25. How many cm in in 120 m?

 12000cm

26. How many mm^2 in 5.1 cm^2?

 $5.1cm^2 = 5.1 \cdot 10^2 mm^2 = 510mm^2$

27. How many cm in 17 km?

 1700000cm

28. How many m in 12392 km?

 12392000m

29. How many mm^2 in 5.1 m^2?

 $5.1m^2 = 5.1 \cdot 10^6 mm^2$

30. How many m^2 in 2.2 mm^2?

 $2.2mm^2 = 2.2 \cdot 10^{-6} m^2$

31. How many cm in 13.12 m?

 1312cm

32. Complete the table:

mm	cm	m	km
14	1.4	0.014	0.000014
650	65	0.65	0.00065
3000	300	3	0.003
5000000	500000	5000	5
12.5	1.25	0.0125	0.0000125
37	3.7	0.037	0.000037
4780	478	4.78	0.00478
1310000	131000	1310	1.31
8000	800	8	0.008

mm^2	cm^2	m^2	km^2
14	0.14	$0.14 \cdot 10^{-4} = 1.4 \cdot 10^{-5}$	$0.14 \cdot 10^{-10} = 1.4 \cdot 10^{-11}$
6500	65	0.0065	$0.0065 \cdot 10^{-6} = 6.5 \cdot 10^{-9}$
3000000	30000	3	$3 \cdot 10^{-6}$
$5 \cdot 10^{12}$	$5 \cdot 10^{10}$	$5 \cdot 10^6$	5
12.5	0.125	$0.125 \cdot 10^{-4} = 1.25 \cdot 10^{-5}$	$0.125 \cdot 10^{-10} = 1.25 \cdot 10^{-11}$
370	3.7	0.00037	$0.00037 \cdot 10^{-6} = 3.7 \cdot 10^{-10}$
4780000	47800	4.78	$4.78 \cdot 10^{-6}$
$1.31 \cdot 10^{12}$	$1.31 \cdot 10^{10}$	$1.31 \cdot 10^6$	1.31
$8 \cdot 10^9$	$8 \cdot 10^7$	8000	0.008

5.2. – COMMON ERRORS

1. $\sqrt{A+B} = \sqrt{A} + \sqrt{B}$

   $\sqrt{16+100} \neq \sqrt{16} + \sqrt{100}$

   True / **False**, Give an example to show your answer.

2. $\sqrt{A^2 + B^2} = A + B$

   $\sqrt{4^2 + 10^2} \neq 4 + 10$

   True / **False**, Give an example to show your answer.

3. $(A+B)^2 = A^2 + B^2$

   $(A+B)^2 = A^2 + B^2 + 2AB$

   True / **False**, if false write the correct version.

4. $(A+B)(A-B) = A^2 + B^2$

   $(3+7)(3-7) \neq 3^2 + 7^2$

   True / **False**, Give an example to show your answer.

5. $(A+B)(A-B) = A^2 - B^2$

   True / False, if false write the correct version..

6. $(x+2)^2 = x^2 + 4x + 2$

   $(x+2)^2 = x^2 + 4x + 4$

   True / **False**, if false write the correct version.

7. $(A-B)^2 = A^2 - B^2$

   $(3+7)^2 \neq 3^2 - 7^2$

   True / **False**, Give an example to show your answer.

8. $(2x-3)^2 = 4x^2 - 6x + 9$

   $(2x-3)^2 = 4x^2 - 12x + 9$

   True / **False**, if false write the correct version.

9. $(\sqrt{a} - 3)^2 = a^2 - 6a + 9$

   $(\sqrt{a} - 3)^2 = a^2 - 6\sqrt{a} + 9$

   True / **False**, if false write the correct version.

10. $x^2 x^3 = x^6$

    $x^2 x^3 = x^5$

    True / **False**, if false write the correct version.

11. $(x^2)^3 = x^{(2^3)}$

    $(x^2)^3 = x^6$

    True / **False**, if false write the correct version.

12. $\dfrac{x^{10}}{x^2} = x^5$ True / **False**, if false write the correct version.

$\dfrac{x^{10}}{x^2} = x^8$

13. $x^1 = 1$ True / **False**, if false write the correct version.

$x^1 = x$

14. $x^0 = 0$ True / **False**, if false write the correct version.

$x^0 = 1$

15. $-3^2 = (-3)^2$ True / **False**, if false write the correct version.

$-3^2 = -3 \cdot 3 = -9; \quad (-3)^2 = (-3)(-3) = 9$

16. $(4x^2) = (4x)^2$ True / **False**, if false write the correct version.

$(4x^2) \neq (4x)^2 = 16x^2$

17. $\sqrt{7x} = 7x^{\frac{1}{2}}$ True / **False**, if false write the correct version.

$\sqrt{7x} = \sqrt{7} \cdot \sqrt{x} \neq 7x^{\frac{1}{2}} = 7 \cdot \sqrt{x}$

18. $\dfrac{0}{2} = \dfrac{2}{0}$ True / **False**, if false write the correct version.

$\dfrac{0}{2} = 0 \neq \dfrac{2}{0} = Undefined\,!$

19. $\dfrac{14+x}{14} = x$ True / **False**, if false write the correct version.

$\dfrac{14+x}{14} = \dfrac{14}{14} + \dfrac{x}{14} = 1 + \dfrac{x}{14} \neq x$

20. $\dfrac{7-x}{7} = x-1$ True / **False**, if false write the correct version.

$\dfrac{7-x}{7} = \dfrac{7}{7} - \dfrac{x}{7} = 1 - \dfrac{x}{7} \neq x-1$

21. $\dfrac{a+b}{a} = 1 + \dfrac{b}{a}$ **True** / False, if false write the correct version.

22. $$\frac{14+x}{14} = x + \frac{x}{14}$$ True / **False**, if false write the correct version.

$$\frac{14+x}{14} = \frac{14}{14} + \frac{x}{14} = 1 + \frac{x}{14} \neq x + \frac{x}{14}$$

23. $$\frac{1}{x+y} = \frac{1}{x} + \frac{1}{y}$$ True / **False**, if false write the correct version.

$$\frac{1}{x+y} \neq \frac{1}{x} + \frac{1}{y} = \frac{y+x}{xy}$$

24. An **expression** and an **equation** is the same thing.   True / **False**

25. $$\frac{\left(\dfrac{a}{b}\right)}{c} = \frac{a}{\left(\dfrac{b}{c}\right)}$$ True / **False**, if false write the correct version.

$$\frac{\left(\dfrac{a}{b}\right)}{c} = \frac{a}{bc} \neq \frac{a}{\left(\dfrac{b}{c}\right)} = \frac{ac}{b}$$

26. $$-a^2 = (-a)^2$$ True / **False**, if false write the correct version.
$$-a^2 \neq (-a)^2 = a^2$$

27. $$a^{-2} = (-a)^2$$ True / **False**, if false write the correct version.
$$a^{-2} = \frac{1}{a^2} \neq (-a)^2 = a^2$$

28. $$a^{-2} = -a^2$$ True / **False**, if false write the correct version.
$$a^{-2} = \frac{1}{a^2} \neq -a^2$$

29. $$a^{-2} = -\frac{1}{a^2}$$ True / **False**, if false write the correct version.
$$a^{-2} = \frac{1}{a^2} \neq -\frac{1}{a^2}$$

30. $$a^{-2} = \frac{1}{a^2}$$ **True** / False, if false write the correct version.

31. $a^{-1} = -\dfrac{1}{a}$ True / **False**, if false write the correct version.

$a^{-1} = \dfrac{1}{a} \neq -\dfrac{1}{a}$

32. $\dfrac{1}{2} + \dfrac{1}{3} = \dfrac{1}{2+3}$ True / **False**, if false write the correct version.

$\dfrac{1}{2} + \dfrac{1}{3} = \dfrac{5}{6} \neq \dfrac{1}{2+3} = \dfrac{1}{5}$

33. $a^{-1} + a^{-1} = a^{-2}$ True / **False**, if false write the correct version.

$a^{-1} + a^{-1} = \dfrac{1}{a} + \dfrac{1}{a} = \dfrac{2}{a} \neq a^{-2} = \dfrac{1}{a^2}$

34. $a^{-1}a^{-1} = a^{-2}$ **True** / False, if false write the correct version.

35. $a^{-2}a^{-3} = a^{-6}$ True / **False**, if false write the correct version.

$a^{-2}a^{-3} = \dfrac{1}{a^2} \cdot \dfrac{1}{a^3} = \dfrac{1}{a^5} = a^{-5} \neq a^{-6}$

36. $a^{-2} + a^{-3} = a^{-5}$ True / **False**, if false write the correct version.

$a^{-2} + a^{-3} = \dfrac{1}{a^2} + \dfrac{1}{a^3} = \dfrac{a+1}{a^3} \neq a^{-5} = \dfrac{1}{a^5}$